James G. Stevens

A digest of the reported decisions in the Supreme Court of New Brunswick

James G. Stevens

A digest of the reported decisions in the Supreme Court of New Brunswick

ISBN/EAN: 9783741190834

Manufactured in Europe, USA, Canada, Australia, Japa

Cover: Foto ©Suzi / pixelio.de

Manufactured and distributed by brebook publishing software
(www.brebook.com)

James G. Stevens

A digest of the reported decisions in the Supreme Court of New Brunswick

A DIGEST

OF

THE REPORTED DECISIONS

IN THE

SUPREME COURT OF NEW BRUNSWICK,

FROM

HILARY TERM, 42 VICTORIA, 1879,
TO
EASTER TERM, 49 VICTORIA, 1886,

WITH

DIGEST OF CASES IN CANADA SUPREME COURT

DECIDED

ON APPEAL FROM SUPREME COURT OF NEW BRUNSWICK

WITH

RULES OF COURT FROM 1881 TO 1886

IN

CONTINUATION OF "STEVENS' DIGEST."

BY

JAMES G. STEVENS, ESQ., Q.C.,

TORONTO:
CARSWELL & CO., PUBLISHERS.
1888.

PRINTED BY
THOS. MOORE & CO., LAW PRINTERS,
32 ADELAIDE ST. EAST,
TORONTO.

SUPREME COURT OF JUDICATURE.

NEW BRUNSWICK.

Chief Justice—	HON. JOHN C. ALLEN.	October, 1875.
Justices—	HON. A. R. WETMORE.	May, 1870.
"	HON. A. L. PALMER,	June, 1879.
"	HON. GEO. E. KING,	December, 1881.
"	HON. JOHN JAMES FRASER.	December, 1882.
	HON. W. H. TUCK.	March, 1885.

ABBREVIATIONS AND REFERENCES.

Vol. 18,	2. Pugsley & Burbidge.
" 19,	3. do. do.
" 20,	4. do. do.
" 21,	5. do. do.
" 22,	1. Pugsley & Trueman.
" 23,	1. Trueman.
" 24,	2. do.
" 25,	3. do.

ADDENDA.

CASES ON APPEAL TO SUPREME COURT OF CANADA.

ERRATA.

On page 11, 5th line from bottom, for "lanes" read "land."
" 12, 15th line from bottom, for "Agreement" read "Amendment."
" 17, 19th line from top, for "vol. 26" read "vol. 25."
" 65, under Number "3," "*Chestnut* v. *Doyle*," for "vol. 25" read "vol. 24."
" 88, 6th line from top, for "after" read "on motion for."
" 95, 20th line from top, after "vol." insert "21."
" 140, 7th line from bottom, for "564" read "364."
" 155, *McDonald* v. *Mayor, etc., of St. John.* Appeal to S. C. C. dismissed. Reports S. C. C., vol. 14, page 1.
" 240, under head "Woodstock," case *ex parte Dibble* is omitted; read "The Act, 45 Vic. cap. 78, providing that no person, who is not a ratepayer in Town of Woodstock, shall engage in any trade, etc., therein without a license from the mayor, is *intra vires* the Provincial Legislature under 92nd section of B. N. A. Act, vol. 25, page 149."
" 245, at foot of note, read "*Coates* v. *Town of Moncton*, vol. 25, 605."

N. B. Some few errors occur in names of cases in Digest, but are correct in Table of Cases. It was not thought necessary to extend the errata in this respect.

The cases that were inserted in the last edition of Stevens' Digest in the Addenda to that edition, being several cases in vol. 18, N. B. Reports, are now included in this present edition, thereby saving the trouble of reference to the Addenda in Stevens' last edition of Digest.

A DIGEST

OF

THE REPORTED DECISIONS IN THE SUPREME COURT OF NEW BRUNSWICK, FROM HILARY TERM 42 VICTORIA, 1879, TO EASTER TERM 49 VICTORIA, 1886.

ABATEMENT.

For matter of form. Action in Justice's Court, section 13, cap. 85, Consolidated Statutes.

An action was brought in a Justice's Court, by the title of "The estate of the late R. K." against the defendant, and a non-suit was granted, because the name of the executrix was not stated in the summons.

Held, that the suit abated for matter of form, and prevented the plaintiffs' claim, being barred by the Statute of Limitations, under section 13, of cap. 85, Consolidated Statutes. *Kerr Executrix, etc. v. Squires*, vol. 22, 448.

Action brought in County Court by a female, does not abate by her marriage. See County Court 5.

ABANDONMENT.

Notice of—Loss of vessel—Waiver. See Insurance, 16.

—Of possession of land where wrongful entry by another. Whether trespass can afterwards be maintained. See Trespass, 8.

—Of excess in particulars filed. *See Certiorari*, 8.

—Not applicable to actions of tort. See County Court 6.

—Giving evidence of separate trespass—No abandonment of joint trespass. See New Trial 2.

—Election of trespass—time for—in judge's discretion. *Ibid.*

ABSCONDING DEBTOR.

1 Consolidated Stat. Cap. 44—Warrant to attach property—Affidavit stating belief of witnesses only—Supersedeas—Certiorari—Delay in applying.

Merely stating belief of absconding or concealment, not sufficient—facts should be stated for grounds of belief, if not, the judge has no authority to issue the warrant. Void proceedings not cured by the appointment of trustees and registry thereof, under the 11th section of Act.

A purchaser of land from the debtor after the issue of a warrant, in such a case, had a right to apply for a *certiorari* to quash the proceedings.

Such an application might be made though two terms had elapsed since the warrant issued.

Ex parte Moore, vol. 23, 229.

ABSENCE.

The mere absence from parish, of parish officer, does not create such a vacancy as will authorise the appointment of a person to fill the office by the councillors. *The Queen v. Close*, vol. 19, 382.

—Meaning of Canada Temperance Act. See Canada Temp. Act 19.

ACCEPTANCE.

—What constitutes such under Statute of Frauds. See Statute of Frauds.

—An acceptance of goods subsequent to time agreed upon for delivery. See Assumpsit 1.

—Order for goods sent by letter. See Contract 10.

Contract for sale of goods—Statute of Frauds—Offer by letter to sell. See Contract 17.

—Necessity of distinct offer and acceptance.

—Where contract for insurance depends upon correspondence. See Insurance 12.

Entire contract—Whether purchaser can accept a part and refuse to pay contract price for whole. See Contract 18.

Accomplice — Testimony of — Corroboration of. See Evidence 16.

ACCOMMODATION NOTE.

1—Liability of maker of, where payee has been discharged.

To an action on a promissory note made by the defendant in favour of F. L. L., or order and by him endorsed to plaintiffs, the defendant pleaded that he made and gave the note F. L. L. for his accommodation, and that there never was any value or consideration for the making or payment of the said note; that the plaintiffs were a banking company, of which L. was president and manager, and that the said note was received by the said L. for the plaintiffs with full knowledge that the note was so given without value and for the accommodation of the said F. L. L., and the plaintiffs while they were holders, discharged the said F. L. L. from all liability on said notes.

Held, by Weldon and Fisher, JJ. (Wetmore, J., doubting), that the plea was no answer to the action. *Bank of New Brunswick v. Brown*, vol. 19, 106.

—Agreement to pay—Bill of sale given in consideration of. See Promissory Notes 6.

ACCORD AND SATISFACTION.

Plea of—Taking defendants' promissory note—Note not stamped—Where given back—Pleading—Departure, duplicity.

1—To a declaration for goods sold and delivered defendant pleaded. 1st. That after the accruing of plaintiff's claim and before the commencement of the suit, he satisfied and discharged the claim by making and delivering to plaintiff his promissory note dated, etc. which promissory note plaintiff accepted and received in satisfaction and discharge of his claim. 2. That after the accruing of plaintiff's claim, etc., (as in first plea) he made and delivered to plaintiff, and the latter accepted and received from him on account thereof, his promissory note for, etc., payable to plaintiff or order on 1st August then next, which period had not elapsed at commencement of the suit. Plaintiff replied to both pleas. 1st. That the notes were not stamped according to provisions of statute, etc. And 2nd. (as to the first plea), that he did not receive the note in satisfaction and discharge of his debt, and that after he received it, he returned it to defendant, who accepted it and cancelled and discharged it, and agreed to remain liable to pay plaintiff's claim whenever required so to do. Defendant demurred to the replications, and plaintiff delivered objections to the pleas.

Held, that the pleas were good, but that the replications were also good on demurrer, and that plaintiff was entitled to judgment.

Held, also, that though the 2nd replication was open to objection for duplicity, that was not a ground of general demurrer. *Cruickshank* v. *McArity*, vol. 20, 352.

2—Where the plaintiffs demand is for a liquidated amount, the payment of a smaller sum will not amount to a satisfaction of the larger sum, even though the plaintiff agreed to accept it in full. Pitfield, App. and Kimball, Resp., vol. 25, 123.

—Plea of—In action against drawer of bill of exchange—What evidence of. See Agreement 7.

—Contract under seal—Breach—New agreement by parol, in settlement of. See Contract 16.

Accounts. Previous settlement with third party—Effect of, as admission of their correctness. See Evidence 11.

Settlement with deceased person—Conclusiveness of. See Settled Accounts 1.

Settlement of accounts by Ship's husband being part owner of vessel. See Ship's Husband 1.

—Between debtor and creditor—Credit of chattels—Whether statement should be registered. See Bill of Sale 4

ACCOUNT STATED.

Evidence of.

1—The defendant, having had dealings with the plaintiff, inquired of the plaintiff's clerk how the account stood. The clerk made out the account from the plaintiff's books, giving the defendant credit at the rate of $3.50 per M. for lumber delivered to the plaintiff, and told defendant the balance was $110.05, to which he said that he ought to be allowed a higher price for the lumber, but made no other remark.

Held, that this was not evidence of an account stated. *Ford* v. *Reid*, vol. 23, 569.

—Sufficiency of evidence—Official of corporation—Cash book kept by—Entries showing balance against self Admission to auditors of correctness. See Evidence 14.

—Action on—A new trial granted where jury, without reason, only allowed half the amount. See New Trial 5.

—Note with stamp uncancelled may be used as evidence in action on. See Evidence 3.

—Evidence of, with reference to former transactions necessary. See Statute of Frauds 1.

—Ship's husband, part owner of vessel—Settlement by. See Ship's Husband 1.

—Where declaration did not disclose wife's interest in account stated. See Husband and Wife 2.

ACKOWLEDGMENT

Of deed taken out of province—Certificate. See Dower 1.

ACQUIESCENCE.

1—Adjoining proprietors—Dividing line run by surveyor mutually agreed upon.

A dispute having arisen between adjoining landowners as to the boundary between them, they mutually agreed upon a surveyor to run the line, which he did. One owner then, without objection on the part of the adjoining proprietor, built a fence on the line so given by the surveyor.

Held, a sufficient acquiescence to establish it as a conventional line. *Steeper* v. *Harding, et al*, vol. 21, 143.

Mortgagor and mortgagee of ship—Agreement by mortgagee not to charter ship without consent of mortgagor—Notice of charter by telegram. See Ship 2.

ACQUITTAL.

Criminal law—Previous—Of principal—Felon—Indictment—Amendment.

1—On the trial of the prisoner on an indictment charging him with receiving property which one M. had feloniously stolen, etc., the evidence showed that he had stolen the property, and that the prisoner was guilty of receiving the same, knowing it to have been stolen. For the defence it was proved that M. had been previously tried on a charge of stealing the same property and acquitted. The counsel for the prosecution then applied to strike out of the indictment the allegation, that M. had stolen the property, and to insert the words "some evil disposed person," etc., which the Judge allowed.

Held, 1st. That the record of the previous acquittal of M. formed no defence on the trial of this indictment, and was improperly received in evidence.

2nd. That the amendment was improperly allowed. *Regina* v. *Ferguson*, vol. 20, 259.

—In an action for negligence when there is no evidence against one of the defendants, he is entitled to have a verdict entered for him at end of plaintiff's case. See Negligence 3.

Acquitted defendant — Joint action of tort—Costs—Time of taxing. See Costs 19.

ACTION AT LAW.

Commencement of—Against a Justice of Peace—*Nisi prius*, record proof of. See Practice 8.

—Refusal of assignor of debt to allow an action in his name—Suit in equity. See Pleading 6.

—Restraining by injunction. See Injunction 2.

—Court House — Injury to person falling down stairway leading to court room, owing to want of light—When fee vested in Mayor, etc., of St. John, in trust, etc. Partial caution in municipality—Principle governing liability. See Municipality of St. John 1.

—Splitting up claim—Whole amount due at time of first suit—Subsequent suit and arrest. See Arrest. *National Park Bank* v. *Ellis*, vol. 18, 547.

—Action on life policy by person beneficially interested. See Stay of Action 2. See Contract 5.

—Action on agreement to indemnify. See Sheriff 2.

—Separate or joint interest—Loss of lumber—Plaintiff's interest—Right to sue. See Contract 11.

Action for goods sold and delivered, and for money had and received, where will lie. See Conversion 1.

ACTION ON THE CASE.

1—Adjoining land owners—Defendant allowing cellar to remain after building destroyed, water collecting and running against plaintiff's wall—Plaintiff's default—When action not maintainable. *Trustees, etc.*, v. *Hutchinson*, vol. 18, 523. See Addenda 12.

2—Tort duty arising out of contract of employment—Traversing the employment;—the proper mode of denying the existence of the duty to use due diligence. See *Danville* v. *O'Brien*, vol. 18, 656.

Joint owners in vessel — Action by owner against joint owner for taking vessel and launching her in a negligent manner—Joint ownership no answer to action. *Ibid.*

3 — Corporation — St. John City — Power to raise level of the streets—Evidence of exercising powers carelessly—Withdrawing evidence of same from jury—Setting aside nonsuit. See *Patterson* v. *Mayor, etc.*, *St. John*, vol. 18, 636.

4 — Obtaining injunction — Averment that same was obtained wrongfully and

maliciously. *Collins v. Everett*, vol. 18, 469. See Addenda 41.

Master and Servant.—Injury to servant—Death of Master—Survival of action. See *Connelly v. Skirs*, vol. 18, 606.

ACTS OF PARLIAMENT

—Should be construed so as to give effect to all parts of the Act. See Inspection 1.

ACTS

—To be performed by seller A. not prevent property from vesting in vendee so as to prevent him from recovering in trover, where goods were seized under execution of the contract of sale. See Property, passing of 1.

Adjoining Land Owners.—Acts of possession—Time agreed upon. See Possession. 1. 2. See Acquiescence 1.

ADMINISTRATION.

Granted in different countries—Rights of Administraters. See Husband and Wife 3.

—Evidence of probable expenses under plea of *plene administravit*, inadmissible. See Evidence 15.

Admission—Accounts—Previous settlement with third party—Effect of—Evidence. See Evidence 11.

—By Counsel, how far client bound by. See Master and Servant 2.

—By Infants—Fraud. See Estoppel 3.

ADULTERY.

Marriage—In foreign state—Necessity of proving marriage law of such state.

1.—On an indictment of E. for adultery with L. R., it was proved that L. R. and J. R., who were citizens of the United States, were married in the State of Maine by a clergyman who testified that it was a part of his duty to solemnise marriages. E. was convicted, but on a motion to quash the conviction, it was held that it should have been proved that the marriage was valid under the law of Maine, and the conviction was quashed. *Regina v. Ellis*, vol. 22, 440.

ADVANCES

Made to testator—Action for part of claim barred by Statute of Limitations—Second action alleging agreement to devise form—*Res Judicata*. See Former Recovery 2.

Future—*Cognovit* given to secure—Application to set aside judgment—Right of creditor to be repaid amount advanced. See Judgment 5

Recovery of—order for goods to be manufactured—Part payment in advance—Refusal to deliver goods without payment of unauthorized extras. See Contract 17.

ADVERSE POSSESSION.

1—Land owned by tenants in common—Partition by consent without deed—Person claiming under, entitled to avail himself of the partition.

A. and B., tenants in common of a lot of land, divided it without a deed of partition, and afterwards occupied their separate portion according to that division. J. came into possession after the division under A. of his part.

Held, that he had a right to avail himself of the partition and of A.'s occupation. *Jones v. Morgan*, vol. 22, 338.

AFFIDAVIT.

1—Foreign company—Attaching order—Right to sue by name, or its incorporation must be shown by the affidavit. See *Avon Stone Co v. Denham*, vol. 18, 460.

Attaching order. See *Ibid*.

2—Attachment law—Omitting to state in affidavit that plaintiff's claim is not secured—Writ good on face, a justification to officer. See *Burke* v. *Clarke*, vol. 18, 662.

3—No statement of total amount—Statements in detail—Statement of no agreement that attachment should not issue—Description of particulars of demands. *Cahill* v. *Cahill*, vol. 18, 438.

4—Hearsay. An affidavit consisting of mere hearsay ought not to be put on the files of the Court. *In re Halstead*, vol. 20, 512.

5—Review—From Justices' Court—Entitling by affidavit—Description of commissioner—Marksman—Jurat.

An affidavit to obtain an order for review of a magistrate's judgment should not be entitled in any court, but if entitled in a County Court, when the application is made to a Judge of that Court, it may be treated as surplusage.

If, in an affidavit so entitled, the commissioner, before whom it is sworn, describes himself as "a commissioner, etc., Supreme Court,"

Held, per Wetmore and Fraser, J. J. (King, J., dissenting), that, as the affidavit was not properly entitled in the County Court, it could not be intended that the words "commissioner, etc.," meant a commissioner for taking affidavits.

If the jurat of an affidavit, made by a marksman, states that it was read over to the defendant by the commissioner, it will be presumed that it was so read before being sworn to. *Ex parte* McQuarrie, vol. 24, 287.

6—Initials. Promissory note. Affidavit to hold to bail.

It is not sufficient in an affidavit to hold to bail in an action on a promissory note, to describe the defendant by the initials of his Christian name without stating that he signed the note in that manner. *Stephenson* v. *Hoar*, vol. 24, 614.

7—Excessive damages—Action of tort.

Affidavits will not be received to shew that the damages are excessive in an action of tort. *Smith* v. *Chapman*, vol. 25, 206.

8—Sworn before prosecutor or his attorney.

Affidavits used in applications on the Crown side of the Court must not be sworn before the prosecutor or his attorney. *Regina* v. *Marsh*, vol. 25, 370.

—To arrest—What need not be stated. See Arrest 1.

—What must be stated to obtain judge's order for second attachment to issue. See Attachment 4.

—The obtaining of—Not a condition precedent to the right to sue for a debt against an estate. See Executors 1.

—On which a rule for costs is obtained—Need not state that cause was at issue. See Costs 15.

—In obtaining writ of *Habeas Corpus*—Surplusage. See *Habeas Corpus* 2.

—For taxation of witnesses' fees—Sufficiency of. See Costs 18.

—For bail—Delay in filing. See Bail Bond 1.

—For review from judgment in the Civil Court of the Town of Moncton—Before whom to be sworn. See Review 4.

—Of justification of surety—For petition under Controverted Elections Act. See Controverted Elections Act 1.

—On which *mandamus* was granted—When objection to can be taken. See *Mandamus* 2.

—On application to be let in to defend on the merits, after judgment signed. See Judgment 7.

—Used on motion to set aside a judgment sworn before the attorney who prepares, but is not the attorney on the record. See Practise 10.

—Application to answer affidavits used on motion. See Practise 20.

—Used on obtaining rule *nisi*—Defect in—When may be objected to. See Practise 21.

—In bankruptcy proceedings—Entitling of. See Bankruptcy.

—*Certiorari*—Filing of affidavits. See Practise 22.

—Act relating to absconding debtors—Witnesses stating their belief only of the absconding. See Absconding Debtor.

—To hold to bail—Made by Attorney—Whether sufficient. See Arrest 4.

—To hold to bail—Time of filing. See Practice 12.

—Where several papers are referred to—What should be stated. See Evidence 12.

AGENT—AGENCY.

Power to refer to Arbitration.

Authority to an agent to settle a matter in dispute between his principal and a third party does not authorise the agent to refer it to arbitration; and an award made under such a reference is not binding on the principal. *O'Regan v. Quebec and Gulf Ports Steamship Co.*, vol. 19, 528.

—Exceeding authority. See Power of Attorney 1; Addenda 33.

—Affidavit by, to hold to bail—What should be stated. See Arrest 4.

—Extent of authority—Appointed by municipal corporation. See Principal and Agent 2.

—Foreign corporation — Proof of agency. See Insurance 14.

—Policy of Insurance—Warranty not to load more than registered tonnage with stone or ore without consent of agent—Verbal consent, whether sufficient. *Ibid.*

—Policy of marine insurance issued by foreign corporation. See Insurance 14.

—Declaration by company's agent. See Insurance 6.

—Crediting by—Not payment of principal. See Ship's Husband 1.

—Hiring — Statute of Frauds. See Statute of Frauds 2.

—Continuing agency. See Pleading 9.

—Ship's Husband — Settlement of accounts by. See Ship's Husband 1.

—If insurance company has no authority to waive the condition requiring payment of premium. See Insurance 1.

—Employment of surgeon to attend a servant of his principal. See Master and Servant 2.

—Right of action. See Agreement 5.

After acquired property. Conveyance of, by bill of sale. See Equity.

AGREEMENT—(See Contract).

Rescission of — Trover — Conversion — Third party having property.

1—B. agreed with C. to give the latter a sleigh in exchange for a sewing machine and delivered the sleigh to C. The latter finding that the sleigh required some repairs which B. should have made, sent it back for the purpose of having the repairs made, but not intending to rescind the agreement. B. sent the sleigh to the shop of D. for the purpose of having the repairs made. Afterwards C. demanded the sleigh of D., who refused to let him have it unless a charge of $9 for work done on it originally for B., besides his charges for the present repairs and storage was paid.

Held, that C. could maintain trover against D. for the value of the sleigh, and that the latter could not complain of the Judge leaving it to the jury to find whether the title to the sleigh was in B. or C. *Bell v. Carlyle*, vol. 22, 453.

2—Written—Charter party—Parol evidence —When admissible.

In an action for a breach of a charter party, which stated that defendant's vessel, then on a voyage from Ireland to S. for orders, would on her arrival there at once proceed to C. and there load from the charterers' agent a full cargo of coal and proceed to St. John and deliver the same to the charterers,

Breach.—That the vessel was not at the time of the agreement on a voyage from Ireland to S. for orders, but was on a voyage from Ireland to St. John, and did not proceed to C. and load with coal, whereby plaintiffs were obliged to charter another vessel for that purpose.

At the trial the charter party was proved as alleged, and also that the vessel did not call at S., but came direct from Ireland to St. John and did not deliver any coal to plaintiffs. Defendants offered evidence to shew a verbal agreement made contemporaneously with the signing of the charter party; and while one of the defendants (by whom it was signed as agent for the other owners) was in the act of handing it over to plaintiffs, and while he had the control of it, he said to plaintiffs, "Now you are not to have the charter party, or it is not to be binding if the vessel does not go to S.;" to which one of the plaintiffs said "yes," or words to that effect. And upon plaintiffs assenting to receipt it on these terms, he gave them the charter party.

This evidence was rejected, and plaintiffs obtained a verdict.

Held, by Allen, C.J., and Weldon, Wetmore, Palmer and Fraser, J. J., (King J., *dubitante*) that the evidence should have been received—that the object of it was not to vary the terms of a written agreement, that the parties had already entered into, but to show that the writing which they had signed, but which was not then a complete agreement, was not to operate at all unless the vessel called at S. *Walters v. Milligan*, vol. 22, 622.

3—Written—What is a sufficient consideration—Averment of consideration—When it may be implied.

The declaration set out an agreement in writing providing that certain acts should be done by the defendant, but neither averred any request by the defendant to the plaintiff, nor any consideration moving from the plaintiff to the defendant, except that the plaintiff should accept a deed from the defendant of certain property, and allow the defendant to remain in possession thereof for a certain specified time.

Held, that the consideration was sufficient to support the agreement, and that in such a case a request might be implied. *Brownell v. Raworth*, vol. 21, 11.

4—Debtor and creditor — Novation — Substitution of liability of third person—Discharge of principal debtor—Consideration—Statute of Frauds.

Defendant being indebted to the plaintiff, it was verbally agreed between them and G., for whom the defendant was cutting lumber, that the plaintiff should discharge the defendant and accept G. as his paymaster, and G. thereupon promised to pay the plaintiff the amount due him from the defendant. G. was not indebted to the defendant at the time or afterwards.

Held, per Allen, C.J., Palmer and King, JJ., that there was a sufficient consideration for G.'s promise, and that the defendant's indebtedness to the plaintiff was extinguished.

Per Wetmore, Fraser and Trick, JJ., that G.'s promise, not being in writing, was void under the Statute of Frauds, and that the defendant's indebtedness was not extinguished. Coulthard, App. and Caverhill, Resp., vol. 25, 81.

5—Sale of land—Deed handed to purchaser by agent of grantor for purpose of examination—Receipt containing promise to agent to return deed or pay purchase money—Whether agent has right of action—Pleading—Non assumpsit—Right to dispute consideration under plea of.

W. sold land to defendant at auction, the terms of sale being 10 per cent. down, and the balance in two annual instalments, to be secured by notes on the delivery of the deed. W. executed a deed of the land, acknowledging the receipt of the purchase money, and gave it to the plaintiff as his agent, who took it to the defendant in order to get the notes; and the defendant, wishing that the deed should be examined by his attorney before completing the purchase, to which the plaintiff assented, but requiring something to shew that the purchase money had not been paid, the defendant signed a writing stating that he had received the deed from the plaintiff only to be examined, and if not lawfully executed, to be returned to the plaintiff; and when lawfully executed to the satisfaction of his attorney, that defendant would pay the balance due on the deed, $572. The deed being satisfactory the defendant kept it; but there being some dispute about the notes offered by the defendant, the plaintiff brought an action for the $572, the balance of the purchase money, to which the defendant pleaded *non assumpsit*.

The jury found that the writing was not intended to create a new agreement with the plaintiff, differing from the agreement made at the sale, but merely as a memorandum to shew the terms on which the deed had been delivered to the defendant, and gave a verdict in his favor.

Held, on application to enter the verdict for the plaintiff, by Weldon, Wetmore and Fraser, JJ. (Allen, J., dissenting). 1. That the writing was an agreement by the defendant to pay the purchase money to the plaintiff, and that he was entitled to recover, there being a sufficient consideration to support the defendant's promise. 2. That evidence was not admissible under the plea of *non assumpsit* to shew that the writing was not intended as an agreement with plaintiff. *Anderson* v. *Fawcett*, vol. 24, 313. See Addenda, 34. Appeal to Supreme Court of Canada allowed.

6—Agreement for sale of lands—Description—Mistake—Specific performance—Sale of lumber—Estimated quantity—Representation.

In November, 1878, defendants agreed in writing to sell to plaintiffs for $50,000 a mill property at Point Wolf, and three other tracts of land (describing them), and all their logs on hand. This agreement was abandoned in April following, in consequence of a disagreement about the quantity of logs at defendant's mill, and a new agreement entered into, by the terms of which the defendants agreed to sell to the plaintiffs for the same price as before, "their real estate known as the Point Wolf property, and all property in connection therewith, and logs and other property there." In describing the quantity of logs agreed to be sold, the agreement stated, "logs said by S. and M. (defendants) to contain 8,462,000 feet; survey bills for these amounts to be furnished by S. and M.; C. & Sons (plaintiffs) to pay for said logs, $26,500;" and it concluded by stating that it "included all the defendants' real estate, licenses, and other property in connection with their mills and lumber operations." At the time of entering into each of the agreements the defendants owned a lot G, which enabled them to control the lumber cut in its vicinity, and to prevent its being diverted from their mill at Point Wolf and sent to other mills, and they had purchased the lot for that purpose. Shortly after the first agreement was made, and for the purpose of performing it, the defendants executed a deed of the lands described therein, but did not deliver it to the plaintiffs till after the second agreement was entered into. Nothing was said at the time of the second agreement about the land to be conveyed, the statement that it was to include all property in connection with the defendants' mills having been inserted by the plaintiffs' solicitor, because his clients told him that they had purchased all the property the defendants had. The defendants did not furnish the plaintiffs with any survey bills of the logs sold, and the quantity, according to the mill survey, fell considerably short of what was stated in the agreement. The defendants refused to convey lot G. to the plaintiffs, alleging that they had not agreed to sell it.

In a suit for specific performance of the agreement respecting that lot, and for compensation for the deficiency of the logs, the defendants swore that they never intended to sell lot G. to the plaintiffs, or to include it in the agreement.

Held, 1. That lot G. was held by the defendants in connection with their mill property. 2. *Per* Allen, C.J., and Wetmore, J. (Weldon, J., dissenting), that so far as related to the real estate, the second agreement was based upon the first case, and that there was evidence of a mistake in the second agreement as to the land intended to be sold; and therefore the plaintiffs were not entitled to specific performance as to lot G. 3. That though the words of the agreement respecting the logs, "said to contain," etc., might, by themselves, amount only to an estimate by the defendants of the quantity, the succeeding words, "survey bills for these amounts to be furnished," etc., amounted to a representation by the defendants that they had that quantity of logs; and therefore the plaintiffs were entitled to compensation for the deficiency. Stephenson, *et al*, App., and Clinch, *et al*, Resp., vol. 24, 189.

7—Settlement of by the note of third party—Whether accepted in satisfaction and discharge of bill—Writing given on receipt of—Accord and satisfaction—Parol evidence—Admission of—Motion for new trial—Ground not taken on trial.

Defendant having drawn a bill of exchange in favor of the plaintiff, which was dishonored; R. gave his note to the plaintiff for the amount of the bill and interest payable in three months, and the plaintiff made out an account in which the bill and interest were charged on the debit side, and R.'s note credited, balancing the account; under which was written, "Settled as above," and signed by the plaintiff. Under this was written, "the above note to be renewed if required by Mr. R."

In an action against the defendant as drawer of the bill, he pleaded accord and satisfaction, and gave evidence by R. without objection, that the plaintiff accepted his note in "full settlement and payment" of the bill. This was denied by the plaintiff, who testified that the note was taken as collateral security for the payment of the bill. A verdict having been found for the defendant on this issue.

Held, per Allen, C.J., Weldon, Wetmore and Fraser, JJ. (Palmer, J., dissenting) that the plaintiff not having objected at the trial, could not move for a new trial on the ground that the parol evidence was improperly received, and that the jury should have been directed that the account signed by the plaintiff contained the agreement on which the note was given; and did not amount to satisfaction of the bill.

Semble, that the account signed by the plaintiff, did not amount to an agreement *inter partes*, but [illegible] a receipt shewing the manner [illegible] the account was settled, and [illegible] [illegible] evidence of the agreement was [illegible] sible.

An agreement to accept a note "in full settlement and payment" of a debt is evidence of accord and satisfaction.

Per Palmer, J. That the amount signed by the plaintiff contained the agreement between the parties, that as it did not shew that the note was accepted in satisfaction of the bill, parol evidence was inadmissible, and the jury should have been directed to find for the plaintiff, though no such contention was made at the trial.

Also that the evidence of R. did not prove that his note was taken in satisfaction of the bill. *Barbour et al. v. Roberts*, vol. 24, 211.

8—Sale of goods—Price subject to be reduced—Recovery under count for goods sold and delivered.

Where, on the sale of a chattel by the plaintiff to the defendant for $130, it was agreed that the price should be reduced to $65, if the defendant produced a deed from the sheriff shewing that he had previously sold the chattel to the defendant under an execution; the plaintiff may recover the price in an action for goods sold and delivered. It is the defendants' duty to produce the sheriff's deed, if he claims to reduce the price to the lesser sum. Woods, App., and McCann, Resp., vol. 25, 253.

—By mortgagee of ship not to charter without consent of mortgagor—Notice of charter by telegram—Acquiescence of mortgagor. See Ship 2.

—Agreement to indemnify. See Sheriff 2.

—Agreement to deliver lumber to be measured by a named surveyor—Survey bills, how far conclusive. See Estoppel 5.

—Conditional sale—Representation—Estoppel. See Trover 6

—Construction of agreement—Property in lumber—ownership and control of lumber until payment of draft given for stumpage under the agreement. See McLeod, App., and N. B. Railway Co., Resp. Addenda 28.

—Of counsel at trial—Power of Court to depart from. See Practice 14.

—Agreement under seal—Subsequent parol agreement. See 16.

—Verbal—To devise form in payment for advances—Statute of Frauds. See Former Recovery 2.

—Agreement for a lease. See Landlord and Tenant 6.

—Written—Work done under—Action for—*Quantum meruit*. See Assumpsit 4.

—Ante Nuptial—Voluntary conveyance. See Husband and Wife 5.

—For towage of raft of lumber made by agent—Where portions of raft owned in severalty by different persons—Loss of portion owned by one—Right of owner to sue alone for the loss. See Contract 11.

—Where property held under—Party holding to repay himself for expenditure from profits—Premises destroyed by fire—Who entitled to insurance money. See Insurance 13.

—As to determination of quantity, where guage has been tampered with. See Sale 3.

Sale of property, agreement to give security—Evidence to jury. See Sale of Goods 5.

ALIENS.

1—Naturalization—Certificate—Person taking oath of allegiance, etc.—Must grant.

The certificate required by sec. 4 sub-sec. 3 of the Act 31, V. c. 66, respecting aliens and naturalization must be signed by the person who administers the oaths of residence and allegiance required by sub-secs. 1 and 2. *Re Doster, an Alien*, vol. 20, 267.

—Juror—Objection to, how taken. See Juror.

ALLEGIANCE.

Oath of—Who must sign certificate. See Aliens.

AMBIGUITY.

In description of lands—Acts of person under deed may be evidence to explain.

1—When there is any ambiguity in the description of the land conveyed by a deed, the acts of a person under a deed would be evidence to explain it; but mere declarations alleged to have been made by former owners offered in evidence with a view of affecting the titles, are not admissible. Defendant conveyed to plaintiff a piece of land described as follows: "One-fourth share or part of that one hundred and sixty-six acre lot conveyed by H. to H. B., J. B. and G. B., which one-fourth contains forty-one and one-half acres more or less, and is bounded west by land conveyed to J. B. by G. B. and J. his wife, north by W., east by D.; and to extend southerly till it comprises said one fourth of said one-hundred and sixty-six acres ot, being forty-one and a half acres more or less."

In the deed, defendant covenanted with plaintiff that he was seised of the premises therein described and thereby conveyed, that he had good right to bargain and sell the same in manner and form therein written, and that he would warrant and defend the same unto the plaintiff his heirs and assigns for ever against the lawful claims and demands of all persons whomsoever.

Held, that this covenant in law amounted to a covenant that the defendant was solely seised of the property described in the deed, and that he had a legal right to grant, bargain and sell the land so described in fee simple to the plaintiff; and that as the whole block contained by actual measurement 171½ acres instead of 166 acres as stated in the deed—the plaintiff's deed from the defendant entitled him to the full one quarter, and the defendant was liable upon his covenant to whatever quantity of land the plaintiff was deficient in such quarter. *Somers* v. *Wilbur*, vol. 20, 502.

AMENDMENT.

Application for—Discharged without costs.

1—On demurrer to defendant's plea, there was judgment for the plaintiff with leave for the defendant to amend on payment of costs. The defendant did not amend, and plaintiff applied to have the rule amended by striking out that part which allowed defendant to amend. After the rule *nisi* was granted the parties went to trial.

Held, that the application was unnecessary, and the rule was discharged, but without costs, as the rule was taken out without costs, and could not be made absolute with costs, and there was no necessity for the defendant to shew cause. *Tower* v. *Outhouse*, vol. 21, 302.

2—Notice under—Practice—Act 42, Vic. Chapter 8.

Where the notice given under Act 42, Vic. Chap. 8, Sec. 10, stated that defendants would move to enter a non-suit or a verdict for the defendants, and leave had not been reserved at the trial, the Court refused to allow the defendants to amend the notice and move for a new trial. *Mullin* v. *Frost*, vol. 20, 122.

—Conviction under Canada Temperance Act, 1887—When penalty imposed is greater than the Act authorises—Whether allowable. See Canada Temperance Act 9.

—Conviction under Canada Temperance Act. See Summary Conviction Act, 3, 4, 7.

—Agreement of conviction. See Can. Tem. Act, 22.

—Of name of defendants—Judge granting order to change. See Practice 2.

—Of declaration—When both lessor of plaintiff and defendant died while suit was pending. See Ejectment 3.

—Bill in Equity—When allowable. See Equity.

—Pleadings—At trial—When proposed amendment would make Court demurrable. See False Imprisonment 7.

—Amendment on appeal. See Addenda 31, 39.

—When judge at *nisi prius* has power to refuse. See Partnership 1.

—Of Bill in Equity—Foreclosure. See Mortgage 2.

—Election petition under Dominion Controverted Election Act—Variance in copy served — Whether may be amended. See Dominion Controverted Election 2.

Ancient Document. — Statement in Crown grant of sale of the land—Admissibility of. See Possession 2.

ANNUITY

To wife of testator—If the particular property upon which it was made a charge should prove insufficient for that purpose, the amount should be paid in full out of the residuary estate. See Will 5.

—Where *corpus* can be sold to pay. See Will 3.

Ante-Nuptial Agreement. — Voluntary deed from husband to wife—Whether can support by proof of. See Husband and Wife 5.

APPEAL—*(See County Court Appeal.)*

Decision of Judge.

—The decision of the Judge in equity on a question of fact will not be reversed on appeal, unless it clearly appears that his decision was not only wrong, but entirely erroneous. *Wilbur v. Jones*, vol. 21, 4.

In questions of fact—Verdict set aside by County Court Judge — Interfering with Judgment of County Court.

2—On an appeal from an order of a County Court Judge granting a rule for a new trial on the ground of the verdict being contrary to evidence, the Court refused to interfere with the decision of the Court below. *Hamilton v. Dunphy*, vol. 21, 214.

3—From order made by a County Court Judge —When appeal will lie —Where Judge sets aside a judgment and allows defendant to come in on terms—Mandamus to compel Judge to certify—Power of Court to grant—Consol. Stat. C. 51, SS. 31 and 51.

An order of a Judge of a County Court setting aside a judgment and allowing the defendant to come in and defend on terms, made under section 31 Consol. Statutes, chap. 51, is not a decision upon a point of law, but depends on the Judge's belief in the facts stated in the affidavits, shewing a defence to the action on the merits; and no appeal lies from the order under the 51st section of that chapter.

The Court will not compel a County Court Judge to certify the proceedings before him, unless his decision is upon a point of law, or comes within the other cases mentioned in section 51 of Consol. Statutes, chap. 51

Semble—If a Judge of a County Court refuses to certify proceedings in a case where he ought to do so, the Court will grant a *mandamus* to compel him to certify. *Ex parte McCully*, vol. 20, 87.

4—From order of a County Court Judge refusing rule for a new trial, on the ground that the verdict was against the evidence, the Court will not interfere with the finding of the Court below. *Sheratin v. Whelpley*, vol. 20, 75.

5—From County Court—Where abandoned by appellant and notice given—Motion to dismiss with costs refused—Power of County Court to give costs.

Where the proceedings on an appeal from a County Court had been certified and filed with the clerk of the pleas, but the case had not been entered on the appeal paper, an application to dismiss the appeal with costs for failure to prosecute was refused, the appellant having previously given notice that he abandoned the appeal, and the respondent having a remedy by application to the Judge of the County Court under Consol. Stat. cap. 51, sec. 52. *Kinnear* v. *Black*, vol. 21, 272.

6 -Chatham Police Act 22 Vic. cap. 46, and 26 Vic. cap 40—Appeal under 11 Vic. cap. 12—When Court will not interfere with decision of Justice.

Where on appeal under 11 Vic. cap. 12, from a conviction before a Justice, the evidence was conflicting, the Court refused to interfere with the decision of the Justice. *Ex parte Belstead*, vol. 21, 227.

7—Probate Court—question of fact—Decision of.

The Court on an appeal from the Probate Court will decide questions of fact from the evidence sent up on appeal, irrespective of the finding of the Judge of the Probate Court. Consol. Stat. cap. 52 sec. 47. *In re Ferguson*, vol. 21, 71.

—Preliminary objections as to sufficiency of petition to prove a bill in solemn form—Decision of Judge. See Probate Court.

8—Equity—Injunction—Dissolution of.

In order to entitle a defendant to have an *ex parte* injunction dissolved on the ground of suppression of fact by the party obtaining it, the facts relied on must be material to the case as presented in the plaintiff's bill.

Held, by Wetmore, J., on appeal from the decision of a Judge sitting in equity, that the Court having stopped the defendant's counsel when he was about to endeavour to sustain the decision of the Court below on grounds not considered by the latter, that judgment ought not to be given allowing the appeal until the respondent's counsel was permitted to present the other grounds, which he had been so estopped from arguing. *Watt* v. *South West Boom Co.*, vol. 19, 646.

9—To Supreme Court of Canada—Extending time.

Held, that a Judge has power from time to time to extend the time for perfecting an appeal to the Supreme Court of Canada.

The fact of the Court having decided what the case on appeal should be, will not prevent a Judge from making an order settling the appeal. *Copp* v. *Reid*, vol. 19, 641.

—Preparation of case, what case must contain. See Supreme Court of Canada 1.

10—Crown has not an appeal to the Supreme Court of Canada from judgment quashing conviction. See Evidence 16.

11—Ex parte order extending time

The time for appeal allowed by the Supreme and Exchequer Court Act Statutes of Canada 38 Vic., cap 11, sec. 21, should not be extended by an *ex parte* order. *Jackson* v. *McLellan*, vol. 18 604.

—Summons for new trial not disposed of—Refusal to set aside taxation of costs. See New Trial 12.

—Dismissal of, when appellant does not appear when case is reached. See County Court Appeal 2.

—Where appeal, County Court allowed—Rule—Costs. See County Court Appeal 3.

—Judgment of the Court appealed from, may be supported on other grounds than those on which it was decided below. See Ship 1.

—Dismissal of—Where appellants' counsel had stated that he did not intend to support the appeal. See County Court Appeal 1.

—Non-suit having been set aside with costs, Court will not grant attachment for costs. See Costs 8.

—Not allowed on question of costs. See Costs 10.

—Can only be in reference to point actually taken and decided in Court below. See Carrier 2.

—From an order of a Judge of County Court relieving bail. See Bail 1.

—Permission to enter cause on appeal proper—Practice. See County Court Appeal 4.

—Serving notice of—Statement of grounds. See Equity Appeal 2.

—Costs—Question of—Whether appeal will lie. See *Sagre* v. *Harris*, vol. 18, 677.

—Procedure on appeal. See Court General Rules.

—County Court—Judge certifying proceedings—Time within which applicant must apply for—Bond. See County Court Appeal 7.

—On Appeal to Supreme Court of Canada—Defendant cannot rely on ground of plea not pleaded. See Addenda 31.

—Jurisdiction—On what grounds appeal will lie—Secs. 20 & 22, Sup. Court Act. See Addenda 48.

Appeal Papers—Equity—When to be printed—Entry of cause—Application to strike cause off docket—Rule of Hillary Term, 1881—Practise.

The Court, (Wetmore, J. dissenting) refused to strike a cause off the Equity Appeal paper by reason of the appeal papers not having been printed and filed as required by rule of Hilary Term, 1881, when good cause was shewn for the delay. *Colwell* v. *Robinson*, vol. 21, 489.

Appropriation—Agreement for—whether payment—Rescission of. See Contract 7.

Appropriating with intent to defraud—Stating value in indictment for. See Intent to Defraud 1.

ARBITRATION—*(See Award)*.

Costs of—Power of Court to review.

1—Where an order of reference to arbitration made at *nisi prius* provided that the costs of the arbitration should be taxed by the clerk as costs in the cause, the Court has no power to review the clerk's allowance of the costs of the arbitrator. *Snowball* v. *Muirhead*, vol. 22, 561.

—Power of agent to refer to, without authority of principal. See Agent 1.

—When clause in Act 34 Vic. cap. 52, to construct lines of Telegraph applies. See Trespass 6.

—When damages reduced to less than two hundred dollars in action brought in Supreme Court, whether plaintiff is entitled to costs. See Costs 5.

—Conditions for, in insurance policy—Where it does not apply. See Insurance 6.

—A submission to—Parties to, must expressly consent and agree to its being made a rule of Court. See Award 1.

Arbitration clause—Marine insurance—Policy. See Insurance 11.

Architect's certificate—Not required to entitle to damages for delay in finishing work under contract. See Contract 2.

Argument of summons—To set aside attachment—What grounds party applying can avail himself of. See Practice 3.

Array—Challenge to—Action pending against sheriff by prisoner's husband—Good ground of. See Challenge 2.

ARREST.

—Previous arrest for same cause of action—*Res adjudicata*—Discharge from custody—Splitting up claims—Whole amount due at time of first suit. See *National Park Bank* v. *Ellis*, vol. 18, 517.

Right to arrest not taken away in actions of *tort* by Consol. Stat. See *Mallen* v. *Frost*, vol. 18, 163.

—Writ of capias—Affidavit to obtain order for arrest under Chap. 38 Consol. Stat. sec. 1, need not state plaintiff's belief—Defendant about to quit the province—

Order to arrest one of several defendants—Attorney's name not signed to notice on copy writ of capias—Effect of—impossible date—When defendant not misled.

An affidavit to obtain an order for the arrest of defendant under sec. 1 Chap. 38 Consol. Stat. (where an order is necessary under that section), need not state an allegation that plaintiff believes the defendant is about to quit the province.

An order may be made to arrest one of defendants—the name of the plaintiff's attorney was stated at the foot of the endorsement required to be made on a writ of capias (Consol. Stat. cap. 37. Schedule A. No. 2, page 278), where the form does not require it and omitted at the end of the notice to the defendant (No. 8), where it is required to be stated.

Held, that as the object in requiring the name to be stated on the copy is to give the defendant the name of the attorney who issued the writ, and as the defendant in this case could not have been misled, or left in any doubt, the deviation from the form was not sufficient to justify the Court in setting aside the arrest.

A considerable part of the copy of the writ of capias was illegible. It appeared to be dated thirty-third day of June, 1869, the word intended for "twenty" looking more like "thirty" than "twenty," though it was neither the one nor the other, the year was plainly written 1869.

The copy of the indorsement which appeared on the copy of the writ stated that "the writ was issued on the 23rd day of June, 1879"—the defendant was arrested on the 25th June.

Held, that the irregularity was not sufficient to justify the setting aside of the arrest, the defendant not having been prejudiced by it. *O'Sullivan v. O'Sullivan*, vol. 19, 386.

2—In an action for malicious prosecution—Consol. Stat. c. 38—Not necessary to state in affidavit that defendant about to quit the province—Or that arrest not made for purpose of vexing or harrassing defendant—Amount for which bail to be given in Judge's discretion.

Held, by Allen, C. J., and Duff, J., Wetmore, J., dissenting, that the right to arrest by a judge's order in action of tort is not affected by the 38th Chap. of Consol. Stat. And it is not necessary to state in the affidavit, to obtain the order, that the arrest is not made for the purpose of vexing or harrassing the the defendant. *Hollis v. Frost*, 2 P. & B. 463 approved.

Held, by Allen, C. J., and Duff, J. (Wetmore, J., dissenting), that an affidavit to obtain a judge's order to hold to bail in an action of tort, it is not necessary to state that the defendant is about to quit the province.

The amount for which the Judge should order, bail in an action of tort must be, to a great extent, a matter of discretion to be exercised by him with reference to the facts disclosed by the affidavits upon which the application is made. *Weldon v. O'Sullivan*, vol. 19, 451.

3—Under a Judge's order for a tort—Examination and disclosure under Consol. Stat. cap. 38, sec. 7—Whether Act applies to such case.

Held, by Allen, C. J., and Duff, J. (Palmer, J., dissenting), that the provisions of the Consolidated Statutes Chap. 38, sec. 7, allowing a debtor to make a disclosure of his affairs, and authorizing his discharge under certain circumstances, do not apply to a case where the defendant is arrested under a Judge's order for a tort. *Bate v. Bernstein*, vol. 20, 106.

4.—Affidavit of agent—Statement that arrest not made for purpose of vexing or harassing debtor—Affidavit of attorney not sufficient.

The agent of an incorporated company made an affidavit for the arrest of the defendant in an action of debt, stating that the amount of the claim was justly due to the company. The plaintiff's attorney also made an affidavit that the arrest was made under his advice, and was not for the purpose of vexing or harrassing the debtor.

Held, that the affidavit of the agent should state that the arrest was not made for the purpose of vexing or harassing the debtor, and it was not sufficient for the attorney to make an affidavit to that effect. *The Star Kidney Pad Company* v. *McCarthy*, vol. 23, 83.

5—Plea justifying an imprisonment under warrant issued by receiver of taxes, St. John, by virtue of 41 Vic., cap. 9—Necessity of setting out in detail the proceedings taken under the Act—An allegation that all things required by the Act were done, not sufficient—Consol. Stat. Cap. 37, sec. 46—Applies only to actions on contract—Appointment of person to receive moneys assessed under Act—Necessary before receiver of taxes can issue warrant—Sec. 14 of 41 Vic., cap. 9.

The plaintiff was arrested on an execution issued by the receiver of taxes of the City of St. John, under 41 Vic. cap. 9. In an action against the corporation and the receiver of taxes for false imprisonment, the defendants pleaded a special plea, setting out the proceedings taken under the Act. There was, however, no allegation in the plea of the appointment of a person to receive the moneys assessed against the plaintiff under the 14th section of the Act; but there were allegations that all things required by the Act had been done, and that the moneys assessed under the Act, by the commissioners against the plaintiff, had been demanded of him.

Held, that the plea was bad. *McSorley* v. *the Mayor of St. John*, vol. 19, 635.

—Under execution issued out of a Justice's Court without search for goods and chattels. See False Imprisonment 3.

Under second execution. For costs of previous execution for taxes. See False Imprisonment 8.

Discharge from—Disclosure by debtor—Consol. Stat. cap. 38, sec. 7. See Debtor 1.

—Where goods stolen—Right to arrest person on whose lands goods are found—Search warrant. See Trespass 9.

—Where justice not justified in issuing warrant to arrest in first instance. See Summary Conviction Act 9.

ASSAULT.

1—Where one enters house of another quietly—Necessity of previous request to leave, to justify assault.

There is a manifest distinction between endeavouring to turn a person out of a house into which he has previously entered quietly, and resisting a forcible attempt to enter: in the first case a request to depart is necessary; but not in the latter.

In a criminal prosecution by the wife of O. for assault made upon her on entering her husband's house, the defence was, that she had no right to go to her husband's house, and that her intention in going there was to take away property which she had no legal right to take; but *held*, on a case reserved: that this would not justify the assault, there being no previous request made of her to leave the house, nor any statement of her intention, or attempt made, to take anything. *The Queen* v. *O'Neil*, vol. 19, 49.

Summary convictions—Under the Consolidated Statutes cap. 62—Evidence that assault was made in defence of title to

land admissible—Magistrate refusing to certify for review—Certiorari.

The defendant in a prosecution for an assault under cap. 62 of the Consolidated Statutes of "summary convictions" has a right to shew that the assault was committed on his land and in defence of his title.

When the magistrate before whom the prosecution was had, refused to certify the proceedings for appeal under cap. 62 of the Consolidated Statutes the court granted a *certiorari*. *Ex parte Estabrooks*, vol. 10, 283.

—When action is brought in the Supreme Court and plaintiff does not recover over $100—Costs refused. See Costs 1.

—Prisoner indicted for murder in short form cannot be convicted of. See Indictment 1.

—Where an indictment charged that the prisoner made an assault upon A. "and him the said A. did beat, wound, and illtreat," and there was no evidence of any wounding, it was held that the prisoner was rightly convicted of a common assault. See Criminal Law 7.

Assault and battery—*Plea of son—Assault Demesne* — Replication justifying assault only. See Pleading 7.

Assent—Necessity of creditor's for whose benefit judgment confessed. See Deed 4.

ASSESSMENT.

1—Statement—Ambiguous and uncertain—Requisite information not furnished—Right of assessors to assess.

Where assessors under authority of Act, 31 Vic., cap. 36, sec. 4, required the manager of a bank to furnish them "a true and correct statement in writing—under oath—setting forth the whole amount of income received for each bank within the City of St. John for a fiscal year preceding May 1st, 1877." And the manager rendered a statement as follows: "Net profits or income derived from business done within the city—*nil*."

Held, that as he had treated the terms "income" and "net profits" as synonymous, the statement was uncertain and ambiguous, and that the assessors were justified in ignoring it, and assessing the manager according to the best of their judgment. Lawless, *ex parte*, vol. 18, 520. See case on appeal. Addenda No. 26.

2—St. John City—Whether party applying for certiorari must give bond required by sec. 110, cap. 100, Consol. Stat.

Held, by Allen, C.J., and Duff, J., that sec. 110 of Consolidated Statutes, cap. 100, relating to rates and taxes, requiring a bond to be given before a party complaining of an assessment shall be entitled to a rule *nisi*, for *certiorari* is not applicable to assessments made in the City of St. John.

Held, by Palmer, J., that the section applied, but if it did not, it would be because it was inconsistent with the 20th section of the Act, 22 Vic., cap. 37, giving an appeal to the common council, and as the applicants had neither given the bond required by the former, nor taken the appeal required by the latter, *certiorari* should be refused. *Ex parte* Lewin, vol. 19, 424.

3—False imprisonment—Action for an arrest by virtue of an execution issued for assessment under 41 Vic., cap. 9—Where plaintiff did not own land on account of which the assessment was made—Execution issued by chamberlain of city—Where it was his duty to issue it—Whether either corporation or chamberlain liable.

The plaintiff was arrested under a warrant issued by the defendant Sandall, the receiver of taxes for the City of

St. John, for non-payment of an amount assessed upon him under the Act, 41 Vic., cap. 9, providing, among other matters, for the extention of Canterbury street.

The assessment was made by commissioners appointed by the Lieut.-Governor-in-Council. The plaintiff was not the owner of the land for which the commissioners made the assessment on him. Sandall, as was his duty under the Act, notified the plaintiff to pay, and in default, issued an execution, and for want of goods the plaintiff was arrested.

Held, that the corporation of the city had nothing to do with the legality of the assessment, and that neither the corporation nor Sandall were liable for doing what by law they were directed to do. *McSorley v. the Mayor of St. John*, vol. 20, 479. Appeal to Sup. Court of Canada allowed. See Addenda No. 10.

4—St. John—Trustees of estate residing out of the city, but employing agents there to collect and pay moneys.

S. being a resident of St. John died leaving property consisting of mortgages, bank stock, debentures, etc., and appointed trustees, none of whom resided in St. John, although some of them carried on their private business there. The trustees employed T., who held the office of pilot commissioner in St. John, and also attended to some other business on his own account, to collect the dividends and interest on the securities, and to make payments of the moneys collected. T. kept the accounts in his office, where some of the trustees came occasionally to make inquiries and give directions in matters connected with the estate; but they kept no office, and did no business as trustees, except what he did as their agent in so collecting and paying the moneys.

Held, that the trustees neither "carried on business" nor had "an office or place of business" in St. John, and were not liable to assessment. *Regina v. Wilson*, vol. 21, 178.

5—"Employment" within meaning of St. John Assessment Act of 1882—"Inhabitant of city"—President of a company attending office in St. John.

The president of an insurance company resided outside the city of St. John, but attended daily at the company's office in the city for the purpose of transacting such business as was assigned to that officer, such as signing policies, etc.

Held, that he had an employment within the meaning of "The St. John Assessment Act of 1882," and was liable to be assessed as an inhabitant. *Ex parte* Tucker, vol. 23, 311.

6—St. John Assessment Act of 1882—Assessment of capital and joint stock of bank—Whether real and personal property belonging to, may be assessed.

By the St. John Assessment Act of 1882, sec. 25, all rates and taxes on the city are to be raised by an equal rate upon the real estate therein, and on the personal estate and income of the inhabitants, and of persons declared to be inhabitants, for the purpose of taxation and upon the capital stock, income or things of joint stock companies or corporations, and shall be levied as follows—viz: by a poll tax of one dollar on all the male inhabitants of 21 years of age, and the residue upon the whole rateable property, real and personal, and rateable income and joint stock, according to its true and real value; provided that joint stock shall not be rated above the par value thereof.

By sec. 28, joint stock companies are to be assessed in like manner as individuals; and the president or manager of such joint stock company, etc., is to be deemed the owner of the real and personal estate, capital stock and effects of such company, and shall be dealt with accordingly.

By the Act incorporating the bank of New Brunswick, the capital or stock was to consist of gold and silver coins to a certain amount to be divided into shares of £50 each; and by a subsequent Act, the capital stock of the bank was fixed at one million dollars. In 1882 the president of the bank was assessed under the 28th section of the Assessment Act on real estate valued at $42,200, and personal estate of $1,057,800, making together $1,100,000.

Held, per Allen, C.J., Wetmore and Palmer, JJ. (Weldon and Fraser, JJ., dissenting), that the real and personal estate and capital stock of the bank were each liable to be assessed under the Act; and that an assessment on the real and personal estate was legal, though the estimated value of such estate exceeded the par value of the joint stock of the bank.

Per Allen, C.J., and Wetmore, J., that the words "capital stock" in the Act, meant the shares into which the capital of the company was divided, and not the real or personal estate of the bank.

Per Weldon and Fraser, JJ., that all the property, real and personal, of a joint stock bank formed its assets, and should be assessed as capital stock, and at the par value thereof. *Ex parte Lewin*, vol. 23, 591. Appeal to Sup. Court of Canada allowed. See Addenda 23.

7.—Municipal taxation—Employee of Federal Government—Income—Assessment of.

A. was employee of the Intercolonial Railway in the capacity of a clerk in the general offices of the railway at the town of M., where he resided. He received from the Government of Canada a salary at the rate of $600 per year, payable monthly, for his services as such clerk, and had been so employed for the space of three years, but such employment might be terminated at any time by the Railway Department, on giving fourteen days' notice. A. did not contribute to the superannuation fund of the Civil Service of Canada, and had not been appointed to such service as provided by the Canada Civil Service Act, 1882, or otherwise. It did not appear whether or not his salary was fixed by the Governor-General in Council. A. was assessed in the said town of M. for municipal purposes on his said income, and on the question being stated for the opinion of the court,

Held, by Weldon, Palmer, King and Fraser, JJ. (Allen, C.J., dissenting), that the case came within the principle of *ex parte Owen* (4 P. & B. 487), and that such income was not subject to assessment.

L. was employee of the Intercolonial Railway, employed as a painter of cars in the works of said railway, at the town of M., where he resided. He was paid by the Government, through the management of the railway, fifteen cents per hour for each hour that he was so employed, and was paid monthly therefor. At the time of the assessment mentioned below, he had been so employed for two years, but his employment might be terminated at any time by the Railway Department, on giving fourteen days' notice. He was assessed in the said town of M. for municipal purposes on his income derived from such labour and employment.

Held, by Allen, C.J., Weldon and Palmer, JJ. (King and Fraser, JJ., dissenting), that L.'s case did not come within the principle of *ex parte* Owen, and that the assessment was rightly made. *Ackman* v. *Town of Moncton*; *Landry* v. *Town of Moncton*, vol. 24, 103.

Assessment for taxes — How made where owner of land dead — Assessment against widow—Warrant to sell land for non-payment of taxes—Effect of including bad assessments in warrant — Whether warrant to sell land a judicial Act—Estoppel by attending sheriff's sale of land without protesting.

G. being the owner of real estate, conveyed it by registered deed in 1868, to three persons in trust for the benefit of his creditors, but remained in possession. In 1873 the trustees executed a deed reconveying the property to G., but it was not acknowledged by them, or registered until after his death, nor was there any proof of actual delivery of it to him. G. died in 1875 leaving a widow and children in possession of the land. Under the Act, 38 Vic. cap. 40, incorporating the town of Moncton, the property was assessed in the years 1875, 1876, and 1877 to "the estate of G.," and in 1878 to "the widow G."

These taxes being unpaid, a warrant issued in 1879 by the chairman of the town of Moncton, to the sheriff of the county under the Act, 41 Vic. cap. 82, reciting that the estate of G. had been assessed for the years 1875, 1876, 1877 and 1878 in a certain sum (the aggregate of the four years), which remained unpaid, and directing the sheriff to sell so much of the real estate as would be sufficient to pay the assessment and expenses. Under this warrant the sheriff seized and sold part of the land on which the assessments had been made, and it was purchased by the defendant. No objection having been made by the heirs, though a person attended the sale at their request for the purpose of bidding in the land. In ejectment by the heirs of G. against the purchaser,

Held, *per* Allen, C.J., King, Wetmore and Fraser, JJ. (Palmer, J., dissenting).

1. That the assessment for 1875 while G. was living, was improperly made against his "estate," and that the assessment for 1878 against "the widow G." did not indicate that it was upon her as the occupier or person having the ostensible control of her deceased husband's real estate; but was merely in her character as widow; and therefore that non-payment by her was not a default by the heirs of G.

2. That the inclusion of the assessment for 1878 in the warrant of the sale of the real estate vitiated the whole, and that no title passed by the sheriff's deed to the defendant.

Per Allen, C. J., and Palmer, J. (Wetmore, King and Fraser, JJ., dissenting).

1. That the order for the sale was a judicial Act, and while it stood unreversed, the validity of the sale could not be disputed.

2. That the heirs of G. having attended the sheriff's sale by their agent for the purpose of bidding on the property, and having seen the defendant purchase it without protest or objection, were estopped from disputing the defendant's title.

Per Fraser, J., *Quære.* Whether where an assessment is against the estate of a deceased person, a sale of the real estate can be made for non-payment of the taxes under 41 Vic. cap. 82. *Doe dem Elliott et al.* v. *Flanagan and wife*, vol. 25, 154.

—This case was affirmed on appeal to the Supreme Court of Canada. See Addenda 38.

—In city of St. John, creating lien on land. See Notes and Taxes 1.

—Warrant against estate of non-residents and minors. See *Certiorari* 5.

—Of damages—Affidavit for—Power of single judge to assess in term. See Practice 10.

—Of damages—Bills of exchange—Fraud—Disclosure to judge.

—Inhabitant — Wife's separate property—Taxes—Partly legal and partly illegal—Whether execution issued for whole is void. See Inhabitant 1.

—Land damages—Where land taken for railway purposes. See Land Damages 1.

— Highway — Assessment for. See Highway Act.

—Of commissioners of sewers for purpose of improving lands—Evidence of possession in party paying. See Possession 2.

ASSIGNEE.

Of bill of lading—Right to instruct agent to hold until payment of bill of exchange drawn for goods mentioned in bill of lading. See Bill of Lading 1.

—Of mortgage—Whether right in judgment obtained by mortgagee passed to assignee. See Ejectment 2.

—Under Insolvent Act of 1869. Title to land. See Insolvent Act 2.

ASSIGNMENT.

Under Insolvent Act—Demand of, made with malice and without probable cause, affords ground of action. See Insolvent Act 1.

—Of debt—Suit by assignee in equity. See Pleading 6.

—Of claim after verdict. See Set Off 1.

—Deed of assignment—Fraudulent. See Deed 2, 3, 4.

—Mortgage of chattels—Not an assignment—Condition in fire insurance policy. See Addenda 45.

ASSUMPSIT.—(See contract—Agreement.)

1—Delivery and acceptance of goods subsequent to time agreed upon for delivery—Cannot be set up as a defence, or in reduction of damages.

Where it is agreed that goods shall be delivered at a certain time, and the defendant, subsequently to the time agreed upon with a full knowledge of all the facts, thinks proper to accept delivery of the goods, he cannot set up the non-delivery at the specified time as a defence to the action, or in reduction of the value of the goods. *Moffat* v. *Lent*, vol. 18.

2—Implied contract to pay freight—Where owner gets possession of the goods—Interest.

In an action for the recovery of the freight of a quantity of iron carried in plaintiff's ship from London to St. John, it appeared that the iron was shipped by D. C. & Co., of England, who received from the master the usual bill of lading, in which the goods were made deliverable to the order of D. C. & Co., on paying freight. On arrival of the ship in St. John, defendant, to whom the bill of lading had been sent, claimed the iron as his own, and explained to plaintiff that D. C. & Co. had omitted to indorse the bill of lading. He also tendered the freight. Plaintiff still declined to deliver the goods without an indorsed bill of lading. The iron, however, was landed on the wharf, and it was shown that one J., a tide waiter, weighed it by defendant's direction, and it was hauled to the railway station by one C., who was paid for the hauling by defendant. Subsequently plaintiff rendered a bill for the freight to defendant, who replied that he had once tendered the freight, and referred the plaintiff to his solicitor.

Held, (by Weldon and Fisher, JJ., Allen, C.J., dissenting), that under these circumstances the jury were justified in finding an implied contract on defendant's part to pay the freight.

Held, also, that plaintiff was not entitled to interest. *Ferguson* v. *Domville*, vol. 19, 576.

3—Master and servant—Wages—Where servant leaves before time up.

If a servant, being engaged for a stated period, has, by the terms of the hiring, a right to leave before the time is up in a certain event, he may sue at once for the time he has worked, unless agreed to the contrary. *Lee* v. *Harding*, vol. 19, 390.

4—Written agreement—Work done under—Action for quantum meruit—Where plaintiff allowed to prove case without producing agreement—Defendant putting in as part of his case denying performance—Onus of proof.

In an action for work and labour done under a written agreement, plaintiff was allowed without objection to prove his case on the *quantum meruit* without producing the agreement.

Held, by Allen, C.J., and Weldon and Fraser, JJ., that this made out a *prima facie* case, and the defendant having put in the agreement as part of his case, the onus was on him to shew that plaintiff had not performed the contract.

Held, by King, J., that at the close of the whole case the question was as to the rights of the parties on the whole evidence, and if it shewed that the work was in fact done under a written contract, it was for the plaintiff to shew the performance of it, rather than for defendant to negative it. *Stevens* v. *Foxwell*, vol. 23, 476.

—Contract repudiated — Recovery under common counts. See Contract 12.

—Sale of goods subject to reduction of price. See Agreement 8.

ATTACHING ORDER.

Under Garnishee Act — Set aside where proceedings vexatious. See Garnishee Act.

ATTACHMENT.

1—Dissolution of—Where defendant has become insolvent—Where property has been released on bond.

Where defendant's property has been attached, and he afterwards becomes insolvent, the court is bound to dissolve the attachment, although the property was released on bond. *McIntosh* v. *Hamilton*, vol. 19, 1.

2—Action on bond given by defendant—Where obligors cannot dispute defendant's ownership of property.

The obligors in a bond given by a defendant, under section 29 of the Attachment Act, cannot, in an action on the bond, raise any question as to defendant's ownership of the property attached. *Botsford* v. *Trites*, vol. 19, 135.

3—Where defendant became a non-resident of the province before cause of action accrued—Whether Act applies.

Held, that the Attachment Act (Consol. Stat. cap. 42) did not apply to non-residents of the province, who had not been within it since the cause of action accrued. *Schofield* v. *Nevins* vol. 19, 399.

4—Whether second may be issued—What affidavit should state.

Held, that a second attachment might issue under cap. 42, Consol. Stat., the first having been set aside, and that the affidavit to obtain a judge's order for attachment to issue during the progress of the suit, need not state more than the affidavit for attachment issued concurrently with the writ in the cause. *Hilyard* v. *Wood*, vol. 19, 572.

5—Sheriff's return — Matter of record — Estoppel.

A sheriff having made return to a writ of attachment issued under the Attachment Act, Consol. Stat. cap. 38, that he had seized certain property (describing it) under plaintiff's attachment, and held it subject to that attachment till the debt and costs were paid, is estopped, while that return stands, from returning *nulla bona* to the execution issued on the plaintiff's judgment; and in an action for a false return, it is no defence to allege that at the time of delivery to him of the attachment in plaintiff's suit, the sheriff had already attached the same property under another attachment, which it was not sufficient to satisfy. *Everitt et al.* v. *Lynds*, vol. 20, 384.

6—Contempt of Court—Injunction order—Disobedience not wilful.

Where a judge sitting in equity, being satisfied that a breach of an injunction order by the defendant was not wilful, declined to make an order for his imprisonment, the Court on appeal refused to disturb the judgment of the Court below. *Sayre* v. *Harris*, vol. 18, 677.

7—Contempt of Court—Constable selling goods after being served with certiorari containing stay of proceedings—Interrogatories—When to be filed—Costs of.

A constable, who had seized goods under a warrant issued by a justice on a conviction made by him, was served with a rule *nisi* for a *certiorari*, containing an order for stay of proceedings, but went on and sold the goods.

Held, that he was guilty of a contempt of Court, and that it was no excuse to say that he did not think the *certiorari* [illegible]strained him from selling, but where [illegible] had made restitution, and paid the [illegible] of the application, he was ordered [illegible] discharged from custody.

[illegible] to an attachment for contempt was ordered by the Court to remain in the clerk's office until the first day of the following term, on the defendant's attorney undertaking that he would then appear in Court, the party obtaining the attachment is not entitled to costs of interrogatories before the time appointed for the defendant to appear. *Ex parte Leone; ex parte Groves*, vol. 22, 629.

—For costs, where costs are taxed on a day later than day named in clerk's appointment of taxation, Court will not grant. See Costs 12.

—For costs against one of two defendants, no demand on the other being shewn. See Costs 12.

For costs on appeal. See Costs 8.

—Writ of—Writ good upon face, while in force a justification to the sheriff. See Insolvent Act of 1869, 2.

—Of property—By order of commissioner under Consol. Stat. cap. 39. See False Imprisonment 7.

—Issued out of County Court. See Criminal Law 7.

ATTESTATION

Of Will. See Will 4.

ATTORNEY.

1—Collecting money.

Although an attorney, who has collected money, may be made to account therefor in a civil action, the Court will compel him to do summary justice without putting the client to the necessity of bringing an action. *Ex parte Kerr* v *Thorne*, vol. 18, 625.

2—Understanding between—Pleading.

A suit was commenced in January, 1876, and declaration delivered in April, with the ordinary notice to plead.

No plea was demanded, and by consent of the attorney the matter was allowed to stand, on an undertaking that the defendant should plead, and that one of the pleas would be "never indebted." The defendant did not plead till November, 1879, previous to which time, and since the commencement of this suit, he had become insolvent, and had agreed with plaintiff that he would pay him $1,000, and his costs in settlement of this suit, if plaintiff did not oppose his discharge. Defendant obtained his discharge, but would not carry out this arrangement; he then pleaded five pleas, the fifth plea being his discharge under the Insolvent Act. The plaintiff joined issue upon the first four pleas, but took no notice of the fifth plea, alleging that it was pleaded against good faith, and gave notice of trial.

Held, *per* Weldon and Wetmore, JJ.: 1st. That the Court would not interfere to aid attorneys in carrying out loose understandings in matters of practice. 2nd. That if the 5th plea was irregularly pleaded, the plaintiff's attorney might have applied to have it struck out, but he could not accept part of the pleas, and treat the 5th as a nullity. 3rd. That the 5th plea, not setting up a matter of defence which had arisen after plea pleaded, was not a plea *puis darrein continuance*, but might be pleaded with the other pleas under Consol. Stat. cap. 37 sec. 64.

Per Fisher, J., That defendant should be allowed to plead the matter of the 5th plea *puis darrein continuance* without the affidavit required by Consol. Stat. cap. 37 sec. 64, but only on condition of his paying the plaintiff the $1,000 and his costs. *Moore* v. *May*, vol. 19, 506; see also *Knox* v. *Gregory*, vol. 21, 196.

3—Misconduct—Witness—Refunding fees where he does not attend.

Where an attorney was subpœnaed four times to attend the trial of a cause as a witness, and only attended once, though he was paid his witness fees—$20 each time—a rule was granted directing him to refund the $20 paid him for the trial which he did not attend.

Semble, that where a charge against an attorney amounts to an indictable offence, it cannot be tried on a summary application calling on him to pay over money. *In re Wetmore*, vol. 19, 639.

4—Firm of—Whether each member must pay library fees—Notice of bail by firm when one in default—Irregularity.

Where two or more attorneys practice as partners, they must all be qualified by payment of library fees under Consol. Stat., cap. 34, or their proceedings will be liable to be set aside.

When special bail was put in and the notice of bail was signed by a firm of attorneys, one of whom had not paid his library fees,

Held, by Allen C.J. and Weldon Wetmore, and Palmer, JJ., that the notice was not a nullity, but an irregularity, and plaintiff's proper course was to have taken advantage of the irregularity by opposing the justification or by applying to set the proceedings aside; but by King J., that the notice was a nullity, and plaintiff was entitled to treat it as no bail, and take an assignment of the bail bond. *Jones* v. *Milliken*, vol. 22, 315.

5—Admission of—When applicant had no notice of new by-laws of the Barristers' Society.

The by-laws of the Barristers' Society relating to the admission of attorneys approved by the Court in Easter term, were not published until May. Two students-at-law, who, under the new by-laws, might have been admitted in Easter term, had no notice of the rules, and came up in following term for examination. The Barristers' Society having recommended their admission, the Court, under the peculiar circumstances of the case, allowed the applicants to be enrolled, stating, however, that it must not be considered a precedent for any departure from the rules in future. *In Re Beckwith*, vol. 21, 104.

6—Firm of—Misappropriation of money by one partner—Liability of co-partner—Summary application to Court.

If an attorney receives money in his character as such, the Court will compel him to perform his undertaking in respect to it.

Where one member of a firm of attorneys receives money for investment, and misappropriates it without the knowledge or consent of the other, it ought to be clearly shown that the latter was guilty of personal misconduct, or at least, of neglect of duty as a member of the firm, in consequence of the misconduct of his partner, before the Court will interfere on a summary application to compel him to pay money. *Ex parte Flood*, vol. 23, 86.

Agency of student-at-law in Barrister's office.

See *Eastern Township Bank* v. *Harrington*, vol. 18, 631.

Liability of attorney for sheriff's fees for executing a *fi. fa.*

The attorney is liable to the sheriff for the latter's fees for executing a *fi. fa.* *Palmer* v. *Harding*, vol. 19, 281.

Attorney's name not signed to notice on copy of *capias*.—Effect of. See Arrest 1.

Absence unavoidable on trial of cause.—Effect of. See Collision 1.

Admission of—Rule as to. See Rules Easter Term, 1881.

Affidavit to hold to bail by—Whether Sufficient. See Arrest 1.

Promise by an attorney to indemnify sheriff—When binding one client. See Sheriff 2.

AUCTIONEERS.

Liability to assignees of bill of lading for selling goods on consignee's account. See Bill of Lading.

AUDITORS.

Admission to, of correctness of entries in cash book, kept by official shewing balances against self. See Evidence 11.

AWARD—(See Arbitration).

1—Submission containing agreement that award may be entered as a postea—But silent as to its being made a rule of Court—Application to make it a rule of Court refused.

Where by a submission containing no agreement that it might be made a rule of Court, the parties to the suit agreed that the award could be entered as a *postea* on the *nisi prius* record, and judgment be signed thereon, the Court refused to make the submission a rule of Court. *McLeod*, assignee, v. *Pye*, vol. 21, 212.

2—Publication—Reference of a suit and all matters in difference—Finding on one issue only—Immateriality of other issues Costs.

A. and B. being the respective owners of mills on the same stream, A. brought an action against B. for damages to his mill by the erection of a dam by B., which it was alleged caused the water to flow back upon A.'s mill further up the mill stream. B. pleaded, 1. Not guilty; 2. That A. was not possessed of the mill as alleged; 3. That A. was not entitled to the flow of water to his mill; That B. was seised in fee of a mill, and for 20 years before the suit enjoyed the right to use the water of the stream to work his mill, which user was the alleged injury complained of. The suit and all matters in difference were referred to arbitration—the costs of the action and of the arbitration to be assessed and allowed by the arbitrators for the party in whose favor they should award—to be paid as they should direct. The arbitrators awarded that B. was not guilty of the grievances laid to his charge in the declaration, and directed that A. should pay him a certain sum as the costs of the action and of the arbitration, which when paid, should be a final end and determination of all matters in difference.

Held. 1. That the award that B. was not guilty of the charge in the declaration was a determination of the suit; and that it was not necessary for the arbitrators to award upon the issues raised by the other pleas which thereby became immaterial. 2. That the arbitrators having power to assess the costs, it was not necessary for them to award specifically upon the several issues raised by the pleas. 3. That B. had a right to withdraw from the consideration of the arbitrators, a claim which he made against A. for injury caused by him to B.'s mill.

An award need not be made in duplicate. If it is duly executed, and delivered to the party in whose favor it is made, it is sufficient to give a copy to the other party. *In re Dalton and Allen*, vol. 25, 19.

3—Refusal to make submission a rule of Court—When action pending on the award.

An application to make a submission to arbitration, a rule of Court was refused, where an action was pending on the award, and where there was a dispute as to the validity of it. *In re Palmer and Calhoun*, vol. 24, 240.

4—Excess of authority—Award bad in part—When bad part inseparable.

A matter was referred to two arbitrators, with power to select a third person to act with them in case they could not agree; the costs to be in their discretion. The arbitrators appointed A. who sat with them on the arbitration and joined in the award, though it did not appear that they had been unable to agree. An award was made in favor of the plaintiff for a sum of money payable by instalments, in which was included an amount for the fees of A.

Held, that under the circumstances, the arbitrators had no right to appoint A., and as the sum included for his fees was so mixed up with the total sum awarded, that it could not be separated from it, the award was bad. *Turner v. Hart*, vol. 24, 547.

—*Of* arbitrators — Amendment — When allowable. See Equity 1.

—Conclusiveness of—As to amount of demand. See Costs 5.

BAIL.

1—Relief of—In action in the County Court—Consol. Stat. C. 37, sec. 31, cap. 38, sec. 5, and cap. 51, sec. 30—Considered—Necessity of issuing ca sa to fix bail—Appeal from order of Judge—County Court relieving bail.

A Judge of the County Court has no power to relieve bail who render their principal after the expiration of thirty days after the service upon them of the writ in the action on the bond.

Semble,—An appeal lies to this Court from an order of a Judge of a County Court relieving bail. *McRory v. McAlpine*, vol. 20, 537.

2—Execution delivered to sheriff to fix bail—Effect of—City Court of St. John—

Consol. Stat. cap. 53, sec. 11.

Held, in an action in City Court of St. John where the execution was delivered to the sheriff "to fix bail" it was not delivered "*to be executed*," and the bail was held not liable. *Young Claus v. Wallace*, vol. 24, 365.

Affidavit for—Delay in filing. See Bail Bond 1.

Notice of, by firm of Attorneys, one of whom had not paid his library fees—Irregularity. See Attorney 4.

Where defendant had entered, and been rendered—Delay in signing judgment. See Discharge 1.

The amount of bail to be given in action of tort—In Judge's discretion. See Arrest 2.

Affidavit to hold to—Time of filing. See Practise 12.

Arrest of Debtor—Affidavits of attorney and agent of company. See Arrest 4.

Arrest on *capias*—Time for giving bail. See Practise 24.

BAIL BOND.

1—Forfeiture of—Delivered up to be cancelled—Affidavit for bail and entry docket—Delay in filing.

Where a defendant had given a bail bond, but did not put in special bail till after the forfeiture of the bond, though before the assignment of it to the plaintiff, the Court ordered the bail bond to be delivered up to be cancelled—the plaintiff not having filed the affidavit for bail, nor the entry docket in the cause till after the special bail was put in, and more than thirty days after the execution of the *capias*. *Jones v. Landry*, vol. 22, 417.

Where signed by only one surety—Sufficiency of. See Practise 24.

BANK.

New Brunswick—Capital and joint stock—Whether real or personal property belonging to, may be assessed under St. John Assessment Act of 1882.

See Assessment 6.

Bankable Currency—Whether a note for a stated sum "payable in bankable currency" is a promissory note—Meaning of. See *Dunn v. Allen*, vol. 24, 1.

BANKING ACT.

Charter—Continuation of—Right to transact business—Proof of Charter.

The Banking Act, 34 Vic. cap. 5, continues the charters of the banks enumerated in a schedule to the Act, and authorises them to discount bills and notes, and to transact business at any place in the Dominion.

In an action by such a bank as indorsees of a promissory note it is not necessary to produce the charter of the bank to shew their right to sue.

Semble, that if the existence of the corporation is not denied by plea, it is admitted. *La Banque Nationale v. Beckett*, vol. 25, 145.

BANKRUPTCY.

1—Under Imperial Act, 12 and 13 Vic. cap. 106—May be pleaded in the Courts of this Province to an action on a judgment obtained prior to 1869 on a cause of action arising here—Sec. 115 of the Insolvent Act of 1875—Not retrospective—What plea should contain—Procedure and pleading—Pleading matters of law only—Departure—Costs as part judgment—Whether discharged with debt.

See *Gilbert v. Raymond*, vol. 19, 315.

2—Partnership—Non-resident partner—English Bankrupt Act—Trustee appointed under property vesting in—Jurisdiction of Supreme Court.

A firm consisting of A. and B. carried on business in England, and also in New Brunswick, A. residing in England and B. in New Brunswick. The firm became insolvent, and petitioned the Court in England for liquidation under "The Bankruptcy Act of 1869," which was adjudged, and a trustee of the estate appointed.

Quære, Whether the provisions of the Bankrupt Act, 1869, applied to this province, and whether property belonging to the firm here, vested in such trustee.

A judgment creditor of the firm in the province issued an execution, under which property belonging to the firm here was seized and sold by the sheriff, who refused to pay the proceeds to the trustee. On an application to the Court, under the 74th section of "The Bankruptcy Act, 1869," for an order to the sheriff to pay the proceeds of the execution to the trustee.

Held, 1. That even if the English Bankruptcy Act did apply to this province, this Court had no jurisdiction as a Bankruptcy or Insolvent Court. 2. That no sufficient application had been made to this Court by the English Bankruptcy Court, under the 74th section, to justify this Court in acting in aid of the English Bankruptcy Court in the matter. 3. That if the property of the firm in this country vested in the trustee under the Bankruptcy Act, he might have brought trover against the sheriff for the seizure under the execution, or, an action for money had and received for the proceeds of the sale; and therefore the Court would not interfere on a summary application.

Held, also, that the affidavit on which the application was made need not be entitled in the suit in which the judgment was obtained. *Ex parte Gliddon; in re Maritime Bank v. Carrill et al.*, vol. 24, 250.

BILL.

In equity—Amendment of—Prayer—General relief—Where inconsistent with specific prayer. See Equity.

Amendment of title. See Equity 1.

BILL OF EXCHANGE.

Action by indorsee—Where payee became insolvent before indorsement—Whether notice to indorsee necessary.

A declaration on a bill of exchange stated that F. drew the bill on the 13th May, directed to the defendant, requesting him to pay to B., or order, $600 on 1st December then next; that defendant accepted the bill; that B. indorsed it to one E., who indorsed it to plaintiff. Defendant pleaded that subsequent to the acceptance of the bill, and prior to the alleged indorsement by B., the latter became insolvent, and a writ of attachment was issued against his estate under the Insolvent Act, whereby the bill of exchange became vested in his assignee; that the alleged indorsement was made without the knowledge or consent of assignee. Plaintiff demurred to this plea on the grounds (1) that it did not appear that at the time B. indorsed the bill, plaintiff had any notice that B. had become an insolvent; (2) that by accepting the bill defendant was estopped from disputing B.'s right to indorse it. But,

Held, that the plea was good, and defendant was entitled to judgment. *Macfillan v. Davidson*, vol. 20, 338.

Stamp Act—Right to affix double stamps—Knowledge—What constitutes. See *Tufts v. Chapman*, vol. 22, 185; see also Addenda No. 12, case on appeal.

Double stamping by payee—Where allowed.

Defence of insufficient stamping—Whether must be pleaded. See *Vaughan v. Roberts*, vol. 23, 343; see also Addenda No. 29, case on appeal.

Double stamping—Reasonable time. See *Bank of Nova Scotia v. Cushing*, vol. 21, 498.

Conditional payment—When considered such. Assessment of damages by single Judge in term. See Practise 10. (See Promissory Notes).

—Parol evidence of agreement.

Accord and satisfaction—What evidence of. See agreement 7.

BILL OF LADING.

1—Rights of assignee of—Right to instruct agent to hold until payment of bill of exchange drawn for goods mentioned in bill of lading—Whether instructions admissible in action against a third party—Consignee obtaining goods without bill of lading and without paying for goods—Liability of auctioneers to assignees of bill of lading for selling goods on consignee's account—Trover—Interest.

The plaintiffs, a banking company doing business at Charleston, S. C., were assignees of a bill of lading, for one hundred casks of spirits of turpentine and five hundred and one barrels of resin, for which they had discounted the shipper's draft on R. of St. John, N. B., the consignee. They forwarded the draft to their agents with instructions to deliver the bill of lading to R. when the draft was paid. The draft was dated August 2, 1875, and was payable twenty days after date. R. accepted the draft, but did not pay the same, and the bill of lading was retained by plaintiffs' agents. The invoice was sent from Charleston to R., to whom the captain of the vessel by which the goods were shipped, delivered the goods without the production of the bill of lading.

Subsequently R. delivered ninety barrels of the turpentine to the defendants, who were auctioneers, for the purpose of being sold by the defendants on account of R., upon which they advanced R. $1,000. The defendants after advertising the sale sold the turpentine at public auction and paid the balance of the net proceeds to R., on September 21, 1875. The turpentine had been taken out of the vessel and landed and warehoused several days before delivery to defendants, and defendants did not know that R. had not possession of the bill of lading until October 21, 1875, when the plaintiffs, by notice in writing, demanded the turpentine of them.

Held, that plaintiffs were entitled in an action of trover to recover from defendants the invoice of the turpentine. The court also gave interest on the amount to the plaintiffs from the day the demand was made.

Held, that the instructions from plaintiffs to their agents to deliver the bill of lading upon payment of the draft, was admissible evidence in an action by plaintiffs against the defendants. *The People's National Bank of Charleston* v. *Stewart*, vol. 18, 298.

On appeal to S. C. C., judgment confirmed, 10th June, 1880.

BILL OF SALE.

1—Passing of after acquired property—Novus actus interveniens—License to grantee to take possession jus tertii—Trover.

The plaintiffs were the grantees, and one H. the grantor, in a bill of sale, which specified certain property conveyed, and contained the following clause:—"And all property owned or to be owned by me, and including all renewal stock or stocks to be purchased by me." H. subsequently acquired possession of a horse and colt. The colt was the progeny of a mare conveyed by the bill of sale. The horse was bought in for H. at a sale had at his direction to satisfy a lien which he claimed for keep. H. made a formal delivery of the horse and colt to the plaintiffs, stating that he delivered them to hold on the terms of the bill of sale; but H. always retained the actual possession.

The defendant (the sheriff) seized and sold the horse and colt under an execution against H., and the plaintiffs claiming that the property was in them, brought trover.

Held, 1. That the property in the horse did not vest in the plaintiffs by the bill of sale, and that the symbolic delivery by H. to them with no ostensible change of possession, was not a *novus actus interveniens*, nor was it an exercise by them of a license to take possession under the bill of sale.

2. That the colt being the progeny of a mare conveyed by the bill of sale, passed to the plaintiffs.

3. That the sheriff having seized and sold the horse and colt under an execution against H., could not set up that H. had no title, in answer to an action by persons claiming through H. *Nicholson et al., v. Temple*, vol. 20, 218.

Appeal to S. C. C. dismissed. See Addenda 37.

2—Action by grantee not in possession—Evidence under not guilty—Measure of damages—Trover.

D. conveyed two horses to the plaintiff by a bill of sale conditioned to become void on the return by D. of a quantity of grain, etc., loaned him by the plaintiff, and on payment of a sum of money. D. retained possession of the horses. During the continuance of the security the defendant took the horses under an alleged distress for rent against D.

Held, in an action of trover by the plaintiff against the defendant for converting the horses,—1. That the property being in the plaintiff, he was not bound under the plea of not guilty to shew a right to prevent possession. 2. That no demand of possession was necessary. 3. That it was not misdirection to tell the jury that they might find as damages the full value of the horses. *Coates v. Gosling*, vol. 20, 323.

3—Registry—Grantor continuing in possession—Whether conclusive evidence of fraud.

When an absolute bill of sale is given, the fact of the grantor continuing in possession, though evidence of fraud, does not necessarily make the transfer void; and it is for the jury to say whether, from all the circumstances, the transaction is *bona fide*, or merely colorable to defeat an execution creditor.

When the bill of sale is registered, one of the circumstances always relied on to shew fraud, namely, the secrecy of the transaction is wanting. *Sheriff v. McKeen*, vol. 23, 181.

4. Consol. Stat. cap. 75—Debtor and creditor accounts—Credit of chattels—Registration.

A. being indebted to B., an account was made out by B. shewing the amount which A. owed him, and crediting certain articles, including a wagon, leaving a small balance in favor of B. The account was signed by A. The wagon was in A.'s possession at the time, in an unfinished state, and was left with him to be completed in consideration of the balance due on the account. There was no other evidence of a sale of the wagon from A. to B.

Held.—Per Palmer, King & Fraser, JJ., (Wetmore, J., dissenting) that as there was no sale of the wagon independent of the written document, it amounted to a bill of sale, and not being registered under Consol. Stat. cap. 75, the wagon was liable to seizure under execution against B.

Per Wetmore, J., that the writing was simply a receipt of the settlement of accounts between A. and B., and did not require registration as a bill of sale.

Shirreff, Appellant, and Vye, Respondent, vol. 24, 572.

—Subject to a defeasance, necessity of filing—Schedule should be attached. See Bills of Sale Act, 1.

—Conditional sale-agreement—Representation when not considered as bill of sale. See Trover 6.

—Whether a bill absolute in its terms, but subject to a defeasance, which is not reduced to writing and filed is void, against the persons named in section 1 of the Bills of Sale Act. See *Sheraton* v. *Whelpley*, vol. 20, 75.

—Insolvency—Future advances—Registry. See vol. 20, 75.

—After acquired property—When Court of Equity would refuse performance. See Equity 1.

—When void under Insolvent Act of 1875. See Insolvent Act of 1875.

—When fraudulent or not—Question properly left to jury. See Evidence 2.

—Effect of—Where boat has been rebuilt and registered—Since given. See Registration 1.

BILL OF SALES ACT.

Ultra Vires—Defeasance—Filing of—Schedule.

1—The Bills of Sale Act Consol. Stat., cap. 75, is not beyond the power of the Local Legislature under the British N. A. Act, 1867, as dealing with matters relating to insolvency.

A bill of sale absolute on its face was made subject to a defeasance or equity of redemption, but the defeasance was not filed under the Bills of Sale Act.

Held, that the bill of sale was inoperative, and vested no title in the grantee as against the assignee of the grantor under the Insolvent Act.

A bill of sale professed to convey all the goods and merchandise of the grantors contained in their store situate etc., consisting of dry goods and groceries mentioned in the schedule annexed. There was no schedule.

Quære—per Allen, C.J., whether the bill of sale was not thereby rendered inoperative. *In re Deveber*, vol. 21, 397.

2—Matters of insolvency—Bill of sale Act not *ultra vires* as dealing with matters of insolvency — Bill of sale taking effect only from time of registry —Future advances—Fraudulent preference—Banking Act 34 Vic. cap. 5, sec. 40. See *in re Deveber, ex parte Bank of New Brunswick*, vol. 21, 401.

Agreement when not considered as bill of sale. See Trover 6.

Boom Company—Incorporation of, no power to obstruct tidal or navigable rivers. See Addenda No. 29.

BOND.

Given by defendant under Attachment Act—Action on. See Attachment 2.

Although property released on—Attachment dissolved if owner after becomes insolvent. See Attachment 2.

For security for costs — Defective—Should be returned to plaintiff's attorney. See Judgment 1.

—For faithful discharge of agent's duties. See pleading 9.

—On appeal from County Court—Perfecting of—Notice to the Judge. See County Court Appeal 7.

—Bail—One surety—Sufficiency of. See Practice 24.

—Bond — Payment on — Statute of Limitations. See Addenda 27.

BOOKS.

Inspection of—Application for—Where particulars previously demanded—Stay of proceedings.

Held, by Wetmore and King, JJ.—(Weldon and Duff, JJ., dissenting), that the fact of defendant having demanded particulars of plaintiff's claim prevented plaintiff from obtaining an order for inspection of defendants' books until an application was made under section 94 of C. L. P. Act (Consol. Stat.), to remove the stay of proceedings created by the demand of particulars. Mr. Justice Duff having referred the matter to the Court yielded his opinion to that of Wetmore and King, JJ., and the order was refused. *Jones v. Maritime Bank of Canada*, vol. 20, 544.

BOOKS OF ACCOUNT.

A creditor has no right to object before County Court Judge that insolvent has not kept proper books when he has not raised objection before assignee. See Insolvent Act.

Insurance company having once examined the books of the insured and adjusted the loss, cannot demand a second examination. See Insurance 6.

Boom Company—Liability of. See Meduxnikik Boom Co.

Boundary line. See Acquiescence.

BREACH OF PEACE.

Assault on wife by husband is breach of peace. See Husband & Wife 6.

BRITISH STATUTES.

Mortmain.

The Statute of Mortmain, 9 Geo. II, cap. 36, is not in full force in this province. *Doe dem Hasen v. Rector, etc., St. James' Church*, vol. 18, 479.

BUILDING.

Overhanging land of adjoining owners —Entry to prevent falling — Justification. See Trespass 1.

—For faithful discharge of agent's duties. See Pleading 9.

—On appeal from County Court — Perfecting of—Notice to the Judge. See County Court Appeal 7.

—Bail—One surety—Sufficiency of. See Practice 24.

—Bond — Payment on — Statute of Limitations. See Addenda 27.

BUSINESS LICENSES.

1—Authorizing the Mayor of St. John to grant business licenses — By-laws imposing penalties on persons not free citizens who engage in any business in St. John without a license—Commercial travellers—Whether Act ultra vires.

The Act of the Provincial Legislature, 33 Vic. cap. 4, authorising the Mayor of St. John to license natural born British subjects, etc., to engage in business, etc., in the city of St. John, and empowering the city council to pass by-laws imposing penalties and forfeitures on persons other than free citizens who carry on business, etc., in the city without a license, is not *ultra vires* as being in conflict with the powers of Parliament to regulate trade and commerce. *Ex parte Fairbairn*, 2 P. & B. 4, approved. *Jones v. Gilbert*, vol. 20, 61; *Jones v. Marshall*, vol. 20, 64.

Appeal to Supreme Court of Canada allowed. See Addenda No. 5.

BY-LAW

of City of St. John—Retrospective operation of—Previous contract for building avoided. See Contract 4.

The common council of St. John have no power to pass a by-law subjecting persons to imprisonment for non-payment of a pecuniary penalty, except contingently, in case goods and chattels cannot be found on which to levy. *Regina v. Gilbert*, vol. 18, 619.

CANADA TEMPERANCE ACT.

1—Certiorari—Whether taken away.

Certiorari is by the Canada Temperance Act of 1878, taken away in all cases where the magistrate has jurisdiction. *Ex parte Gee*, vol. 20, 67.

2 —Conviction—Proof necessary — Proclamation of Act.

Held, by Allen, C.J., and Duff, J. (Palmer, J., dissenting), that in order to convict a person under the Canada Temperance Act of selling liquor contrary to the statute, it must be proved by the production of the proclamation containing the order in council, and by shewing the expiry of the licenses that the second part of the Act is in force.

By Palmer, J., that the Court must take notice, as a matter of law, that the Act is in force; and is also bound to find out and take notice of all facts necessary to determine the question of law.

Held, by Palmer, J., that in a conviction under the Act costs may be awarded against the defendant. *Ex parte White*, vol. 20, 552.

3 —Conviction under—Must prove second part of Act in force—Evidence that licenses have expired.

Where the proclamamation in the *Canada Gazette* contained an order in council declaring the second part of the Canada Temperance Act shall be in force [upon, from, and after the day on which the annual or semi-annual licences would expire, in order to sustain a conviction under the Act, it must be proved that the licences have expired, except in cases where from the time which had elapsed between the publication of the proclamation and prosecution for the alleged breach of the law, all previously existing licences must necessarily have expired. *Ex parte McDonald*, vol. 20, 542.

4 —Gazette containing proclamation must be put in evidence to show second part of Act is force —Certiorari where magistrate acts without jurisdiction.

Before a person can be legally convicted of selling liquor under the Canada Temperance Act 1878, it must be proved before the magistrate that the second part of the Act is in force by the production of the *Gazette* containing the proclamation. Without such proof the magistrate has no jurisdiction, and the Court will grant *certiorari* to remove the conviction.

The Act does not take away *certiorari* where the magistrate acts without jurisdiction or in excess of it. *Ex parte William Russell*, vol. 20, 536.

5—City within meaning of — Licenses — Expiration of.

The town of Moncton, in County of Westmoreland, was incorporated by Act of Assembly, whereby the whole local government of the town, and the exclusive power to grant licences for, and to regulate the sale of spirituous liquors in the town, was vested in the town council. The County of Westmoreland was afterwards incorporated as a municipality. The Canada Temperance Act 1878, provided that the proceedings for bringing the Act into force in any county or city should be by petition to the Governor-General in Council, of at least one-fourth of the electors of any county or city, on which a proclamation might issue for taking a poll of the votes for and against the petition. By section 96, if the petition was adopted by the electors of the county or city named therein, and to which the same related, the Governor-General in Council, might by order in council declare "that the Act shall be in force and take effect in such county or city from and after the day on which the annual or semi-annual licenses for the sale of spirituous liquors then in force in such county or city will expire." A petition from the requisite number of electors in the County of Westmoreland having been presented to the Governor-General, and a vote having been taken adopting the petition, an order in council was made declaring that the Act should be in force and take effect in the County of Westmoreland from and after the day on which the annual or semi-annual licences for the sale of liquors then in force in the said county expired.

At the time this order in council issued, there were licenses for the sale of liquors in force in Moncton granted by the town council, and in the County of Westmoreland granted by the municipality, such licenses expiring at different periods.

Held, by Allen, C.J., and Duff, J., (King, J., dissenting) that Moncton is a city within the meaning of the Canada Temperance Act, and as no separate vote of the ratepayers of the town had been taken, the order in council bringing the Act in force in the county did not apply to Moncton.

Held, by King, J., that Moncton is not a city within the meaning of the Act, and that the Act came in force in the county, including Moncton, on the termination of the latest expiring licences either in the town or county.

The licences granted by the town council of Moncton expired on the 15th December, 1880. A by-law of the municipality declared that all tavern licenses should expire at the annual meeting of [illegible] council, which was on the third Tues[illegible] in January. Licences were granted by the muncipality on the 24th January, 1880, for one year.

Held, per Weldon and Wetmor, JJ., that even if the Act were in force in Moncton, such licences would not expire till the 24th January, 1881; and that the Canada Temperance Act would not be in force in Moncton till that day.

Per King, J., that the licences should be read in connection with the by-law, and that they would not run for 365 days from their issue, but would expire at the annual meeting of the municipality, (the 18th January, 1881) and therefore a conviction for selling liquor in Moncton on the 23rd January was sustainable. *Ex parte McCleave*, vol. 21, 313.

6—Certiorari—In what cases taken away—Sec 111—Construction of—Penalties under sec. 110—How recoverable.

Held, per Allen, C.J., Duff and King, J.J., (Weldon Wetmore and Palmer, JJ., dissenting) that by section 111 of the Canada Temperance Act, a *certiorari* is taken away in all cases of conviction for offences against part II of the Act, except where there is an excess or want of jurisdiction.

Per Wetmore and Palmer, JJ., that the *certiorari* is not taken away where the conviction is before two justices of the peace, but only where it is before the officers named in sec. 111.

Per Allen, C.J., Wetmore, Duff, Palmer, and King, JJ., that the convictions, etc., mentioned in sec. 111, related to offences against part II of the Act, and not where offences created by sec. 110.

Per Allen, C.J., Duff and Palmer, JJ., that the penalties for offences under sec. 110, were not recoverable by summary conviction, but by action of debt.

Per Allen, C.J., Duff and King, JJ., that as a *certiorari* would still lie in some cases as in excess or want of jurisdiction, the recognition of the *certiorari* in sec. 118, was not inconsistent with the prohibitory words of sec. 111.

Per Wetmore and Palmer, JJ., that as the *certiorari* was not taken away by sec. 111, where the conviction was before two justices of the peace, the 118th sec. might apply to such cases. *Ex parte Hackett* vol. 21, 513.

7—Proclamation declaring second part of Act in force—Must be put in evidence before Magistrate—Information.

Held, (following *Ex parte Russell*, vol. 21, 526) that before a person can be legally convicted of selling liquor under Canada Temperance Act, 1878, it must be proved before the magistrate, that the second part of the Act is in force by the production of the *Canada Gazette*, containing the proclamation.

Held, that the information under the Act must be taken before two justices, although one may sign the summons. *Reg. v. Historn*, *Reg. v. Burtt*, vol. 22, 51.

8—Election under—Scrutiny—Parties to—Writ of prohibition.

By a return of a poll held on a petition to bring the Canada Temperance Act into operation, it appeared that the votes for and against the petition were equal. An application to the Judge of the County Court, under section 61 of the Act, praying for a scrutiny of the votes polled, charged that there had been bribery, and corruption, and treating; that persons who had no right to vote, voted against the petition by personating voters; that ballots against the petition were improperly allowed, and ballots in favor of it improperly rejected by the returning officers; and that there was a legal majority in favor of the petition. That B. was the secretary of a committee who opposed the petition, and that F. was prominent at the election in opposing it, and was a proper person against whom the petition might be brought.

The Judge thereupon appointed a time for hearing the application, and directed notice to be given to B., F. and S., and at the hearing decided that B. and F. were proper parties against whom the petition should be brought, and ordered the petitioners to enter into a recognisance to prosecute the petition, and to pay B. and F. any costs that might be adjudged them, and appointed a day for the scrutiny.

Held, *per* Allen, C.J., Palmer and King, JJ.; (Weldon, J., dissenting), that the Judge of the County Court had jurisdiction over the subject matter of the petition, and power to name a party against whom the same should be brought; that F. was properly named as such party, and therefore the recognisance was sufficient, even if B. should not have been included; but—*Semble*, that B. was also properly named as a party.

Held, also, that as the petition contained sufficient allegations to authorise the Judge to proceed, it was immaterial that it asked for the scrutiny on other grounds into which he might not have a right to enquire.

Per Weldon, J. 1. That the petition should have been brought against the officer whose return was complained of, or, against the agent of a party at the polling. 2. That the petition stated no act done by B. to justify his being made a party. 3. That the authority of the County Court Judge was only to order a re-count of the ballots, and as the petition asked for a scrutiny of the votes polled on other grounds, not authorised by the Act, the Judge had no jurisdiction, and a prohibition should issue to restrain him from proceeding. *Ex parte Bogue*, vol. 22, 228.

9—Conviction under—Excessive penalty imposed—Conviction invalid—Court has no power to amend.

Under sections 117 and 118 of the Canada Temperance Act, 1878, the Court has no power to amend the conviction when the penalty imposed is greater than the Act authorises; but such conviction is invalid. *Regina* v. *Rose*, vol. 22, 309.

10—Town of Milltown—Whether "city" or "county" within meaning of Act.

The town of Milltown is neither a city nor a county within the meaning of the Canada Temperance Act, 1878, and is not entitled to a separate vote under the Act, from the rest of the county of Charlotte. *Ex parte Maher, Ex parte Coughlin*, vol. 22, 632.

11—Prosecutor for offences under—Deputy Collector of Inland Revenue—Police Magistrate of Woodstock—Jurisdiction over offences committed outside the town.

Held, by Allen, C.J., and Wetmore, Palmer and King, JJ.: 1st. That the Police Magistrate of the town of Woodstock has power under the Act, 43 Vic. cap. 48 to try offences against the Temperance Act, 1878, committed in any part of the county of Carleton. 2nd (Weldon, J., dissenting). That a Deputy Collector of Inland Revenue was not necessarily a prosecuting officer under the Act sec. 101; and, therefore, that the Police Magistrate, holding such office, was not disqualified from trying offences under the Act. *Regina* v. *Dibble, ex parte Shaw*, vol. 23, 30.

12—Whether Woodstock is a city within meaning of Act—Deputy Collector of Inland Revenue—Prosecuting officer—Power of Town Council to assess for expenses of prosecutions under Canada Temperance Act—Conviction for second offence—Whether defendant must be present in person.

Held, by Wetmore, Palmer, King and Fraser, JJ., that the town of Woodstock is not a "city" within the meaning of the Act.

Held, by Wetmore, Palmer, King and Fraser, JJ., (Weldon, J., dissenting), that the fact of the Police Magistrate being Deputy Collector of Inland Revenue did not disqualify him from trying offences under the Act.

The town council of Woodstock has no power to assess the inhabitants of the town for the expenses of carrying on prosecutions under the Canada Temperance Act, and the Police Magistrate being a ratepayer of the town, is consequently not disqualified from trying offences under the Act.

In a prosecution under the Act, where the defendant appeared by attorney,

Held, by Palmer, King and Fraser, JJ., (Weldon and Wetmore, JJ., dissenting), that the defendant might be convicted of a second offence under the 122nd section of the Act, though he was not present at the trial. *Ex parte Groves*, vol. 23, 38.

13—Summary Conviction—Place of Sale—Evidence of.

A summons headed "County of York, parish of S., required the defendant to appear before a justice to answer the complaint for illegally selling liquor "in the said parish." The trial took place in the parish of S., and a witness proved a sale by the defendant at his shop "in this village."

Held, sufficient evidence of a sale in the parish of S. *Ex parte Hayes*, vol. 23, 313.

14—Prosecution before two Justices—Information.

Where a prosecution is brought before two justices under sec. 105 of Act, the information must be laid before both justices. *Ex parte Mawer*, vol. 23, 315.

15—Adoption of Act in counties where no licenses issued—Whether can be brought

into force—Newcastle Civil Court—Commissioner of—Jurisdiction to try offences under Act.

Held, (Allen, C.J., dissenting) that the Canada Temperance Act, 1878, can be brought into operation after its adoption by a county, notwithstanding no licenses are in force there at the date of the Order in Council. *Ex parte Farrell*, vol. 23, 467.

16—Section 100—Imprisonment—In default of goods—What time allowed.

The provisions of the 57th [illegible] sec. [illegible] the Summary Con[illegible] 32 and 33 Vic., cap. 31, are ap[illegible] convictions under the Canada Temperance Act, sec. 100, where [illegible] mode is provided for enforcing payment [illegible] fine—therefore in default of goods, imprisonment not exceeding three months may be imposed. *Ex parte Pourrier*, vol. 23, 544.

17—Liquor License Act 1883—Sale of liquor without license—Whether procedure must be under the Liquor License Act—Repeal of Statute by implication.

Prosecutions for selling liquor without license in towns and counties where the Canada Temperance Act, 1878, is in force, must, since the passing of "The Liquor License Act 1883," be regulated in the mode of procedure and punishment by the 91st and 104th sections of the latter Act, and not by the 100th and 106th sections of the former Act.

Per Palmer J., that where the mode of procedure provided by "Liquor License Act, 1883," is imperative, it must be followed in prosecutions for violation of "The Canada Temperance Act, 1878," but when the mode of proceeding is only permissible, it does not take away the right of the prosecutor to proceed according to the provisions of "The Canada Temperance Act, 1878." *Ex parte Coleman*, vol. 23, 574.

18—Ultra vires.—Mandamus to compel the City of Fredericton to grant license to applicant to sell spirituous liquors by retail.

Held, by Allen, C.J., Weldon, Fisher and Wetmore, JJ., (Palmer, J., dissenting) that the C. T. Act, 1874, which prohibits the sale of spirituous liquors in those counties or cities where the Act is brought in force is *ultra vires*. *The Queen v. Fredericton*, vol. 19, 139.

Appeal to Supreme Court of Canada followed. See Addenda No. 1.

19—Justices of the Peace—"Absence" within meaning of sec. 103 of the Canada Temperance Act—Summons to witness—Who may issue—Conviction—Where made by justices acting without jurisdiction, but having jurisdiction over the subject matter—Whether justification to parties for anything done under it.

A prosecution under the Canada Temperance Act was commenced by two justices, A. and B., and a summons issued. At the return of the summons, another justice of the county, on application of the defendant, issued a summons for A. and B. to give evidence for the defendant on the hearing; whereupon two other justices, at the request of A. and B., under the provisions of sec. 105 of the Act, heard the case, and convicted the defendant.

Held, *per* Allen, C.J., Weldon, Palmer and Fraser, JJ. (King, J., *contra*), that the Word "absence" in sec. 105 did not necessarily mean actual absence from the place of trial, but would apply to a case where the original justices had, for some cause, become incapable of acting on the hearing.

Per Allen, C.J., Weldon, King and Fraser, JJ., that under section 16 of the Summary Convictions Act, only a justice before whom the case is to be heard, has authority to issue a summons for a witness; therefore A. and B. were not legally summoned as witnesses, and were not "absent" within the meaning of the Act, and that the other justices acted without jurisdiction.

Per Palmer, J., that A. and B. having been summoned as witnesses on the request of the defendant he could not object that they were not legally summoned.

Held, also (King, J., *dubitante*), that as the convicting justices had jurisdiction over the subject matter of the complaint, and the conviction was good on its face, it was a justification for them, until set aside, for anything done under it. *Byrne* v. *Arnold*, vol. 24, 161.

(Affirmed on appeal to Sup. Court of Canada). See Addenda 36.

20—Election under—Scrutiny of votes—Extent of inquiry by Judge.

On a scrutiny of votes given at an election held under "The Canada Temperance Act 1878," a County Court Judge has power under secs. 61 and 62 of the Act to go into an inquiry affecting the validity of the election, and not merely to inspect the ballots and so determine their validity and then recount them. (King, J., dissenting). *Ex parte Rand*, vol. 24, 374.

Above case reversed on appeal to Sup. Court of Canada. See Addenda 25.

21—Keeping liquor for sale—Partners—Joint conviction.

A conviction of A. and B. who were in partnership, for an offence several in its nature (keeping intoxicating liquor for sale), adjudging that they for their said offence should forfeit and pay $50, and in default of payment, be imprisoned for forty days, is bad. The penalty ought to be imposed on the parties severally. *Ex parte Howard and Crangle*, vol. 25, 191.

22—Conviction for violation of, and Acts in amendment thereof—Liquor License Act 1883—Amendment of conviction—Surplusage—Refusal to grant certiorari—Where conviction amendable.

Before the disallowance of "The Liquor License Act, 1883, by the judicial committee of the privy council, a conviction was made for selling liquor "contrary to the Canada Temperance Act 1878, and the Acts in amendment thereof."

Held, after the disallowance of the Liquor License Act, that the words "and the Acts in amendment thereof," might be treated as surplusage, and the conviction amended accordingly under secs. 117 and 118 of the Canada Temperance Act; and therefore that a *certiorari* should not issue to bring up the conviction in order to quash it on account of the addition of these words. *Ex parte Russel*, vol. 25, 437.

23—Order in Council bringing Act into force—Evidence of.

The introductory part of the annual statutes of Canada containing a statement that an order in council had been made bringing the Canada Temperance Act into force in a county, is not evidence of the making of such order. *Ex parte Mercer*, vol. 25, 517.

— Witness — Summons for — Who authorized to issue under sec 16 of Sum. Convictions Act. See above, No. 19.

—Liquor sold in violation of Act. See Contract 15.

—Liquor bought for sale in violation of—Onus of proof. See Contract 8.

—Parish Court has jurisdiction to try offences under. See Parish Court Commissioner.

—Second offence — Defendant's presence at trial not essential to conviction for selling liquor. See Sum. Con. Act 6.

—Uncertainty as to time of offence—Amendment. See Sum. Con. Act 6.

—Identity of offence. *Autrefois* convict. See Sum. Con. Act 12.

—Certificate of dismissal, subsequent prosecution for same offence. See Sum. Con. Act 8.

—Form of conviction must be adopted. See Sum. Con. Act 7.

—Intoxicating—Spirituous—Whether synonymous terms. See Sum. Con. Act 4.

—*Procedendo* when will issue to enforce conviction. See *Procedendo*.

CAPIAS.

Issuing wrong form of—Irregularity. See Practice 12.

CAPITAL STOCK.

Bank of New Brunswick—Assessment under St. John Assessment Act of 1882. See Assessment 6.

CARRIER.

1—Liability—Forwarding by company beyond terminus contract—Conditions—Notice—Right of carrier to impose conditions—Loss by fire. See *Armstrong* v. *Grand Trunk Railway*, vol. 18, 445.

2—Steamboat owners — Loss of goods—Action for negligence—Onus of proof—37 Vic. cap. 25—Effect of evidence—Rebuttal—Hearsay—Statement by master regarding cause of accident — Whether admissible — Where improper evidence admitted without objection, and left by Judge to consideration of jury—Whether ground for new trial.

In an action against the owner of a steamboat as a common carrier for the loss of goods, the plaintiff proved the delivery of goods to the defendant, and their non-delivery at the place of destination. The defendant then (without objecting that the plaintiff had given no evidence of negligence), called witnesses to disprove negligence, and the plaintiff gave evidence of negligence in reply.

Held, per Allen, C.J., Weldon, Wetmore and Fraser, JJ. (Palmer, J., dissenting). 1. That no such objection having been taken at the trial, the defendant could not afterwards move to enter a non-suit on the ground that the plaintiff had not given any evidence of negligence in his *prima facie* case. 2. That the plaintiff having relied in the first instance on the receipt of the goods by the defendant, and their non-delivery at the place of destination, was properly allowed to give evidence of negligence in answer to the case set up by the defendant.

Quære, Whether the Dom. Stat. 37 Vic. cap. 25, has changed the onus of proof in actions against carriers for loss of goods, and requires the plaintiff to give affirmative evidence of negligence.

Semble, per Allen, C.J., Weldon, Wetmore and Fraser, JJ., (Palmer, J., dissenting), that it does not, but that the defendant to excuse himself must prove that the loss happened without any negligence on his part.

Where the loss of the goods was caused by the steamboat running on a bar, and afterwards sinking, the declaration of the master of the boat, made at the time that the grounding of the boat was an act of carelessness is not evidence against the defendant; but *per* Allen, C.J., Weldon, Wetmore and Fraser, JJ., that the evidence having been received without objection, the judge was not bound to withdraw it from the consideration of the jury.

Per Palmer, J., that it was misdirection to tell the jury they might consider the declaration of the master with the other evidence. *Small, et al.*, applicant, and *Belyea*, respondent, vol. 24, 16.

CERTIFICATE.

Under 37 Vic. cap. 94, Acts of Parliament—Shareholder of company. See Evidence 16.

CERTIFICATE FOR COSTS.

Where action brought in the Supreme Court, on being submitted to arbitration, is reduced to less than $200. See Costs 5.

—For costs where party sues in Supreme Court, but does not recover more than he might have recovered in County Court. See Costs 9.

In action in Supreme Court for trespass—Title to land not in question—Verdict less than $100. See Costs 13.

CERTIFICATE OF DISMISSAL.

Under Summary Convictions Act—Whether granted *bona fide* — Inquiry into. See Summary Convictions Act 8.

CERTIORARI.

1—Copy of proceedings — Production — Necessity of.

Quære.—Whether a party applying for a *certiorari* should not produce a copy of the proceedings before the justice, or account for his not doing so. *Ex parte Abel*, vol. 18, 600.

2—Where rule once refused—Second application—Refusal of Court to hear a second application.

A motion having been made for a *certiorari* and refused, the court declined to hear a second application. *Ex parte Abel*, vol. 19, 2.

3—Application for—Whether necessary to produce copy of proceedings.

Although it is not necessary on an application for a *certiorari* that a copy of the proceedings sought to be removed should be produced, the substance should be set out. *Ex parte Nevers*, vol. 19, 5.

4—Debtor—Order of discharge—When Refusal to answer proper questions.

When a debtor who was being examined before a commissioner, on an application for his discharge from custody, refused to answer proper questions put to him, and the commissioner ordered his discharge, the court granted a *certiorari* to remove the order. *Ex parte Wright*, vol. 20, 509.

5—Judicial and Ministerial Acts—Will not lie to remove proceedings purely ministerial—When objection may be taken—Void proceedings — Issuing Warrant against real estate of non-resident minors without order of County Court Judge. Con. Stat. c. 100, ss. 17, 74, 75 and 77.

The issuing of a warrant by the secretary of the municipality under the 74th section of chapter 100 of the Consolidated Statutes, to sell the real estate of non-residents for the purpose of collecting the amount of an assessment against them, is not a judicial act, and the court has no power to grant a *certiorari* to remove the warrant.

The objection that the act of the secretary is a ministerial and not a judicial one, may be taken when shewing cause against the rule to quash the warrant.

Semble, *certiorari* may be granted to remove proceedings which are void.

Semble, the issuing of a warrant under Consol. Stat. cap. 100. sec. 77, against the real estate of non-resident minors under an assessment made against their guardian without the order of the County Court Judge as provided in sec. 17, is bad. *The Queen v. Simpson*, vol. 20, 472.

6—Judge Supreme Court—Review—New trial.

A *certiorari* will not be granted to bring up the proceedings in *review* before a Judge of this Court under the Consol. Stat., cap. 60, the proper remedy being by motion to set aside the order.

A Judge has no power to order a new trial in a review case under Consol. Stat. cap. 60, sec. 43. (Weldon and Palmer, JJ., dissenting). *Ex parte Kane*, vol. 21, 370.

7—New trial in review under Consol. Stat. cap. 60, sec. 45—County Court Judge.

A *certiorari* will lie to bring up the proceedings in *review* had before a County Court Judge under Consolidated Statutes, cap. 60, if he had no jurisdiction to make the order—(Weldon, J., dissenting).

Per Weldon, J , the order of a judge in a review case is final.

A judge has no power to order a new trial in a review case under Consol. Stat. cap. 60, sec. 45.

(Weldon and Wetmore, JJ., dissenting). *Ex parte Fahey*, vol. 21, 392. See Acts of Assembly, 45 Vic., cap. xii.

8—Review — Costs — Abandonment of excess upon particulars.

In an action in a parish court where the plaintiffs' claim exceeds the amount over which the court has jurisdiction, he may by abandonment of excess upon the particulars filed, bring the case within the jurisdiction of the court. Where the plaintiff in an action of debt in a parish Court was improperly nonsuited—no evidence having been given by the defendant.

Held, per Wetmore and King, JJ., (Palmer, J., dissenting) that a judge on review had power to order judgment to be entered for the plaintiff for the amount proved at the trial.

Held, per Weldon, J., that an order of a judge of a County Court in a case of review, was final, and that a *certiorari* would not lie to remove it into this Court.

Per Wetmore and King, JJ., that a *certiorari* would lie in such a case.

Per Palmer, J., that though the order of the judge of the County Court was wrong, if he had jurisdiction to make it, a *certiorari* would not lie to remove it into this Court.

The Court has no power to grant costs in discharging a *rule nisi* for a *certiorari*, unless such power is given by statute. *Ex parte Simpson*, vol 22, 132.

9—County Court Judge—Review—Where Judge does not exceed his jurisdiction.

The decision of a County Court Judge in a review case, under the Consol. Stat. cap. 60, is final, if he has jurisdiction over the matter, or has not exceeded his jurisdiction, and a *certiorari* will not be granted to bring up the proceedings. *Ex parte Turner*, vol. 22, 634.

10—Where right of review exists—Delay in applying.

Where a right of review exists, *certiorari* will be granted under very exceptional circumstances.

Where there has been delay in applying for a *certiorari*, such delay must be satisfactorily explained. *Ex parte Price*, vol. 23, 85.

11—Removal of proceedings under the Highway Act—Unreasonable delay in applying for.

A *certiorari* to remove proceedings for the alteration of a road under the Highway Act, Consol. Stat. cap. 68, was refused where two terms had elapsed since the filing of the commissioners' return. *Ex parte Lipsett*, vol. 25, 66.

Granted where magistrate refused to certify the proceedings for appeal. See Assault 2.

Whether party applying for, must give bond required by Consol. Stat. cap. 100, sec. 110. See Assessment 2.

—Taken away by Canada Temperance Act, where magistrate has jurisdiction. See Canada Temperance Act 1.

Not taken away where magistrate acts without jurisdiction. See Canada Temperance Act 6, Summary Convictions Act 11.

In what cases taken away. See Canada Temperance Act 6.

—Containing an order for stay of proceedings — Constable selling goods after having been served with—Contempt of court—See Attachment 7.

—When too late to read affidavits. See Seaman's Act 1873.

—Right to apply for, to quash the proceedings under Act, relating to absconding debtors—Application allowed, though two terms have elapsed since the warrant issued. See Absconding Debtor 1.

—Filing affidavits on which rule granted by Judge at Chambers. See Practice 22.

—Amending return. See Seaman's Act 1.

—Garnishee Act—Whether proceedings under, are subject of appeal, under County Court's Act, or by *certiorari*. See County Court, Appeal 9.

—Conviction under Canada Temperance Act, where amendable *certiorari* will not issue. See Canada Temperance Act 22.

—*Procedendo* will issue when proceedings affirmed on *certiorari*. See *Procedendo*.

Cestui que Trust.

Relation of trustee, and *Cestui que trust* created. See Equity.

CHALLENGE.

1. Of juror after hand has been placed on book.

On the trial of cause when the first four jurymen came to the book, the clerk at once commenced to administer the oath, and had got as far as "you shall, well and truly try the issues," when the Judge interposed, and called the attention of plaintiff's counsel and the clerk to the fact that there was only one issue upon the record. The plaintiff's counsel then challenged L., one of the four jurymen, whose hand was on the book, and the counsel persisting, L. was ordered to stand aside. The record was then amended by adding another plea; and the jury was sworn to try the issues then upon the record—the plaintiff having obtained a verdict.

Held, that the allowance of the challenge under the circumstances was no ground for a new trial. *Somers* v. *Wilbur*, vol. 20, 502.

2—For favor—Should contain an allegation of sheriff's partiality—Venire to a coroner.

When the facts stated in the challenge would not of necessity disqualify the sheriff from summoning the jury, and might or might not render him partial, the challenge is to the favor, and it should, in addition to the facts relied on, contain an allegation that the sheriff was not impartial, otherwise it is bad.

Semble. A *venire* may be issued to a coroner on a suggestion on a record that the sheriff, for the reasons stated, is not impartial. *Brown* v. *Maltby, et al*, vol. 20, 92.

3—To array—Where prisoner's husband has action pending against the sheriff.

Held, on an indictment against R. M., that it was ground of principal challenge to the array that the prisoner's husband had an action pending against the sheriff for assault committed on the prisoner. *The Queen* v. *Rose Milne*, vol. 20, 394.

4—The fact of a juryman who is open to challenge, having served on the jury, is not *per se* a ground for a new trial.

A party challenging a juror should make his objection in such a manner that the Judge or the clerk of the court can hear him; and unless he does so, he cannot raise the objection after the juror is sworn. *Pitfield*, appellant, and *Kimball*, respondent, vol. 25, 193.

—Juror—An alien—Objection when must be taken. See Juror.

CHAMBERLAIN.

Of Saint John—Not liable for arresting a person on execution for taxes assessed by the commissioners, who was not owner of the land on which he was assessed. See Assessment 3.

CHARGES.

Railway Company—Action to recover back excessive charges. See Railway Company 3.

CHARTER PARTY.

1—Damage to ship—Unavoidable delay—Refusal of charterers to load—Action by ship-owners for.

By a charter-party of December 11, 1878, it was agreed that the plaintiff's vessel, then on her way to Shelburne, N. S., should proceed with all possible despatch, after her arrival at Shelburne, to St. John, and there load from the charterers a cargo of deals for Liverpool; and if the vessel did not arrive at Shelburne on or before 1st of January, 1879, the charterers were to be at liberty to cancel the charter-party.

The vessel arrived at Shelburne in December, and sailed at once for St. John.

At the entrance of the harbour of St. John, she got upon the rocks, and was so badly damaged that it became necessary to put her upon the blocks for repairs. Although she was repaired with all possible despatch, she was not ready to receive her cargo until 21st April following, prior to which time—on 26th March—the charterers gave the owners notice that they would not furnish a cargo for her. The owners sued for breach of the charter-party, and on the trial defendants gave evidence, subject to objection, that freights between St. John and Liverpool were usually much higher in winter than in summer, that lumber would depreciate in value by being wintered over at St. John, and also as to the relative value of lumber during the winter, and in the spring in the Liverpool market: and it was contended that the time occupied in repairing damage was unreasonable, and entirely frustrated the object of the voyage. The Judge directed the jury that if the time occupied in getting the vessel off the rocks and repairing her, was so long as to put an end, in a commercial sense, to the commercial speculation entered into by the ship-owners and charterers, they should find for the defendants. The verdict being for the defendants.

Held, on notice for a new trial that this was a misdirection, there being no evidence to warrant the case being left in this way, and a new trial was ordered. *Schofield* v. *Carvill*, vol. 21, 558.

Appeal to Supreme Court of Canada dismissed. See Addenda No. 14.

2—Charter-party—Voyage from England to New Brunswick—Ship not ready for sea—Danger of the seas—Damage to ship—Deviation for repairs—Questions for jury.

By a charter-party, stating that the ship was tight, etc., and in every respect ready for sea, and the defendant agreed to sail from Liverpool with all convenient speed to B., in New Brunswick, and there load a cargo of deals for the plaintiff, and thence proceed to Liverpool — the dangers of the seas and navigation excepted. The ship was not ready for sea at the time the charter-party was entered into—not having any sails—and repairs were made to her while her ballast was being taken in, but she sailed as soon as she had completed her ballasting. On the voyage, the ship was damaged by storms, and became leaky, and when off the coast of Cape Breton, and within about a day's sail from the port of Sidney, the master determined that he could not proceed to B. without repairing the ship, and he sailed to St. John, N. B., for that purpose, thinking, as he stated, that the repairs could be best made there. Repairs were made at St. John, but it was then too late in the season to go to B., on account of the ice, and the voyage was never completed. There was evidence that the ship could have been repaired at Sydney, and at other ports in Nova Scotia nearer than St. John. The plaintiff recovered damages for not loading his deals and carrying them to Liverpool.

Held, 1. That there was a breach of the charter-party in the ship not being ready for sea at that time, though if she sailed as soon as the ballast was completed, the plaintiff might only be entitled to terminal damages for such breach. 2. That it should have been left to the jury to find whether the necessary repairs to the ship could have been made at Sydney, or the other ports of Nova Scotia, and whether the master was justified in going to St. John for that purpose, and also, whether if the repairs could have been made at Sydney, &c., it would have then been too late in the season for the ship to proceed to B. and take in the cargo. *Burns v. Cassels*, vol. 25, 13.

—Parol evidence—When admissible as to. See Agreement 2.

—Loss of freight—Voyage frustrated by ice. Whether one of the perils insured against. See Insurance 18.

—Where signed by mortgagee of ship under instructions received by telegram from mortgagor—Meaning of telegram—How ascertained. See Ship 3.

CHOSE IN ACTION.

An indorsement in insurance policy to pay loss to third party, is not an assignment of. See Insurance 4.

Bill of sale of Act does not apply to. See Bills of Sale Act 2.

Property of wife — Assignment by husband and wife—Effect of. See Husband and Wife 3.

CITATION.

1. The heir at law, though not entitled to any of the personal estate of the deceased, may file a petition to have an alleged will of deceased proved in solemn form under Consolidated Statutes cap. 52, sec. 34. *In re Annie R. Fox*, vol. 20, 391.

Proof of will in solemn form. See Probate Court 2.

CITY.

Within meaning of Temperance Act. See Canada Temperance Act 5.

CLERK OF COURT.

Writ signed and sealed by, but issued after appointment of successor. See Practice 12.

Client—Liability of, on promise by attorney. See Sheriff 2.

CLAIM OF PROPERTY.

Setting aside defective claim. See Replevin 6.

CASE.

Whether railway company bound to barn. See Railway Company 5.

COGNOVIT.

—Future advances—Dispute as to intention—Right of creditors to be repaid. See Judgment 5.

—Judgment on motion to set aside on ground of fraud—Application by judgment creditor—Contradicting affidavits. See Judgment 4.

COLLISION.

1—**Carrying lights—31 Vic. cap. 58—Onus of proof—Plaintiff must shew his default did not contribute to injury—Interest in an action of trespass on the case—Consol. Stat. cap. 37, sec. 119—Reducing verdict—Trial of cause in unavoidable absence of attorney and counsel—New trial—On terms—Whether ground for or not—Waiver of objection.**

The plaintiff's vessel was lost in a collision in which the defendant's vessel was at fault. At the time of the collision the plaintiff's vessel was not carrying lights as required by 31 Vic. cap. 58, it being a bright moonlight night. On the trial the judge directed the jury that the onus was on the plaintiff of showing that the absence of lights did not in any way contribute to the accident.

Held, by Weldon and Wetmore, JJ., that the direction was correct.

In an action of trespass on the case for the loss of the plaintiff's vessel by collision with the defendant's vessel, interest on the value of the vessel and freight is not recoverable as part of the damages under the 119 section of the Consolidated Statutes, chapter 37, and where in such a case the jury allowed interest, a new trial was ordered, unless the plaintiff should consent that the verdict should be reduced to the value of vessel and freight as proved on the trial.

This cause was tried in the unavoidable absence of P., the attorney and counsel for the defendants, an application to postpone having been refused by the presiding judge. P., by his agent, protested against the trial, but instructed counsel to appear in case the cause was forced on and keep the cause going until his return.

This was done, but on his return P. refused to take any part in the cause. It appeared also that P. was led from a conversation with one of the counsel for the plaintiff to believe that the cause would not be forced on in his (P's) absence.

Held, by Allen, C.J., and Fisher, J., that there ought to be a new trial on terms, but by Weldon and Wetmore, JJ., that the rule for a new trial should be discharged. *Jackson* v. *McLillan*, vol. 19, 432.

COMMERCIAL TRAVELLER.

Power of corporation of St. John to tax for business licenses. See Business Licenses.

COMMISSIONS.

Evidence—Where not objected to before commissioner—Whether can be objected to on trial—Rule as to.

A commission, in which defendant joined, was addressed to two commissioners, with power to either of them to act. One commissioner only acted and took the depositions of the witnesses produced by plaintiff, the defendant not being present or represented by counsel. Some of the evidence given by plaintiff's witnesses was legally inadmissible, and when offered on the trial, the defendant's counsel objected to its reception, but the presiding judge admitted it.

Held, on a motion for a new trial, that the fact of the evidence not having been objected to on behalf of the defendant at the time the witnesses were examined before the commissioners, did not preclude defendant from objecting to it on the trial, and that it should have been rejected. *Boston Belting Co.* v. *Gobel*, vol. 20, 347.

2—To Examine Witnesses—Return—Address to Supreme Court.

A commission for the examination of witnesses in England was returned endorsed with the title of the court and cause signed by the commissioners, and addressed to the clerk of the circuits of the county in which the venue was laid.

Held, sufficiently addressed to the court. *Moran* v. *Taylor*, vol. 26, 30. See Act 48 Vic. cap. 18.

3—Commission for examination of Witnesses—Return—Whether should shew how commissioners were sworn—Interrogatories—Answer extending to matters not inquired of—Whether will be suppressed.

On a commission to examine witnesses, if the answer to an interrogatory extends to matters not enquired of, and which the opposite party could not have anticipated, and therefore did not file a cross interrogatory, the answer will be suppressed.

A commission directed that before proceeding to examine witnesses, the commissioners should take an oath in the form indorsed on the commission. The return stated that the commissioners were severally duly sworn, and that all things were had, done, taken, and performed by them as required by the commission.

Held, sufficient. *Barbour* v. *Robert*, vol. 24, 211.

Examination of witnesses abroad—Return by one commissioner—Omission of defendants commissioner to put cross interrogatories—Effect of—Endorsement of return of commissioners—Whether necessary. See Insurance 16.

Examination of witnesses abroad—Interrogatories not returned with depositions—See Practice 15

Depositions taken under—Sufficiency of endorsement on envelope enclosing. See Depositions.

Commission in equity. See Court General Rules 10.

COMMISSIONER.

Under Consolidated Statutes, cap. 38. —Power of—See False Imprisonment 5.

— Commissioner — Parish Court — Jurisdiction. See Parish Court Commissioners.

—For taking affidavits—Description. See Affidavit 5.

COMMISSIONER OF SEWERS

Assessments by — Payment of, by parties claiming land. See Possession 2.

COMMITTEE.

Appointed by municipal corporation —Limited powers. See Principal and Agent 2.

COMMON CARRIERS.

Railway company must be taken to hold themselves out as. See Railway Company 3; see Carrier.

COMMON COUNCIL.

Of city of St. John—Power to reduce pay of policeman. See Policeman.

Common counts — Recovery under, when contract repudiated. See Contract 12.

COMMON SCHOOLS ACT.

Summary remedy to compel Secretary of Trustees to give up property of incorporation. See Injunction 1.

—Notice of action, when party entitled to. See Notice of Action.

—Meaning of words in section 81. See Notice of Action.

COMPANY.

Incorporated under Joint Stock Companies Act—Action by—Necessity of obliging incorporation. See Joint Stock Companies Act 1.

—Action on foreign judgment—Necessity of stating incorporation. See Pleading 8.

—Admissibility of statements of President to shew appointment of Agent. See Insurance 15.

—Admissibility of declarations of members to shew who compose the company. See Landlord and Tenant 3.

—President attending office in St. John — Whether inhabitant of city within the meaning of the St. John Assessment Act of 1882. See Assessment 5.

COMPENSATION.

Railway company entitled to—Where no special agreement. See Railway Company 3.

COMPOSITION DEED.

When creditor may oppose application for discharge under. See Insolvent Act.

COMPUTATION OF TIME.

Day of arrest should be included in. See Supersedeas.

CONDITIONAL SALE.

Lease — Monthly rent — Not bill of sale. See Contract 6.

CONDITIONS.

Of sale must be strictly performed. See Sale of Land 2.

—Precedent, whether condition in insurance policy, that amount of loss shall be determined by arbitration, is a condition precedent to plaintiff's right of action. See Insurance 8.

CONDUCTOR OF RAILWAY.

Right to eject passengers who refuse to pay fare. See Railway Passenger 1.

—His duty as to waiting for passengers to get on train. See Railway Conductor 1.

CONFESSION.

Given by one partner for himself and his co-partner with his consent—Effect of. See Execution.

Judgment by. See Judgment 4, 5.

CONFIRMATION.

Of discharge — Necessity of filing objections with assignee. See Insolvent Act of 1875.

CONSIDERATION.

What sufficient amount of, to support written agreement. See Agreement 3.

—Transfer of property alleged to have been made to defraud creditors. See Judgment Creditor 5.

—Illegal in part—Lease. See Railway Company 1.

—Right to dispute, under plea of non assumpsit. See Assumpsit 5.

—Original—May sue on, when note given for, is unstamped. See Promissory Note 2.

—Promise to third party. See Agreement 4.

—Sufficiency of, to sustain promise. See Agreement 5.

—Deed in trust. See Deed 2, 3, 4.

CONSIGNEE.

Obtaining goods without bill of lading and without paying for goods—Liability of. See Bill of Lading 1.

—Passing of property. See Sale of Goods 5.

Consolidation — Of Mortgages. See Mortgage 2.

CONSTABLE.

His duty when executing a warrant to levy on a person's goods or take his body. See False Imprisonment 1.

Arresting, without search for goods and chattels—Execution issued out of Justice's Court. See False Imprisonment 1.

—**Contempt of Court.** See Attachment 6.

Construction of Acts of Parliament—Rule for. See Inspection 1.

—Of Will. See Will 1.

CONTEMPT OF COURT.

Disobedience not wilful. See Attachment 6.

Constable selling goods after having been served with *certiorari* containing stay of proceedings. See Attachment 7.

—Warrant of commitment for—Irregular—Justification to officer. See Criminal Law 7.

CONTESTATION.

Of claim by assignee—County Court Judge has power to award costs against assignee on. See Costs 10.

CONTINUING TENANCY.

Evidence of—Should be left to the jury. See Landlord and Tenant 1.

CONTRA ACCOUNT.

Allowance of, as part payment—Sufficient to take case out of Statute of Frauds. See Statute of Frauds 1.

CONTRACT—(See Agreement.)

1—Novation—Sale of land—Delivery of deed for inspection—Receipt for—Action on.

A new contract by novation cannot be created without the assent of the original creditor. *Anderson* v. *Fawcett*, vol. 19, 34. See Addenda 34.

2 — Building — Forfeiture clause — Liquidated damage—Architect's Certificate.

Plaintiff, in June, 1876, entered into a contract to build a house for the defendant on his (defendant's) land and to complete it by 1st December following, the defendant to pay a certain sum when the house was boarded in, and $200 monthly thereafter, if in the opinion of the architect the work progressed with sufficient speed to ensure its completion by the 1st December, and it was provided that if the house was not finished by the 1st December the plaintiff should forfeit $10 per day for each day's delay, to be deducted from the last payment.

The house was not complete till the latter part of January, 1877, when the defendant got possession.

Held, in an action to recover an alleged balance on the contract, that the defendant was entitled to deduct $10 per day as stipulated damages, and that he need not obtain certificate of the architect that the work was not progressing with sufficient speed. *Carter* v. *Leudy*, vol. 19, 516.

3 — Under Seal — Variance — Substituted parol agreement — Building contract—Extra work—Architect's Certificate.

Plaintiff contracted under seal to erect a building for defendant according to plans and specifications. The contract provided that if any change in the plans were desired, their value should be agreed upon and endorsed on the contract, otherwise no allowance should be made for them. The plaintiff was to be paid a certain percentage on the value of the work as it progressed, on the certificate of the architect; but the last payment was not to be made until all the claims for extras had been agreed upon. The plaintiff proceeded with the building, and did a considerable amount of extra work, but before the completion of the building it was destroyed by fire.

Held, in an action on the contract, 1. That plaintiff was entitled to recover the percentage on the value of the work done, though the building was never completed. 2. That he could not recover for the extra work, because its value had not been agreed upon and indorsed on the contract. 3. Plaintiff having contended that the contract under seal had been abandoned, and a parol contract substituted, he should have asked the judge to submit the question of abandonment and substitution to the jury; and not having done so, the court could not consider it on an application to increase the amount of the verdict pursuant to leave reserved at the trial. *Flood* v. *Morrisey* vol. 20, 5. *McMillan* v. *Walker*, vol. 21, 31. See Addenda 32.

4—Void—By-law—Pleading.

A contract was made on the 26th September to erect a proper and legal building in the city of St. John. Two days afterwards a by-law of the city of St. John was passed prohibiting the erection of buildings such as the one contracted for, and declaring them to be nuisances.

Held, per Weldon, J., that the by-law avoided the contract, and the building erected under it was a nuisance. *Per* Wetmore, J., that even the by-law did not make the building a nuisance, the plaintiff could not, under the pleadings in the case, have the benefit of it.

5—Parties to—Policy of insurance—Beneficiary not entitled to bring action in her own name.

By a policy of insurance on the life of the husband, effected by him for the plaintiff his wife, the defendant company agreed to pay the sum assured to the plaintiff or her executors, administrators or assigns, and in the case of her death in his life time to his executors, administrators or assigns. By her application for the insurance, the husband agreed that his answers to certain questions should form the basis of the contract, and he agreed to pay the premiums.

Held, by Allen, C.J., Wetmore, Duff and King, J.J., (Weldon, J., dissenting) that the plaintiff could not maintain an action on the policy on her own name. *Abbott* v. *North Western M. L. Ins. Co.*, vol. 21, 216.

6—Written — Fraudulent misrepresentation —Tender—Consol. Stat., cap. 75—Bill of sale under.

A. being in treaty with the plaintiffs for the purchase of a sewing machine, signed an agreement, stating that he had received the machine of the value of $65.00, which the plaintiffs had leased to him for nine months, at the rent of $6.00 per month, $15.00 being paid in advance at that time; that he would take care of the machine, and not part with the possession of it, and in case he made default in paying the rent, or in the performance of the agreement, that the plaintiff's might take possession of the machine, and he would forfeit any rent paid; and the plaintiffs agreed if A. paid the rent they would sell the machine to him for one cent at the expiration of nine months. A. having made default in paying the monthly rent, the plaintiffs demanded the machine, which was in possession of the defendant under a bill of sale from A. Defendant refused to give it up, but afterwards, and before action brought, tendered the plaintiff $14.00, the balance of the $65.00 unpaid. In trover for the machine, A. swore that there was a verbal sale of the machine to him for $65.00, of which he paid $15.00 at the time; that he did not read the agreement, and the plaintiff's agent told him at the time he signed it that it was an agreement to secure the balance of the purchase money by monthly instalments. The jury having found a verdict for the defendant on a question left to them whether the plaintiff's agent had fraudulently represented to A. the contents of the written agreement.

Held, per Weldon, Wetmore, Palmer and King, JJ., (Allen, C.J., *dubitante*) that if there was fraudulent misrepresentation respecting the writing, the property in the machine passed to A. under the verbal agreement, and he had a right to transfer it to the defendant.

Per Weldon, Palmer and King, JJ., that even if the property did not vest in A. till the whole price was paid, the tender of the $11.00 before action would prevent the plaintiff from recovering.

Per Allen, C.J., that the evidence of misrepresentation of the contents of the writing was unsatisfactory.

Per Allen, C.J., and Wetmore, J., that if the property in the machine did not vest in A. till the whole price was paid, there was a wrongful conversion by the defendant, which would not be affected by the subsequent tender of the balance of the purchase money.

An agreement for a conditional sale of a chattel, with a lease of it in the meantime at a monthly rent, is not a bill of sale under Consol. Stat. cap. 65. *Wheeler & Wilson Manuf. Co., v. Charters*, vol. 21, 1869.

7—Sale of goods—Payment—Appropriation—Rescission of contract.

The Albert Mining Company brought action to recover for coal sold and delivered to defendants during the years 1866, 1867 and 1868. The action was commenced on 1st September, 1873. Defendants were partners carrying on business under the name of the Albertine Oil Company—the defendant furnishing the capital. The contract for the coal was made by S., w was a large stockholder in the plain 's company, and entitled to yearly dividends on his stock. The agreement, as proved by plaintiffs, was, that S. purchased the coal for the Albertine Oil Company, the members of which he named; that the then president of the plaintiff company told S. they would look to him for payment, as the other partners were poor; that the terms of sale were cash on delivery on board the vessels; and that S. agreed that the dividends payable to him on his stock, should be turned in in payment for the coal, that in consequence of this arrangement the plaintiffs credited the Albertine Oil Company with the amount of S.'s dividends, as they were declared from time to time down to August, 1869, leaving a balance of $912.00 due to S. In the latter part of the year 1868, S. repudiated the agreement to appropriate his dividends to the payment of the coal, and refused to sign the receipts therefor in the plaintiff's books. He had signed the receipt for the dividend of 1866. He afterwards brought an action against the plaintiffs for the dividends; the action was referred to arbitration, and an award was made in favor of S. for upwards of $15,000, which the plaintiffs paid in July, 1874. The receipt given for the payment stated that it was in full satisfaction in the judgment in the suit of S. against the Albert Mining Company, and it appeared (though the evidence was objected to) that it included the dividends for the years 1867 and 1868. It appeared that the coal delivered was charged in the plaintiff's books to the Albertine Oil Company, and that the bills of lading on the shipments of the coal were also made out in their name, and that some time afterwards a notice, signed by S. and M., (the other defendant) was given to the plaintiffs, complaining of the inferior quality of the coal, and claiming damages in consequence. Weldon, J., before whom the cause was tried, was of opinion that the coal was sold to S. alone; that the agreement by him for the appropriation of his dividends to the payment of the coal had not been rescinded when this action was brought, and that the subsequent payment of the dividends by the plaintiffs had no effect: he accordingly nonsuited the plaintiffs.

Held, by Allen, C.J., Wetmore and King, J.J., (Weldon, J., dissenting) that the nonsuit was improperly granted. *Albert Mining Co. v. Spurr*, vol. 22, 316.

Appeal to Supreme Court of Canada allowed. See Addenda, No. 14.

8—Illegal—Money paid—Liquor bought for purpose of sale in violation of Canada Temperance Act—Onus of proof.

Plaintiff purchased and paid for liquor at the request of the defendant, and sent it to him in the County of C., where the "Canada Temperance Act, 1878," was in force. In an action to recover the money paid, it was proved that the plaintiff knew the defendant was in the habit of selling liquor, and that he knew the purpose for which the liquor in question was bought,—not stating what the purpose was.

Held, that it did not necessarily follow that the plaintiff knew the defendant intended to sell the liquor in violation of the law; and that the burthen was on the defendant to shew that the plaintiff knew that it was to be so sold. *Hotham v. Phillips*, vol. 23, 136.

9—By correspondence—Construction of.

Where it is sought to establish a contract from a correspondence, the whole of the correspondence which has taken place between the parties must be taken into consideration; accordingly where a letter written by plaintiff to defendant, and replied to by the latter, made a complete contract, but before the contract was performed or there was any breach, other letters passed between the parties from which it appeared that both parties still treated the matter as being in negotiation.

Held, that there was no binding contract. *Jones v. Dewolf*, vol. 23, 336.

Appeal to Supreme Court of Canada dismissed. See Addenda 54.

10—Order for goods—Acceptance.

Where an order for goods is sent by letter, the acceptance of it to create a contract must be unconditional. The answer to the letter must be a simple acceptance of the offer without any new terms. *Clarke v. Kimball*, vol. 23, 412.

11—Agreement to tow raft of lumber—Where portions owned in severalty by different persons—Loss of portion owned by one—Right of action.

Defendant agreed with A. to tow a raft of lumber through the falls of the river of St. John for a certain fixed sum. A. in making the agreement, was acting as the agent of the plaintiff, and four other persons who severally owned portions of lumber in the raft, but this was not communicated to the defendant who knew nothing about the ownership of the lumber. In going through the falls the raft was broken up, and part of the lumber lost.

Held, *per* Weldon, Wetmore and Palmer, J.J., (Allen, C.J., and King, J., dissenting) that as the plaintiff's interest in the subject matter of the contract was separate, he could sue alone for the loss of his lumber.

Held, *per* Allen, C.J., and King, J., 1st. That as there was a distinct joint contract for the towage of the entire raft for a certain sum, one of the owners of lumber in the raft could not sue alone for the loss of his part of it. 2nd. That the fact of one of the owners having taken his lumber out of the raft after the towing was commenced, did not put an end to the express contract, and create a new implied agreement with the plaintiff as to the towage of his lumber. *Elliott* v. *Parks*, vol. 23, 611.

12—Voidable contract—Repudiation by one party—Recovery under common counts by other party for work done under the contract—Statute of frauds.

Defendant agreed verbally to advance money to plaintiff to enable him to build a house on land of which he was to obtain a lease for a term of years; the lease to be made in the defendant's name as security for the money advanced, and to be assigned to the plaintiff on his paying the advances. The defendant advanced the money which was expended in building the house, the plaintiff contributing towards it labor and materials, and the lease was made to the defendant as agreed. The defendant then repudiated the agreement, claiming the property as his own.

Held, that the plaintiff was entitled to recover on the common counts for his work and materials expended on the house. *McHugh* v. *Murray*, vol. 24, 12.

13—Sale of two descriptions of goods—Entire contract—Acceptance of part—Inferior quality of remainder—Action for contract price.

Plaintiff agreed to sell defendant a quantity of Muscatel raisins, and a like quantity of London Layer raisins—both to be of the best quality. Before receiving the raisins the defendant sold a portion of the Muscatels, and on their receipt, and before he had an opportunity of examining them delivered them to the purchaser. He soon afterwards discovered that the London Layers were of inferior quality, and so informed the plaintiff, stating that he would not accept them, but offered to pay for the Muscatels. The plaintiff refused this, and brought an action for the contract price of the whole.

Held, 1. That as the contract was entire, and one of the conditions on the part of the plaintiff was not performed he could not recover. 2. That the defendant by accepting the Muscatels, did not preclude himself from objecting that the others were not according to contract. *Henry* v. *Botsick*, vol. 21, 111. See *Thomas* v. *Dymont*, Supreme Court Canada, vol. 13, 305.

14—Contract to deliver portable steam engine and mill machinery—Failure to deliver within specified time—Nominal damages — Defect in machinery — Evidence—Former statement of plaintiff as to quality of mill—Whether admissible—Expert testimony.

Defendants contracted to make for plaintiff one of their portable steam engines with mill machinery complete to be delivered by a certain day, and put the mill in complete operation—the plaintiff to provide the building, foundation, stone and mason work — defendants not to be responsible for delays caused by fire, or disturbance among employees. In an action for breach of the agreement, in furnishing defective machinery, and not delivering at the time agreed upon, the plaintiff gave evidence of the bad quality of the machinery, and that it would not manufacture good lumber, nor lumber of a certain length stated in the agreement; also, that he had been delayed in getting his mill in operation for want of the machinery; and that the mill was of very little value.

The defendants in answer gave evidence that there had been a disturbance among their workmen shortly before the time when the machinery should have been delivered, and that the plaintiff on being told of it, did not object to the delay in the delivery; but it did not appear that the work had been delayed by the disturbance among the workmen, or that the defendants had delayed their efforts to complete the work by anything the plaintiff had said. Evidence was also given of the good quality of the machinery; that it was capable of cutting lumber of the size specified, that the plaintiff on applying to insure the mill, had represented it to be first-class in every respect, and the machinery to be valuable. In order to account for the lumber cut in the mill being defective, evidence was given that the bed of the carriage was not level; and a witness who owned a mill of the defendant's manufacture in another part of this province, and who had examined the foundation of the plaintiff's mill, gave it as his opinion that the foundation was insufficient, and that part of it would be liable to heave with the frost, and throw the mill out of level.

Held, 1. That the plaintiff's declaration of the value of the mill when he applied for insurance, was evidence to contradict him as to the inferior character of the mill. 2. That without evidence to the effect that the defendants relaxed their efforts to complete the machinery in consequence of what the plaintiff said about the delay, it should not have been left to the jury to find whether they did so or not. 3. That though the plaintiff would have been entitled to nominal damages for non-delivery of the machinery at the time agreed upon. No evidence of actual damage having been proved, a new trial ought not to be granted on that ground.

4. *Per* Allen, C.J., and King, J. (Wetmore and Palmer, JJ., dissenting), that the opinion of the witness as to the sufficiency of the foundation of the mill, was admissible. *Morrow* v. *Waterous et al.*, vol. 24, 412. Appeal to Supreme Court of Canada allowed. See Addenda 38.

15—Illegality—Canada Temperance Act, 1878.

A person who sells spirituous liquor, knowing that the purchaser intends to sell it in violation of law in a county where the Canada Temperance Act is in force, cannot recover the price of the liquor. *Furlong* v. *Russel*, vol. 24, 478.

16—Contract under seal—Breach—New agreement by parol—Accord and satisfaction—Order for goods to be manufactured—Part payment in advance—Refusal to deliver—Recovery of advances—Tender of contract price.

Plaintiff ordered from defendant, a manufacturer, goods which were to be according to specification, and made a part payment in advance, the defendant refused to deliver the goods unless unauthorized extra work was paid for.

Held, that the plaintiff could recover the amount advanced in an action for money had and received, without tendering the contract price of the goods.

Defendant made a contract under seal to build fifty railway cars for plaintiff according to specification. After twenty-four of the cars had been delivered, and after the plaintiff was aware that they were not according to the contract, he agreed verbally to abandon all claim for damages for breach of the contract if defendant would, make certain alterations in the remainder of the cars, which the defendant did.

Held, that this amounted to accord and satisfaction of the plaintiff's claim for damages in respect of the twenty-four cars. *Greeney* v. *Harris*, vol. 21, 496.

17—Contract for sale of goods—Statute of frauds—Offer by letter to sell—Acceptance.

Action for breach of agreement to sell two car loads of potatoes.—Defendant, who lived at Restigouche, wrote to plaintiff at St. John, stating that he could load one or two car loads of Early Rose potatoes, and one or two of Jacksons, and asking if plaintiff would take a couple of car loads of each kind, and how much he would give per barrel for them. Plaintiff answered this the next day, stating the prices he would give for two car loads of each kind, and asking defendant to let him know in two or three days if he would accept the offer. On the 13th the defendant replied that he would have one car load of Early Rose ready to leave by train on the 15th, and would send another car load of the same kind the next week; but that he could not get the Jacksons at the price named by plaintiff: and asking plaintiff to send him $200. On the 15th defendant wrote to plaintiff that potatoes were coming in very slowly, that he could not get loaded before the middle of the next week, and that he would advise plaintiff when the potatoes were loaded. On the 22nd defendant wrote to plaintiff that a car load of potatoes had left that day, and that he would be in St. John on a day named (about the time of the arrival of the potatoes there.) Defendant went to St. John and told plaintiff that he had the car load of potatoes for him, and plaintiff offered to pay him for them, but defendant wished him to see the potatoes first, which he did, and approved of them, telling defendant to call at plaintiff's store and be paid. The next day the defendant refused to deliver the potatoes.

Held, per Allen, C.J., Palmer, King and Fraser, J.J. (Wetmore, J. dissenting). 1. That though the defendant's letter of the 13th April was not an acceptance of the plaintiff's offer of the 11th, it might be treated as a counter offer by defendant of two car loads of Early Rose potatoes, and if verbally accepted by plaintiff created a binding contract. 2. That the agreement by plaintiff to accept the car load that had arrived and to pay for them, was an acceptance of the defendant's offer of the 13th April of two car loads of Early Rose, and created a contract for that quantity. *Connacher*, Appellant, and *Parker*, Respondent. Vol. 21, 585.

—Made by partners not binding on firm unless partner had authority so to contract. See Co-partners 1.

—For insurance—Depending on correspondence—Distinct offer and acceptance necessary. See Insurance 12.

—On demise of an unfurnished house there is no implied contract that it is tenantable. See Landlord and Tenant 2.

—Contract to cut lumber—Vesting of property. See Replevin 4.

—When required to be in writing by Statute of Frauds. Evidence adding to or varying not admissible. See Sale 2.

—To pay freight—Implied, when owner got possession of goods. See Assumpsit 2.

—Of Sale. What constitutes executed contract See Property, passing of 2.

—Safe carriage of passengers—Through

ticket — Injury on intermediate ferry owned by another company — Implied contract. See Railway Co. 6.

Building contract — Enforcement of — Violation of city by-law — Liability of owner — Effect of by-law passed after contract was made. See Addenda 9 and 32.

CONTRADICTORY EVIDENCE.

Question for jury — Plaintiff and his witnesses. See Evidence 10.

Contributory Negligence. See Negligence.

CONTROVERTED ELECTION'S ACT

1 — Petition — Surety — Defective affidavit of justification — Removal from files of court.

The provisions of section 4, sub-sections 5 and 6, and section 5 of the Controverted Election's Act, (Consol. Stat. cap. 5) are imperative and not merely directory, and where a petition was filed with an affidavit of the sureties to the recognizance which was defective in substance, it was held that an order to remove the petition from the files of the court was rightly made.

Sub-section 6 of section 4, provides that the sureties in all cases before entering into recognizance, severally justify by affidavit made before a person authorized, etc., that they are severally worth double the sums for which they are respectively bound by such recognizance, after payment of all their just debts. In this case the affidavit of each surety was in these words,—"I am surety in the matter of, etc, that the sum about to enter into a recognizance as a for which *I shall be bound* by such recognizance is that of five hundred dollars. That I am worth at least double the sum for which I *am bound* by such recognizance, after payment of all my just debts."

Held, by Allen, C.J., and Weldon, Palmer, and King, J.J., that the affidavit was ambiguous, and therefore defective.

Held, by Wetmore, J., that as at the time the affidavit was made the surety had not entered into any recognizance, and was therefore not bound in any amount, it could not be read as stating that the surety was worth any amount, and was clearly bad. *Lynds v. Turner*; *Hoar v. Lewis*, vol. 22, 286.

2 — Petition under Consol. Stat. cap. 5 — Resignation of respondent — Whether petition thereby abates.

Where a member elected to the Local Legislature against whom a petition has been presented under the Consol. Stat. cap. 5, relating to controverted elections, voluntarily resigns his seat, the petition is thereby abated, and a judge has no power to proceed with the trial. *Sayre v. Le Blanc*, vol. 23, 147.

— Dominion. See Dominion Controverted Elections Act.

CONVERSATION.

When admissible the papers spoken of are also admissible. See Sale 3.

Between husband and wife. See Married Woman 2.

CONVERSION.

1 — Of goods — Waiver of Tort — Action for goods sold and delivered — Money had and received — Particulars of demand.

Plaintiffs and defendant negotiating about the sale of lumber, they write to him offering to sell at a certain price. Before the receipt of this letter the defendant's servant without his knowledge shipped the merchantable part of the lumber. In answer to the letter the defendant offered to give the price asked for so much of the lumber as was merchantable and a lesser price for the rest, which offer the plaintiffs refused. The defendant admitted that he had got returns for the lumber shipped. In an action for goods sold and delivered, and also for money had and received.

Held, that an action for goods sold and delivered would not lie.

The plaintiffs' particulars claimed for a quantity of lumber at a certain price but made no reference to either of the counts of the declaration.

Held, sufficient to entitle the plaintiffs to claim under the count for money had and received, as they gave the defendant substantial information of the plaintiffs demand. *Flewelling* v. *Lawrence*, vol. 21, 529.

—When goods were delivered under a verbal agreement which was not fulfilled. See Trover 2.

—What constitutes, when property held subject to a lien for charges. See Trover 3.

—Third party having property. See Agreement 1.

—Sale of property by one defendant and purchased by another, evidence of a joint conversion. See Trover 5.

CONVEYANCE.

1—Reservation of life estate in portion of land conveyed—Whether good.

A. the grantee of a lot of land distinguished as lot No. 10, containing 100 acres and described by metes and bounds, made a conveyance to B. in the following words:—"All that certain lot or parcel of land situate and bounded as follows: (describing it by same courses and bounds as in the grant,) containing 100 acres more or less distinguished as lot No. 10, reserving for himself (the said A.) the east half of the said lot No. 10 from the front to the rear during his natural life, then after his decease the said east half of the said lot reserved to revert and return to B., his heirs and assigns.

Habendum, the said lot and parcel of land thereby granted be or meant and intended so to be, and every part thereof with the appurtenances unto the said B., his heirs and assigns for ever. A. afterwards conveyed all his right, title and interest in lot No. 10 to the plaintiff.

Held, that the exception in the deed to B. was not repugnant to granting part of the deed and that the east half of the lot was reserved to A.

Quære, Whether a life estate in A. could be created by the exception in the deed. If it could not, the title to the east half of the lot remained in him as it was before the deed to B., and in either case his right vested in the plaintiff. *Rowat* v. *Murdock*, vol. 20, 317.

—Must be prepared by vendor of land. See Sale of Land 3.

—When conveyance void, agent exceeding authority. See Power of Attorney.

CONVICTION.

Admissible in evidence, though defective. See False Imprisonment 1.

—Joint indictment—Where jury disagree as to guilt of one prisoner and find the other guilty. See Criminal Law 8.

—Joint conviction—Partners—Penalty must be separate. See Summary Conviction Act. 21.

—Before a Justice of the Peace to what court to be returned. See Justice of the Peace 1.

—Conviction by Supreme Court of Nova Scotia—Warrant to commit. See Warrant 1.

—Whether court has power to amend where penalty imposed is greater than Canada Temperance Act authorizes. See Canada Temperance Act 9.

—Disqualifying interest in justice. See Justice of the Peace 3.

—Justification under. See Canada Temperance Act 19.

—Uncertain as to time of offence. See Canada Temperance Act.

—Under Seaman's Act. See Seaman's Act, 1873. See Summary Convictions Act.

COPY OF PROCEEDINGS.

Not necessary on an application for a *certiorari*—The substance should be set out. See *Certiorari* 3.

Co-partners—See Partners—Partnership.

1—Money borrowed by one partner — Liability of firm for.

Held, by Allen, C.J., and Wetmore and Duff, J.J., that the mere fact that money borrowed by a member of the firm has been applied to partnership purposes, is not sufficient, of itself, to render the firm liable, at law, to repay it when there is no actual or implied authority to borrow, and there has been no ratification of the loan. The authority of one partner to bind the others by his contracts, is a branch of the law of agency; and the test of the partnership liability is—not whether the money came into the business of the firm, but whether the partner had any authority, express or implied, to borrow it.

Held, by Weldon and Fisher, J.J., that where money belonging to the plaintiff was received by one partner, and by him handed to the cashier of the firm, who deposited it in a bank to the credit of the firm, plaintiff was entitled to recover it from the firm, irrespective of what might be the private agreement between the partners. *Robertson v. Jones, & Co.*, vol. 20, 267.

CORONER.

When *venire* may issue to. See Challenge 1.

Fees—*Mandamus* to compel municipality to pay. See *Mandamus* 2.

CORPORATION.

Not liable for doing what by law they are directed to do. See Assessment 3.

—Official of—Cash book kept by—Entries shewing balance against self—Admissions to auditors. See Evidence 11.

—Municipal — Committee appointed with specific duties—Extent of authority. See Principal and Agent 2.

—St. John—Power to raise level of street and erect fence. See Addenda 40.

CORPUS.

Whether it should be sold to pay annuities. See Will 3.

CORRESPONDENCE.

Contract for insurance depending on —Offer and acceptance. See Insurance 12.

—Letter—Making evidence for one's self. See Evidence 9.

—Contract by—Construction of. See Contract 9.

COSTS.

1—Certificate for—Action for assault—Where plaintiff does not recover over $100—Refusal.

In an action by a constable [illegible] defendants for assaulting him [illegible] endeavoring to arrest a person [illegible] whom he had an execution, the jury gave a verdict for the plaintiff for [illegible] damages.

Held, by Allen, C.J., and Weldon, Fisher and Duff, JJ., (Wetmore J., dissenting) that the judge who tried the cause was right in refusing to certify for costs. *Tait v. Sherrack*, vol. 19, 93.

2—Certiorari to remove a rate levied under St. John Assessment Act, 1859—Discharging rule for, Where grounds previously decided.

Section 111 of Chapter 100 of the Consolidated Statutes which authorizes the court in discharging any rule for a *certiorari* to remove any rate to award costs against the person or persons obtaining such rule, applies to cases where the rate is levied under the St. John Assessment Act, 1859.

Where the grounds upon which the rule for a *certiorari* to remove a rate had already been decided by the court, the rule was discharged with costs. *Ex parte Jones*, vol 19, 101.

3—Of the day—Witnesses fees—Several suits by same plaintiff.

Where the trials of two causes at the suit of the same plaintiff against different defendants are put off on the payment of costs of the day, and the same persons attend as witnesses in both the cases, plaintiff is entitled to tax their mileage and attendance in both cases. *Chapman v. Providence W. Ins. Co. Same v. Delaware M. In. Safety Ins. Co.*, vol 19, 496.

4—Taxation of—Where takes place on different day from that appointed—Execution.

On a motion for an execution against defendant for non-payment of costs on setting aside an attachment, it appeared that the clerk's appointment to tax was on the 8th while the taxation actually took place on the 10th. It did not appear that defendant was represented at the taxation, nor was any explanation given of the taxation taking place on a later day than that appointed.

The court were equally divided as to whether the taxation was sufficient to entitle plaintiff to the execution. *Maclellan v. Barnes*, vol 19, 590.

5—Consolidated Statutes, cap. 51, sec. 50—Certificate for—Award—Conclusiveness as to amount of demand.

An action of assumpsit for work and labor, brought in the Supreme Court, was referred to arbitrators who awarded the plaintiff a sum less than $200.

Held, per Weldon, Fisher, Wetmore and Palmer, JJ., (Duff, J., dissenting) on an application for a certificate for costs under Consol. Stat., cap. 51, sec. 50, that if upon the whole evidence there appeared reasonable ground for bringing the action in this court, the amount of the award was not conclusive as to the amount of the demand, though the evidence as to the amount was conflicting, and that a certificate should be granted.

Per Duff, J., that if the evidence as to the amount of the demand was conflicting, and the award was consistent with any view of the evidence, it was conclusive as to the amount of the demand and no certificate should be granted. *Smith et al v. Morrissey*, vol 20, 1.

6—Of showing cause against rule nisi for new trial not taxable where plaintiff reduces his verdict on one count to nominal damages rather than submit to new trial—Notice of motion—When necessary.

The plaintiff in accordance with the terms of the rule of this court made on motion by the defendant for a new trial, consented to reduce his verdict on the 5th count to nominal damages rather than submit to a new trial.

Held, that as he was substantially unsuccessful in resisting the application for a new trial, he was not entitled to the costs of showing cause against the rule *nisi*.

Semble, where the clerk refuses to tax costs claimed by the plaintiff, the latter need not give notice of motion to review the taxation. *Derry* v. *Derry*, vol 20, 90.

7—Execution for Consolidated Statutes, cap. 38, sec. 27—Court cannot give execution against a corporation.

Section 27 of Chapter 38 of Consolidated Statutes does not authorize the court to grant an execution against a corporation for the non-payment of costs ordered to be paid. *Chapman* v. *The Providence W. Ins. Co.*, vol. 20, 91.

8—Appeal—Attachment.

Plaintiff sued defendant in the county court and was nonsuited. The nonsuit was set aside with costs on appeal. Plaintiff applied for an attachment under Consol. Stat., cap. 38, sec. 26, for non-payment of the costs.

Held, the court had no power to grant the attachment. *Law* v. *Harding*, vol. 20, 120.

9—Certificate for — When party suing in Supreme Court, and not recovering more than might have been recovered in County Court.

The plaintiff having made use of abusive language to the defendant, the latter laid an information before the police magistrate of Portland, upon which a warrant issued, and the plaintiff was arrested and imprisoned in the lock-up for several hours before he obtained bail. He was afterwards convicted, but the conviction was set aside. The plaintiff paid out thirty dollars for expenses in procuring his discharge. In an action against the police magistrate the plaintiff recovered one hundred and fifty dollars. The right of the magistrate to issue the warrant, and his right to try the complaint were both raised by the pleadings. The question of granting a certificate for costs, having been referred to the Court, it was *held* by Weldon, Wetmore and Duff (Allen, C.J., and Palmer, J., dissenting), that this was not a case in which a certificate should be granted. *Robinson* v. *Clarke*, vol. 20, 156.

10—Insolvent Act of 1875—Sec. 95—Power to award—Appeal.

Held, on appeal, that the County Court Judge had power to award costs under section 95 of Insolvent Act of 1875, against the assignee on his contestation of a claim filed against the estate; and as the judge had such power, the appeal was dismissed, it being a well settled rule of practice that an appeal will not be allowed on a question of costs. *Tait* v. *Dowling*, vol. 20, 265.

11—Demurrer — Taxation of costs while other issues are pending—Setting aside taxation.

When the plaintiff obtained judgment on demurrer under the Rule of Michaelmas Term, 9th Victoria, because the defendant had not delivered demurrer books, and taxed his costs under the 208th section of cap. 37 of the Consol. Stat. And there were at the time of taxation issues in fact to be disposed of, the court set aside the taxation on the ground that the costs of the demurrer should not have been taxed until the final determination of the case. *Anderson* v. *Fawcett*, vol. 20, 83.

12—Attachment for—Delay in applying for attachment — Costs taxed on day other than that appointed for taxation—Irregularity — When court will grant attachment.

When as appeared by the clerk's *allocatur*, costs were taxed on a day later than that named in the clerk's appointment for taxation, and no explanation of the irregularity was offered, the court refused an attachment for contempt in not paying the costs so taxed.

In *Hilary Term*, the plaintiff applied for an attachment for non-payment of costs taxed on a rule of court of the preceding term. The application was withdrawn, it being doubtful whether the *allocatur* which was in the clerk's handwriting expressed the amount to be $77.70, or $27.70. The application was renewed in Easter.

Held, by Weldon, J., that the second application was too late; but by King, J., that neither the lapse of a term nor the absence of an affidavit accounting for the delay, was an objection to the application as the facts were within the knowledge of the court, and the delay was not caused by the fault of the plaintiff.

Held, by Weldon, J., that as the application was against one of two defendants, and no reason was shown why a demand for payment was not made on the other defendant, the attachment ought not to be granted. *Sinclair* v. *Sinclair*, vol. 20, 506.

13—Certificate for—Where action is in this court and jury find less than $100—Title to land not brought in question—Certificate granted.

The defendant having leave to cut lumber on land adjoining the plaintiff's, was warned by the plaintiff to be careful that he did not cut on his land. The defendant paid no attention to the warning, and took no trouble to ascertain where the line was, but told his men to continue cutting, saying that he would make it all right.

In an action brought for the trespass, the defendant did not question the plaintiff's title. The plaintiff recovered less than $100. The Chief Justice granted the plaintiff a certificate for costs.

Held, by Allen, C.J., and Weldon and Duff, J.J., (Wetmore and King, J.J., dissenting) that the certificate was rightly granted. *Carnier* v. *McKee*, vol. 21, 1.

14—Court below—Appeal.

Direction as to costs not a ground of appeal even though this court might not have come to the same conclusion as the court below. *Merrit* v. *Wright*, vol. 21, 135.

15—Of the day—Affidavit not disclosing that the cause was at issue—Where cause had been noticed for trial and entered at the circuit—Court will presume cause was at issue.

The plaintiff gave notice of trial and entered the cause on the docket at the circuit. An application to set aside a rule for costs of the day for not proceeding to trial, was made on the ground that the affidavit on which the rule for costs was obtained did not show that the cause was at issue.

Held, that as against the plaintiff the court must presume that the cause was at issue. *McCarthy* v. *Providence W. Ins. Co.*, vol 21, 165.

16—Death of judge before certificate granted.

Certificate for—Where judge who tried the cause has died without giving the plaintiff a certificate for costs, he is without remedy, as another judge cannot grant the certificate. *Nicholson* v. *Temple*, vol. 21, 172.

17—Taxation of—On a day other than that appointed for taxation—Review of.

When it appeared that the clerk by his appointment to tax costs obtained by the plaintiff, appointed the 8th as the day for the taxation, and the costs were not taxed until the 10th, and it did not appear that the defendant was represented at the taxation, and no explanation was given of the taxation taking place later than that appointed, the court made absolute a rule to review the taxation. *McLellan* v. *Barnes*, vol. 21, 226.

18—Offer to suffer judgment by one of several defendants in trespass—Of making cause a remanet part of the general costs of the cause—Affidavit for taxation of witness fees—Sufficiency of—Cost of writing letters to each of several defendants—Whether taxable—Costs of discharging rule where point raised is new.

Where in an action of trespass one of several defendants offered under Con. Stat., cap 37, sec 127, to suffer judgment by default for $50, and the plaintiff recovered against all the defendants for that sum. It was held that the plaintiff was entitled to costs against all the defendants.

The cause had been made a remanet at the circuit preceding that at which it was tried. A new trial was granted on payment of costs.

On the second trial the plaintiff again had a verdict.

Held, that the plaintiff was entitled to the costs of making the cause a remanet as part of the general costs of the cause.

The affidavit of the attendance of witnesses stated that a paper annexed "was a statement of the number of the witnesses who attended for the plaintiff on the trial of the cause, the number of the days each one travelled, and that the plaintiff believed they were material and necessary witnesses."

Held, sufficient (Allen, C.J., doubting.)

Semble, that the plaintiff is entitled to the costs of sending a letter to each of several defendants.

The point raised being new, the rule was discharged without costs. (Wetmore and Palmer, J.J., dissenting.) *Gogson* v. *Chapman*, vol. 21, 251.

19—Of acquitted defendant—Joint action of Tort—Time for taxing.

An acquitted defendant in a joint action of tort is *prima facie* entitled to an aliquot portion of the joint costs though all the defendants appeared by the same attorney and counsel and pleaded jointly.

The acquitted defendant's costs should be taxed at the same time the plaintiff's costs are taxed. *Kerney* v. *Trustees re Baptist Church*, vol. 23, 11.

20—Trespass to land—Action in Supreme Court—Offer to suffer judgment by default for $8—Whether plaintiff entitled to full costs.

In an action for trespass to land brought in the Supreme Court, defendant filed an offer and consent to suffer judgment by default for $8.

Held, by Allen, C.J., and Weldon, Palmer and King, J.J., (Wetmore, J. dissenting,) that in order to deprive plaintiff of full costs, and bring him within the provisions of the Act, 45 Vic., cap 9, sec. 7, the onus was on the defendant of showing that the action could have been brought in the county court and that the title to land was not in dispute. *Connell* v. *McLeod*, vol. 23, 310.

21—Taxation of—Without notice—Where defendant only pleads to one count of declaration — Judgment — Setting Aside of.

A declaration contained two counts, to only one of which the defendant pleaded, and plaintiff therefore had his costs taxed without notice to the defendant's attorney and signed judgment on the other count for want of a plea.

Held, irregular, as notice of taxation should have been given, and the judgment was set aside with costs. *Deforest* v. *Holland*, vol 23, 411.

22—Reserving question of allowance of costs—Appeal.

Where a judge in equity reserved the question of costs on refusing to make an order for imprisonment for breach of an injunction order, it was held that the court on appeal could make no order concerning the costs in the court below. *Sayre* v. *Harris*, vol. 18, 677.

23—Action in Supreme Court—Where amount recovered is within the jurisdiction of county court—45 Vic. cap. 9, sec. 7.

If in an action in the Supreme Court the plaintiff recovers an amount within the jurisdiction of the county court, the costs of the proceedings are to be taxed under the Act, 45 Vic. cap. 8, according to the scale of fees in county courts; and not county court costs only. *Good* v. *Merrithew*, vol. 21, 160.

24—Telegraph company—Cutting trees—Justification under Act of incorporation—Title to land—Costs.

In trespass for cutting trees, the defendants (a Telegraph Co.) justified the cutting under an Act of parliament, authorizing them to enter on land and cut trees, if it was necessary to do so, for the purpose of constructing their line; and this was the only issue in the case.

A verdict having been found for the plaintiff for less than $200 damages, the court were equally divided in opinion whether on this issue the title to land was in question, and whether the plaintiff was entitled to Supreme Court costs under the Act, 45 Vic. cap. 9, sec. 7. *Taylor* v. *The Dominion Tel. Co.*; *Raymond* v. *The Dominion Tel. Co.*, vol. 21, 337.

25—St. John City Court—Costs—Taxation of.

In actions in the St. John city Court, the city alderman and common clerk should tax the costs of the successful party at the time of giving judgment.

Where a judgment was signed on the 22nd November, including in the costs an amount paid for witness' fees, and there was no affidavit made of the payment of the fees to the witness, as required by the Consol. Stat. cap. 119, until the following day, the court, on review, reduced the judgment by the amount taxed for witness fees. *Intercolonial Express Co.*, v. *McKenzie*, vol. 21, 618.

26—When costs on appeal not allowed—Decision of county court judge on case overruled.

Costs not allowed on appeal from the county court, where the judge had decided on the authority of a case in this court, which was overruled on the appeal. *Russel*, Appellant, and *Buckley*, Respondent, vol. 25, 261.

27—Security for costs—Nominal plaintiff insolvent.

If the plaintiff in a suit is insolvent, and the action is brought solely for the benefit of a third person, the defendant will be entitled to security for costs. *Grew* v. *Providence W. Ins. Co.*, vol. 25, 279.

28—Summons not moved with costs.

Costs will not be given on granting application when summons not moved with costs. *Allen* v. *Allen*, vol. 25, 360.

—Where plaintiff gives notice of hearing in equity suit, but does not attend, costs of the day should be ordered. *Wilbur* v. *Jones*, vol. 19, 526.

—Costs as part of judgment—Whether discharged with debt. See Bankruptcy.

—Should be allowed defendants, when trial postponed in order to allow name of defendant to be amended. See Practice 2.

—Treble—Whether takes away common law—Remedy. See Insolvent Act 1.

—On conviction under Canada Temperance Act may be awarded against defendant. See Canada Temperance Act 2.

—On action for slander where plaintiff recovered $8. See Slander 3.

On motion to appeal from county court—Refused. See Appeal 5.

—Refused on motion to amend Rule. See Amendment 1.

—Court has no power to grant in discharging a rule *nisi* for a *certiorari* unless such power is given by statute. See *Certiorari* 8.,

—Attachment for contempt of court—Interrogatories. See Attachment 7.

—Respondent may move to dismiss county court appeal with, if appellant does not appear when case is reached. See County Court Appeal 1.

—The court on an appeal from a county court has no control over the costs in the court below. See County Court Appeal 3.

—Notice of motion for a new trial—Party not appearing to support motion. See Practice 11.

—Of arbitration—Whether court has power to review. See Arbitration 1.

—Of execution for taxes—Arrest for, under second execution. See False Imprisonment 6.

—Of review from justices court—Where not in discretion of judge—Judgment "wholly reversed." See Damages 2.

—By reason o. increased jurisdiction. See County Court 3.

—Action in Supreme Court—Where amount recovered is within jurisdiction of county court. See Costs 23.

—Of former suit—Second suit for same matter. See Stay of Proceedings 2.

—Costs in equity—Right of court of appeal to vary. See Injunction 3.

COUNCILLORS.

Of parish—When they may appoint an officer to fill vacancy. See Parish Officer.

COUNSEL.

Where defendants appear by same attorney and are represented by separate counsel—Whether both counsel have right to cross examine witnesses and address the jury. See Practice 6.

—Right to examine witness on matters brought out on cross examination. See Ships' Husband.

—Argument of—Whether parties to suit bound by. See Practice 16.

—Agreement at trial—Power of court to depart from. See Practice 14.

—Admission of—How far client bound by. See Master and Servant 2.

—A party arguing his own cause cannot be heard by. See Bankruptcy.

COUNTY COURT.

1—Replevin — Jurisdiction — Statement of value of goods necessary in declaration—Power of court to give judgment.

In actions of replevin in the county court, the declaration should shew that the value of the goods does not exceed $200, otherwise it will be demurrable.

Though a county court has no jurisdiction to try a cause, it may nevertheless give judgment for the defendant on that ground with costs. *Morrice*, Appellant, and *Fisher*, Respondent, vol. 25, 1.

2—Acceptance to offer to suffer judgment by default for $8—Costs.

Where in an action for debt in the county court, the plaintiff accepted an offer of the defendant to suffer judgment by default for $8, the court was equally divided as to whether the costs necessarily followed the judgment, or whether the plaintiff's right to costs depended upon his having reasonable ground for bringing the action in the county court. *Fraser*, Appellant, and *Ulloch*, *et al*, *Executors*, Respondent, vol. 25, 55.

3—Offer to suffer judgment—Notice of, before filing Act, 45 Vic. cap. 9—Additional costs by reason of increased jurisdiction.

An offer and consent to suffer judgment by default under the Consol. Stat. cap. 37, sec. 127, must be filed in the clerk's office before giving notice of it to the plaintiff.

Per Wetmore, J., that the Act, 45 Vic. cap. 9, giving additional costs by reason of increased jurisdiction, applies to the successful party, whether plaintiff or defendant. *Chestnut*, Appellant, and *Boyle*, Respondent, vol. 25, 505.

4—Jurisdiction — City court of St. John having.

In an action brought in the King's county court, it appeared on the trial that the sum claimed did not exceed $80, and the cause of action arose in the city of St. John, and that the plaintiff and defendant both resided there.

Held, that the county court had no jurisdiction, the city court of St. John having jurisdiction in such a case, to the exclusion of the county court. *Thompson*, Appellant, and *Simonson*, Respondent, vol. 25, 122.

5—County Court Act section 44—Abatement of suit.

An action brought in a county court by a female does not abate by her marriage. *White*, Appellant, and *Riley* Respondent, vol. 24, 476.

6—Jurisdiction in action of tort—Damages—Abandonment—Action for escape—Proof of drainage.

The writ and particulars in an action in a county court against a sheriff for not arresting D. on a *capias*, and for a false return of *non est*, claimed $200 damages. In order to prove the damage he had sustained by the neglect to arrest D., the plaintiff testified that he had lost his debt of $393. The jury gave verdict for $150.

Held, (Wetmore, J., dissenting), 1 That as the writ and particulars shewed the case to be within the jurisdiction of the court, it was not taken away by the plaintiff's statement that in consequence of the sheriff's neglect to arrest D. he had lost the amount of his debt which exceeded the jurisdiction in actions of tort.

2. That the power given to a plaintiff by Consol. Stat. cap. 51, sec. 41, to abandon part of his claim, did not apply to actions of tort.

3. That to sustain the action, the plaintiff must prove actual damage, or delay of his suit; and in the absence of such evidence, the verdict for $150 could not stand, as the jury might have been influenced by the plaintiff's statement that he had lost his debt by the neglect to arrest D. *Chapman*, appellant, and *Doherty*, respondent, vol. 25, 271.

7—Pleading—General issue.

Held, (Palmer, J., dissenting), that *non assumpsit* was a good plea in an action on a promissory note in a county court; that neither the provisions of the Consol. Stat. cap. 37, relating to pleading, nor the Act, 43 Vic. cap. 8, applied to county courts; and that whatever was the general issue in suits in these courts before the Act, 36 Vic. cap. 31, could still be pleaded. *McCatherine* v. *Lewis*, vol. 25, 429.

—Remitting cause to Supreme Court where title to land is brought in question. See Trespass 10.

— Power to give costs. See Appeal 5.

— Plea of never indebted — Whether applicable to county courts. See Plea 4.

COUNTY COURT APPEAL.

1—Where appellant does not support—Dismissing appeal.

A cause having been entered on the county court appeal paper before it was reached, the counsel for appellant and for respondent appeared in the case, and when the respondent's counsel requested that the case be heard out of its turn, the appellant's counsel stated that he did not intend supporting the appeal.

The respondents' counsel then asked to have it struck off the paper, which was ordered accordingly without objection.

Held, that the respondent was entitled on the next common motion day to have the appeal dismissed with cost. *Burns v. Botsford*, vol. 19, 5.

2—Dismissal of—Rule 2 Mich. T. 40 Vic.

If the appellant in a county court appeal does not appear when the case is reached on the paper, the respondent may move to dismiss it with costs, and is not obliged to wait until a common motion day. (Wetmore, J., dissenting.) *McLellan* v. *Rankine*, vol 22, 146.

3—Rule—Where Appeal allowed—Costs.

Where an appeal is taken to the Supreme Court from an order of a county court judge granting a nonsuit, and the Supreme Court directs that the nonsuit be set aside, it is not necessary for the rule to go further than state that the court allows the appeal and orders that the nonsuit granted in the court below be set aside. *Easterbrooks* v. *McGowan*, and *Ward* v. *Reed*, vol. 22, 455.

4—Omission of appellant's attorney to enter cause on the appeal paper.—Dismissing appeal.

A defendant in a county court case having given the bond and completed the other proceedings necessary for an appeal, afterwards attended at the clerk's office to enter the cause on the appeal paper, but was unable to do so because the judges of the county court had not returned the proceedings. At the next term he again attended for the same purpose, but being still unable to enter the cause he requested the deputy clerk to do so when the return should be filed. A few days afterwards the return was filed but the deputy clerk forgot to enter the cause, and on the last day of the term on application of the respondent, the appeal was dismissed because the cause had not been entered.

Held, that the order dismissing the appeal was regular; that it was the duty of the attorney to see that the cause was entered, and having made the deputy clerk his agent for that purpose, he was responsible for the clerk's omission. *Ferguson* v. *Saroy*, vol 23, 87.

5—Entry of Appeal—Summary Conviction Notice of appeal in service of—Duty of judge to hear Mandamus.

Under the Dominion Act, 33 Vic. cap. 27, it is sufficient to serve a notice of appeal on the convicting justice without stating that it is for the prosecution.

If the appellant has taken the proper steps to perfect his appeal under the Act, it is the duty of the clerk of the county court to make any necessary entry of the appeal, and the judge of the court cannot refuse to hear the appeal because the appellant's attorney has entered it without authority and improperly named a party as respondent.

The judge may direct how an appeal should be entered. *Ex parte Doherty*, vol. 25, 98.

6—County court appeal—Dismissal where appellant neglects to appear—Subsequent leave to hear.

Where an appeal was dismissed because no counsel appeared to support it when it was reached on the paper, the court was equally divided on an application in the following term to restore the case to the paper, and to allow the appeal to be argued. The only ground for the application being, that the appellant's counsel had forgotten to attend at the proper time.

Quære, whether after an appeal had been dismissed, the court had power to restore it to the paper. *South-West Boom Co.*, v. *Farley*, vol. 25, 41.

7—Judge certifying proceedings — Time within which appellant must apply for—Bond on appeal—Perfecting of—Notice of to judge.

A county court judge cannot refuse to certify proceedings on appeal to the Supreme Court, although the appellant does not apply to him to do so until more than thirty days have elapsed after the filing of the bond with the clerk.

Held, by Allen, C.J., and Fraser, J., (Weldon and Wetmore, JJ., dissenting) that when a party is desirous of appealing from the decision of the county court, it is his duty to furnish the judge with evidence that the bond on appeal has been perfected and deposited with the clerk. *Ex parte Clarke*, vol. 24, 128.

8—Return of proceedings—If defective—Amendment.

If the return on an appeal from the decision of a judge of a county court omits to state any of the grounds taken before the judge, and intended to be relied on by the appellant, he should apply to have the return amended. *Woods*, Appellant and *McCann*, Respondent, vol 25, 253.

9—Grounds available on agreement.

On an appeal from an order of a county court judge, the appellant will be confined to the objections taken in the court below, as stated in the return. *Herrick*, appellant, and *Wry*, respondent, vol. 25, 258.

Quære — Whether the proceedings under the Garnishee Act, 45 Vic. cap. 17, are the subject of an appeal under the County Courts Act, Consol. Stat. cap. 51, and whether they should be brought up by *certiorari*. *Ibid.*

COUNTY COURT JUDGE.

Jurisdiction of—Under Seaman's Act 1873. See Ship 1.

— Review — Where judge does not exceed his jurisdiction—Whether *certiorari* will lie. See *Certiorari* 9.

COUNTERFEIT NOTES.

False pretences — Obtaining money by. See Criminal Law 6.

COUNTERSIGNING.

Policy of marine insurance issued by foreign corporation—Whether countersigning by agent may be waived. See Insurance 14.

COUPONS.

Interest on, is not recoverable. See Debentures.

CREDIT.

To whom given—Evidence. See Evidence 30.

CREDITORS' ASSIGNEE.

Title is derived from sheriff in case of compulsory liquidation. See Insolvent Act of 1869, 2.

—Necessity of calling meeting of, to consider consent to discharge. See Insolvent Act of 1875.

Trust deed—Assent of trustees. See Deed 2, 3, 4.

CRIMINAL LAW.

1—Indictment—Omission of word "feloniously"—Effect of—Reserving question for consideration of court—Words "during trial in Rev. Stat. cap. 129, sec. 22.

An indictment charged that the "prisoner did steal, take and carry away," etc., without charging that it was done feloniously. Before pleading, the prisoner's counsel moved to quash the indictment. After argument, the presiding judge allowed the indictment to be amended under 32 & 33 Vic., cap. 29, sec. 32, by adding the word "feloniously." The prisoner was found guilty upon the amended indictment.

Held, on a case reserved that the indictment without the "feloniously" was bad.

Held, by Allen, C.J., Weldon, Fisher and Duff, JJ., (Wetmore, J. dissenting) that although the objection to the indictment in this case was taken before plea pleaded, and that technically the trial does not begin till after the prisoner has pleaded to the indictment, and the jury are being called and sworn, yet that such a liberal construction should be put upon the words "during the trial" in Rev. Stat., cap. 159, sec. 22, Consol. Stat., p. 1088, that the provisions of this chapter relating to reserving questions for the consideration of the court should be held to apply to any of the proceedings in the court below after the indictment has been found. *Regina v. Morrison*, vol. 18, 682.

2—New trial—Right of crown.

A new trial will not be granted to the crown in a criminal cause; neither has the crown an appeal to the Supreme Court of Canada from a judgment quashing a conviction. *The Queen v. Tower*, vol. 20, 168.

3—Acts of Canada 32 & 33 Vic., cap. 21—Larceny of an unstamped promissory note—Whether valuable security within the meaning of the Act.

Held, by Allen, C.J., Duff and King, JJ., (Weldon and Wetmore, JJ., dissenting) that an insufficiently or defectively stamped promissory note, the holder being ignorant of the insufficiency of, or defect in the stamping, may be the subject of larceny, as a valuable security under the Act, 32 & 33 Vic., cap. 21, sec. 15. *Regina v. Dewitt*, vol. 21, 17.

4—Jury—Separation of, during trial—What sufficient to avoid verdict—Order under cap. 41, Consol. Stat.—Court can inquire into facts although return shows prisoner to be properly in custody.

The prisoner was tried before the York county court on a charge of larceny and found guilty. During the trial the jury, while in charge of two constables, were allowed to separate by walking on different sides of the street. One or two other separations of a similar nature were complained of, but there was nothing to shew that any of them had any conversations with any person, not a juror, in reference to the case. This was brought to the notice of the county court judge, and an application was made to him to delay passing sentence, and to treat the verdict as a nullity. This application was refused.

and the prisoner was sentenced and remanded to jail, pending his removal to the penitentiary. An order to the keeper of the gaol having been obtained under the provisions of cap. 41 of the Consol. Stat., upon the return of this order,

Held, by Allen, C.J., Wetmore, Duff, and Palmer, JJ., (Weldon and King, JJ., dissenting) that the separation of the jury was such as to avoid the verdict.

Held, by Allen, C.J., Wetmore, Duff and Palmer, JJ. (Weldon and King, JJ., dissenting), that although the return of the gaoler showed that the prisoner was properly in custody under the sentence of a court of competent jurisdiction, the court has power to inquire into the facts of the case, and that the prisoner is not bound to proceed by a writ of error. *Ex parte Ross*, vol. 21, 257.

5— Indictment — Misjoinder of counts — Amending reserved case.

An indictment contained two counts, one charging the prisoner with murdering M. on the 10th November, 1881; the other with manslaughter of the said M. on the same day. The grand jury found "a true bill." A motion to quash the indictment for misjoinder was refused, the counsel for the prosecution electing to proceed on the first count only.

Held (Palmer, J., dissenting), that the indictment was sufficient.

The prisoner was convicted of manslaughter in killing his wife, who died on the 10th November, 1881. The immediate cause of her death was acute inflammation of the liver, which the medical testimony proved might be occasioned by a blow or a fall against a hard substance. About three weeks before her death the prisoner had knocked his wife down with a bottle. She fell against a door, and remained on the floor insensible for some time. She was confined to her bed soon afterwards and never recovered. Evidence was given of frequent acts of violence committed by the prisoner upon his wife within a year of her death, by knocking her down and kicking her on her side.

Held, per Allen, C.J., Wetmore, Duff and King, JJ. (Palmer, J., dissenting), that there was evidence to leave to the jury that the disease which caused her death was produced by the injuries inflicted by the prisoner, and that the evidence of violence committed within a year of the death was properly received.

Where it was objected at the trial that there was not evidence against the prisoner to leave to the jury, but the judge was not asked to reserve the point, the case reserved was allowed to be amended at the argument in order to raise the point. (Weldon and Wetmore, JJ., dissenting). *Regina v. Theal*, vol. 21, 449. Appeal to Supreme Court of Canada dismissed. See Addenda No. 11.

6—False pretences—Obtaining property by —Whether necessary to complete the offence.

The prisoner wrote to the prosecutor to induce him to buy counterfeit bank notes. The prosecutor in order to entrap the prisoner and bring him to justice pretended to assent to the scheme, arranged a meeting, of which he informed the police, and had them placed in position to arrest the prisoner at a signal from the prosecutor.

At such meeting the prisoner produced a box which he said contained counterfeit bank notes, which he agreed to sell the prosecutor on payment of a sum agreed upon. The prisoner gave a box to the prosecutor which he pretended to be the one containing the notes, who then gave the prisoner $50 and a watch as security for the balance which he had agreed to pay.

The prosecutor immediately gave the signal to the police and seized the prisoner and held him until they arrested him, and took the money and watch from him.

On examining the box given the prosecutor, it was ascertained that the prisoner had not given him the one containing the notes as he pretended, but a similar one containing waste paper. The box containing the notes was found on the prisoner's person. It was clear and undisputed that the motive of the prosecutor in parting with the possession of the money and watch, as he had done, was to entrap the prisoner.

The prisoner was found guilty of obtaining the money and watch of the prosecutor by the false pretence of giving him the counterfeit notes, which he did not give.

On a case reserved for the opinion of the court,

Held, by Allen, C.J., and Palmer, J., that in order to complete the crime of obtaining property by false pretences, there must not only be the false pretence but an actual parting, and intention to part with the property of the party imposed upon by the pretence; that the prosecutor here never intended to part with his property in the money and watch, and that the conviction should be quashed.

They were also of opinion that as the prosecutor only expected to receive from the prisoner counterfeit notes, which were of no value, it was extremely doubtful whether he could be said to have been defrauded because he received worthless goods of another kind.

Held, by Weldon, Wetmore, King and Fraser, JJ., that the prisoner was rightly found guilty, and that the conviction should be affirmed. *Regina* v. *Carey*, vol 22, 543.

7—Indictment—Assault—Warrant.—Where irregular—Justification to officer—Attachment.

A prisoner was found guilty on an indictment charging that he made an assault upon A., "and him, the said A. did beat, wound and ill-treat," etc. There was no evidence of any wounding.

Held, by Weldon, Wetmore and King, JJ., that the indictment was substantially one for a common assault, and that the conviction was right.

Where a county court has jurisdiction to issue a warrant of commitment for contempt under the Consol. Stat. cap. 38, sec. 20-22, the warrant, though irregular, is a justification to the officer for arresting the party under it, and he is guilty of an assault if he resists the officer. S. was served with an order to appear before a commissioner to be examined under the Consol. Stat. cap. 38, sec. 20, and neglected to appear. A notice was afterwards served upon him that an application would be made to the county court on a certain day, for an attachment against him for contempt in disobeying the order of the commissioner. S. did not appear in the county court pursuant to this notice, and the judge thereupon ordered an attachment to issue against him, directing him to be imprisoned for thirty days for his contempt.

Held, *per* Weldon, Wetmore and King, JJ., (Palmer, J., dissenting) that the county court had power to issue the attachment—that the direction in it to imprison S. for thirty days was at most an irregularity; and that he was not justified in resisting the officer in executing it.

Per Palmer, J., that the attachment was a nullity; that the court had no authority to order S. to be imprisoned for thirty days; and that he was justified in resisting his arrest. *Regina* v. *Shavson*, vol. 23, 1.

8—Joint indictment — Where jury disagree as to guilt of one prisoner and find the other guilty—Conviction — Whether warranted.

H. and W. were jointly indicted and tried for stealing. On the trial H. was found guilty, but the jury were unable to agree upon a verdict as to W., and were discharged from giving a verdict as to him.

Held, that the verdict warranted the conviction of H. *Regina* v. *Hamilton and Walsh*, vol. 21, 540.

9—Previous acquittal of principal felon—When no defence—Indictment—Amendment.

On the trial of the prisoner on an indictment charging him with receiving property which one M. had feloniously stolen, etc., the evidence showed that he had stolen the property, and that the prisoner was guilty of receiving the same, knowing it, to have been stolen

For the defence, it was proved that M. had been previously tried on a charge of stealing the same property and acquitted. The counsel for the prosecution then applied to strike out of the indictment the allegation that M. had stolen the property, and to insert the words "some evil disposed person," etc., which the judge allowed.

Held, 1st. That the record of the previous acquittal of M. formed no defence on the trial of this indictment, and was improperly received in evidence.

2nd. That the amendment was improperly allowed. *Regina* v. *Ferguson*, vol. 20, 259.

10—Taking with intent to defraud—Stating value in indictment—Bona fide claim of right.

An indictment under 32 & 33 Vic. cap. 21, sec. 110, for unlawfully taking and appropriating property with intent to defraud, need not state the value of the property taken; although perhaps a prisoner could not be tried under the second clause of the section if the value was not stated.

Held, also, on the trial of such an indictment, to be a proper direction, to tell the jury they should acquit the prisoner if they thought he *bona fide* believed he had a claim of right in the property taken. *Regina* v. *Horseman*, vol. 20, 529.

11—Habeas corpus—Returnable forthwith—Prisoners brought in once — Whether orders to bring in again can be made without issuing new writs.

Writs of *habeas corpus* were made returnable forthwith. The prisoners were brought into court on Tuesday, and the matter directed to be argued on the following Saturday. The same day the sheriff took the prisoners back to the gaol from which he had brought them. The writs and returns had been filed the day the prisoners were brought in, and by order of a judge taken off file again and returned to the sheriff.

Held, by Allen, C.J., Fisher and Duff, JJ., (Weldon and Wetmore JJ., dissenting) that the court could direct the sheriff to bring in the bodies of the prisoners on the day set for the argument, without directing new writs to issue. *Regina* v. *Tower*, vol. 20, 178.

12—Crime committed in a foreign country.

Murder being an extraditable offence under the treaty of Washington, 1842, the courts of this country will take notice that it is punishable as a crime in the United States. *Porter* v. *McMahon*, vol. 23, 211.

—Extradition—Treaty of Washington, 1842—Trial for offence other than that for which prisoner was surrendered. See Extradition.

— Indictment for murder — Short form—Whether prisoner can be convicted of assault under. See Indictment 1.

— Joinder of offences. See Indictment 2.

—Intent to defraud — Statement of value. See Intent to Defraud.

—Confession of prisoner. See Evidence 23.

—Adultery — Indictment for — Marriage in foreign country. See Adultery.

Criminate — Refusal of witness to answer questions tending to. See False Imprisonment 4.

Crown grant — Statement upon, in handwriting of grantee's agent that he had sold the land — Admissibility of. See Possession 2.

COURT—GENERAL RULES.

1 — Appeals — Demurrer books — Hilary Term, 1881.

1. It is ordered that all appeals from the decision of a judge in equity and all special cases, be printed and filed with the clerk of the pleas before the opening of the court on the first day of the term at which such cases are to be argued, and that copies for each of the judges be filed with the clerk at the same time; and that until such appeals and special cases are so filed no entry thereof shall be made on the respective papers.

2. That the attorneys for the respective parties shall deliver to the clerk of the pleas before the opening of the court on the first day of term, the copies of the demurrer books required to be delivered to the judges by the Rule of Hilary Term 6th, William IV.; and that no entry of the cause shall be made on the special paper until the party demurring shall have delivered to the clerk the demurrer books which by the practice he is required to deliver.

3. So long as the court shall sit in two divisions under the provisions of the Act, 42 Vic. cap. 8, it shall not be necessary to deliver more than three demurrer books, two of which shall be made up and delivered by the plaintiff's attorney.

4. That no entry of any appeal from a probate court or from any county court, shall be entered on the appeal paper until the return of the judge of the court appealed from shall be on file in the office of the clerk of the pleas.

5. That hereafter all entries upon the motion, crown, special, or appeal papers, shall be made before the opening of the court on the first day of each term, and that no entry shall afterwards be allowed, except for good cause shown by affidavit, and upon motion made to the court on one of the common motion days.

6. Crown cases reserved shall come on for argument immediately after the Crown paper, or if there should be no Crown paper, then immediately after the conclusion of the motion paper.

1 a—General rule of—Issues in law and fact —Trial—Hilary Term, 43 Vic.

It is ordered that no cause in which issues in law and in fact are joined, shall hereafter be entered for trial at any circuit unless the plaintiff, when he enters the cause, intends to try it in its order when it is reached on the docket.

2—Michaelmas Term, 45 Vic.—Admission of Barristers.

1. Whenever any attorney of this court shall desire to be called to the Bar as a barrister, he shall apply by petition to the court, stating the date of his admission as an attorney, which petition

shall be filed with the clerk on or before the first day of the term in which he intends to apply.

2 Thursday in the first week, and Thursday in the third week of each term, at the opening of the court on such days shall be times for the admission of barristers, and no attorney shall be admitted to the Bar at any other time, unless it shall be shewn by affidavit to the satisfaction of the court that the person applying was prevented by reasonable cause from being present at the time appointed.

3—Hilary Term, 46 Vic.—Filing docket.

Whereas the rule of Hilary Term 7th, William IV., relative to the filing of entry dockets, is inapplicable to writs of summons and *capias* issued under the Con. Stat. cap. 37.

It is ordered that in all actions commenced after the end of the present term, and which have not been settled or discontinued, the attorney shall enter the return, and make and file with the clerk of the court a docket of the return to such writs of summons or *capias*, together with the said writs, within thirty days after the expiration of the two months within which such writs are required to be executed or served; and that the clerk of the court do not in future receive or file any docket, or enter any such cause, after the said thirty days without the order of a judge to be obtained on affidavit properly accounting for the delay.

4—Easter Term, 46 Vic. (1883)—Equity appeals.

Whenever hereafter an appeal is made from a decree or order of a judge sitting in equity, such judge, or in case of his absence or inability to attend, some other judge of the court shall, on the application of the appellant and on notice to the solicitors of the respondents, settle and order which part of the pleadings, evidence, judgments, and other proceedings shall be printed for the use of the Appellate Court; and the court may at the hearing of the appeal refer to and use any other part of the pleadings, evidence, and other proceedings in the suit as they may think necessary.

5—Divorce Court appeals.

On appeals from the Court of Divorce and Matrimonial Causes, the judge of such court may, where in his opinion a copy of the pleadings and evidence is not necessary for the hearing of the appeal, state a case for the opinion of the Court of Appeal, subject, however, to be amended by such further return of the pleadings, evidence, judgment, and other proceedings in the cause as the Court of Appeal may think necessary. See Rule 3, Trinity Term, 1868. Easter Term, 46 Vic., 1883.

6—Practise in Equity.

That from and after the present term all bills, interrogatories, answers, pleas, demurrers, and other pleadings in suits in equity shall be written or printed on foolscap paper, instead of parchment as heretofore used.

6 a—It shall not hereafter be necessary to issue any commission in suits for partition or for dower; but the commissioners to be appointed in any such suits shall act under the order of the court appointing them, and directing the partition or assignment of dower in the same manner as has been heretofore done under commissions issued for that purpose. Easter Term, 46 Vic., 1883.

7—Plea—Time allowed to file—Service—Hilary Term, 1884.

Where the attorneys for the respective parties reside in the same county, but more than ten miles distant from each other, the defendant's attorney shall be allowed four days after demand of plea wherein to file the plea and serve a copy thereof on the plaintiff's attorney, unless the demand be accompanied by a direction to deliver the copy of plea to some person resident in the same place in which the defendant's attorney resides; in which case such copy of plea must be delivered within twenty-four hours, according to the present practice.

8—Election Court.

The following fees shall be taken by the clerk under the Dominion Controverted Elections Act, 1874:

EASTER TERM, 1884.

Entering petition	$	60
Receiving and care of deposit 2½ per cent.		
Certificate of deposit		40
Comparing and forwarding copy of petition for publication, per folio		05
Entering appointment and address of agent		40
Signing and sealing every process		30
Certified copies of all papers, per folio		20
Copies of all papers, per folio		10
Taxing costs in contested cases	1	50
Taxing costs in all other cases		70
Each notice		60
Filing each paper		20
Entering every order or dismission		50
Each search		20

9—Con. Stat. cap. 38—Fees under Michaelmas Term Act, 1884.

It is ordered that the fees to be taken for the several services of attorneys, counsel, witnesses, clerk, and sheriff, under the provisions of chapter 38 of the Consolidated Statutes, be the same as provided for similar services on the law side of the Supreme Court by chapter 119 of the Consolidated Statutes.

10—Commission to examine witnesses.

Con. Stat. cap. 49. Supreme Court in Equity. General rules. Hilary Term 1885. See vol. 24, page 515.

11—County Court appeals—Easter Term, 1885.

1. It is ordered that rule 1 of Michaelmas Term, 1876, relating to County Court appeals, be rescinded, and the following rule be substituted therefor:

That the appellant from the decision of a Judge of a County Court shall enter the cause on the appeal paper of the term immediately succeeding the receipt of the proceedings by the Clerk of the Pleas; but when any such proceedings are received after the opening of the court in any term, the causes shall be entered by the appellant on the appeal paper of the next succeeding term. See Earle's Rules 195.

2. It is ordered that the stamp now used in the office of the Clerk of the Pleas, bearing the representation of a crown encircled with the words "*Sigil. Cur. Sup. Nov. Bruns.*" may be used as the seal of the court upon all writs, processes, and other documents required to be under seal, either on the crown side, or on the common law or equity sides of the court.

12—Michaelmas Term, 1885—County Court appeals.

Rule 1. It is ordered that no appeal from the decision of a County Court shall be entered on the appeal paper, unless the proceedings duly certified by the judge have been received in the office of the Clerk of the Pleas seven days before the first day of the term at which it is intended to be entered.

2. It shall be the duty of the appellant to prepare and file with the Clerk of the Pleas for the use of the court, on or before the first day of the term, a brief statement of the material facts in the

case, plainly and legibly written, together with the grounds of the appeal, numbering the same consecutively, and referring to the page or pages of the proceedings to which the several grounds respectively relate; and such statement shall be framed as near as may be as the notices of motion for new trials required by the Rule of Hilary Term, 1867, and the appellants on the argument of the appeal shall be confined to the grounds so stated. A copy of such statement and grounds of appeal shall be filed for each of the judges of this court.

3. Rule 1 of Michaelmas Term, 1876, Earle's Rules 195, relating to County Court appeals, is hereby rescinded, and in lieu thereof it is ordered that the appellant, having filed the statement hereinbefore required, shall enter the cause on the appeal paper of the term in which such statement is so filed.

4. In case the appellant shall neglect to enter the appeal on the appeal paper, according to the last preceding rule, or having entered it, shall not argue it when reached in due course on the paper, or pursuant to any order of the court made in respect thereof, then and in either of such cases, the respondent may, on the case being reached on the paper, or upon any subsequent common motion day, move that the said appeal be dismissed. Rule 2 of Michaelmas Term, 1876, is hereby rescinded.

5. The Clerk of the Pleas shall, on the application of the attorney of any appellant, deliver to him the proceedings, certified by the Judge of the County Court (taking a receipt therefor), in order that the statement required by Rule 2 may be prepared, and such attorney shall return such proceedings to the said clerk before the opening of the court on the first day of the term.

13—Easter Term, 1885.

1. It is ordered that Rule 1 of Michaelmas Term, 1876, relating to County Court appeals, be rescinded, and the following rule be substituted therefor:

That the appellant from the decision of a Judge of a County Court shall enter the cause on the appeal paper of the term immediately succeeding the receipt of the proceedings by the Clerk of the Pleas; but when any such proceedings are received after the opening of the court in any term, the causes shall be entered by the appellant on the appeal paper of the next succeeding term. See Earle's Rules 195.

COURT HOUSE.

Control of building—Personal injury—Principle governing liability. See Municipality of St. John 1.

COVENANT.

In insurance on stock that amount of claim shall be settled by arbitration, does not apply where there has been a total loss. See Insurance 8.

—Not to assign—Mortgage of chattels. See Addenda 45.

—Action for breach of—Necessity of setting out in declaration the agreement sued on. See Pleading 4.

DAMAGES (See Land Damages.

1—Action on the case—Maliciously inducing one to record deed.

Held by Duff, J., that where defendant had induced a person with whom a deed had been entrusted as an escrow to prove and record it; and the jury found that in so inducing her, he was actuated by a fraudulent and malicious motive towards the plaintiff, the latter had a good cause of action, and the jury were not confined to the actual pecuniary damages which plaintiff had sustained in consequence.

Held by Weldon and Wetmore, JJ., that the deed though registered could not operate to pass the title, and as plaintiff had proved no actual legal damage the verdict should be reduced to nominal damages.

Derry v. *Derry*, vol. 19, 621.

2—Costs of review from Justices' Court—Where not in discretion of Judge—Res Judicata.

On review from a judgment of nonsuit in a justice's court, the county court judge set aside the nonsuit, without costs. Previous to the order for review being obtained, an execution had been issued by the justice on which plaintiff had been arrested, but on the order for review being granted, he was released.

In an action for false imprisonment—

Held by Allen, C.J., and Weldon, Palmer, King and Fraser, JJ., (Wetmore, J., dissenting) that as the county court judge had "wholly reversed" the judgment of the magistrate, the awarding of costs to him should have followed, and was not a matter in the discretion of the judge, and that the plaintiff was entitled in this action to recover the expenses to which he had been put in securing such reversal of judgment.

Carman v. *Dunn*, vol. 20, 335.

3—Defective Machinery—Bad Sawing therefrom—Limitation of damages after defect known.

Where plaintiff claimed damages for bad quality of lumber sawed, in consequence of defective machinery sold by defendants, it was

Held, that the damages must be confined to the sawing for a reasonable time after the plaintiff had an opportunity of judging of the defects and notifying defendants to have them remedied.

Morrow v. *The Waterhouse Engine Co.*, vol. 18, 569. See Addenda, 38.

—When doubtful as to what trespass damages have been given by jury. See *Eagan* v. *Chapman*, *et al.*, vol. 18, 410.

—Adjoining land owners—Defendant not filling up cellar—Plaintiff's default—When defendant not liable. See *Trustees*, *etc.* v. *Hutchinson*, vol. 18, 523. See Addenda 42.

—Acceptance of goods subsequent to time agreed upon for delivery—When cannot be set up as defence or reduction of damages. See *Moffat* v. *Lunt*, vol. 18, 673.

—Liability of town for, when town raises level of streets and neglects to fence. See Streets 1.

—Granted under forfeiture clause on building contract. See Contract 2.

—If excessive, a new trial might be granted by county court judge. See Husband and Wife 1.

—Two cents—Section 11, Consol. Stat. cap. 90, does not apply when arrest and imprisonment took place before conviction of plaintiff. See False Imprisonment 1.

—Special—Test whether action of slander will lie without proof of. See Slander 2.

—Light and air—Interruption of. See Addenda 51.

—Excessive—Where jury must have acted under influence of undue motives—New trial. See Trespass 11.

—Injury to person falling down stairway leading to court room owing to want of light. See Municipality of St. John.

—Liability of town of Portland for—Hole in sidewalk. See Portland, Town of.

—Measure of, in action of trover for promissory note by executor, where executor maker of note. See Trover 1.

— Prospective — Action by husband and wife, for injuries to wife—Loss of wife's services. See Husband and Wife 1.

—Railway company—Action against for killing horse. See Railway Company 4.

—Fire set by sparks from locomotive.

—When property insured — Whether an answer to company's liability. See Railway Company 5.

—When plaintiff entitled to nominal damages and no actual damage shewn New trial refused. See Contract 15.

—Accord and satisfaction. See Contract 16.

—Interest not recoverable as damages on loss of vessel and freight. See Collision 1.

— Stipulated damages — When such. See Contr[illegible]

— Contract to deliver steam engine and mill machinery—Failure to deliver within specified time. See Contract 14.

— Tort — Necessary to prove actual damage. See County Court 6.

— Injunction, obtaining of. See Addenda 41.

DATE.

Impossible date, effect of, where parties are not misled. See Arrest 1.

DEBENTURES.

1.—Issued under 38 Vic. cap. 85—In hands of third parties—Coupons—Interest on.

Held, adhering to the opinion expressed in this case in 4 P. & B. 78, that debentures issued under 38 Vic. cap. 85, sealed with the seal of the general sessions of the county of Albert, acquired by the 4th sec. of the Act, a negotiable character like promissory notes payable to bearer and that in the hands of third parties, their validity could not be questioned.

Interest on coupons is not recoverable. [illegible] v. *Municipality of Albert*, vol. 21, 200.

—Issued by sessions, must be redeemed by municipality. See Municipality.

DEBT.

—Extinguishment of accommodation note. See Promissory Note 6.

—Assignment of—Suit in equity by assignee. See Pleadings 6.

—Bills of Sale Act does not apply to debts. See Bills of Sale Act 2.

DEBTORS.

1—Consol. Stat., cap. 38, sec. 7—Disclosure by debtor—Discharge from arrest—Second application for examination—Res judicata.

If a debtor applying for examination under the Consol. Stat., cap. 38, sec. 7, is unable to make a full disclosure of the state of his affairs, and to answer all proper interrogatories without reference to his books, it is his duty to produce them at the examination; and an order made for his discharge without the production of his books, will be set aside.

If the plaintiff in the suit, or his attorney, resides within 30 miles of the place where the examination is to be held, 48 hours' notice of such intended examination is sufficient.

Per Palmer, J. If a debtor applies for examination, and after a hearing before the proper tribunal his discharge is refused, the matter is *res judicata*, and he cannot make a second application. *Ex parte Clerke, in re Harvey*, vol. 24, 623.

2—Disclosure by debtor—Consol. Stat., cap. 38, sec. 7—Discharge from arrest where debtor on gaol limits.

Section 7, of cap. 38, Consol. Stat., providing for disclosure and discharge of a debtor from arrest, is applicable to a defendant who has been rendered in discharge of his bail, and is on the gaol limits at the time of making his disclosure. *Manchester ex parte*, vol. 25, 552.

—Order of discharge — Refusal to answer questions. See *Certiorari* 1.

—Examination of—Consol. Stat. cap. 38—Attachment. See Criminal Law 7.

—Attachment and sale of property of —Order of commissioners under Consol. Stat. cap. 38. See False Imprisonment 7.

Deceased person — Accounts settled with. See Settled Accounts.

DECLARATION.

Where only one trespass laid, whether more can be proved. See Trespass 2.

—Does not require to be filed as well as served under sec. 52, cap. 37, Consol. Stat. See *Supersedeas*.

—In trespass when premises not set out—Defendant's remedy. See Trespass 5.

—In ejectment—Service of when door of house is locked. See Ejectment 1.

DECREE.

—Of Equity Court—Parties assenting to must be bound by it. See Will 5.

DEED.

1.—Voluntary conveyance—Deed to son—Bona Fides of consideration—Question for jury—Secondary circumstances considered in determining matter.

No certain rule can be laid down as to what is an honest transaction, or the opposite. Every case must stand on its own footing, and the Court or jury must consider whether, having regard to all the circumstances, the transaction was a fair one, and was intended to pass the property for a good and valuable consideration. *Doe dem Jones and wife v. Neeels*, vol. 18, 677.

2.—Trust deed for benefit of creditors—Further assurance—Judgment to defraud creditors—Want of consideration.

S. being indebted to a number of persons conveyed to the plaintiff property in trust to sell, and pay certain creditors named in the trust deed, and to pay any surplus to such of his creditors as should execute the deed within a certain time; and he covenanted that he would on request execute such further assurance of the trust property as counsel should advise. The deed contained a release by the creditors who executed it of all their claims and demands against S. Afterwards, certain creditors of S. who were not named in the trust deed, and who had not signed it, filed a bill in equity to set aside the deed as fraudulent, the proceedings in which suit were pending. Soon after this, S. confessed a judgment in favour of the plaintiff for a large amount—the proceeds of which were to be divided among the creditors named in the trust deed, upon which judgment execution was issued against the property of S.

Held, 1. That the judgment was fraudulent and void against the creditors of J. who had not signed the trust deed—the persons for whose benefit it was given, having previously released all their claims against S.

2. That the judgment was not a further assurance within the terms of the trust deed—it being a security on other and different property than that conveyed thereby.

3. That the pending of the suit to set aside the trust deed did not affect the application to set aside the judgment. *Ensury et al v. Sherman*, vol. 25, 521.

3 — Release of debts — Fraudulent judgment—Failure of consideration—Trustee and cestui que trust.

S. executed a deed of property in trust for the benefit of certain creditors, who thereby released him from all claims and demands. A suit in equity having been afterwards brought to set aside the deed as fraudulent, he confessed a judgment to one of the creditors named in the trust deed, who signed a paper stating that he held the judgment for the benefit of himself and other persons named (who were also named in the trust deed as creditors of S.) for specified sums. It did not appear that those persons knew that the judgment had been given, nor was there any proof that the sums specified were due to them. On an application by a subsequent judgment creditor of S., to set aside the judgment as fraudulent.

Held, 1. That there was no consideration to support the judgment in the case of any creditor who had signed the trust deed.

2. That until the persons for whose benefit the judgment professed to have been given assented to it, the relation of trustee and *cestui que trust* did not exist between them and the holder of the judgment.

3. When it is not clearly shewn that a person in whose favour a judgment as confessed is a *bona fide* creditor for a certain sum, the judgment will not be sustained against a subsequent judgment creditor. *Sheraton* v. *Sheraton*, vol. 25, 534.

4 —Trust deed —Trust for benefit of husband and wife—Release by husband—Fraudulent conveyance.

A. S. conveyed property in trust for the benefit of his creditors preferring (*inter alia*) R. S. for the sum of $6,281, and his wife for $1,853. By the terms of the deed, the creditors who signed it released A. S. from all claims and demands up to that date. R. S. signed the deed. The trustees having offered the property for sale, it was bought in for R. S. for the sum of $21,050, but differences arising between him and the trustees, he commenced a suit in equity to compel them to complete the sale, whereupon an order was made by consent in September, 1883, appointing a receiver of the proceeds of the sale, R. S. guaranteeing the trustees that the property would produce $21,050, in certain stated sums, in three, six and nine months; and on that sum being realised from the sales, it was agreed that the receiver should transfer to R. S. any balance of the property that might remain. The property was sold and the proceeds paid to the receiver from time to time; but it did not appear, after the lapse of nine months, how much had been realised from the sales. Immediately after making the order appointing the receiver, R. S. commenced an action against A. S. And recovered a judgment by default for the amounts claimed by R. S. and his wife, being the sums directed to be paid to them by the trust deed. On an application by a subsequent judgment creditor of A. S. to set aside this judgment as fraudulent;

Held, 1. That R. S. having released A. S. by the trust deed from all debts, there was no consideration to support the judgment as to his claim.

2. That it not being shewn what amount had been realized by the sale of the property under the order in equity, or the value of the property unsold, there was no proof that the debt due to R. S.'s wife had not been paid by such sales or property; and that the onus of proving that fact was on R. S.

Quære — Whether the debt due to R. S.'s wife was not released by his executing the trust deed it not being shewn to be her separate property under the Consol. Stat. cap. 72. *Sheraton* v. *Sheraton*, vol. 25, 511.

5—Effect of words "to A. B. forever"—Necessity of words "heirs" to convey fee.

Held, that a deed of land to "A. B. forever" will not convey the fee, but only a life estate. *Jack* v. *Lyons*, vol. 19, 336.

—Given under Insolvent Confined Debtor's Act or by sheriff under execution does not defeat a previous voluntary deed executed by the debtor. See Voluntary Conveyance.

—Delivery of for inspection—Agents' right of action. See Contract 1.

—Maliciously inducing one to record. See Damages 1.

—Effect of covenant that grantee has a right to grant bargain and sell. See Ambiguity 1.

—By Infant—Evidence of confirmation after coming of age. See Infant 2.

—Effect of words "warrant and defend." See Estoppel 4.

—Acknowledgement taken out of province. See Dower.

—Of partition—Mutual—Reservation of common right to quarry in one moiety. See Partition.

—Registered — Purchaser under — Whether actual entry necessary in order to maintain trespass. See Trespass 10.

—Composition and discharge under Insolvent Act—Title to land. See Insolvent Act of 1869, 2.

— Voluntary — Husband to wife through medium of third party—*Ante* nuptial agreement. See Husband and Wife 5.

—Where agent in giving exceeds his authority—Whether void. See Power of Attorney.

—Relation to date of deed, when not recorded till after death of grantor. See *Doe dem Elliott* v. *Flanagan*, vol. 25, 154.

Defect. In affidavits used on obtaining a *rule nisi*—When may be objected to. See Practice 21.

DELAY.

Unavoidable — When charterers relieved. See Charter Party 1.

—In moving to set aside a judgment for irregularity. See Judgment 1.

—In signing judgment — When defendant had entered special bail and had been rendered. See Discharge 1.

—In applying for *certiorari*. See *Certiorari* 10.

—*Certiorari* to set aside proceedings under Absconding Debtors Act. See Absconding Debtor 1.

DEMAND OF PARTICULARS.

Plaintiff cannot have order for inspection of books until application to remove stay of proceedings created by. See Books.

—In ejectment—Effect of. See Ejectment 6.

DEMURRER.

In action for trespass, insufficient description of *locus in quo*—Not a ground of—Withdrawal of. See Trespass 5.

—If plea professes to answer the whole cause of action and answers only a part, plaintiff may demur. See Plea 1.

—Costs must not be taxed on, while other issues are pending. See Costs 11.

—When defendant's proper remedy was by, a new trial will not be ordered. See Husband and Wife 2.

—On ground that the declaration does not disclose any consideration for the making of the promise therein alleged. See Agreement 3.

—Bill—Want of Equity—Multifariousness. See Equity.

—Declaration—Action by incorporated company—Not alleging incorporation. See Joint Stock Companies Act.

—Issues in law and fact—*Ex parte* order directing trial of. See Practice 23.

DEPOSIT.

On land bought at auction under agreement that vendor should have a clear title is recoverable if such title is not given. See Sale of Land 3.

DEPOSITIONS.

1.—Endorsing on envelope enclosing—What sufficient entitling of cause—Con. Stat. cap. 37, sec. 194.

The parties to the action were—*La Banque Ville Marie*, plaintiffs, and *Albert J. Lordly* and *Sterling R. Lordly*, defendants. The depositions taken under a commission were returned addressed to the Court and endorsed *La Banque Ville Marie v. A. J. Lordly et al.*

Held, that the endorsement was not sufficient. *La Banque Ville Marie v. Lordly* vol. 21, 273.

DEPUTY COLLECTOR OF INLAND REVENUE.

Whether necessarily a prosecuting officer under the Canada Temperance Act 1878, sec. 101. See Canada Temperance Act 1878, 11.

DESCRIPTION OF LAND.

If no ambiguity, reference cannot be made to a plan annexed, or to any other grant. See Trespass 4.

—Insufficiency of, not a ground of demurrer. See Trespass 5.

Dividing line—Surveyor mutually chosen. See Acquiescence 1.

DEVISE.

Of income and profits to widow—Right of widow to lease. See Will 9.

DISCHARGE.

1—From custody—Where unnecessary delay in signing judgment—Where defendant had entered special bail and been rendered.

The fact that a defendant had entered special bail, and had been rendered by his bail does not deprive him of his right to be discharged for unnecessary delay under sec. 4, cap 38, of Consol. Stat. *McManus v. Walsh*, vol. 22, 332.

—Order of—Under Consol. Stat. cap. 41—Whether court has power to set aside. See *Habeas Corpus* 3.

—Under Insolvent Act—Plea of. See Attorney 2.

—Consent to—Necessity of calling meeting of creditors to consider. See Insolvent Act of 1875.

—Confirmation of—Under deed of composition—When creditor may oppose application for. See Insolvent Act of 1875.

—By statutory majority of creditors when insolvent is without assets. See Insolvent Act of 1875.

—Of Jury—Whether a judge has power without defendant's consent. See Practice 15.

—Order of commissioner for debtor's discharge—What it should set out. See Limit Bond 1.

—From arrest—Disclosure by debtor—Second application for examination—Consol. Stat. cap. 38, sec. 7. See Debtor 1.

DISCLOSURE.

Examination under Consol. Stat. cap. 38, sec. 7—Arrest for a tort. See Arrest 3.

—Refusal to answer questions on examination for. See *Certiorari* 4.

See Debtor—Discharge.

DISCONTINUANCE

Of possession of land. See Possession 2.

DISCRETION.

Exercise of by judge—Certifying—Review by court. See Review 1.

DISQUALIFICATION.

Police magistrate being ratepayer of town—Whether disqualified from trying offences under Canada Temperance Act. See Canada Temperance Act 11. See Justice of Peace 3.

DISTRESS.

Privilege from—Logs delivered to mill-owner to be sawn into deals—Whether privilege destroyed by mill-owner being jointly interested. See Landlord and Tenant 3.

Sufficiency of agreement to warrant distress. See Landlord and Tenant 4.

Distress after sunset—Breaking doors. See Landlord and Tenant 6.

Divorce Court Appeals. See Court General Rules 5.

Docket. Application to strike cause off. See Appeal Papers.

DOMINION CONTROVERTED ELECTIONS ACT.

1.—Petition withdrawn and deposit returned pending preliminary objections — Refiling petition.

A petition alleging corrupt practices by the respondent was filed against the return of a member of the House of Commons under "The Dominion Controverted Elections Act, 1874." Preliminary objections were taken to the petition, and while they were pending the judge of the Election Court made an order, with the consent of the attorneys of both parties, that the petition might be taken off the files and the deposit returned to the petitioner. The petitioner afterwards obtained an order from the judge that the petition might be re-filed, and the petitioner's attorney changed, on condition of his repaying the deposit to the clerk.

Held, by Allen, C.J., and Weldon, Palmer and King, JJ., that when the deposit was withdrawn the judge had no authority to make an order to proceed in the matter, and that the order should be rescinded.

Per Wetmore, J., that the petitioner having withdrawn the petition (though in a different manner from that described by the statute), was estopped from taking any further proceedings. [illegible] v. *[illegible]*, vol. 22, 573. Appeal to Supreme Court of Canada quashed. See Addenda 12.

2.—Election petition—Variance in copy served—Amendment—Preliminary objections.

By "The Dominion Controverted Elections Act, 1874," sec. 9. A copy of an election petition is required to be served on the respondent within five days after its presentation; and by sec. 10 the respondent may present preliminary objections to the petition within five days after the service thereof. A petition was filed charging the respondent with having corruptly given to electors, meat, drink, etc., on the day of nomination, and on the polling day; also, with hiring, promising to pay, and paying for horses, carriages, etc., to convey voters to the polls. The paper served on the respondent as a copy of the petition omitted from the first allegation the words "and on the following days," and from the second the words, "and paying for."

Held, per Allen, C.J., Wetmore and Palmer, JJ., (Fraser, J., dissenting), 1. That no copy of the petition had been served on the respondent the words omitted being material allegations in the petition—and that the judge had no authority to proceed in the matter.

2. That a copy of the petition not having been served, the case was not within sec. 10, and the respondent was not bound to object to the omissions in the copy within five days after service.

Per Fraser, J., that the omission from the copy of the petition only amounted to irregularities, and that it might be amended; and that the only effect of the omission would be to prevent the petitioners from giving evidence of the charges omitted. *Rogers*, petitioner, and *Wallace*, respondent, vol. 21, 459.

—Fees in election court. See Court General Rules 8.

DOMINION OFFICIAL.

1—Income—Whether subject to taxation for municipal purposes.

Held, by Weldon, Wetmore and Duff, JJ. (Allen, C. J., *dubitante*), that an income of an officer in the customs, who resided in the city of St. John, was not subject to taxation for municipal purposes. *Ex parte Owen*, vol. 20, 487. See also Assessment 7.

Dominion Penitentiary — Warrant to commit. See Warrant 1.

DONATIO MORTIS CAUSA.

What constitutes.

A., a few days before his death, and while in good health, handed to one F. a box with a letter addressed to the defendant, and requested F. to forward the box to the defendant "in case anything should happen" to him A.

The box contained a number of debentures and other valuables labelled for different persons, and also a will insufficiently executed, disposing of the same articles in substantial accordance with the labelling of them. A. a few days afterwards committed suicide. After his death F. delivered the box to the defendant.

Held, that this did not constitute a valid *donatio mortis causa*. *Eade v. Botsford*, vol. 23, 107.

DOWER.

1—Whether widow has estate of freehold before assignment — Conveyance — Acknowledgment—Taken out of Province—Officer taking must certify that person acknowledging is the grantor.

A deed acknowledged out of the province had on it the following certificate of the notary public taking the acknowledgment:

"City of Boston, etc., April 10, 1876.

"There personally appeared I. T., and acknowledged the aforegoing instrument to be his free act and deed. I. A., notary public." The name I. T. was the same as that of the grantor.

Held, that the acknowledgment was bad, because the notary had not certified that the person appearing before him was the grantor.

A widow has not previous to her dower been assigned an estate of freehold in the lands of her deceased husband. *Torrens v. Carvor*, vol. 22, 342.

—Suit for procedure. See Court, General Rules of, 6 a.

DOUBLE STAMPS.

Bill of exchange—Reasonable time. See Stamp Act.

Double stamping, when allowable—Pleading. See Bill of Exchange.

DREDGE.

Belonging to government Liability of master for negligence of his fellow servants. See Negligence 2.

DRIFTING FOR SALMON.

When under the Fisheries' Act Officer may seize boat and nets. See on View.

DUPLICITY IN PLEADING.

Not ground for general demurrer. See Accord and Satisfaction.

EASEMENT.

1—Flowage — Mill privilege — Deed — Construction of—Estoppel.

On trial of an action on the case for overflowing plaintiff's land, it appeared that many years ago D. V. was seized of a considerable tract of land, through which ran a small stream of water. On part of this land, about fifty years ago, D. V. erected a small mill, which was driven by water obtained from a pond formed by damming the stream. This mill was several times destroyed, and as often rebuilt on the original site by D. V. or his sons, until it was finally destroyed in 1854. This tract of land embraced as well the land overflowed, as that now owned by the defendants. D. V. died intestate in 1842, leaving a son D. V. the younger, and several other children. In July of that year all the other children joined in a conveyance of the whole tract to D. V. the younger, who subsequently made a division of it amongst his father's heirs, and conveyed to each his share. In that division he conveyed to S. V. the homestead and piece of land in which it stood. In the conveyance from D. V. the younger to S. V. what is therein described as the "mill seat" was expressly excepted. The land adjoining S. V. on the west was retained by D. V. the younger till his death, when his executors conveyed it to the female plaintiff. It was upon this land that the flowage complained of took place.

From 1854 to 1863 there was no mill or dam on the premises. In the latter year defendants agreed with D. V. the younger for the purchase of the mill privilege, and erected a new mill and dam on the site of the old one. On 29th January, 1864, defendants obtained a conveyance of the mill site and privilege (describing it by metes and bounds), together with all the privileges and appurtenances to the same belonging. After running the mill for about three years, defendants found the supply of water in the dam they had erected on the old site insufficient to keep the mill during the whole season. They accordingly erected another dam further up the stream on the land which had been conveyed to S. V., so as to secure a reserve supply of water. This was the dam which caused the flowage complained of on plaintiff's land. It was proved that the water from the old dam had never overflowed any portion of the land now owned by plaintiffs.

Held, that the grant of the mill privilege by D. V. the younger to defendants must be confined to such a privilege as was previously used and enjoyed by their grantor, and that they had no right to overflow plaintiffs' land. *Colhoun et ux* v. *Hoarke et al.*, vol. 19, 591.

2—Obstructions interfering with — Executed parol license—Revocation of—Harbour of St. John—Power of corporation to erect wharves.

The corporation of St. John being the conservators of the harbour of St. John and owners of the soil thereof, with power to amend and improve the harbour, leased to the European and North American Railway Company the right to the ferry across the harbour, with the ferry slips and landings, and a wharf on the south side of the slip, built by the corporation, with power to extend such wharf to the harbour line. The railway company, in the exercise of this power, extended the wharf further into the harbour, and in doing so deflected that portion of the wharf to the south of the line of the old wharf, so as, to some extent, to narrow and encroach upon the entrance to the slip on the south side of the wharf. At the time the wharf was so extended B. was the owner of the land in rear, or to the east of the wharf, and also lessee of the slip to the south of it; he was also the manager of the railway company, and knew that they were building the extension of the wharf, being present from time to time while the work was being done.

The plaintiff afterwards purchased B.'s right to the land and slip, and brought an action against the defendants (who had come into possession of the wharf and ferry on the expiration of the lease) for the obstruction of, and encroachment upon, his slip by the extension built upon the wharf. A verdict having been taken for the plaintiff for nominal damages, with leave to defendants to move to enter a nonsuit, the court took the liberty to draw inferences of fact;

Held, 1. That the court was justified in inferring that B. had consented to the railway company placing the wharf where it was placed.

2. That B. having given a parol license to erect the wharf, and the company having built it there, neither B. nor the plaintiff claiming under him could complain of the encroachment on his slip.

3. That as the soil of the harbour on which the wharf was built belonged to the defendants, and they were by the city charter conservators of the harbour, with the sole power of amending and improving the same, the plaintiff had no right to require them to remove the wharf.

Quære, Whether the defendants would be liable to an action if the wharf, in consequence of a defective foundation, or by means of the ferry boat striking against it, had sagged over to the south and obstructed the plaintiff's slip. *Magee v. The Mayor, etc., of St. John*, vol. 23, 275.

—Light and air—Twenty years uninterrupted possession—Prescription. See Addenda 13.

EJECTMENT—(See Possession.)

1—Judgment against casual ejector—Setting aside for irregularity.

In ejectment where judgment was signed against the casual ejector, but plaintiff's proceedings were irregular, the judgment was set aside. *Doe dem. Barnett v. Roe*, vol. 19, 102.

2—Mortgage—Where he obtains judgment and afterwards assigns mortgage—Whether right in judgment passes to assignee of mortgage.

Where a mortgagee brought ejectment to recover possession of the land mortgaged, and obtained judgment, and, before the writ of *habere facias* issued, assigned his mortgage;

Held, that the assignment did not give to the assignee of the mortgage any right in the judgment, and a *habere facias* issued by his authority was set aside. *Doe dem. Ferguson v. Roe*, vol. 19, 337.

3—Where lessor of the plaintiff and defendant both die pending suit—Application to amend declaration—To compel parties in possession to come in and defend—Second application on amended affidavits.

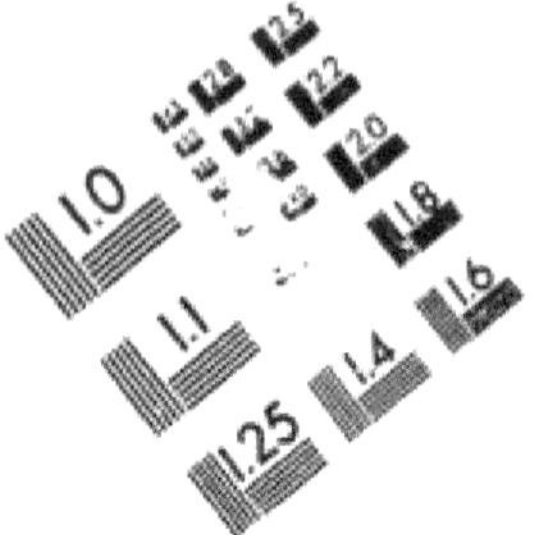

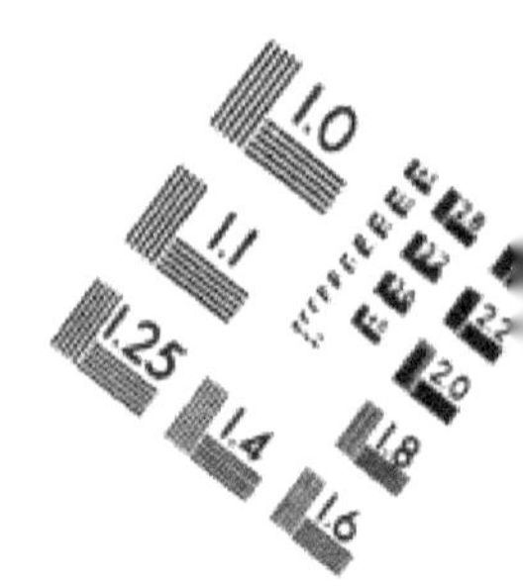

IMAGE EVALUATION
TEST TARGET (MT-3)

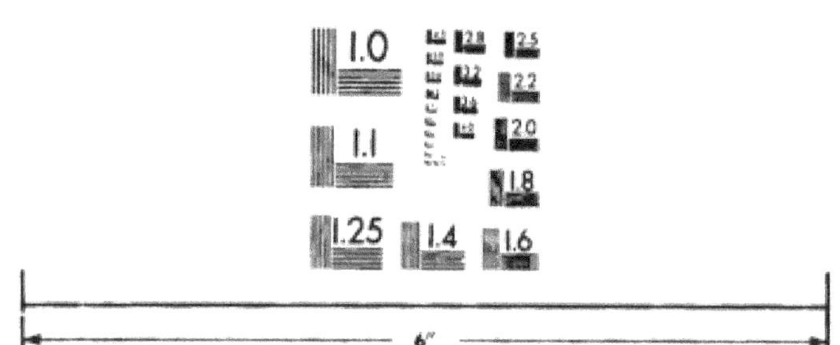

The lessor of the plaintiff and the defendant both died after the commencement of the action and before trial.

This being admitted when the case was called on for trial, the judge struck the case off the docket.

Subsequently a rule *nisi* to amend the declaration by making E. McL. J., and C. E. L. J. lessors of the plaintiff, and calling upon certain parties to come in and defend was obtained, the affidavit on which the rule was granted did not disclose the interest of E. McL. J. and C. E. L. J., nor did it shew that the right of the deceased lessor of the plaintiff would be barred by the Statute of Limitations, if the amendments were not made.

Held, that even if the amendments could be made in such a case, the affidavits did not disclose facts which would justify the court in making the amendments.

Quære.—Whether under the circumstances an amendment can be made.

Where all the material facts set forth in the affidavits on a second application to the court were within the reach of the parties when the first application was made the court refused to entertain the second application. *Doe dem. Jarvis v. Trites*, vol. 19, 471.

4—Meaning of words "centre line of railway"—Instrument affecting lands—Certified copy of—Description of railway lands—Signed by two out of three commissioners—Evidence—Rebutting—Where plaintiff has been cross-examined as to facts sought to be rebutted.

In an action of ejectment, the question in dispute was one of boundary between adjoining lots, and turned on the meaning of the words "the centre line of the railway" in the description of the lands taken and dedicated for the European and North American (now part of the Intercolonial) railway.

The land, the boundary line of which was in question was described in the instrument of dedication as follows:—"A further portion of the said tract beginning on the division line between the said I. V. and I. S. on the northwestern side line of lands owned by the said S., and on the centre line of the said railway, thence by the Magnet N. 40° 30', west on said line 44 feet 2 inches, or a sufficient distance to make 43 feet 6 inches at a right angle from the said centre line of the railway, thence northeasterly by a line parallel to the said centre line, seven chains and fifty links," etc.

Held, that by the centre line of the railway was meant the centre of the railway track itself, and not the centre of the lands taken for the railway track.

Held, that the description of lands laid off by the railway commissioners and registered under the Act, 19 Vic. cap. 17, is an instrument affecting lands, and a certified copy may be received in evidence.

Held, also, that the description was sufficient, though only signed by two of the three commissioners. The fact of plaintiff having denied on cross-examination a fact afterwards testified to by the defendants, will not prevent plaintiff calling witnesses to rebut defendant's testimony on the point as to which plaintiff had been cross-examined. *Doe dem. Barnes v. Delgro*, vol. 19, 541.

5—Declaration—Service of—House locked.

Service of a declaration in ejectment is sufficient where the door of the house was locked, and the tenant's wife refused to open it, and the officer at a closed window in the hearing of the wife read and explained to her the declaration and notice, and then affixed a copy thereof to the door of the house. *Doe dem. Dorion v. Roe*, vol. 23, 307.

6—Demand of particulars of premises—Stay of proceedings.

Where there were several tenants in possession, and one of them filed a memorandum of appearance and gave notice thereof to the plaintiff's attorney, and demanded the particulars of the premises, which the plaintiff's attorney promised to give, but afterwards, without giving the particulars, signed judgment against the casual ejector and turned the tenants out of possession, the court set aside the judgment and *habere facias*.

A demand of particulars in ejectment operates as a stay of proceedings. *Doe dem. Gallant* v. *Roe*, vol. 22, 423.

7—Estoppel.

In an action of ejectment the lessor of the plaintiff relied upon a title derived through T. from one J., and defendant claimed to hold by possession. It was proved by T. that before he purchased the property, defendant with a view to inducing him to buy it, told him it belonged to J., that he (J.) was heir to it and entitled to sell it, and that if he (T.) got a deed of it from J. he would have a good title. Soon after this conversation T. went to examine the land, and while there defendant told him he had been put on the place to watch it, and in case he (T.) bought from J. he would not give up the possession of it unless he got a portion of it—he said about 200 acres. In consequence of what defendant had said to T., and after examining the land, the latter went to see J., but no agreement to purchase was arrived at on that occasion, J. wanting $600, and T. offering $400. A week or a fortnight afterwards J. concluded to accept the $400, and sent word to that effect. Thereupon T. said he would see what could be done with defendant. He swore—"I sent word by my brother to see if defendant would take 150 acres. My brother brought a message to me, in consequence of which I bought the property." T. then obtained from J. a deed of the property, and, as he said, went up to the land with a surveyor "to run off defendant's 150 acres" which he "had arranged to give him." When they got on the land defendant wanted 220 acres, which T., having purchased and paid for the title, finally assented to, and 220 acres were run off. It was thereupon arranged that defendant should give T. a quit claim deed of the land, except the 220 acres which had been surveyed off to him, and that T. should give defendant a deed of the 220 acres. The deeds never were executed; and finally, after the lessor of plaintiff purchased from T., defendant repudiated the transaction altogether, and claimed to retain the whole land.

Held, by Fisher and Duff, JJ. (in which judgment Weldon, J., being opposed to a new trial also concurred, waiving his own opinion), that defendant was estopped from disputing J.'s, and (consequently the lessor of the plaintiff's) title to the whole land.

But by Wetmore, J., that in the absence of evidence of what the message was that T.'s brother brought back from defendant, the estoppel was not made out. *Doe dem. Doherty* v. *Brown*, vol. 19, 605.

8—Service of declaration—Non-payment of rent—Widow of lessee in possession—Judgment.

Where a lessee, under a lease containing a clause of re-entry for non-payment of rent, died intestate, leaving his widow in possession, though letters of administration had not been granted; service of declaration upon her is sufficient to entitle the landlord to a rule for judgment in ejectment for non-payment of rent. *Doe dem. Mayor of St. John* v. *Roe*, vol. 24, 357.

9—Non-payment of rent—Judgment against casual ejector—Whether necessary to shew how the tenant holds.

In ejectment for non-payment of rent, under the Con. Stat. cap. 80, sec. 19, after judgment against the casual ejector, where the tenant in possession is not the lessee, it is not necessary to shew that he claims under the lessee, or how he holds possession. *Doe dem. Mayor, etc., St. John* v. *Roe*, vol. 25, 149.

—Recovery by mortgagee by default and obtaining possession after right extinguished—Effect of. See Limitations 3.

—Recovery of vacant possession—Practise. See Practise 1.

Landlord and tenant—Summary ejectment. See Summary Ejectment. See Further Possession.

Election under Canada Temperance Act, 1878—Scrutiny—Parties to. See Canada Temperance Act 8.

—Extent of inquiry by Judge County Court. See Canada Temperance Act 20.

Election Court—Petition withdrawn while preliminary objections pending. See Dominion Controverted Elections Act 1.

Petition under Con. Stat., cap. 5—Resignation of respondent. See Controverted Elections Act 2.

"Employment"—Meaning of word within St. John Assessment Act, 1882. See Assessment 5.

Employee of Crown—Not liable except for misfeasance. See Railway Conductor 1.

—Federal Government—Income—Assessment of—Principles governing. See Assessment 7.

Entry Docket—Filing of—Where wrongly entitled. See Practice 9.

Time of filing. See Court General Rule of, 3.

Entry of Cause—What constitutes. See Practice 9.

Entry on Land—When right of, accrues to heir—His father in possession as tenant by curtesy. See Limitations 2.

—Whether a purchaser under a registered deed is obliged to make an actual entry in order to maintain trespass. See Trespass 10.

Under colour of right—Extent of possession. See Possession 2.

Endorsement—On envelope enclosing depositions. See Depositions 1.

EQUITY.

Bill—Description of defendant in title—Amendment—Insolvent Act of 1875—Creditors remedy under section 125—Court of Equity—Objection to jurisdiction—How taken—Bill of sale—Registry—After acquired property. See *Vassie* v. *Vassie*, vol. 22, 76.

Jurisdiction—When parties are residents of foreign country, but subject matter of suit is in this province—Pleading—Multifariousness. See *Franks* v. *McGrath*, vol. 22, 456.

1—Practice—Amending award—Prayer—General relief—When inconsistent with specific prayer.

The plaintiffs and defendant having submitted to arbitrators the matter of certain actions at law brought by the plaintiffs in right of the female plaintiff against the defendant, and an award having been made in plaintiffs' favour for $993, which (as was alleged) had been improperly reduced to that sum by the arbitrators taking into consideration certain dealings between the defendant and the male plaintiff, which were no part of the matters referred; upon a bill filed to amend the award by adding the amount allowed to defendant in respect of his claim against the male plaintiff.

Held, that the power of the court to rectify an award extends at most to errors whereby the award does not express what the arbitrators intended it should, and that as the award in this case expressed what the arbitrators intended, the court could not interfere.

The bill prayed that the award might be amended (as above) and that the defendant should be decreed to pay to the plaintiffs the whole amount coming to them upon the award being so rectified, and that in all other respects the award should stand and be forthwith acted upon, and be binding upon the parties, and that the plaintiffs should have all other relief in the premises to which they were entitled.

At the hearing the plaintiffs counsel claimed that in the event of his failure to have the award rectified as prayed he was entitled to have the award set aside because of the arbitrators having exceeded their authority.

Held, that the plaintiffs were not entitled to this relief as it was inconsistent with the relief specifically prayed for.

Held, also, that an amendment should not be allowed to convert a bill filed for one purpose into a bill for a wholly opposite purpose. *Vernon* v. *Oliver*, vol. 23, 302.

Appeal to Supreme Court of Canada allowed. See Addenda No. 17.

2—Bill in Equity—Prayer for alternate relief—Exceptions.

Defendants bound to answer all interrogatories when discovery asked for is material to enable court to determine as to representations made, and whether plaintiff entitled to the relief prayed for.

The defendant is not bound to answer any interrogatories not founded on charges in the bill. *Union M. Life Ins. Co.* v. *Gilbert*, vol. 25, 221.

—In a suit where plaintiff gives notice of hearing, but does not attend—Costs of day should be allowed. See Practice 5.

—Appeal—*Ex parte* injunction—Dissolution of. See Appeal 8.

—When decision of judge in equity on a question of fact will be reversed on appeal. See Appeal 1.

—Pleadings—Setting out documents at full length. See Will 9.

—Right of judge in granting an injunction to restrain an action at law to require the money to be paid into court. See Injunction 2.

—Suit by assignees of debt, where assignor refuses to allow an action at law to be brought in his name. See Pleading 6.

—Foreclosure of mortgage—Defendant entitled to statement of amount due before appearance. See Mortgage 3.

—Injunction—Dissolution of, on giving security—New security affected by dismissal of bill—Costs. See Injunction 3.

—Whether jurisdiction in Equity Court to restrain secretary of school trustees from retaining property of school corporation. See Injunction 1.

—Foreclosure of mortgage—Consolidation of mortgages—Tender of interest and costs after commencement of suit—Amendment of bill. See Mortgage 2.

EQUITY APPEAL.

1—Serving notice of appeal.

Where there are several defendants in a suit in equity, and one of them appeals from the decree, notice of the appeal must be served on the other defendants as well as on the plaintiff. *Morrison* v. *Bank of Montreal*, vol. 23, 100.

2—Notice of appeal—Statement of grounds.

A notice of appeal from a decision of a judge in equity, under the Con. Stat.

cap. 49, sec. 61, must state the grounds of appeal. *Robertson* v. *Armstrong*, vol. 21, 102.

—*Ex parte* injunction—Dissolution of. See Appeal 8.

—Equity appeal papers—When to be printed. See Appeal Papers 1.

—Appeals—Procedure. See Court, General Rules 1-4.

EQUITY COURT.

1—General Rule of—Easter Term, 44 Vic.

It is ordered that where leave is given to introduce facts and circumstances into a bill filed, by way of amendment, or where the plaintiff has liberty to state such circumstances on the record, pursuant to the provisions of the 50th section of chapter 49 of the Consolidated Statutes, such amendment or statement shall be made by filing with the clerk a printed or written statement thereof, to be annexed to the bill, and such proceedings by way of answer, evidence, or otherwise, shall be had and taken thereon, as if the same were embodied in a supplemental bill; provided that the judge may make such order for accelerating the proceedings as may be agreeable to justice.

2—Whenever a judge receives notice of appeal under the 61st section of chapter 49 of the Consolidated Statutes, he shall, on the application of either party, order that the same be set down for hearing at the term of the Supreme Court next after such application, and the clerk shall thereupon enter the same upon the proper paper, and the same shall be heard when reached; and if not then prosecuted, such appeal shall be dismissed with costs, unless the court shall, upon good cause shewn, postpone the hearing of such appeal. See Court, General Rules, 4, 6.

ESTATE.

Reservation of life—In conveyance—Whether good. See Conveyance 1.

—Claims against, need not be sworn to before action. See Executors 1.

—Of freehold—Whether widow has, previous to her dower being assigned. See Dower 1.

ESTOPPEL.

1—Ejectment.

In an action of ejectment the lessor of the plaintiff relied upon a title derived through T. from one J., and defendant claimed to hold by possession. It was proved by T. that before he purchased the property, defendant, with a view to inducing him to buy it told him it belonged to J., that he (J.) was heir to it, and entitled to sell it, and that if he T. got a deed of it from J. he would have a good title. Soon after this conversation T. went to examine the land and while there defendant t[illegible] him he had been put on the place to watch it, and in case he T. bought from J. he would not give up the possession of it, unless he got a portion of it—he said about 200 acres. In consequence of what defendant had said to T., and after examining the land, the latter went to see J., but no agreement to purchase was arrived at on that occasion, J. wanting $600, and T. offering $400. A week or fortnight afterwards J. concluded to accept the $400 and sent word to that effect. Thereupon T. said he would see what could be done with defendant. He swore—"I sent word by my brother to see if defendant would take 150 acres. My brother brought a message to me, in consequence of which I bought the property." T. then obtained from J. a deed of the property and, as he said, went up to the land with a surveyor—"to run off defendant 150 acres"—which he "had arranged to give him." When they got on the land defendant wanted 220 acres, which T. having purchased and paid for the title finally assented to, and 220 acres were run off. It was therefore arranged that defendant should give T. a quit claim deed of the land, except the 220 acres which had been surveyed off to him and that T. should give defendant a deed of the 220 acres. The deeds never were executed; and finally after the lessor of plaintiff purchased from T. defendant repudiated the transaction altogether and claimed to retain the whole land.

Held, by Fisher and Duff, (in which judgment, Weldon, J., being opposed to a new trial also concurred, waiving his own opinion) that defendant was estopped from disputing J.'s (and consequently the lessor of the plaintiff's) title to the whole land,

But by Wetmore, J., that in the absence of evidence of what the message was which T.'s brother brought back from defendant, the estoppel was not made out. *Doe dem. Doherty v. Brown*, vol. 19, 608.

2—In pais—Evidence.

O. being agent of the plaintiff company, and having a quantity of stone consigned to him, sold it to defendant ostensibly as his own. Subsequently the price of the stone remaining unpaid, was garnisheed by a creditor of O., who, although he had notice of the garnishee proceedings took no steps to have the money released from the attaching order, or to shew before the judge that the money was due to the company and not to him, and judgment was given against defendant as garnishee.

Held, that plaintiffs were estopped from saying that O. sold the stone as their agent.

Held, also, that evidence of the garnishee proceedings was admissible under the general issue. *The Wallace Huestis Greystone Co. v. Farwell*, vol. 20, 68.

3—Admissions by an Infant—Appeal—On questions of fact.

In a Court of Equity an infant stands in no different position from a person of full age in relations to matters of fraud, and therefore if he makes a representation upon which another person acts, he will not be allowed to impeach the validity of it on the ground of his minority. *Wilbur v. Jones*, vol. 21, 4.

4—Words "Warrant and defend"—Effect of in deed.

D., while residing on Crown land, and after he had applied for a grant under the Labour Act, conveyed it by a warranty deed to S., who afterwards conveyed it to the defendant. D. after obtaining the grant conveyed the land in question to B., who conveyed to the plaintiff. It appeared on the trial that both B. and the plaintiff had notice of the deed to S. before the deeds were given to them respectively.

Held, that D. was estopped from denying that he had title to the land when he made the conveyance to S., and that the plaintiff claiming under him as his assignee was bound by the same estoppel which runs with the land.

Held, also, that the words "warrant and defend" are words creating a covenant of warranty. *Guigain v. Langer*, vol. 21, 549.

5—Agreement to deliver lumber to be measured by a named surveyor—Survey bills—How far conclusive—Estoppel by conduct.

A. agreed to cut and deliver to B. a quantity of logs to be measured on the booms by a surveyor named by B. The surveyor delivered a survey bill of the logs to each party. The logs were delivered in a mill pond, where they became mixed with other logs belonging to B., and logs belonging to C. In dividing these logs between B. and C., a portion of which were unmarked, B. claimed and was allowed a proportion of the unmarked logs, according to his survey bill.

Held, in an action by A. against B. for the price of the logs, that B., by naming the surveyor to measure the logs, was not estopped from disputing the correctness of his measurement; and that B.'s claiming by the survey bill in his transaction with C. could not be taken advantage of by A. as an estoppel.

In order to create an estoppel by conduct the representation must be made with the intention that another party should act upon it, and he must have been induced to do so. *McManus v. Blakeney*, vol. 23, 216.

—Plea of—Bad for departure—Being inconsistent with averments in declaration. See Pleading 3; Ejectment 7.

—In order to make a person's declaration operate as, it must be made for the purpose of inducing a party to act upon it, and he must act upon it. See Easement 1.

—Of sheriff from returning *nulla bona* an execution while he at the same time holds goods of defendant under attachment, and has made return of writ of attachment. See Sheriff's Return.

—Sheriff having seized goods under execution against H. cannot set up as defence that H. had no property in the goods. See Bill of Sale 1.

—Municipality cannot deny liability for debts for which county sessions would have been liable. See Municipality 1.

—**Representations.** See Evidence 12.

—Where plaintiff agrees to give defendant credit for amount of receipt found, and afterwards refuses—Defendant's remedy—delay. See Judgment 2.

—Return of sheriff to writ of replevin. See Sheriff.

—Attending sheriff's sale of land without protesting. See Assessment 8.

—Conditional sale of goods—Representation. See Trover 6.

EVIDENCE.

1—Improper admission of—Action for false imprisonment—New trial.

On the trial of an action for malicious prosecution and false imprisonment, plaintiff was allowed to prove (subject to objection) that at the time of his arrest the constable, who was not a party to the suit, told him "his orders were to look for fees."

Held, improperly admitted, and as it was impossible to say the jury were not influenced by this evidence in estimating the damages, a new trial was ordered unless plaintiff consented to reduce the verdict to nominal damages. *Dowling v. McNeilly*, vol. 19, 42.

2—Admitted improperly—May be withdrawn—Right of judge in charging jury to express his opinion—Fraud—Finding of jury—Refusal of court to disturb.

The judge may withdraw from the consideration of the jury evidence that has been improperly admitted.

The judge may express his opinion on the case if he thinks proper to do so.

Where the question as to whether a bill of sale was fraudulent or not was fairly left to the jury, the court refused to disturb the verdict. *Ferguson v. Johnston*, vol. 19, 279.

3—Promissory note—Stamp not cancelled—Account stated.

Where the judge on the trial refused to receive in evidence the note on which the action was brought, as the stamp was not cancelled, the plaintiff not offering it as evidence of an account stated, but attempting by other evidence to prove the stating of the account, and the jury found for defendant, the court refused to disturb the verdict. *Carey v. Hannington*, vol. 19, 282.

4—General objection to admission of—New trial.

On the trial of a cause plaintiff recalled a witness who previously gave evidence for him and left the stand. Defendants' counsel objected to plaintiff being allowed to recall, and upon the objection being overruled, objected generally to any of witness' testimony being received.

Held, that this general objection did not enable the defendants, on a motion for a new trial, to claim that a part of the evidence was improperly received, but that the particular evidence complained of should have been objected to. *Allen v. McDonald et al.*, vol. 20, 533.

5—Hearsay—Res gestæ.

On the trial of an indictment for obstructing a street, C., a surveyor, stated, subject to objection, that he measured certain distances from a post which he said was pointed out to him by B. as the Gesner line, and that he ran a course from that, and tested his line from four points given him by B. and found them correct, and also stated what the result of that measurement would be in regard to defendant's house. B. was not called.

Held, that the evidence was improperly received. *The Queen v. Budge*, vol. 20, 531.

6—Former suit—Trial—Way to prove.

The only way which a suit can properly be proved is by the proceedings themselves, or the admission of a party against whom the evidence is offered; and if it is material to show what was in dispute and what was decided, the record must be produced. It cannot be shewn by the evidence of a person who was present at the trial. *Appleby v. Secord*, vol. 20, 460.

7—Slander—Husband and wife—Action for words of wife—What witness understood the words to mean—Damages.

In action of slander a witness cannot be asked what he understood to have been meant by the words used unless it is first shewn that there was something to prevent the words from conveying the meaning they would ordinarily convey.

In an action of slander against a husband and wife for the slander of the wife, evidence of a statement of the wife made subsequent to the slander that her husband compelled her to utter it, and his object in compelling her, is improper—*per* Weldon, J. *Wood v. Mackay and wife*, vol. 21, 109.

8—Expert—Opinion involving truth of evidence.

A witness, skilled in diseases of the eye, who had heard the testimony of the defendant and the other witnesses, in an action against a surgeon for malpractice in operating upon plaintiff's eyes, was asked (*inter alia*) the following question: "Is the statement of the medical case, as given by the defendant in evidence, reconcilable with the facts (assuming them to be true) as given by the other witnesses?"

Held, that the question was improper, as the answer to it would involve an opinion by the witness, not only as to the truth of what the other witnesses had sworn to, but also the meaning of the words they had used. *Briggs v. Don*, vol. 22, 107.

9—Letter written by party seeking to put in.

A tenant cannot, by writing a letter accompanying the key of the premises stating his reasons for giving up the premises, make evidence for himself by having the contents of the letter admitted in evidence in an action brought to recover the rent. *Gibbs* v. *Morrison*, vol. 22, 247.

10—Where evidence of plaintiff and his witnesses contradictory.

Where plaintiff proved a trespass committed by defendant, and then called a witness whose evidence, if true, shewed that no trespass had been committed:

Held, that the question should be submitted to the jury. *Getchell* v. *Burchill*, vol. 22, 631.

11—Accounts—Previous settlement with third parties—Effect of, as an admission of correctness.

P. entered into an agreement with A. to get out lumber for him, and also to take charge of supplies furnished by A., and other operators under contracts with A. All supplies were to be charged against P., and he was to be credited with what he delivered to A.'s other operators. A book was kept by P. in which he entered all supplies delivered by him to the other operators, and A. settled with them according to the entries in this book.

Held, in an action by P. for a balance due him on account of the lumber, that the book was evidence of the supplies delivered by him to the defendant's operators, the settlement by the defendant with them according to the entries in the book being an admission by him of their correctness. *Pheeny* v. *Aiken*, vol. 21, 632.

12—Certified copies of deeds—Uncertainty of affidavit where copies of several deeds are referred to—Estoppel—Representations.

Where copies of three deeds were offered in evidence under the Consol. Stat. cap. 74, sec. 34, on an affidavit of the plaintiff, stating that the original deeds, copies of which were annexed (describing each of them separately), were not under his control, and he did not know where the same might be found.

Held, by Allen, C.J., Weldon and Palmer, JJ., (Wetmore, J. dissenting) that the affidavit was insufficient, as it should have stated that neither of the deeds was under his control, etc.

In trespass to land the defendant justified under a deed from A. (who had no right to convey) and gave evidence of statements by the plaintiff that he had no claim to the land, and proposed that the defendant should purchase it from A., expressing his satisfaction that A. had an opportunity of selling it. On the question whether the defendant had a title of estoppel as against the plaintiff under the deed from A.

Held, by Allen, C.J., Weldon and Palmer, JJ., (Wetmore, J., dissenting) that the defendant should have been allowed to state whether he purchased the land from A. in consequence of the representations made to him by the plaintiff. *McCormick* v. *McBride*, vol. 23, 12.

13.—Negligent driving—Opinion of witness.

In an action for negligent driving, the defendant was asked by his counsel whether anything more could have been done than was done to prevent the collision which occurred.

Held,—improper as being the point which the jury had to decide; and that the defendant should have stated the facts—without giving his opinion—and left it to the jury to determine whether he could have done anything more than he did to avoid the collision. *Cowie* v. *Kirkbride*, vol. 23, 404.

14—Official of municipal corporation—Cash book kept by—Entries shewing balance

against self—Admission to auditors of correctness—Whether sufficient evidence against official in action for money had and received and on account stated.

Defendant was chairman of commissioners of water supply in the city of St. John, and as such, kept the cash book, showing his receipts and disbursements. In it he made entries in his own handwriting, charging himself with the receipts of moneys for the use of the plaintiffs, (the city corporation) and also made entries by way of discharge, and when the balance between his receipts and outlays was ascertained by auditors appointed by the corporation, under the powers given the latter by Act of Assembly, he did not dispute its correctness. When asked if he could explain the balance against him, he said he could not. The auditors then told him they would have to report it to the plaintiffs, to which he replied, "Well, you will just have to report it."

Held, sufficient evidence to recover such balance either on a count for money had and received or an account stated. *Mayor, etc., of St John* v. *Lockhart*, vol. 23, 430.

15—Irrelevant.

The defendants under the item "Expenses of administration," in the notice given with the plea of *plene administravit* under Consol. Stat. cap. 52, sec. 21, offered evidence of the probable expenses of this and other suits.

Held, that the evidence was properly refused. *Marshall* v. *Armstrong*, vol. 21, 152.

16—Certificate under 37 Vic., cap. 94—Acts of parliament—Necessity of showing defendant to be a shareholder before certificate is evidence against him.

By the 5th section of the Act incorporating the Stadacona Fire and Life Insurance Company, it is provided that in an action against a shareholder for calls, a certificate under the seal of the company, and purporting to be signed by one of their officers, to the effect that the defendant is a shareholder, that such calls have been made and that so much is due by him, shall be received in all courts of law as *prima facie* evidence to that effect. The certificate put in evidence on the trial certified that defendant was the holder of fifty shares, that certain calls had been made, and that he was indebted to the company in a sum named, being the amount of the calls.

Held, that the certificate was not evidence against the defendant, in the absence of other evidence that the defendant was a shareholder in the company. *Stadacona Ins. Co* v. *Rainsford*, vol. 300.

16—Criminal law—Reading to witness from paper not in evidence, and cross-examination as to—Intent—Log book—Admission of—Accomplice, corroborative evidence—Comparison of handwriting—Admission of previous signature by subsequent indorser—Rebutting evidence—Effect of words "weight and contents unknown" in criminal charge.

Held, that on the trial of the master of a vessel, indicted for scuttling her, (by Allen, C.J., and Fisher and Duff, JJ.), adhering to the old rule of the common law, the contents of a written instrument, if it be in existence, can be proved only by the instrument itself, and council will not be allowed to read from a paper not in evidence, and found a question upon the paper so read, that this cannot be done even on cross-examination for the purpose of testing the credibility of the witness; also that sec. 64 of the Statutes of Canada, 32 & 33 Vic., cap. 29, allowing a witness to be cross-examined as to previous statements made by him in writing, or reduced into writing would not apply to protests made by the prisoner, or to policies of insurance issued to the witness, or to receipts, which it did not appear the witness had either written, signed, or even seen until they were shewn to him in the witness box, but

Held, by Weldon, J., that it was competent on the cross-examination of the witness to put into his hands a policy of insurance not in evidence, and ask him if he did not see certain words in it, also, to read from a paper purporting to be a protest made by the prisoner, and to ask the witness if he did not write the protest, and if certain words were not in it.

Held, by Allen, C.J., and Fisher and Duff, JJ., that where the indictment in certain counts charged the destruction of the vessel with intent thereby to prejudice the underwriters, and in others simply charge the crime, without alleging the intent, and the prisoner was found guilty on all the counts, even if it was necessary to show that the prisoner had knowledge of the insurance, as to which they expressed no opinion, the court could, if necessary, alter the verdict to a finding on the counts which did not allege the intent.

Held, by Weldon, J., that it was not necessary to show the prisoners knowledge of the insurance, as he must be presumed to have intended the necessary consequence of his Act, which was to prejudice the underwriters. It appeared on the trial that the prisoner, with the greater portion of his crew, including the mate, had gone before a naval court and given a false account of the loss of the vessel, also that the prisoner had persuaded the mate to suppress the log book and swear that it was lost.

Held (Fisher *dubitante*), that the log book was properly received in evidence.

Held, that proof of the receipt by the prisoner of drafts for large sums of money, drawn by parties in C., from which the vessel, which the prisoner was charged with scuttling, sailed, was properly received, and being unexplained by the prisoner they were properly left to the jury as evidence against him.

Held, also, by Allen, C.J., and Duff, J. (Weldon, J., dissenting), that the signature of one R. to an invoice was properly proved by a witness comparing it to a signature purporting to be by R. as endorser of a bill of exchange, his endorsement being prior to that of the prisoner. But by Weldon, J., that the evidence being immaterial, the reception was not sufficient to warant the quashing of the conviction of the prisoner.

The principal witness for the Crown who had himself done the act of scuttling the vessel at the instigation of the prisoner on his examination in chief, stated that he bored auger holes in the air streak. On cross-examination he was asked how far below the water he bored, etc. On the part of the defence it was sworn by several witnesses that the air streak of the vessel alleged to have been scuttled, was also the load line, and that if the holes were bored in the air streak they must have come out above the water. The Chief Justice allowed the Crown to call rebutting evidence for the purpose of showing that the air streak was below the load line.

Held, that the evidence was properly allowed.

There is no positive rule of law that the testimony of an accomplice must receive direct corroboration, and the nature and extent of the corroboration required depend a great deal upon the character of the crime charged. Therefore where the judge directed the jury "that it was not necessary that J. (the accomplice) should be corroborated as to the very act of boring the holes in the vessel; if the other evidence and circumstances of the case satisfied them that he was telling the truth in the account which he gave of the destruction of the vessel, that would be sufficient.

Held, a proper direction.

Held, that the words in a bill of lading, "weight and contents unknown," would not prevent a jury from having the right to draw whatever inference of guilt they please against the prisoner, from his knowledge that the cargo was not what the bill of lading represented it to be.

A new trial will not be granted to the Crown in a criminal case; neither has the Crown an appeal to the Supreme Court of Canada from a judgment quashing a conviction. (Wetmore, J., doubting as to the right of appeal.) *Regina* v. *Tower*, vol. 20, 168.

17—Destroyed letter—Secondary evidence of the contents of part—Inability of Witness to remember the rest—Handwriting—Expert testimony.

A person who has received a letter, part only of which, he stated, related to the subject matter of the suit, may after the destruction of the letter, testify as to the contents of that part, though he cannot state the words of the remainder of it, except generally, that it had no reference to the question involved in the suit.

Quære, whether a witness who has no knowledge of the handwriting of a party can, after comparing a signature with a writing admitted to be genuine, speak as an expert as to his belief whether such signature and the genuine writing were made by the same person. *McGibbon* v. *Burpee et al*, vol. 25, 81.

18—Judgment creditor—Transfer of property—Consideration—Account between debtor and claimant—Evidence of date of transfer.

In an action against a sheriff for seizing under an execution against B. property which the plaintiff claimed under a prior purchase from B., but which the judgment creditor alleged was made without consideration, and to defraud B's. creditors; an account between the plaintiff and B., in the handwriting of B., and dated at the time of the alleged transfer in which the plaintiff was debited with the property and credited with payments on account, is evidence for the plaintiff that the account was made at the time it bears date without any other proof of the fact. (Wetmore J., dissenting.) *Armstrong* v. *Botsford*, vol. 21, 284.

19—Action for loss of a scow—Evidence of negligence—Expert testimony.

In an action for loss of a scow used in conveying deals to a ship lying in a harbour, it appeared that the scow in question, with two others, was fastened to the ship and broke adrift during a gale of wind and was lost.

Held, that a witness could not be asked for the purpose of proving negligence, "whether it was good or bad management for the defendant to have three scows fastened to the ship at the same time?" the question not being a matter of science, art or trade. *McNair* v. *Stewart*, vol. 24, 471.

20—Goods sold and delivered—To whom credit given—Evidence—Statement by witness to plaintiff.

In an action for goods sold and delivered, in which the question was, whether the credit was given to the defendant or to D. F., to whom the goods were actually delivered, and who carried on a retail trade near the defendant's shipyard, and supplied the men in defendant's employ, in part payment of their wages—the evidence for the plaintiff being that by agreement the credit was given to the defendant, and that the goods were to be paid for by D. F.'s notes at three months, to be taken up at maturity by the defendant's notes at four months.

Held, that D. F.'s statement to the plaintiff when he gave him a note of the defendant's to take up D. F.'s note given for the price of goods, was admissible without producing the defendant's note.

Held, also, *per* Wetmore and Fraser, JJ., (Palmer, J., dissenting) that the plaintiff could be asked for the purpose of shewing part performance of the alleged agreement by the defendant, how long the defendant continued to carry out his part of the arrangement.

Per Palmer, J., that the question assumed that something had been done by the defendant under the agreement; and that the answer to it stated no facts from which the court could determine whether there had been a part performance of the agreement or not. *Stephenson* v. *Fraser*, vol. 24, 482. See Addenda 50.

21—Fraud—Purchase of property in name of another to defraud creditors—Subsequent agreement between same parties relative to other matters—Admissibility of evidence.

In an action against a sheriff for seizing a horse under an execution against the plaintiff's father, the defendant sought to shew that the horse, which was purchased from W., was really bought for plaintiff's father, and that the purchase was nominally made in plaintiff's name to defraud the father's creditors. In order to establish fraud, defendant offered evidence of an agreement subsequently made between plaintiff and W., having reference to fishing business in which the father and son were engaged, and which the horse was in some way employed.

Held, admissible. *Shirreff*, App., and *Campbell*, Resp., vol. 24, 554.

22—Exemplification of judgment.

In an action brought by the judgment debtor against the sheriff for seizing goods, the exemplification of a judgment is evidence against the judgment creditor in a promise to indemnify. *Sheriff* v. *Muirhead*, vol. 25, 196.

23—Confessions of the prisoner.

M. was convicted of stealing goods the property of S. The evidence to connect M. with the crime was his statement to a policeman who had him in charge, that if he went to a particular place he would find the goods. This statement was made in consequence of his being told by the policeman that S. was a good-hearted man, and he (the policeman) thought that if he got his goods back he would not prosecute. The goods were afterwards found in the place described by the prisoner.

Held, (Allen, C.J., and King, J., dissenting), that the prisoner's statement was improperly received, and that the conviction should be quashed. *Regina* v. *McCaffrey*, vol. 25, 396.

—Admissibility of papers spoken of between parties to an agreement—When conversation admissible. See Sale 3.

—Declaration of third parties—Admissible as part of the *res gestæ*. See Trespass 4.

—Admissibility of instructions from assignee of bill of lading to agent to deliver the bill upon payment of the draft given for the goods mentioned in the bill of lading in an action by assignee against a third party. See Bill of Lading 1.

—When improperly received and afterwards withdrawn by judge, not ground for new trial. See New Trial 7.

—On ground of verdict against—Rule as granting new trial. See New Trial 8.

—In prosecution for assault the defendant has a right to shew that assault was committed on his land in defence of his title. See Assault 2.

—Parol evidence not admissible to shew a subsequent variation in contracts required to be in writing by Statute of Frauds. See Sale 2.

—Claim of wife to separate property must be clear and satisfactory. See Married Women 1.

—Rebutting—When plaintiff has been examined as to facts sought to be rebutted. See Ejectment 4.

—Subscription paper shewing how the money was obtained to purchase property claimed by wife—Admission of. See Husband and Wife 1.

—A certified copy of description of railway laid off by commissioners and registered may be received. See Ejectment 4.

—A conviction, though defective, is admissible in action against the justice of the peace. See False Imprisonment 1.

—Acts of a person under a deed may be evidence to explain it, but declarations made by former owners, with a view to affect the title, are not admissible. See Ambiguity 1.

—In a plea of not guilty in trover, where property is in plaintiff, he need not shew a right to present possession. See Bill of Sale 2.

—Taken before commission and not objected to, may be objected to on trial. See Commission 1.

—That previously existing licenses have expired. See Canada Temperance Act 5.

—Proclamation of second part of Canada Temperance Act being in force must be produced and expiry of license proved. See Canada Temperance Act 4.

—Garnishee proceedings admissible in evidence under general issue. See Estoppel 2.

—Declarations of company's agents made while adjusting a loss under a policy issued by the company, are admissible in action against the company. See Insurance 6.

—Statements by administrator before assuming that character, tending to contradict his evidence, were properly received. See Insurance 7.

—Contrariety of—Where there is contrariety of evidence the court will not grant a new trial, although of the opinion that the strength of the evidence was against the verdict. See New Trial 10.

—A declaration by one partner is inadmissible to prove partnership. See Partnership 1.

—To prove reasonableness of claim on special agreement is admissible. See Settled Accounts 1.

—Reading to jury on second trial, the former judgment improper, but not ground for new trial. See Settled Accounts 1.

—In action for slander, to shew that plaintiff suffered loss of custom from having been charged with keeping false weights and measures, customers must be called to prove. See Slander 2.

—Where there was no positive evidence that line of telegraph was constructed by defendants, but that they were authorized to build, and did operate line when completed, jury were right in finding that they did construct it. See Trespass 6.

—Asking a witness if he wrote a letter containing certain statements which were read to him, is improper. See Settled Accounts 1.

—Mere omission to disaffirming a conveyance made by infant after coming of age is not sufficient evidence to warrant a jury in finding a confirmation. See Infant 2.

—Leave and license. See Sheriff's Sale 1.

—Certificate under 37 Vic. cap. 91—Acts of Parliament—Necessity of shewing defendant to be a shareholder before certificate is evidence against him. See *Stadacona Insurance Co. v. Rainsford*, vol. 21, 309.

—Action for false imprisonment—Arrest under warrant issued by justice of the peace—Where plaintiff puts warrant in evidence—Whether it should be left to the jury to find whether recitals in warrant are true. See False Imprisonment 2.

—Adultery—Marriage in foreign state—Necessity of proving marriage law of such state. See Adultery.

—Marriage—Presumption of. See Marriage.

—Certified copy of will under sec. 15, cap. 74, Con. Stat.—*Prima facie* proof of validity. See Will 10.

—Cumulative—Right to rebut. See Will 10.

—Right of counsel to re-examine witness on matters brought out on cross-examination. See Ship's Husband 1.

—Slander—Where words complained of applied to the plaintiff—Necessity of judge pointing same out to jury. See Slander 5.

—Where improperly admitted but unimportant—New trial refused. See Sale of Goods 4.

—Where not objected to on trial. See Agreement 7.

Written agreement—When parol evidence admissible. See Agreement 2-7.

—Absolute bill of sale, grantor continuing in possession—Fraud—Question for jury. See Bill of Sale 3.

—Account stated. See Account Stated 1.

—Admissibility of declarations of members of company to shew who were the persons composing the company. See Landlord and Tenant 3.

—Canada Temperance Act—Conviction for sale of liquor—Proof of place of sale—Sufficiency of. See Canada Temperance Act 1878, 13.

—Circular stairway—Whether want of light at, is proof of negligence. See Municipality of St. John.

—Commission for examination of witnesses abroad—Interrogatories not returned with depositions—Whether admissable. See Practice 15.

—Declarations of president of company—Whether admissible to shew appointment of agent. See Insurance 51.

—Accord and satisfaction—What evidence of. See Agreement 7.

—Cross-examination—Right to explain on rebuttal. See Insurance 14.

—Liquor brought for purpose of sale in violation of Canada Temperance Act—Onus of proof. See Contract 8.

—Sufficiency of—Action against railway company for killing a horse. See Railway Company 4.

—Voluntary deed from husband to wife through medium of third party—Whether can support by proof of antenuptial agreement. See Husband and Wife 5.

—Where mortgagor and mortgagee both dead—Alleged payment on mortgage—Onus of proof. See Mortgage 1.

—Where fire set by sparks from railway company's locomotive—Frequency of fires along company's line—Fuel used on other railways. See Railway Company 5.

—What will constitute a case of necessity in order to justify—Sale of vessel by master—Question for the jury. See Insurance 16.

—Whether phosphate rock known to commercial world as "stone"—Question for the jury. See Insurance 2-14.

—Whether plaintiff should be allowed to state what he told the underwriters at the time of effecting the policy sued on, as to nature of interest he was insuring. See Insurance 14.

—Where jury might find for either party—Refusal of court to interfere with verdict. See New Trial 13.

—Written agreement—Work done under—Action for—*Quantum meruit*—Where plaintiff allowed to prove case without producing agreement—Defendant putting in agreement as part of his case, denying performance—Onus of proof. See Assumpsit 4.

—Licensed tavern-keeper—Defendants admission of being such, admissible against him—Purchasers of liquor competent witnesses to prove selling, vol. 18, 364. *Ex parte Birmingham.*

—Corporation of St. John—Filling in street and erecting fence—Evidence of negligence should be left to jury. *Pattman v. Mayor, etc., St. John*, vol. 18, 636.

—Trespass—Joint and several—Giving evidence of separate trespasses, no abandonment of joint trespass proved. *Gagnes v. Chapman*, vol. 18, 440.

—British subject—Evidence of minister of congregation being. See Slander ii.

—Entries in family Bible or record not evidence of place of birth. See Slander 6.

—Declaration of master of boat at time of accident, regarding. See Carrier 2.

—Evidence received without objection, judge not bound to withdraw it from jury. See Carrier 2.

—Plaintiff's right to rebut case set up by defendant. See Carrier 2.

—Declaration against interest. See Possession 2.

—Effect of assessment on land charged by commissioners of sewers against party. See Possession 2.

—When sale and conveyance may be presumed. See Possession 2.

—Statement of plaintiff. See Contract 15.

—Expert—Testimony of. See Contract 14, Evidence 13.

—Conversations between husband and wife—Trover—Joint conversion. See Married Woman 2.

—Loss of goods—Action for—Negligence—Onus of proof—Hearsay—Statement of master of boat regarding cause of accident—Whether admissible—Evidence admitted without objection. See Carrier 2.

—Action for defect in mill machinery—Statement of plaintiff as to quality of mill when effecting insurance—Admissibility of—Declaration against interest. See Contract 14.

—Ancient documents—Statement on Crown grant of sale of the land to party in possession. See Possession 2.

—Parol evidence of agreement—Accord and satisfaction. See Agreement 7.

—Conversations between husband and wife. See Married Woman 2.

—Landlord and tenant—Evidence of value of goods seized. See Landlord and Tenant 5.

—Eviction—What is evidence of. See Landlord and Tenant 7.

—Telegram—Construction of—Right of court to look at subsequent acts of party sending. See Ship 2.

—Transf r of property—Date of. See Judgment Creditor 18.

—Verdict against weight of evidence. See New Trial.

—Bank charter—When not necessary to produce. See Banking Act.

—Through ticket issued by railway company—Injury to passenger on landing from intermediate ferry owned by another company. See Railway Company 6.

—Onus of proof—Selling and keeping liquor for sale—Identity of offence. See Summary Conviction Act 12.

—Eviction—What evidence of. See Landlord and Tenant 7.

—Order in Council—Statement in annual Statutes of Canada. See Canada Temperance Act 23.

—Reasonable and probable cause—Order of judge annulling demand not *prima facie* evidence of—Insolvent Act of 1869. See Addenda 44.

Eviction—Evidence of. See Landlord and Tenant 7.

EXECUTOR.

1—Claim against estate—Need not be sworn to before action.

By Consolidated Statutes cap. 52, sec. 19, it is provided that no debt shall be paid by an executor until the same be certified by affidavit.

Held, that the obtaining of the affidavit was not a condition precedent to the right to sue for the debt, and if it was, to be available as a defence it would have to be specially pleaded. *Marshall* v. *Armstrong*, vol. 21, 102. See also *White*, App., and *Riley*, Resp., vol. 24, 476.

—Debt due as such—Liable to be attached under Garnishee Act. See Garnishee Act 1.

—Penalty for not proving will—Action for—Excuse. See Will 7.

—Promissory note—Action of trover for, by executor—Measure of damages where executor maker of note. See Trover 4.

—Widow without administering passing note. See Promissory Note 5.

EXECUTION.

Priority lost by instructions to sheriff—Confession signed by one partner for himself and his co-partner with copartner's consent—One partner acknowledging service of summons for himself and co-partner with latter's consent—Summons filed without affidavit of service—Irregularities—Third parties cannot take advantage of, in absence of fraud—Confession signed May 2nd authorizing judgment to be signed on "the fifth day of May next"—When due. See *Record* v. *Record*, vol. 21, 277.

—Where taxation of costs takes place on different day from that appointed—Whether sufficient to entitle party to. See Costs 4.

—For taxes—Under St. John Assessment Act of 1859—Necessity of notice and demand. See Inhabitant 1.

—Assessment partly legal and partly illegal—Whether execution issued for whole is void. See Inhabitant 1.

—Issued out of Justice's Court—Enlargement of return. See False Imprisonment 3.

—Taxes—Costs—Arrest for, under second execution. See False Imprisonment 8.

—Against husband—Levy on wife's property—No removal or touching of goods—Nominal sale—Effect of. See *Smith and wife* v. *White*, vol. 18, 443.

—Duty of constable when executing warrant to search for goods before taking body. See False Imprisonment 3.

EXTRADITION.

Treaty of Washington, 1842—Canadian Extradition Act, 1877—Trial of offence other than that for which prisoner was surrendered.

The 10th Article of the Treaty of Washington between Great Britain and the United States, provides for the delivery up to justice of persons charged with the commission of certain crimes in one of these countries, who shall be found in territories of the other; and directs what shall be sufficient evidence of criminality to justify the issue of a warrant for the surrender of the fugitive. The Canadian Extradition Act, 40 Vic., cap. 25, sec. 23, enacts that when any person accused of an extradition crime is surrendered by a foreign state in pursuance of any arrangement, he shall not, until after he has been restored to, or had an opportunity of returning to the foreign state, be subject, in contravention of any terms of the arrangement, to any prosecution in Canada for any other offence committed prior to his surrender for which he should not, under the arrangement, be prosecuted. A person imprisoned in this province on a charge of having committed the crime of arson (an extraditable crime), escaped and fled to the States, and on requisition made to the government of that country, under the Treaty of Washington, was surrendered to this province, the warrant of surrender stating that he was to be tried for the crime of which he was so accused. He was convicted here of the crime charged, and while he was a prisoner under that conviction was tried for the breach of prison (not an extraditable crime) committed before he escaped to the United States.

Held, per Allen, C.J., Fraser and Tuck, JJ. (Wetmore, Palmer and King, JJ., dissenting), 1. That there being no provision in the Treaty of Washington on the subject, such trial was not "in contravention of any terms of the arrangement" for the surrender of fugitives between Great Britain and the United States.

2. That the warrant stating that the fugitive was surrendered to be tried for the crime of which he was accused, was the act of the United States authorities only, and not an "arrangement" within the Canadian Extradition Act of 1877, and therefore that the trial for prison breach was sustainable.

Per Wetmore, Palmer and King, JJ. that the trial of the prisoner for breach of prison was in contravention of the fair construction of the Treaty of Washington, as it had always been claimed by Great Britain; and was also contrary to the express terms of the warrant on which the fugitive had been surrendered. *Regina* v. *Waddell*, vol. 25, 93.

Extraditable offence under.

Murder being an extraditable offence under Treaty of Washington, 1842, the courts of this country will take notice that it is a crime punishable in United States. See Slander 7.

Executory Contract—Goods not specified. See Property, passing of.

Experts—Opinion involving truth of what other witnesses had sworn to. See Evidence 8

—Evidence of. See Evidence 19, Contract 14.

— Comparison of handwriting by See Handwriting.

—As to reason of ships course. See Insurance 17.

Exporting — What constitutes under Statute Canada, 37 Vic. cap. 45. See Statute of Canada 1.

Extra work—Where written contract provided that if extra work were desired the value should be agreed upon and indorsed in the contract, and this is not done, plaintiff cannot recover it. See Contract 3.

—Unauthorised extras — Refusal to deliver goods without payment for. See Contract 16.

FALSE IMPRISONMENT.

1—Action for—Justice of the Peace—Conviction—Where defective—Notice of action—Constable.

A justice having issued a warrant to a constable directing him to a levy on plaintiff's goods, and for want of goods to take the body, and the latter having illegally arrested plaintiff without searching for goods, plaintiff applied to a judge for his discharge, and the justice appeared before the judge and opposed the application.

Held, that he thereby adopted the act of the constable in arresting plaintiff, and that the arrest and imprisonment was in law their joint act, and a notice so alleging it was sufficient.

In order to entitle a constable to have a demand made on him for a copy of a warrant under cap. 130, Revised Statutes, he must shew that he acted in obedience to the warrant.

It is the duty of a constable having a warrant directing him to seize goods and for want of them to take the body, to make a reasonable effort to find goods before making arrest.

A conviction though defective is admissible in evidence in an action against the justice in order to repel any inference of malice and want of probable cause, and also to entitle him to the benefit of the section of the statute in reference to the twopence damages.

Quære—Where the provisions of the statute restricting damage to twopence in actions against justices will apply to a case where the justice has gone beyond his judicial duty. *McGilvery v. Gault*, vol. 19, 217.

2—Justice of the Peace—Recitals in warrant—Proof of conviction.

In an action for false imprisonment against a justice of the peace, the declaration charged that he acted without jurisdiction, and also maliciously and without reasonable and probable cause—plea justifying the imprisonment under a conviction under the Act, 32 & 33 Vic. cap. 22, for maliciously destroying trees—the plaintiff put in evidence the warrant under which he was arrested, reciting that he had been convicted before the defendant of maliciously destroying trees as stated in the plea, and was adjudged to be imprisoned for twenty days, and he proved his imprisonment under the warrant, and that he had been discharged on *habeas corpus*; but the reason for the discharge was not shewn. The defendant called no evidence.

Held, per Weldon, J., that the plaintiff by putting in the warrant in evidence did not relieve the defendant from the necessity of proving the conviction.

Per Palmer and King, JJ., that though the recital in the warrant was *prima facie* evidence of a conviction, it should have been left to the jury to find under all the circumstances whether the recital was true.

Per Allen, C.J., and Wetmore, J., 1. That the recital being evidence for the defendant of a conviction, the plaintiff was bound to prove either that there was no such conviction, or that it was in a matter beyond the justice's jurisdiction; and 2. There being no evidence throwing doubt upon the recital in the warrant, it should have been left to the jury to find whether it was true or false. *Ward v. Osthouse*, vol. 22, 220.

3—Execution—Omission of name of parish—Imprisonment for lesser number of days than justice might award—Enlargement of return—Search for goods and chattels

In an action for false imprisonment brought against a constable for arresting upon an execution in form K, issued out of a justice's court;

Held, 1. That as the naming of the county appeared in the execution, the omission of the name of the parish was not a substantial deviation from the prescribed form.

2. That a debtor cannot complain that the execution directed him to be imprisoned for a lesser number of days than the justice might have awarded.

3. That the date of the enlargement of the return of an execution need not appear on the execution, but may be shown by oral evidence.

4. That if a debtor states that he has no property wherewith to satisfy an execution, the constable is justified in arresting him without searching for goods and chattels. *Marks* v. *Newcombe*, vol. 22, 419.

4—Witness refusing to answer questions tending to criminate—Husband and wife—Privileged communication—Statute of Canada, 32 & 33 Vic., cap. 21—Arrest under—Damages.

Plaintiff, a teller in a bank in New York, absconded with funds of the bank and came to this province. He was arrested here without warrant by a police officer of Halifax, N. S., upon information obtained by a telegram from New York; and while he was in prison the officer demanded and obtained from his wife money in her possession, telling her that it belonged to the bank, and that her husband was in custody.

Held, in an action for false imprisonment, that the defendant had no reasonable ground for believing that the plaintiff had committed a felony, and was therefore not justified in arresting him; and *per* Weldon and Fisher, JJ. (Wetmore, J., dissenting), that evidence of the forcible manner in which the defendant entered the wife's room to demand the money was admissible.

Held, also that the plaintiff could recover, on a count for money had and received, the money taken by this defendant from the plaintiff's wife, there being no evidence that it was the identical money which the plaintiff had taken from the bank; and that it was no answer to the action that the defendant had paid the money over to the bank before he was sued.

The plaintiff on cross-examination refused to state whether he was teller of the bank at the time he left New York; and also refused to state on what ground he refused to answer the question.

Held, *per* Weldon and Fisher, JJ. (Wetmore, J., dissenting), that he was not bound in order to claim the privilege to state his belief that his answering the question would tend to criminate him.

A statement made to a wife by her husband, who was travelling under an assumed name, as to his reasons for doing so, is a privileged communication; and she is not bound to answer it in an action brought by her husband wherein the fact of the commission of a crime is involved. *Ellis* v. *Power*, vol. 20, 40. Appeal allowed to Supreme Court of Canada. See Addenda No. 7.

5—Justification under attachment for non-payment of costs on review from justice's court—What the plea should allege.

In an action for false imprisonment defendant justified under an attachment granted by a county court judge for non-payment of costs in a case on review from a justice's court, but the plea did not set forth the suit in the justice's court, nor the making of the affidavit necessary to give the judge jurisdiction to hear the cause.

Held, bad on demurrer. *Tower* v. *Outhouse*, vol. 20, 113.

6—Suit against justice of the peace—Notice of action—Whether plaintiff can state he suffered in mind—Provision as to two cents damages—Evidence—Hearsay.

A notice of action against a magistrate for false imprisonment alleged both that the defendant did the acts complained of maliciously and without any reasonable and probable cause, and also that he acted without jurisdiction.

Held, that although the action included two grounds of action, proof of either one or the other would be sufficient, provided there was a count in the declaration to which such proof would be applicable.

In an action for false imprisonment the plaintiff may be asked if he suffered in mind from the imprisonment.

Held, that where the arrest and imprisonment complained of took place before the trial and conviction of the plaintiff, the provisions of sec. 11 of Con. Stat. cap 90, as to a plaintiff being only entitled to recover two cents damages in an action against a justice of the peace, do not apply.

Held, that the following question put to the defendant on cross-examination, "Did you hear any one of these parties say Clark (the plaintiff) was a villain and rascal," was properly rejected.

Quære, whether case will lie against a justice for extortion in exacting illegal fees. *Robinson* v. *Topley*, vol. 20, 361.

7—Amendment at trial—Where proposed Amendment would make count demurrable—Slander—Publication—Attachment of property—Con. Stat. cap. 38, and Act 43 Vic. cap 9.

On the trial of an action in which the declaration contained a count for assault and false imprisonment, the plaintiff put in evidence the *capias* under which he had been arrested at the suit of the defendant, and the affidavit of debt upon which the *capias* issued, and proposed to prove that he was not indebted to the defendant in the amount sworn to in the affidavit; but the evidence was rejected. Plaintiff's counsel then applied for leave to amend his declaration by adding a count for malicious arrest, stating that the present defendant had commenced an action against the plaintiff, and made an affidavit that the plaintiff was indebted to him in the sum of $3300 for goods sold and delivered, etc.; and that the arrest was not made for the purpose of vexing or harrassing the plaintiff; that the *capias* was endorsed for the said sum of $3303, and was delivered to the sheriff to be executed; and that the defendant caused the plaintiff to be arrested by virtue thereof, averring that the said sum of money was not due from the plaintiff to the defendant at the time of making the affidavit of debt and of the arrest; and that such affidavit was falsely and maliciously made by the defendant for the purpose of vexing and harrassing the plaintiff, and by reason thereof the defendant wrongfully and fraudulently caused the *capias* to be issued, and the plaintiff to be illegally arrested and imprisoned.

This application was resisted by the defendant on the ground that the proposed count was demurrable because it did not state that the action in which the *capias* had issued was terminated; and also that the defendant would be prejudiced by the amendment, as it would introduce a new cause of action, which he was not prepared to answer; and that he required time to determine what he should plead. An affidavit of the defendant's attorney was produced supporting these objections. The amendment was refused.

Held, that it was properly refused.

An action of slander will not lie for words spoken to the plaintiff, unless in the hearing of the third party.

A commissioner has power under the Con. Stat. cap. 38, and the Act, 43 Vic. cap. 9, to order property disclosed on examination to be sold. *Gallant* v. *Calder*, vol. 23, 73.

8—Taxes—Costs of execution—Arrest for, under second execution.

An execution having issued against the plaintiff for non-payment of taxes, he paid the amount of the tax to the receiver under the Act, 21 Vic. cap. 29, but refused to pay the costs of the execution. A second execution was afterwards issued for the costs, under which the plaintiff was arrested.

Held (Weldon, J., dissenting), that the first execution was not satisfied till the costs were paid, and the second execution was legal. *Howard* v. *Mayor, etc., of St. John*, vol. 23, 317.

—Action for—Admission of improper evidence. See Evidence 1.

—Action against corporation and receiver of taxes of St. John for. See Arrest 5.

—Chamberlain of St. John and corporation not liable for, while acting as the law directs. See Assessment 3.

—Execution from Justice's Court—Judgment reversed on review—Measure of damages. See Damages 2.

FALSE PLEAS.

1—Setting aside—Judge—Relationship of wife to wife of party.

In order to justify the setting aside of the plea under sec. 88 of the Con. Stat. cap. 37, as a general rule it should be a plea which is false to the knowledge of the defendant.

It is no legal disqualification to a judge taking part in a cause that his wife is the niece of the wife of one of the parties to the cause. *Harris* v. *Fowle*, vol. 22, 388.

FALSE PRETENCE.

Obtaining property by—What necessary to complete the offence. See Criminal Law.

FALSE RETURN.

By sheriff—Nulla bona.

When he held goods of party under writ of attachment. See Attachment 5.

FALSE SWEARING.

Must be wilful to constitute breach of condition in insurance policy that it should become void upon false swearing. See Insurance 5.

FALSE WEIGHTS AND MEASURES.

Action for charging plaintiff with use of. See Slander 2.

FAVOR.

Challenge for—What allegations it must contain, and when used. See Challenge 2.

FEE.

Necessity of word "heirs," to convey. See Deed 2.

FEES.

See Witness Fees.

—Extortion of illegal fees by justice. See False Imprisonment 6.

—In election court. See Court 8.

—Under Con. Stat., cap. 38. See Court 9.

FEME COVERT.

Replevin bond executed by, with husband and another as sureties. See Replevin 5.

FEME SOLE.

Action by—Marriage pending suit. See County Court 5.

FENCES.

Act 33 Vic. cap. 49—Where fences had been erected by railway company—Action against company for killing a horse. See Railway Company 4.

FERRY BOAT.

Effect of registration—Where bill of sale previously given. See Registration of Vessel 1.

—Acts shewing invitation to land—Negligence. See Negligence 4.

FIRE.

Set by sparks from locomotive—Coal or wood—Whether railway company bound to burn coal, being less dangerous. See Railway Company 5.

FISHERIES ACT.

1—Regulation and protection of Fisheries—Provincial right—Granted land—Grantee's right in bed of rivers.

The general power of regulating and protecting the fisheries in this province is in the Parliament of Canada, but a license by the Minister of Marine and Fisheries to fish in fresh water rivers, which are not the property of the Dominion, or in which the soil is not in the Dominion, is illegal.

Where the lands on fresh water rivers have been granted, the exclusive right of fishing is in the riparian owner, and where they have not been granted (with the exception of land owned by the Dominion), the right is in the Crown for the people of New Brunswick.

The right of fishing does not depend upon the ownership of the bed of the river, but of the bank; it depends upon the lateral and not the vertical contract of the water of the river. The title to the bed and waters of the North-west Miramichi, where it runs through lands granted to the Nova Scotia and New Brunswick Land Company, is in that company, with the exception of those places where the lands on the river had been previously granted. *Steadman v. Robertson*, vol. 18, 580.

2—Regulation—Riparian owner—Right of fishing—Fishery officer—Not protected by cap. 89, Con. Stat.—Notice of action—Not entitled to.

The regulation, "Fishing for salmon in the Dominion of Canada, except under the authority of leases or licenses from the Department of Marine and Fisheries, is hereby prohibited;"

Held, not authorized by section 19 of "The Fisheries Act," so far as it might extend to riparian proprietors on non-tidal rivers.

A person in possession of land bordering on a non-tidal river, as a tenant at will of the owner, is entitled to be treated as a riparian owner, so far as regards the right of fishing.

A fishery officer who wrongfully prevented a riparian owner from exercising his right of fishing, was not protected by cap. 89, Con. Stat., nor entitled to notice of action under cap. 90. *Phair v. Venning*, vol. 22, 362.

3—The provisions of sec. 3, sub-sec. 7, of the Fisheries Act, 31 Vic. cap. 60, do not apply to riparian owners in this province whose titles were acquired prior to July 1st, 1867. *Delany v. McDonald*, vol. 23, 139.

4—Dominion Fisheries Act, 31 Vic. cap. 60 Interference with private rights—Harbour of St. John—British North America Act, 1867, secs. 91 and 92.

Though the charter of the City of St. John grants the right of fishery in the harbour of the corporation for the benefit of the inhabitants, the Dominion Parliament has the right under the British North America Act, 1867, sec. 91, to regulate the times and manners of setting nets. *Ex parte Wilson*, vol. 25, 209.

—When officers may seize on view—Materials unlawfully in use. See On View.

FLOWAGE.

Mill privilege—Right of. See Easement 1.

FORECLOSURE.

See Mortgage.

FOREIGN COMPANY.

See Company.

FOREIGN JUDGMENT.

Action against company. See Pleading 8.

FOREIGN SAILORS.

Conviction for harbouring—Consent of consul. See Seaman's Act.

FORFEITURE.

Effect of, in building contract. See Contract 2.

—Of bail bond. See Bail Bond.

FORMER SUIT.

Way to prove. See Evidence 6.

FORMER RECOVERY.

1—Judgment—In former action—When a bar to subsequent suit—Amount not recoverable in former action—Set-off.

To an action of plaintiff the defendants pleaded the general issue and gave notice of a set-off of a promissory note made by plaintiff in favor of defendants. Upon the trial it was shewn that after the note had become overdue the defendants had brought an action against the present plaintiffs on the common counts for goods sold and delivered, and work and labor, etc. The amount of the promissory note was not recoverable under the declaration in the former action, nor had the then plaintiffs (the present defendants) attempted to prove the promissory note as part of their demand in that action.

Held, that by the recovery in the former action the defendants were not precluded from setting up the promissory note in this action. *Miller v. Ross*, vol. 23, 189.

2—Advances made to testator—Part of claim barred by Statute of Limitations—Second action for sums disallowed—Alleging agreement to devise form in payment for advances—Res Judicata—Agreement verbal—Whether action would lie on—Statute of Frauds.

Plaintiff sued in *indebitatus assumpsit* for money and goods supplied to the defendant's testator at different times between the years 1860 and 1877; but under the judge's direction to the jury recovered only the items proved to have been delivered since 1871—being six years before the testator's death. He afterwards brought an action to recover for the moneys, etc., disallowed on the former trial, declaring on a special agreement of the testator to pay at his death.

Held, that the matter was *res judicata*. And even though the plaintiff's right of action on the agreement might not have accrued till the testator's death, the former judgment was a bar to his now recovering for the sums then disallowed.

The declaration stated that the defendant's testator agreed that if the plaintiff would supply him from time to time during his life with money and goods, and would labour for him on his (testator's) farm, the plaintiff should be paid therefor at the testator's death, and that the testator would devise to the plaintiff the testator's farm in payment for such money, etc.

Averment that the plaintiff, in consideration of such agreement, did advance to the testator money and goods, and did perform labour for him at his request, but that he had not paid the plaintiff therefor, nor devised the farm to him, but had devised it to A. The plaintiff was the testator's son, and the agreement stated in the declaration was verbal, and, as proved, was to pay the plaintiff with the farm.

Held, per Allen, C.J., that no action would lie on the alleged agreement; 1st, because it showed that the testator never intended to incur any personal liability to the plaintiff; and 2nd, because it related to an interest in land, which, under the Statute of Frauds, could not be enforced. *Fries v. Wilmot*, vol. 21, 546.

FORMER SUIT.

Way to prove. See Evidence 6.

FOREIGN ADMINISTRATION.

Home administration — Rights of each to assets administered upon. See Husband and Wife 3.

FOREIGN CORPORATION.

Marine insurance agent — Proof of agency. See Insurance 14.

—Policy—Countersigning by agent—Waiver. See Insurance 15.

FOREIGN MARRIAGE.

Adultery. See Adultery.

— Foreign parties to suit, subject matter in this province. See Equity.

FRAUD.

Where question was fairly left to the jury, the court refused to disturb the verdict. See Evidence 7.

—The issue of, being fairly and properly left to the jury—New trial refused. See New Trial 8.

—Bill of sale — Absolute — Grantor continuing in possession — Evidence. See Bill of Sale 3.

—Voluntary conveyance—Honesty of transaction. See Deed 1.

FRAUDULENT MISREPRESENTATIONS.

Written contract. See Contract 6.

—When court bound to determine fact of. See Judgment 4.

—Right of judgment creditor to dispute confession of judgment. See Judgment 4.

FRAUDULENT PREFERENCES.

See Bills of Sale Act 2.

—Trust deed for benefit of creditors. See Deed 2-3-4.

FRAUDS.

Statute of. See Statute of Frauds.

—Agreement to devise farm. See Former Recovery 2.

—Contract for sale of goods—Offer by letter to sell—Acceptance. See Contract 17.

—Voidable contract—Recovery under common counts. See Contract 12.

FREDERICTON.

Power of city council to impose tolls in market. See Market.

FREIGHT.

Implied contract to pay when party takes possession of goods. See Assumpsit 2.

—As subject matter of insurance—What contract of insurance means. See Insurance 16.

—Insurance on — Whether within prior insurance clause in policy. See Insurance 14.

—Interest—Loss and adjustment—Proof of—Necessity for. See Insurance 16.

—Policy on—Where cargo forwarded to destination by another vessel at same rate of freight — Whether total loss. See Insurance 16.

Whether owner of vessel in *prima facie* entitled to. See Insurance 16.

—Railway company only entitled to reasonable compensation in the absence of a rate of freight established according to statute. See Railway Company 3.

—Loss of, by vessel being frozen in—Whether peril insured against. See Insurance 18.

FUTURE ADVANCES.

Bill of sale given to cover—Not accepted, rests in assignee of grantor. See Bills of Sale Act 1.

GARNISHEE ACT.

1—Con. Stat. cap. 43—Debt due executor as such—Liable to be attached.

Held by Allen, C.J., Wetmore and Palmer, JJ., (Weldon and Duff, JJ., dissenting) that a debt due to the primary debtor, as executor, is liable to be attached under the Garnishee Act, Con. Stat. cap. 43, at the suit of a creditor who has obtained judgment against the executor in his representative character.

Semble, that the Act would apply whether the claim of the primary creditor were a judgment or not. *Jones* v. *McMillan*, vol. 19, 378.

2—Attaching order—Setting aside—Where proceedings vexatious.

Where the first having been set aside the plaintiff obtained a second attaching order under the Garnishee Act, Con. Stat. cap. 43, under circumstances which led the judge hearing the matter to believe the proceedings were vexatious and unwarranted, the court refused to disturb his order setting aside such last mentioned attaching order. *Scott* v. *McKenzie*, vol. 19, 470.

3—Insolvent Act of 1878.

Where writ of attachment in insolvency is issued against primary debtor—To whom garnishee shall pay—Primary creditor entitled to the debt to amount of his claim as against assignee of insolvent. See *Harrison* v. *Atton*, vol. 20, 371.

4—Garnishee process.

Act 45 Vic. cap. 17, applicable to existing judgments, applies to judgments recovered as well before as after the passing of the Act. *ex parte Fawcett*, vol. 24, 228.

GAZETTE.

Containing proclamation of second part of Canada Temperance Act being in force, must be put in evidence. See Canada Temperance Act 4.

GENERAL ISSUE.

Garnishee proceedings may be given in evidence under. See Estoppel 2.

GENERAL OBJECTIONS.

To admission of evidence—Does not entitle party on motion for new trial to claim that evidence was improperly received. See Evidence 4.

GOODS NOT SPECIFIED.

What constitutes passing of property in. See Property, Passing of 2.

GOODS SOLD AND DELIVERED.

Action for—Waiver of tort. See Conversion 1.

—Subject to reduction in price—Agreement. See Agreement 8.

—To whom credit given—See Evidence 20.

GRANT.

See Crown Grant.

GRANTEE.

Under registered deed having notice of prior unregistered deed—Legal title not affected. See Trespass 3.

GROUNDS OF ACTION.

Where notice of action against a justice of the peace contains more than one ground of action, it will be sufficient if one of them be proved, if declaration contains a count to which such proof is applicable. See False Imprisonment 6.

GUARANTEE.

On whose credit goods are sold—Question for jury. See Sale 1.

GUARDIAN.

In socage—Infant under fourteen years of age—Who entitled to maintain action of trespass to property of infant. See Infant 1.

HABEAS CORPUS.

1—Returnable forthwith—Prisoners brought in once—Whether orders to bring in again can be made without issuing new writs.

Writs of *habeas corpus* were made returnable forthwith. The prisoners were brought into court on Tuesday, and the matter directed to be argued on the following Saturday. The same day the sheriff took the prisoners back to the gaol from which he had brought them. The writs and returns had been filed the day the prisoners were brought in, and by order of a judge taken off file again and returned to the sheriff.

Held, by Allen, C.J., Fisher and Duff, JJ. (Weldon and Wetmore, JJ., dissenting), that the court could direct the sheriff to bring in the bodies of the prisoners on the day set for the argument, without directing new writs to issue. The *Queen* v. *Tower*; *Same* v. *Mulholland*, vol. 20, 478.

2—Practice—Affidavit—Surplusage.

It is not a ground for setting aside a writ of *habeas corpus* that affidavits on which the *fiat* for the writ was granted were entitled, "In the supreme court *ex parte*," etc., the words after "supreme court" being mere surplusage.

Where a judge granted a *fiat* for a writ of *habeas corpus* against two persons to bring up the bodies of two infant children, the court would not set aside the writ merely on the ground that it did not clearly appear from the affidavits that they were in the custody of both.

It is not a ground for setting aside a writ of *habeas corpus* that two original writs were issued exactly alike, though such a proceeding was quite unnecessary. The fiat being endorsed on the writ and signed by the judge is sufficient. It is not necessary for him also to sign the writ.

The writ of *habeas corpus* issues by common law, except in cases of imprisonment on charges of crime to which only the Statute, 31 Charles II, applies. *In re Shaughnessy*, vol. 21, 182.

3—Order of discharge under cap. 41 Con. Stats.—Whether court has power to set aside.

An order of a judge made under the Con. Stat. cap. 41, discharging a prisoner from custody cannot be set aside or revised by the court. *Ex parte Byrne*, vol. 22, 427.

4—Exclusive right to issue.

The judges of the supreme court of this province have the exclusive right to issue writs of *habeas corpus* to enquire into the legality of the imprisonment of a person confined in the Dominion penitentiary at Dorchester, though he was committed there by the court of another province. *Ex parte Strather*, vol. 25, 374.

—To recover custody of infant. See Infant 3.

HACKNEY COACHES.

Portland town council—Power of, to regulate hackney coaches, etc., under 34 Vic. cap. 11, sec. 57, sub-sec. 45—By-law requiring hackmen to take out license valid—That hackmen have license from city council of St. John makes no difference—Conviction for offence against by-law held valid. *Ex parte Lemon*, vol. 20, 563.

HANDWRITING.

—Proof of comparison. See Insurance 6.

—Comparison by expert. See Evidence 17.

HARBOUR.

St. John—Power of corporation to erect wharves. See Easement 2.

HEARSAY.

Affidavit consisting of, not good. See Affidavits 4.

—When surveyor stated that he measured certain distances from a post pointed out to him by B., and ran his course from that, and tested his line from four points given him by B., and found it correct, the evidence was improperly received. See Evidence 5.

HEIRS.

A deed without the word "heirs" will only convey a life estate. See Deed 2.

—Construed same as "children" or "issue" where such was clear intention of testator. See Will 6.

HEIR AT LAW.

Right of entry—When it accrues—When father in possession as tenant by curtesy. See Limitations.

—Next of kindred. See Next of Kindred 1.

HIDES.

Inspection of, compulsory. See Inspection of, 1.

HIGHWAY.

1—Obstruction of—Right of action—Particular damage.

There is a distinction between the mere right to use a highway and the attempt to use it, as giving a right of action in the one case, and not in the other; and where a highway was obstructed by defendant, and plaintiff hearing of the obstruction went to attend to his business by another route and was thereby put to expense, but did not actually attempt to go upon the road;

Held, that there was no obstruction to the *exercise* of the plaintiff's right of way, and that he had no right of action, the only remedy being by indictment. *Burton v. Dougherty*, vol. 19, 51.

HIGHWAY ACT.

1—Alteration of road extending into two parishes—Damages awarded in both parishes—Power of county council to vary.

On an application under the Highway Act, Con. Stat. cap. 68, for the alteration of a road running through the parishes of S. and W. the jury found the alteration to be necessary, and assessed the damages caused thereby to an owner of land in W. at $120, and to an owner of land in S. at $80.

The county council on the application of one of the commissioners of highways for the parish of S. ordered an assessment upon each of the parishes for an equal amount.

Held, 1. That the application to the council should have been made by a majority of the commissioners in each parish.

2. That the council had no authority to vary the amounts awarded by the jury in each parish, and to direct assessments upon such parishes for equal amounts.

Per Wetmore, J. That the order for assessment should be made by the council at the meeting when the award of damages was laid before them. *Ex parte Parlee*, vol. 25, 51.

—*Certiorari* to remove proceedings in—Delay in applying for. See *Certiorari*, 11.

HIRING.

Verbal promise—Whether primary or collateral. See Statute of Frauds 2.

HUSBAND AND WIFE.

1—Property bought by or for wife—Where part of purchase money belonged to husband—Liability for his debts—Evidence—Damages.

In an action brought in a county court for the alleged wrongful seizure of a cow claimed to belong to the female plaintiff, seized under an execution against her husband, a subscription list on which money was raised to buy the cow for the wife was held to have been properly received in evidence.

The value of the cow was put by the plaintiff at $30, and the jury gave a verdict for $60.

Held, on appeal, that while the damages were so excessive under the circumstances as to have justified the county court judge in granting a new trial, it was not usual for a court of appeal to interfere with a verdict on the ground of excessive damages, and the court was not prepared to say the judgment in this case should be interfered with.

Held, also, that where part of the purchase money belonged to the husband, if the property was bought by, or for the wife, it vested in her. *Bell* v. *Wetmore et al*, vol. 19, 534.

2—Action by—Where wife's interest not set out—Proper remedy—Pleading—County court—Cause tried without jury—Effect of adjudication.

In an action in the county court by a husband and wife the first count set out a promissory note in favour of the female plaintiff. There were also the common counts, including an amount stated, but it did not allege that it was stated with the female plaintiff. The note not being stamped plaintiffs failed in the first count, but offered the note as evidence of the amount stated and obtained a verdict. The cause was tried without a jury. The judge afterwards ordered a new trial, upon the ground that the declaration did not sufficiently disclose the wife's interest in the amount stated;

Held, on appeal, that the defect being apparent on the face of the declaration, the defendant's proper remedy was by demurrer, or motion on arrest of judgment, and that there was no ground for a new trial.

Held, also by Palmer, J., that when a cause is tried by a county court judge without a jury, his adjudication is final so far as the court below is concerned, and he has no power in such case to order a new trial. *Estabrooks* v. *Law*, vol. 20, 310.

3—Chose in action—Assignment by husband and wife—Administration in different countries.

A married woman being entitled to a share of money in England, joined with her husband in a power of attorney to the defendant, an attorney-at-law, authorizing him to collect it. They afterwards assigned their interest in the money to A., but before it was collected the wife died and administration on her estate was granted in England to N. as attorney for the husband, and for his use and benefit. N. collected the money and sent it to B. in this province, who paid it to A. by direction of the husband. There was some evidence to connect the defendant with the receipt of the money by B. The husband afterwards died, and administration of the estate of his deceased wife was granted in this province to the plaintiff, who brought this action for the money received from England.

Held, (1) that the right to the money in England, being a *chose in action*, the assignment to A. did not vest the property in him, but merely transferred to him any right the husband had.

(2) That N., having collected the money as administrator of the wife, it belonged to him as such administrator, and the defendant receiving it was only liable to account to N., and was not liable for it to the personal representative of the wife in this province.

When administrators are granted in different countries, each portion of the estate must be administered in the country in which possession of it is taken and held under lawful authority; and the administrator under a foreign grant has a right to hold the assets received under it against the home administrator even after they have been remitted to the country of the domicil of the deceased. *Dorsey v. Connell*, vol. 22, 364.

4—Action by for injuries to wife—Loss of wife's services—Prospective damages.

In an action by husband and wife for injuries to the wife, the husband may recover damages not only for the loss of his wife's services previous to the commencement of the action, but also prospective damages resulting from her injury. *Fox and wife v. The Mayor, &c., of St. John*, vol. 23, 244.

5—Voluntary deed from husband to wife through medium of third party—Whether can support by proof of parol ante-nuptial agreement—Subsequent conveyance avoiding—Husband's interest in real estate of wife—Sale of. See *Doe dem Chambers v. Douglas*, vol. 23, 484.

6—Assault by husband on wife.

An assault is none the less a breach of the peace because it is committed by the husband upon the person of his own wife, and the wife is a competent person to make the complaint. *Ex parte Abel et al*, vol. 18, 600.

—Privileged communications. See False Imprisonment 4.

—Replevin bond executed by wife, with husband and another as sureties. See Replevin 5.

—Slander—Action for words of wife. See Evidence 7.

—Liability of husband for taxes on wife's property. Assessment Act of the City of St. John. See Inhabitant 1.

—Conversations between husband and wife—Evidence. See Married Woman 2.

—Separate property of married women. See Married Woman.

—Non-abatement of suit by marriage. See County Court 5.

ILLEGAL CONTRACT.

Liquor bought for the purpose of sale

in violation of Canada Temperance Act—Onus of proof. See Contract 8.

—Building Contract by-law of St. John. See Addenda 32.

ILLEGITIMATE CHILD.

Action for support of, Town of Upper Mills. See Overseer of Poor.

IMPERIAL ACTS.

Bankruptcy Act, 12 & 13 Vic. cap. 106, does not extend to this Province so far as relates to the rules of pleading and evidence. See Bankruptcy 1.

IMPOUNDING.

A person is not liable under the Con. Stat. cap. 110, sec. 14, for setting at large a cow from pound, unless the the impounding was by an authorized officer. The *Queen* v. *Close*, vol. 19, 592.

IMPRISONMENT.

For lesser number of days than justice might award—Justice's Court. See False Imprisonment 3.

—Fines imposed for offences against the Canada Temperance Act, 1878—Default of goods—What term allowed. See Canada Temperance Act 16.

—**Taxes**—Cost of execution—Arrest for, under second execution. See False Imprisonment 8.

INCOME.

Dominion officials—Whether subject to taxation for municipal purposes. See Dominion Officials 1.

INCORPORATION.

Under the Canada Joint Stock Companies Act, 1877—Necessity of alleging incorporation in declaration. See Joint Stock Companies Act 1.

Foreign judgment against company—Stating incorporation. See Pleading 8.

Indemnity—Promise to indemnify sheriff—Recovery by sheriff on. See Sheriff 2.

Indian Act of 1880—Selling liquor to Indian—Conviction for. See Summary Convictions Act 11.

INDICTMENT (See Criminal Law).

1—For murder—In short form—Whether prisoner can be convicted of assault under.

Held, by Weldon, Wetmore and King, JJ. (Allan, C.J., and Duff, J., dissenting), that on an indictment for murder in the short form given in Schedule A, to cap. 19 of 32 & 33 Vic. a prisoner cannot be convicted of an assault under sec 51 of that chapter.

Held, also, by all the Judges, that the fact of the prisoner's counsel having at the trial contended that he could be so convicted, and requested the Judge so to direct the jury, did not preclude him from afterwards objecting to the validity of the conviction on this ground. The *Queen* v. *Mulholland* vol. 20, 512.

—Charging an assault and with having beaten, wounded and ill-treated a person—Where no wounding—Whether properly convicted of a common assault. See Criminal Law 7.

2—Joinder of offences—Riot and assault. Revised Statutes cap. 147.

Counts for riot and unlawful assembly under the Rev. Stat., Title xxxix. cap. 147, Consol. Stat. p. 1081, being misdemeanours, may be joined in an indictment with a count for assault. *Regina* v. *Lang et al*, vol 24, 208.

—Stating value in, in an action for taking with intent to defraud not necessary. See Intent to Defraud 1.

—Joint—Where jury disagree as to guilt of one prisoner, and find the other guilty—Conviction. See Criminal Law 8.

—Misjoinder of counts. See Criminal Law 5.

INDORSEE OF BILL OF EXCHANGE.

Action by, where payee became insolvent before indorsement — Whether notice to, is necessary. See Bill of Exchange 1.

INDORSEMENT.

On fire insurance policy that loss should be paid to A. B. is not a contract by the company to pay A. B. See Insurance 7.

—Of promissory note before delivery renders indorsee liable as maker. See Promissory Note 2.

INFANT.

1—Under fourteen years of age—Guardian in socage—Who entitled to maintain action of trespass to property of infant.

Whether an infant under fourteen years of age, and her mother living, can maintain an action for trespass to land, or whether the mother as guardian in socage is not alone entitled to sue.

Such a question cannot be raised under the pleas of not guilty, and that the land was not the plaintiff's, but the defendant's should traverse the plaintiff's possession of the land. *Brewer* v. *Brewer*, vol. 22, 450.

2—Conveyance of land by—Confirmation after coming of age—Evidence.

A conveyance of land by an infant is voidable only, and may be avoided by him after coming of age. Mere omission to disaffirm such a deed is not sufficient evidence to warrant a jury in finding a confirmation. *Doe dem Nesby* v. *Charlton*, vol. 21, 119.

—Fraud — In a court of equity an infant stands in no different position from a person of full age in relation to matters of fraud. See Estoppel 3.

3—Infant—Right of father to custody of.

A father being in poor circumstances left his infant daughter then aged seven years with her uncle and aunt, upon the understanding that she should be considered as their child, and that they should support and educate her as such. She remained with her uncle and aunt until she was nearly fifteen years of age, and was educated by them, became much attached to them and was unwilling to leave them—her father contributing nothing toward her support, nor interfe[illegible] with her in any way during that time.

Held, per Allen, C.J., Wetmore, King and Tuck, JJ. (Palmer and Fraser, JJ., dissenting), on an application by the father for a *habeas corpus* to obtain the possession of the child. That he had the legal right to resume the custody of her, there being no imputation against her father's character, or that she would not be properly cared for in his house. *In re Eva Cowen*, vol. 25, 404.

INFORMATION.

If an Act requires a particular person to prosecute, information must be laid by him. See Summary Conviction 1.

—Under the Canada Temperance Act—Whether to be taken before two justices—Prosecution before. See Canada Temperance Act 14.

—To obtain a search warrant—What should allege. See Trespass 9.

—Wife competent to make complaint against husband for breach of the peace.

—Duty of justice to examine as to substantiation of. See Summary Conviction Act 9.

INHABITANT.

1—Of City of St. John—What constitutes for purposes of taxation—Wife's Separate property—How far husband liable for taxes on—Notice and demand—Necessity before execution issues—Assessment partly legal and partly illegal—Whether execution issued for whole, void.

A. was a resident of the city of St. John up to June, 1877, when he went with his family to Nova Scotia. In 1878 he returned to the province with his wife and family, and after leaving them in the town of Portland went to Boston in search of employment. He remained in Boston until the spring of 1880, having been employed in business and paid taxes there. While A. was absent, his wife's father assigned to her a lot of leasehold property in the City of St. John. In the fall of 1878 she and family moved into the city, and resided on her property until the spring of 1880 when A. returned from Boston and lived with his wife. He was afterwards arrested for the taxes for 1879, assessed against him in respect of his wife's property, and for an income tax against himself, both being included in one assessment.

Held by Allen, C.J., and Wetmore, Palmer and King, JJ. (Weldon, J., dissenting), that A. was constructively an inhabitant of the city of St. John in 1879, and was liable to be assessed as such.

Held also, by Allen, C.J., and Wetmore, Palmer, and King, JJ. (Weldon, J. dissenting), that a husband when in the [illegible] or constructive occupation of [illegible] (which, by the St. John [illegible] Act of 1859, includes lease-[illegible]) of his wife is liable by [illegible] to be assessed in his name in respect of such property, and his liability to be so assessed is not affected by the 17th section of the Act, which enacts that "the estate of deceased persons under contract of their executors, administrators or trustees, the separate property of married women and the property of minors, or other property under the control of agents or trustees, may be rated in the name of the principal party or parties ostensibly exercising control over them, but under such description as will keep the rating separate and distinct from any assessment on such parties in respect of property held in their own right."

Quære, whether, when an assessment is legal in respect to real estate, but illegal in respect to income, the including both assessments in one individual sum would render an execution for taxes void. *Edwards* v. *the Mayor, etc., of St. John*, vol. 22, 237.

Appeal allowed S. C. C. See Addenda 35.

INHERITANCE.

Where a lot of land was divided by mutual deeds of partition and one reserved a right to quarry on the moiety of the other, such right at his death vested in his heirs though there were no words of inheritance in the reservation. See Partition 1.

Initials. See Affidavit 6.

INJUNCTION.

1—Mandatory—Common Schools Act—Summary Remedy.

Held, by Palmer and King, JJ., on appeal from the decision of the former, made in equity, granting a mandatory injunction in this cause, that where a person who has been secretary to a board of school trustees, on being dismissed, refuses to give up the records and other property of the corporation, the court of equity has jurisdiction to grant a mandatory injunction to restrain him from retaining such property; but held by Weldon and Wetmore, JJ., that section 92 of the School

Act, Consol. Stat. cap. 65, has provided a summary remedy by application to the inspector, and that that remedy should be pursued.

Held, by Allen, C.J., that there might be cases where the remedy given by section 92, would be inadequate as where a secretary of a district had a considerable sum of school money in his possession which he refused to account for or give up; but as it was by the bill and not by arguments or objections on the motion for the injunction that the right of plaintiffs to institute the suit, must depend and as there was no allegation in the bill that the books and papers which defendant refused to deliver up were of such character and value as to require the interposition of a court of equity, or that there were special circumstances in the case requiring the interference of the court, he thought the plaintiffs should have resorted to the remedy provided by section 92, and the injunction ought not to have been granted. *West v. Trustees of School District of Johnston*, vol. 22, 56.

2—Restraining action of law—Discretion of judge.

A bill in equity was filed to obtain a decree of partnership between the plaintiff and defendant and for an account, and an *ex parte* injunction obtained restraining the defendant from interfering with the plaintiff (*inter alia*) in making the assets available for payment of the debts. The defendant denied the partnership. Before the hearing the plaintiff collected money belonging to the alleged partnership, which he appropriated to his own use, whereupon the defendant brought an action against him to recover the money. On application by the plaintiff for an injunction to restrain that action;

Held, that the judge in granting it was justified in requiring the present plaintiff to pay the money into court. *Sayre v. Harris*, vol. 22, 142.

3—Dissolution of, on giving security—How security affected by dismissal of bill—Discretion of judge as to costs on dismissal—Right of Court of Appeal to vary.

A. and B. residing in New York, entered into partnership in March 1880, for the purpose of cutting and storing ice in this province, and shipping it to New York or elsewhere for sale, provision being made for the advance of money by B., and the division of the proceeds on the sale of the ice; B. to have the option of purchasing out A.'s right at a fixed sum per ton of the ice. After part of the ice had been cut they entered into a new agreement in April, whereby the partnership was dissolved, and A. was to superintend the cutting, storing and shipping of the ice, which was to be B.'s property, who was to sell it to such parties, and on such terms as he should think advisable, and out of the first sales pay all expenses, including the expense of sending the ice to market, after which he was to pay half the profits to A. Soon after making the second agreement, and while the ice was in store in this province, B. sold it to C., who had notice of the agreements between A. and B., and that A. claimed an interest in the ice, and disputed B.'s right to sell it. A. then filed a bill against B. and C., alleging the sale to have been made for the purpose of defrauding him; and he obtained an *ex parte* injunction to restrain the removal of the ice.

The injunction was dissolved on C.'s giving security to pay any amount which might be found to be due to A. At the hearing of the case the bill was dismissed as against C., the charge of fraud not having been proved, but it was dismissed without costs, the judge being of opinion that by the agreements between A. and B., the ice was to be shipped abroad, and that C. having purchased with notice of the agreements, was bound to know that B. in selling the ice here was violating his agreement. The jury also refused to deliver up the security to C.

Held, on appeal by Wetmore, King, Fraser and Tuck, JJ. 1. That B.'s right to sell the ice was unlimited, and he was not bound to ship it abroad; and that there was no equity making C. responsible for B. paying to A. his share of the purchase money. A.'s only remedy being a money demand against B. on the agreement.

2. That A. was not entitled to the injunction to restrain C. from removing the ice; and therefore the security given by C. to obtain the dissolution of the injunction, ought to be given up to him.

3. That the bill should have been dismissed as against C. with costs, he having been a *bona fide* purchaser of the ice, and the charge of fraud against him not having been proved.

4. That, though ordinarily, costs in equity are in the discretion of the court, such discretion must be governed by certain fixed principles; and that the court of appeal could vary the order of the court below in respect to the costs. *Frank* v. *McGrath*, vol. 25, 499.

—*Ex parte* — Dissolution of — What will entitle a defendant to. See Appeal 8.

—Judge exercising discretion in granting—No sufficient grounds shewn for dissolution of—Damages. See Addenda 41.

INJURIES.

Arising from non repair of streets in the town of Portland. See Streets 2.

INQUISITION.

Of sheriff's jury may be set aside by court. See Replevin 3.

INSOLVENCY.

Admission by one partner—Effect of. See Insolvent Act of 1875.

Where defendant's property has been attached, and he afterwards becomes insolvent, the court is bound to dissolve the attachment, although the property was released on bond. *McIntosh* v. *Hamilton*, vol. 19, 1.

INSOLVENT ACT OF 1869.

1—Demand to assign—When made by a firm upon a firm—Admissible in evidence in action for and against one partner—Where demand annulled—Action for making same—Malice—Reasonable and probable cause—Want of—Treble costs—Whether takes away common law remedy—Evidence—Damages.

See *Gleeson* v. *Domville*, vol. 19, 17.

2—Issue of writ of attachment—Writ good upon face while in force a justification to the sheriff—Title of assignee—In an action of trespass the court will not go behind proceedings in insolvency which have not been set aside in the usual way—Leave and license—Evidence to support plea of.

See *Bourgeois* v. *Gilbert*, vol. 19, 353.

3—Title of assignee to real estate—*Proof* of deed of composition and discharge.

The title of an assignee to real estate under the Insolvent Act of 1869 is only statutory, and a purchaser from him under the authority of a deed of composition and discharge executed by the insolvent and his creditors, in order to establish his title, must prove the execution of the deed of composition and discharge, and that the conveyance was conformable to its terms. *Doe dem Rankin* v. *Andrew*, vol. 22, 425.

—Demand of assignment, when annulled, action for making—Reasonable and probable cause—Order of judge annulling demand not *prima facie* evidence of. See Addenda 44.

INSOLVENT ACT OF 1875.

1. Fraud—Charge of, under section 136. Averment not necessary that defendants have gone into insolvency. *Berry* v. *Hogan*, vol 18, 465.

2. Power of parliament to deprive persons of common law remedies. See *Robinson* v. *Ellis*, vol. 19, 6.

Admission of insolvency—By one partner—Effect of—See *Bank of New Brunswick* v. *Flaherty*, vol 19, 549.

When assignee may terminate lease. See *McLaughlin* v. *McLeod*, vol 19, 539.

Consent to discharge, necessity of calling meetings of creditors to consider. See *In re Seelye*, vol 19, 549.

Confirmation of discharge under deed of composition, creditors opposing—Necessity of filing objections with assignee. See *Bank of Nova Scotia* v. *Sterres*, vol. 20, 333.

Whether a consent to discharge where there are no assets, binds the minority of creditors—Contesting discharge—Ground that insolvent did not keep proper books—Necessity of filing objections with assignee. See *ex parte Clementson*, vol. 20, 413.

Costs — County Court Judge has power to award costs against assignee in contestation of claim under section 95 of Act. *Tait, assignee, etc.*, v. *Dowling*, vol. 20, 265.

When one partner purchases from assignee estate of insolvent firm *en bloc*—Right to sue for debts due firm in his own name—Payment—What constitutes—Where money received by person being partner in two firms. See *Leonard* v. *Griffin*, vol. 21, 188.

Bill of sale — What necessary to make it void under section 130—See *Barry* v. *Logan*, vol. 22, 165.

Creditors' remedy under section 125, See *Vassie* v. *Vassie*, vol. 24, 76.

Power of assignee to sell debts—Promissory note given to assignee—Statute when directory. See *Rowe*, appellant, and *Schofield*, respondent, vol. 25, 127.

INSPECTION.

1. Of rawhides. 37 Vic. cap. 45, ss. 78, 97.

INSPECTION COMPULSORY.

An Act of parliament should be so construed as to give effect to all parts of the Act, and assure the attainment of its objects, even although it exposes individuals to penalties and forfeitures. *Clarke* v. *Catkin*, vol. 20, 98.

—Of books of defendant where he has demanded particulars. See Books 1.

INSURANCE.

1—Life—Conditions—Waiver of—Power of agent to bind company—Payment of premium.

A policy of life insurance contained a condition that it should not be binding until the advance premium was paid and the policy delivered to the applicant for insurance; and that no agent of the company, except the president or secretary, should have any authority to waive or alter any of the conditions. The premium never was in fact paid, nor was the policy delivered; and although the assured did tender the premium to the agent, who declined to receive it and agreed to give time for the payment of it till it was demanded, and to hold the policy in the meantime for the assured.

Held, that as the agent was neither the president nor secretary of the company, he had no authority to waive the condition requiring payment of the premium.

There being no binding contract, an acknowledgement in the policy that the advance premium had been paid amounted to nothing, because the intention of the parties was that the policy should not be delivered till the premium was paid, and it was no admission of payment so long as the policy remained in the hands of the agent awaiting payment by the assured to give validity to the contract. *Calhoun v. Union Mutual Ins. Company*, vol. 19, 13.

2—Marine — Warranty against carrying stone or ore—Phosphate rock—Whether a stone or ore—Question of fact—Pleading.

In a policy of marine assurance the vessel was warranted "not to load more than registered tons with stone, marble, lead, ores or bricks." In an action brought on the policy, defendant pleaded that there was on the voyage on which the vessel was lost, laden on the vessel so insured, more than her registered tons of stone or ore, that is to say, phosphate rock, contrary to the terms of the policy. To this plea, plaintiff replied that the phosphate rock in the plea named was not stone or ore within the true intent and meaning of the condition or warranty in the said policy. Defendant demurred to the replication on the ground that it attempted to put in issue a question of law, the meaning of the words of the condition being for the court and not for the jury; but

Held, that the replication was good, and the demurrer was overruled. *Chapman v. Pror. Washington Ins. Co.*, and *Chapman v. Mutual Safety Ins. Co.*, vol. 19, 28. See Addenda 46.

3—Policy—Condition—Where building on leased ground—Practice—Pleading.

Where one of the conditions of a policy of insurance which by the policy were to be referred to in order to explain the right of the parties when not otherwise therein provided for, was, that if the building insured stood upon leased ground, and it was not so represented to the company and expressed in the policy, the policy should be void;

Held, that a breach of this condition rendered the policy void, even though in the company's printed forms of application signed by the assured, no question was asked as to this.

There cannot be a judgment of nonsuit, and also a judgment for plaintiff on some of the issues. *Ross v. Citizen's Ins. Co.*, vol. 19, 126.

4—Against loss by fire—Where by policy, loss, if any, payable to the person other than the assured—Who may bring action for loss—The assured the proper party—Burnham v. Walls, 3 Kerr, 377, commented upon.

H. and A. insured against loss by fire, certain merchandise their own property, or held by them in trust or on commission, with the defendant company, for one month. The insurance was continued by renewal premiums paid by H. & A., to whom also the receipts were delivered. By the policy, the loss, if any, was payable to the Maritime Bank (the plaintiff company) who had an interest in the merchandise. The property insured being destroyed by fire, the plaintiff company brought an action in its own name to recover the loss.

Held, on demurrer to the declaration that the plaintiff company could not maintain an action in its own name. *Maritime Bank v. Guardian Ass. Co.*, vol. 19, 297.

5—Policy of — Conditions—Breach of—Misrepresentation—Must be material—False swearing—Must be wilful.

A policy of insurance provided that the application for insurance should form part of the policy, and one of the conditions, providing what application for insurance should state, declared that if any person insuring should make any material misrepresentation or concealment, the insurance should be void and of no effect. In an action on the policy, defendants pleaded that in the application for insurance, plaintiff represented that the property to be insured was mortgaged, and that the amount of such mortgage was $900. Whereas the amount of the mortgage was a greater sum.

Held, that the plea was bad for not alleging that the misrepresentation was material.

Another condition provided for the proofs to be furnished in case of loss, and declared "if there appears any fraud or false swearing in the proofs, declarations or certificates," the insured shall forfeit all claim under the policy;

Held, that this meant wilful, false swearing; also, that a false statement, to avoid the policy, must be material.

A further condition required that the insured should within thirty days after loss deliver a full and detailed account in writing, etc., and stating (*inter alia*) what was the whole actual cash value of the subject insured.

Held, that a plea alleging that in an affidavit made by plaintiff in relation to the alleged loss "he falsely swore that the actual cash value of the property insured was $500" was bad, because it did not state that knowingly and wilfully he swore falsely. *Steers v. The Sovereign Fire Ins. Co.*, vol. 20, 394.

6—Action on—Evidence—Proving handwriting by comparison—Declaration of company's agents—Insurance on stock in trade consisting of tin, stoves, etc., only covers the articles mentioned—Conditions as to waiver of conditions—To what confined—Waiver of requirements of proof—Whether an independent stipulation—Pleading—Whether a second examination of books can be demanded—Office of company—What meant by arbitration—Condition for—Effect of—Where want of.

A letter signed "Henry Lye," as secretary of the defendant company, received by the plaintiffs in due course from the head office of the company, Montreal, on the subject of the insurance, was admitted in evidence for the purpose of proving by comparison Mr. Lye's signature to other letters on the same subject.

The policy of insurance which the plaintiffs had received from the defendant company, and upon which the former had paid and the latter received the premiums, and under which the loss was sustained, purported to be signed by "Henry Lye, secretary." The policy had been destroyed by fire.

Held, that as the company would not be permitted to deny Mr. Lye's signature to the policy, his letter written from the company's office, on the subject of the loss under the policy was properly used to prove his handwriting by comparison.

Held, the declarations of the company's agents made while engaged in adjusting a loss under a policy issued by the company are admissible in evidence in an action against the company. What the effect of the evidence under the conditions of the policy may be is another question.

The defendant company agreed to insure the plaintiff against loss or damage by fire to the amount of $4,000 on their stock in trade consisting of stoves, tin and ironware and mantels (slate and marble) contained in their four storey building, etc. Other companies had insurance on the entire stock in trade. The defendant company were liable to pay *pro rata* with the other companies.

Held, that the policy did not cover the plaintiff's entire stock in trade, but only that part which consisted of stoves, tin, and ironware and mantels (slate and marble) but that the question was immaterial as the value of goods of this description exceeded the total amount insured in all the companies.

The stipulation in a policy of insurance that nothing "less than a distinct specific agreement clearly expressed and endorsed on the policy shall be construed as a waiver of any printed or written condition therein" is confined to those conditions which are involved in the creation of the contract itself, and does not extend to those relating to the steps to be taken by the assured for the recovery of a loss upon the policy, especially where in the clause of the policy which deals with the question of proofs, it is agreed that no "act of the company except their written declaration, shall operate to waive the requirements of such proofs."

By Palmer, J. This clause has no application to the subject of the proofs and settlement of loss, but operates where the company places blank policies in the hands of an agent to restrict his authority and as notice to the assured that the agent cannot make verbal changes in the policy or strike out any of the conditions. If more is meant the clause is void, for a man cannot agree that he will not make a contract which the law allows him to make.

By the terms of the policy it was agreed that, "until such proofs, declarations, and certificates were produced and examinations and appraisals permitted by the claimant, the loss should not be payable; nor shall any act of the company, except their written declaration, operate to waive the requirements of such proofs." Defective proofs of loss were put in after the fifteen days named in the condition of the policy had expired. No better proofs were demanded.

The company's agent subsequently advertised for parties suffering loss by the fire, which destroyed the assured's goods, to come to his office to have the same adjusted, and the assured attended and produced his books and gave the required information, after which one of the company's agents adjusted the loss at a sum which the assured would not accept; subsequently the secretary of the company wrote the assured sanctioning the adjustment so made, and making no objection to the delay in delivering the proofs, or to the proofs themselves.

Held, a sufficient written declaration to constitute a waiver.

By Palmer, J. Where there is in a contract for insurance a stipulation that the assured will make proof in fifteen days, and there is no distinct stipulation that doing so in such time is a condition precedent to the assured's right to recover and the contract is not declared void for the non-appearance of it within such time, such stipulation is in that respect an independent one and not such a one as would if not complied with defeat the assured's claim.

By Palmer, J. The clause that nothing but the written declaration of the company shall operate as a waiver of the requirements of such proof, refers to the requirements of the proofs only, that is, what they shall contain and to the time when they shall be presented, and if proofs are presented after the limited time therefor, and no better proofs are demanded, and the company's agents examine and inspect the assured's books and adjust the loss, then the time limited for payment begins to run.

By Palmer, J. Where a plea stated that the proofs were not made according to the conditions of the policy of insurance, and not that they were not made in fifteen days after the loss, and the making of the proofs in fifteen days is not declared to be a condition precedent to the assured's right to recover, the plea does not raise the question that the failure to make proof in fifteen days after loss will avoid the policy. If the doing so had been alleged as a distinct condition of the policy, the company by themselves or agents could have waived it, of which in this case there was ample evidence.

By Palmer, J., when the company's agents once demand and have such an examination of the assured's books and papers, etc., as they think proper and adjust the loss, the company are not entitled to have a further examination of the assured's books, much less to require them to be sent from St. John to Montreal for the purpose of re-examination.

By Palmer, J., where proofs are required to be delivered at the office of the company, a delivery at the office from which the policy finally issued is sufficient.

By Duff, J., where the condition of the policy of insurance provided for a submission to arbitration "in the event of dispute arising after proof of loss and damage is given in due form," and no proofs are given in due form the condition does not apply.

By Palmer, J. (1) The defence that the assured's loss had not been ascertained by an award and arbitration could not be set up under a plea that the assured did not furnish proofs of loss, etc., and the loss had not been ascertained and proved according to the condition of the policy. (2) Before an arbitration could be had, the defendant company, after receiving proofs, etc., would have to admit their liability, but disputing the amount make a request for an arbitration. (3) As the assured had asked for an arbitration, and the company had refused, the latter could not set up this defence. (4) A condition that no action will be brought for a breach of the contract until the defendant did something depending on his own will, would be void as against the policy of the law; and (5) A plaintiff is discharged where performance is prevented by defendant himself. *Burrs* v. *The National Ins. Co.*, vol. 20, 438.

7—Indorsement of consent to pay loss to third person—Conditions—Breach of—Contract—Chose in action—Evidence.

An indorsement on a fire insurance policy that the loss (if any) should be payable to A. B., a mortgagee of the insured premises to the extent of his interest, is not a contract by the company to pay A. B., nor is it an assignment of a chose in action, and when the policy has been avoided by a breach of its conditions A. B. has no claim against the insurers in his own right, nor in the name of the insured for his benefit.

In an action by an administrator on a fire insurance policy one of the issues was, whether the occupation of the insured house had been abandoned. The administrator stated in his evidence that the occupation of the house had not been abandoned, and that he had occupied it.

Held, that statements of the administrator before assuming that character, tending to contradict his evidence, were properly received. *Cormier* v. *The Ottawa Agricultural Ins. Co.*, vol. 20, 526.

8—Fire—Amount of claim to be fixed by an award—Condition precedent—Total loss.

The plaintiffs effected with the defendants an insurance against loss by fire on their stock of dry goods. The stock was totally destroyed by the fire of June, 1877. The policy contained among others the following provisions: 1st. That, in case of damage to personal property, the amount of damages should be determined by appraisal by competent parties, to be mutually appointed by the assured and the company. 2nd. That, in case of any difference arising touching any loss or damage, the same should, at the written request of either party, be submitted to impartial arbitrators. 3rd. That defendants should not be sued for any claim until after an award fixing the amount of the claim in the manner above prescribed. In an action on the policy for a total loss, the defendants pleaded that the action was commenced before any award had been obtained fixing the amount of the claim.

The plaintiffs replied: 1st. That the defendants did not make any written request to submit any difference between them to arbitration. 2nd. That the plaintiffs, before the commencement of the suit, requested the defendants to submit the differences between them to arbitration, and they neglected and refused to do so.

Held, on demurrer to the replications, *per* Weldon, J., 1st. That the amount of the claim should be fixed by arbitration, did not apply when the claim was for a total loss. 2nd. That the covenant was collateral, and was not a condition precedent to plaintiffs' right of action.

Per Wetmore, J. That the covenant was a condition precedent, and would have to be performed before plaintiffs would have any right of action, and the fact that defendants refused to appoint an arbitrator would not relieve them from performance. *Adams et al. v. the National Ins. Co.*, vol. 20, 569.

9—Marine—Loss or damage—Limitation of time within which to bring action for recovery of—Condition—Pleading.

A policy of marine insurance provided that all losses and damages which should happen, should be adjusted and paid in sixty days after proof of loss and adjustment, and that no suit or action against the company for the recovery of any claim under the policy should be sustainable unless such suit or action be commenced within twelve months next after any loss or damage occurred. In an action on the policy the defendants pleaded that the loss or damage to the vessel did not occur within twelve months before the commencement of the action. Replication—that the loss, without the plaintiffs' fault, was not adjusted till a certain day, and that the action was brought within twelve months thereafter.

Held, on demurrer, that the plea stated a good defence, and that the replication was no answer to it. *Dickie v. the Western Ass. Co.*, vol. 21, 544.

10—Fire—Conditions—Waiver.

In an action on a policy of insurance for damage to the appellant's house by fire no evidence was given that the preliminary proof required by the policy had been furnished, the only dispute being the amount of damage. The appellant relied upon the fact that the sub-agent had had the damage estimated, and that he consented to accept the estimate as a waiver.

The 13th condition declared that none of the conditions in the policy should be taken as waived by the company unless the waiver was endorsed on the policy and signed by the agent at St. John.

Held, on appeal (King, J., *dubitante*), that the court below was right in ordering a non-suit to be entered on the ground that there was no evidence of a waiver of the preliminary proof. *McKean v. Commercial Union Ins. Co.*, vol. 21, 583.

11—Marine loss or damage—Matters in dispute — Arbitration clause — Ousting the court of its jurisdiction—Pleading.

A policy of marine insurance provided (*inter alia*) for adjustment in case of loss, and that payment would be made in sixty days after delivery at the office of the company of the usual proofs in writing of loss and interest in the insured, together with the adjustment papers; that if any difference arose between the company and the insured arbitrators should be appointed; that the insured should not be entitled to maintain any action at law or suit in equity on the policy until the matters in dispute had been referred to the arbitrators so appointed; and that the obtaining of the decision of such arbitrators should be a condition precedent to the right of the insured to maintain any such action or suit. In an action on the policy the defendants pleaded that a difference had arisen between them and the plaintiff as to the alleged loss or damage, and that although arbitrators had been appointed, they had not settled the matters in dispute, nor made any award. To this the plaintiff replied that the defendants did not admit their liability under the policy, but wholly denied it. On demurrer to this replication, the question was whether the arbitration clause applied except where the company admitted a liability and only disputed the amount.

Held, that the replication was no answer to the plea, and that until the arbitrators determined the matters in difference referred to them, no action was maintainable. *Lautalum* v. *The Anchor Marine Insurance Company*, vol. 23, 14.

12—Contract—Depending on correspondence — Distinct offer and acceptance necessary.

Defendants were incorporated in the Province of Ontario, and did business in this province by S., their agent. J. was the agent of another company called "The North British and Mercantile Insurance Company," both agents being resident in St. John.

Plaintiff had been insured for a term of three years in a company called "The Canada Agricultural Insurance Company," which was understood to have failed before the expiration of the policy. On the 14th of January, 1878, S. wrote to W., of Chatham, who appeared to have acted in the matter as the sub-agent of both the defendants and the North British Companies, stating that the Canada Agricultural Insurance Company had failed, and asking W. to ascertain whether plaintiff would not insure in the defendants' company and in the North British, stating that J. and he were willing to take the whole of the insurance at the rate of one per cent. on wooden buildings and three-fourths on brick.

W. answered on the 16th of January, stating that he had seen plaintiff, and if it turned out that the property was not insured he would probably send an application. S. replied on the following day, stating that W. could take anything offered at from one to three years, and at such rates as plaintiff had been in the habit of paying, or whatever W. considered a fair premium.

On January 31st W. wrote J. and mentioned the subject of S.'s letter relative to obtaining insurance on plaintiff's buildings, stating he did not know whether any insurance had been effected, and requesting J. to let him know if he had heard anything about it. J. answered this letter on February 4th, stating that he would see S. about the plaintiff's buildings.

On February 7th, plaintiff wrote W., describing him as agent of the North British and Mercantile Insurance Company, and referring to a statement of

W.'s that the company would be willing to insure the buildings at the same rate for which they had been insured in the Agricultural Company, requested him to effect insurance on them for $10,000 in favor of one Z., a mortgagee; that it was the same risk which the Canada Agricultural Insurance Company had for three years at two per cent., and that the policy was in the hands of L., from whom J. could get it to draw the new policy. He also stated that he would like to have a similar amount insured on the buildings in his own favor, at the same rate, and he referred to a plan of the town of Chatham for position of the buildings where they were marked as the "convent" and the "cathedral." On the same day W. wrote J. as follows: "Enclosed find the Bishop's (plaintiff) application just received, 6.30 p.m. He has misunderstood me as to rate. I told him, as authorized by S., at the rate of one per cent., which wo. l be about fair. If the 'North British' and 'Western' will do it, and plan furnished is sufficient, telegraph me in the morning. The meaning of application is $5,000 on each of blocks—that is $10,000 in favor of L. to secure mortgage, and an additional $10,000—five thousand on each in favor of the Bishop (plaintiff)." On the next day, the 8th, J. telegraphed to W. as follows: "S. and J. take ten thousand each."

Held, that this constituted no completed contract of insurance. *Bishop of Chatham v. The Western Assurance Company*, vol. 22, 242.

13—Where property held under agreement that party holding should repay himself for expenditure from profits—Premises destroyed by fire—Who entitled to insurance moneys.

The plaintiffs, a tanning company, requiring money to carry on their business, obtained a loan on a mortgage of their property, covenanting to keep the buildings insured for the security of the mortgage. Afterwards requiring further assistance in their business, they agreed with T., one of the stockholders of the company, that he should take possession of the property, pay all the debts, carry on the business, and make all necessary improvements and have full control until he was re-paid the money he should expend; that the policy of insurance should be assigned to him subject to the lien of the mortgagee, and that all money which he should pay for the debts of the company, or expend in improvements, should be re-paid as a first charge on the business; but that if he abandoned the business or ceased to work the tannery, he should have no claim on the company for any improvements; that the buildings were to be kept insured by him and the premiums charged to the company; and that subject to these charges and payments, the profits of the business should be equally divided between the company and T. until the company's half had re-paid him all sums paid for the company's debts and expended by him for the buildings, machinery, etc., and his commission. T. went into possession under this agreement in September, 1873, and carried on the business, renewing the policy of insurance in the plaintiffs' name, charging them with the premium and making the loss payable to himself. The business not turning out profitably, and T. becoming involved and unable to carry it on, assigned in January, 1876, all his interest in it and in other property to trustees for the benefit of his creditors; and in April following he was declared an insolvent under the Insolvent Act. The tannery buildings, etc., were destroyed by fire in February, 1876.

Held, (affirming the judgment of the court in equity) that the insurance was for the benefit of the plaintiffs as owners of the real estate, and that after paying off the mortgage, they were entitled to the balance of the insurance money, and that T.'s assignee had no claim to it under the agreement with the plaintiffs as a lien for the amount expended by T. in carrying on the business. *Schofield v. New Brunswick Patent Tanning Co.*, vol. 22, 509.

14—Marine—Policy issued by foreign corporation—Agent—Countersigning — Proof of agency—Consol. Stat., cap. 45, sec. 16—Prior insurance clause—Meaning of words—"Premises hereby assured"—Insurance on freight—Whether came within clause—Warranty not to load more than registered tonnage with stone or ore without consent of agent — Verbal consent of agent — Whether sufficient — Phosphate rock — Whether known to commercial world as "stone."—Question for jury—Vessel—Registered owner — Equitable owner — Evidence—Statement to underwriters as to nature of interest.

A policy of insurance of a foreign corporation declared that it should not be valid unless countersigned by R., the company's agent at St. John, N. B. In an action on the policy, proof that it was countersigned by R. as agent, and issued to the plaintiff on his application, and that he had previously dealt with R. as agent of the company, and received a policy from him purporting to have been issued by the company and countersigned by R. as such agent, is sufficient evidence under the Consol. Stat. cap. 46, sec. 16, to prove that R. was the accredited agent of the company, and that the policy was executed by them.

Plaintiff insured $5,000 on a vessel valued in the policy at $40,000. The policy stipulated that if the assured had made any prior insurance, the underwriters should be answerable only for so much as such prior insurance was deficient towards fully covering the premises thereby insured. The plaintiff's interest in the vessel amounted to $15,000. And he had prior insurance to the extent of $5,350; there was also insurance by other persons on the freight and disbursements of the vessel, and on advances made to the plaintiff.

Held, 1. That the words "premises hereby insured" meant the plaintiff's interest in the vessel; and that as the value of his interest exceeded the amounts of the prior insurance, and of the sum insured by the policy sued on, he was entitled to recover the whole of the latter sum.

2. That the insurance on freight did not come within the prior insurance clause in the policy.

By the terms of a policy of insurance, a vessel was warranted not to load more than her registered tonnage "with stone, marble, lead, ores or bricks," without the consent of the agent of the underwriters.

Held, per Allen, C.J., Wetmore and King, JJ., (Weldon, J., dissenting), that a verbal consent of the agent to load beyond the registered tonnage of the vessel was sufficient.

A vessel was loaded with a substance known in commerce as phosphate rock, or phosphate which was used for fertilising purposes; and scientific witnesses were not agreed as to a definition of it.

Held, per Allen, C.J., Wetmore and King, JJ., (Weldon, J., dissenting), that it was a proper question for the jury whether it was known to the commercial world as "stone" at the time the policy issued—there being a warranty against loading with stone beyond the vessel's registered tonnage.

Plaintiff being the registered owner of one-fourth of a vessel, and also the equitable owner of one-eighth insured $5,000 upon her—the policy not specifying his interest. He admitted on cross-examination that he had prior insurance on the vessel, but stated that it was upon his one-eighth interest.

Held, that he was entitled, on being afterwards called to rebut the defendant's evidence, to explain the circumstances connected with the prior insurance.

Quære, whether he should have been allowed to state that he told the underwriters at the time of effecting the policy sued on, that he was insuring the share of which he was the registered owner. *Chapman* v. *The Providence Washington Insurance Co.* (Appeal to Supreme Court of Canada, dismissed.) See Addenda 16, vol. 23, 165.

15—Marine—Policy issued by foreign corporation — Agent — Countersigning by—Pleading—Whether objection that policy not countersigned by agent, available under plea of non est factum—Waiver—Evidence—Conversation with person represented to be the president of the company at a place purporting to be the company's head office—Whether admissible in action against company.

A policy of insurance of a foreign company, sealed with what purported to be the corporate seal and signed by the president, declared that it should not be valid unless countersigned by R., the company's authorized agent at St. John, N.B. The plaintiff agreed with R. to effect insurance on a vessel, and paid him the premium, and R. at the plaintiff's request sent the policy to C., but omitted to countersign it.

Held, by Allen, C.J., Wetmore and King, JJ., (Weldon J., dissenting); 1st. That the countersigning might be waived, and that R. had waived it by receiving the premium and issuing the policy. 2nd. That this objection to the policy was available under the plea of *non est factum*.

The holder of a policy of insurance issued by R. as the agent of a foreign company, went to what purported to be the head office of the company in Philadelphia, to enquire about payment for a loss under the policy, and conversed with H. a person there, who was represented to him as the president of the company, and who produced a paper which he said was a copy of the policy, and spoke about the loss and payment of it by R., the company's agent.

Held, that this was evidence that H. was the president of the company, and that his declaration was evidence of the agency of R. *Chapman* v. *The Delaware Mutual Ins. Co.*, vol. 23, 121. Appeal allowed. See Addenda 46.

16—Freight—Policy on—Where cargo forwarded to destination by another vessel at same rate of freight—Whether total loss—Owner of vessel—Whether prima facie entitled to freight — Preliminary proofs—Necessity for—Sale of vessel by master—When allowable—Abandonment to underwriters—Whether owner entitled to reasonable time to make enquiries after hearing of loss—Waiver of notice of abandonment—What constitutes—Examination of witnesses abroad—Commission for—Return of one commissioner—Omission of defendant's commissioner to put cross-interrogatories—Effect of—Endorsement of return on commission—Whether necessary.

Freight as a subject matter of insurance, means the benefit derived by the ship owner from the employment of the ship; and the contract of insurance against loss of freight is that the ship shall not be prevented from earning it by the perils insured against.

Where a vessel (the freight of which was insured) was lost, and the master forwarded the cargo to its destination by another ship, paying therefor the same freight which he was to receive.

Held, that the ship owner was entitled to recover for a total loss of freight.

The owner of a vessel is *prima facie* entitled to her freight.

When the conditions of a policy on freight required that proof of interest, and of the loss and adjustment should be given to the underwriters before bringing an action, the plaintiff cannot recover unless such preliminary proof is given.

In order to justify the sale of the vessel by the master, there must be urgent necessity for it, and what circumstances will constitute a case of necessity in a mercantile sense is a question for the jury.

The owner of a vessel which has been damaged by the perils insured against, is entitled to a reasonable time to make enquiries after hearing of the damage, before giving notice of abandonment.

Where the owners of a vessel so damaged gave notice of abandonment, which the underwriters refused to accept, and the owner then telegraphed to the master to "follow best advice," whereupon the master having had a survey of the vessel, by which it was found it would cost more to repair her than she would be worth, sold her by auction.

Held, *per* Allen, C.J., Wetmore and King, JJ., (Weldon, J., dissenting) that these instructions did not constitute a waiver of the notice of abandonment, and that there was evidence of a constructive total loss to leave to the jury.

Per Weldon, J., that the plaintiff was only entitled to nominal damages.

A commission for the examination upon interrogatories of witnesses abroad, was taken out by the plaintiff directed to two commissioners, (one named by each party) and authorizing plaintiff's commissioner to return the depositions certified by him, also to proceed *ex parte* with the examination of the witnesses and the execution of the commission in case the defendant's commissioner refused or neglected to attend. The defendant's commissioner attended the examination, cross-examined the witnesses, and asked some of the cross-interrogatories, but, without giving any reason, refused to sign the certificate of their examination.

Held, *per* Allen, C.J., and King, J., 1. That the certificate of the plaintiff's commissioner was sufficient.

2. That if the signing of the certificate was a part of the execution of the commission, the refusal of the defendant's commissioner to sign, authorized the plaintiff's commissioner alone to sign.

3. That the omission of the defendant's commissioner to put some of the cross-interrogatories was no ground for rejecting the depositions.

Per Wetmore, J., that the plaintiff's commissioner should have put the cross-interrogatories to the witnesses; but the omission to do so was only an irregularity which should have been taken advantage of by an application to a judge to quash the depositions.

It is not necessary that the commissioner should endorse a return on the commission. *Driscoll* v. *The Millville Marine Ins. Co.*, vol. 23, 160.

Appeal to Supreme Court of Canada allowed. See Addenda, No. 18.

17—Marine Insurance—Whether damage to ship must be re-paired at port of discharge—Particular average—Plan of adjustment—Policy—Warranty not to enter or attempt to enter Gulf of St. Lawrence before day named—Meaning of—Amendment.

A ship was insured for a voyage from Liverpool to Quebec. The policy contained a clause that a ship should not enter, nor attempt to enter, or use the Gulf of St. Lawrence before the 10th May, nor after the 30th October, and the seaward line of the Gulf was defined. The ship sailed from Liverpool in April, and on the 7th May ran into field ice near Newfoundland, about 60 miles to the east of the defined line of the Gulf, and the weather being stormy, she was injured by the ice. After getting clear of the ice, she proceeded to Quebec (not entering the Gulf till after the 10th), where her injuries were examined, and she was partially repaired and sailed for Liverpool with a cargo of timber. It did not appear that she had received any injury on the voyage to Liverpool. On her arrival there she was put into dock, [illegible] fully [illegible]amined, and her in[illegible] to be such as would probabl[illegible] by her being in the ice.

Held, 1. *Per* Allen, C.J., Wet[illegible], Palmer and Fraser, JJ., (Weldon, J., dissenting), that, though the ship was proceeding towards the Gulf of St. Lawrence at the time she got into the ice, she was not attempting to enter the Gulf, within the meaning of the clause in the policy, and that the underwriter was liable for the damages sustained.

Per King, J., that the clause against entering the Gulf was not applicable to a voyage policy.

2. That it was not necessary that the amount of damage to the ship should be adjusted at Quebec; but it might be done at Liverpool.

3. That there was evidence that the injury to the ship was caused by the ice during the voyage to Quebec, and not on the return voyage to Liverpool.

4. That a skilled witness could not be asked whether, in his opinion, considering the course and position of the ship and the state of the wind at the time she got into the ice, She was not attempting to enter the Gulf? or where was she bound, etc? *Moran* v. *Taylor*, vol. 24, 39.

In above case, appeal to Supreme Court of Canada, allowed. See Addenda, No. 22.

18—Marine insurance—Charter party—Loss of freight—Perils of the seas—Voyage frustrated by ice—Whether a peril insured against.

Plaintiff, the owner of a vessel, effected insurance on her freight 1st December, on a voyage from London to the Bay Chaleur, thence to Maramichi, and thence to Norfolk, Virginia, to load cotton for Liverpool. The policy was in the usual form against perils of the seas, etc. On the 25th November—the vessel being then on her voyage from London—the plaintiff chartered her to persons in New York, and undertook [illegible] on her arrival at Miramichi she [illegible] direct to Norfolk, and there load for the charterers a cargo of cotton, and proceed therewith to Liverpool. The ship arrived at Miramichi on 25th November, and sailed therefrom for Norfolk on the 28th, and while proceeding on her voyage ran into floating ice near the entrance to the river Miramichi, and being unable to get to sea, was taken to a place of safety, where she remained, frozen in, till the 7th May following. She could not, after that, have reached Norfolk before the 1st June.

The charterers, on being informed in December that the vessel was frozen in, notified the plaintiff's agent at Norfolk, that in consequence of this they considered the charter at an end, and would ship the cotton by another vessel, and an endorsement to that effect was made on the charter party, and signed by the agents of the plaintiff and the charterers respectively, and the plaintiff afterwards acquiesced in this.

By the course of trade at Norfolk, no cotton sufficient for a cargo of the plaintiff's vessel, was shipped there between the 1st May and 1st October.

Held, per Palmer, King and Fraser, JJ., (Wetmore, J., dissenting). 1. That the plaintiff having commenced the voyage, and incurred expense towards earning the freight, it was lost if his interest was destroyed by one of the perils insured against.

2. That it must have been the intention of both parties to the charter that the vessel should reach Norfolk during the shipping season for cotton ; and if it became impossible to do so, the object of the voyage was frustrated, and the contract was at an end, and the freight was lost—the vessel not being bound, under the circumstances, to sail for Norfolk after being released from the ice.

3. That the freezing in of the vessel was one of the perils insured against by the policy, and not one of the ordinary occurrences of navigation. *Jordan v. The Great Western Ins. Co.*, vol. 24, 421.

—As to right of trustees of estate under will to insure new buildings or increase the insurance when directed to insure in about the amount in which testator insured. See Will 5.

—Policy of—Beneficiary not entitled to bring action in his own name. See Contract 5.

—Whether the fact that property burnt by railway company's locomotive was insured is an answer to company's liability. See Railway Company 5.

—Action by person to whom life policy payable. See Stay of Action 2. See Contract 5.

—Statement as to quality of mill when effecting insurance. See Contract 14.

—Assignment—condition in policy not to assign.—Mortgage of chattle property not an assignment. See Addenda 45.

INTENT TO DEFRAUD.

1—Taking with intent to defraud—Stating value in indictment—Bona fide claim of right.

An indictment under 32 & 33 Vic. cap. 21, sec. 110, for unlawfully taking and appropriating property with intent to defraud, need not state the value of the property taken, although, perhaps a prisoner could not be tried under the second clause of the section if the value was not stated.

Held, also, on the trial of such an indictment, to be a proper direction, to tell the jury they should acquit the prisoner if they thought he *bona fide* believed he had a claim of right in the property taken. *The Queen v. Horsman*, vol. 20, 520.

Intercolonial Railway—Liability of conductor for accident to passengers. See Railway Conductor 2.

INTEREST.

In an action of trespass on case, not allowed as part of damages. See Collision 1.

Not allowed after amount due has been tendered. See Assumpsit 2.

Not recoverable on coupons. See Debentures 1.

INTERFERENCE.

By parties to suit—with jury during a view. See Jury 1.

INTERLOCUTORY JUDGMENT.

Date of the entry of cause on memorandum—Omission of—Not ground for setting aside the judgment. See Practice 9.

INTERROGATORIES.

Attachment for contempt of court—When to be filed—Costs of. See Attachment 7.

—Answers to matters not enquired of—Suppression of. See Commission 3.

INTESTATE.

Next of kindred—Who entitled to real estate. See Next of Kindred 1.

Intoxicating — Spirituous — Whether synonymous expressions. See Canada Temperance Act.

IRREGULARITY.

In entering up judgment on confession. See Execution 1.

—Issuing wrong form of *capias*. See Practice 12, Arrest 2.

—Warrant for commitment—Justification to officer. See Criminal Law 7.

—Judgment—Delay in moving to set aside. See Judgment 1.

—Notice of special bail by firm of attorneys, where one has not paid his library fees. See Attorneys 4.

JOINDER.

When judge who tried cause has certified that there was reasonable cause for joining a defendant, Court refuses to review. See Review 1.

Joint Conversion—Evidence of—Trover. See Married Woman 2.

JOINT MAKERS.

Payment of interest by one will not prevent Statute of Limitations from operating in favor of others. See Limitations 5.

JOINT OWNERSHIP.

Distress—Logs delivered to mill-owner to be sawn into deals. See Landlord and Tenant 3.

JOINT OWNERS.

Misuse of property by one joint owner—When action maintainable. See Action on the Case 2.

JOINT STOCK.

Capital stock—Bank—Assessment of under "St. John Assessment Act of 1882." See Assessment 2.

JOINT STOCK COMPANIES ACT, 1877.

Action by — Pleading — Declaration, not enough merely to state corporate name.

In an action brought by a company, incorporated by letters patent under the Canada Joint Stock Companies Act, 1877, it was held (on demurrer to the declaration) by Allen, C.J., and Weldon, Wetmore and King, JJ., that the declaration was bad, for not alleging the incorporation of the plaintiffs by letters patent under the Act; but by Palmer, J., that it was sufficient merely to describe plaintiffs by their corporate name. *The Waterous Engine Works Co. v. Campbell*, vol. 22, 503.

JUDGE.

His right in charging jury to express his opinion on the case. See Evidence 2.

1. Jurisdiction to try a cause at a circuit court to which he has not been assigned, not necessary that he should have been assigned to that circuit. *Earle v. Botsford*, vol. 23, 407.

Relationship of wife of party in suit. See False Pleas 1. Discretion of, See Injunction 2.

JUDGE'S ORDER.

1—Discharging a person in custody under a warrant of a magistrate—Made ex parte in a summary way—No lawful authority for making such order.

Held, by Wetmore, Duff, Palmer and King, JJ., (Weldon, J., dissenting), that a judge of the court has no power on the application of one in custody, under a warrant of commitment made by a magistrate in due form of law, to make an *ex parte* order, in a summary way for the prisoner's discharge. The prisoner must proceed by writ of *habeas corpus*, or by proceedings under cap. 41, of the Consolidated Statutes. *Ex parte Woodward*, vol. 21, 221.

2—Copy of—Made rule of court.

A judge's order may be made a rule of court, on production of a copy of it served on the party moving, verified by affidavit. *Powell v. Hunnington*, vol. 22, 559.

3—A Judge's order can be made a rule of court on production of the order with counsel's signature, but only during term. *McLeod v. Jones*, vol. 18, 439.

4—Stay of proceedings—Cause directed to be entered on motion paper—Whether can give notice of motion to set aside award pending stay.

A cause was referred to arbitration and an award made in favor of defendant. Plaintiff then obtained an *ex parte* order from a judge directing that all further proceedings in the case be stayed until an opportunity was afforded plaintiff of moving court in the ensuing term, and that the cause be set down on the motion paper of said term for argument without further order. A copy of this order was served on defendant. Subsequently, plaintiff gave notice of motion to set aside the award, and for a new trial, the notice also stating that he abandoned that part of the judge's order which directed the cause to be entered on the motion paper.

Held, that, while the judge's order stood containing the stay of proceedings, plaintiff could not give the notice of motion for new trial, and the application was, therefore, refused. *Jones v. Tuck*, vol. 23, 447.

Appeal to Supreme Court of Canada allowed. See Addenda, No. 19.

For review from justices' court—Time for granting. See Review 6.

JUDGMENT.

1—Irregularity — Delay in moving to set aside—Waiver—Affidavit of merits.

In July, 1881, an order for security for costs was obtained by defendant with a stay of proceedings till security given. On the 5th September the plaintiff's attorney sent the defendant's attorney a bond for security for costs with a demand of plea, but the time for pleading not having expired, he sent another demand on the 27th September. No plea having been delivered, the plaintiff's attorney soon afterwards asked the defendant's attorney if he had received the bond, and if it was right and if he intended to plead, and he swore that he understood the defendant's attorney to say that the bond was sufficient and that there was no defence to the action; and in consequence of this he signed interlocutory judgment on the 29th November and final judgment on the 21st December following; and that before signing final judgment he told the defendant's attorney that the interlocutory judgment was signed.

On an application to set aside this judgment for irregularity it appeared that there was an error in the bond, the condition being that plaintiff should pay *such costs as the defendant should be liable to pay in case he should discontinue, etc.* The affidavit of the defendant's attorney denied that he had told the plaintiff's attorney that the bond was sufficient, or that there was no defence to the action. He admitted that the plaintiff's attorney had told him that interlocutory judgment was signed in the action, but stated that for certain alleged reasons he did not believe it, having searched the clerk's office in the latter part of October. In the latter part of March following, the defendant's attorney searched again and discovered that interlocutory judgment had been signed in November previous. Upwards of a month after this he applied to set it aside for irregularity, or to be let in to defend on the merits. The defendant's affidavit stated that he had, he believed, "a good defence to the action on the merits."

Held, (Palmer, J., dissenting), that the application was too late, the plaintiff having lost a trial.

Per Allen, C.J., Wetmore and King, JJ., that it was the duty of the defendant's attorney when told that interlocutory judgment had been signed, to search, and not having done so, but having allowed two terms to elapse before applying to set aside the judgment, it was too late.

Per Weldon and Wetmore, JJ., (Palmer, J., dissenting), that it was the duty of the defendant's attorney, if he considered the bond for security for costs defective, to return it to the plaintiff's attorney, or notify him of the objection to it, and his omitting to do so was a waiver of the objection.

Per Wetmore, J., that the defendant's affidavit, stating his belief that he had a good defence on the merits, was insufficient. (Palmer, J., dissenting.) *McDonald v. Potts*, vol. 22, 146.

2—Defendant claiming to have judgment entered on the roll on payment of less sum than amount of—Receipt—Where mislaid—Agreement before action brought to give credit for, if found—Refusal of plaintiff to credit—Defendant's remedy—Estoppel.

Defendant being indebted to the estate of J. M., but the amount being disputed, gave his promissory note to W. M., the administrator of J. M., for $300, in 1877—it being agreed that if the defendant could find J. M.'s receipt for money which he claimed to have paid him, the amount should be credited on the note. W. M. died in 1879 and the note came into the hands of the plaintiff as his administratrix, who brought an action on it in August 1879, and signed interlocutory judgment by default. After this and before final judgment the defendant found a receipt of J. M.'s for $80, and applied to the plaintiff to credit the amount on the note, but she refused to do so, or to recognize it as a payment on account of the transaction for which the note was given. The defendant being then asked what he intended to do said that his son would settle the matter. Final judgment was signed in November, 1879, and a *fi. fa.* execution issued in January following, but no actual levy was made, the defendant's son promising to pay the amount in a short time, and in May 1880 he paid $200, and promised to pay the balance soon.

In August, 1882, the defendant obtained a judge's order to set aside the execution and enter satisfaction on the judgment on payment of the balance due after crediting the $80 claimed as a payment. On application to rescind this order.

Held, *per* Allen, C.J., that the defendant having acquiesced in the plaintiff's refusal to credit the $80, and having allowed final judgment to be signed in the suit, and having paid part of the amount, and promised to pay the balance, was precluded from asking to have the execution stayed.

Per Allen, C.J., Wetmore and Fraser, JJ., that the defendant knowing of the refusal by plaintiff to credit the $80, should have applied to set aside the interlocutory judgment, and to be let in to defend the action, and having allowed final judgment to be signed against him for the whole amount of the note could not afterwards apply on affidavits to reduce it by the amount of $80.

Per Palmer and King, JJ., that under the agreement of the defendant and W. M., the defendant was entitled to have the $80 credited on the execution, and was not bound to enter a defence to the action. *Keiller* v. *Charters*, vol. 23, 493.

3—Action on—Release—Where obtained before judgment—Whether plea available.

In an action brought on a judgment obtained in a county court, defendant pleaded a release from plaintiff after the commencement of the suit, in which the judgment was recovered.

Held, on demurrer, that the plea was bad. *Estabrooks* v. *Sears*, vol. 23, 543.

4—Judgment by confession—Motion to set aside on ground of fraud——Application by judgment creditor—Contradictory affidavits.

Defendant, being indebted to plaintiff, and also to M., gave plaintiff a confession of judgment for a sum equal to both debts, on which judgment was signed. An application by B., a judgment creditor of defendant, to set aside the judgment on the ground that M.'s debt had been fraudulently included in the confession, was refused, because the applicant had not established the fraud.

Held, by Palmer, King and Fraser, JJ., (Wetmore, J., dissenting), that the court was bound to determine the question of fraud.

Quære, whether a judgment creditor could object that M.'s debt was improperly included in the confession—the amount being due to M. *Hickson* v. *Lobes*, vol. 24, 338.

5—Judgment by confession—Future Advances—Intention—Right of Creditor.

A., being indebted to B. in the sum of $395, gave him a confession of judgment for $1,000. B. afterwards made further advances, amounting in the whole to $996, and signed judgment for $1,000, and issued execution for that sum. A. then applied to set aside the judgment and execution, alleging in his affidavit that the confession was only intended as a security for his then existing indebtedness to B. This was denied by B.

Held, per Palmer, King and Fraser, JJ., that the judgment should stand for the amount advanced.

Per Wetmore, J., that an issue should be directed to try fact. *Muirhead* v. *Lobes*, vol. 24, 360. See Deed 2.

Refusal of court to reconsider its judgment *Ex parte Abel*, vol. 19, 2.

—Signed against casual ejector—Set aside for irregularity. See Ejectment 2.

—Of non-suit—There cannot be, and also judgment for plaintiff in some of the issues. See Insurance 3.

—Where judge sets aside, and allows defendant to come in on terms, is not a decision upon a point of law. See Appeal 3.

—A motion in arrest of—Cannot be argued until after the verdict is entered. See Assessment 3.

—When entered up for more than is due from the defendant to the plaintiff, the court will, on the application of a subsequent judgment creditor, reduce. See Execution 1.

—Final—When more than a year has elapsed since the signing of interlocutory judgment—Terms—Notice of plaintiff's intention to proceed. See Practice 9.

—Motion to set aside—Power of court to reduce. See Practice 10.

—Signed, while a summons for a new trial not disposed of. See New Trial 12.

—Set-off of judgments. See Set-off 1.

—Unnecessary delay in signing where defendant had entered special bail and been rendered—Discharge from custody. See Discharge 1.

—Exemplification of—When evidence in suit. See Sheriff 2.

—In former action—When a bar to subsequent suit. See Former Recovery 1.

—Setting aside—For want of notice of motion of cost. See Costs 21.

—Pendency of suit—When will not affect application to set aside judgment. See Deed 2.

—Fraudulent judgment—Failure of consideration. See Deed 2-3-4.

JUDGMENT BY DEFAULT.

Offer to suffer—By one of several defendants—In an action of trespass—Effect of. See Costs 18.

—In an action for trespass to land in Supreme Court—Where defendant filed offer and consent to suffer judgment for $8—Costs. See Costs 20.

JUDGMENT CREDITORS.

Transfer of property—Consideration—Account between debtor and claimant—Evidence of date of transfer. See Evidence 18.

—Lien of a judgment creditor of a mortgagor. See Mortgage 2.

JUDGMENT DOCKET.

Date of filing—Whether necessary to contain. See Practice 9.

Judgment, offer to suffer. See County Court 2.

Judicial—And ministerial acts.

—When *certiorari* will lie. See *Certiorari* 5.

—Warrant to sell land—Whether judicial or not. See Assessment 8.

—**Jurat**—When affidavit made by a marksman. See Affidavit 5.

JURISDICTION.

—Court of Equity—Objection to—How taken. See *Cassie* v. *Cassie*, vol. 22, 76.

—Court not legally constituted—Review of judgment. See Review 5.

—Of Court of Equity—Where parties are residents of foreign country, but subject matter of suit is in this province. See *Fraske* v. *McGrath*, vol. 22, 436.

—Ousting the court of—Arbitration clause in marine insurance policy. See Insurance 11.

—Of county court judge to try cause under "The Seamen's Act, 1873." See Ship 1.

—Where plaintiff's claim in an action in a parish court exceeds the amount over which the court has jurisdiction—Abandoning the excess upon the particulars filed. See *Certiorari* 8.

—Of court—Rule *nisi*—Service on party residing outside of province. See Practice 17.

—Of judge to try a cause at a circuit court to which he has not been assigned. See Judge 1.

—Police magistrate of town of Woodstock—Offences against Canada Temperance Act, 1878, committed outside the town. See Canada Temperance Act, 1878, 11.

—Where none to try cause, may, nevertheless, give judgment for costs. See County Court 4.

—Justice of peace—Title to land—Easement—Jurisdiction. See Title to Land.

—Writ and particulars showing jurisdiction—Plaintiff's statement showing damage exceeding jurisdiction of county court. See County Court 6.

—Justice of peace—Relationship. See Justice of Peace 3.

JURORS.—(See Challenge.)

In debt to defendant, who obtained verdict—Whether ground for new trial. See Will 10.

Ju[illegible] alien—Objection, when to be taken.

It is not a ground for new trial that one of the jurors was disqualified, being an alien. The objection should be taken by challenge. *Stephenson v. Fraser*, vol. 24, 482.

Subject to challenge, having served not ground for new trial. See Challenge.

JURY.

View—When should be allowed—Interference by parties to suit—Misconduct of jury—Affidavit of juror.

[illegible] defendant in an action of trespass [illegible] *re clausum fregit*, while the jury were [illegible]wing the *locus in quo*, conversed and otherwise interfered with them, and provided refreshments for them at his house.

Held, a good ground for setting aside a verdict, though no protest was made till after verdict, and plaintiff himself had been guilty of improperly interfering with the jury during the view.

Held, *per* Weldon, J., that it was improper to allow a view after the judge had charged the jury.

Per Fisher and Wetmore, JJ., that the view was properly allowed. *Anderson v. Mowatt*, vol. 20, 255.

—Cause tried without, in county court cannot have a new trial in that court. See Husband and Wife 2.

—Separation of during trial—Sufficient to avoid verdict. See Criminal Law 4.

—Acting under influence of undue motives—Excessive damages. See Trespass 11.

—Discharge of. See Practice 15.

—When not unanimous in answering special questions left—Whether verdict can be entered within two hours. See Verdict 1.

JURY FEES.

Payment of—Time.

Held, *per* Allen, C.J., and Duff, J., (Wetmore, J., dissenting), that the 40th section of the Consol. Stat., cap. 45, requiring payment of a jury fee, is only directory as to the time of payment, and does not prohibit the payment at a later period of the trial than the opening of the court on each day.

Held, also *per* Allen, C.J., and Wetmore and Duff, JJ., that where a trial began on the 20th and plaintiff's case continued during that day and part of the 21st, when the defence was gone into and occupied remainder of that day and principal part of 22nd, plaintiff then beginning his rebutting case, the latter was not bound to pay for that day.

Held, *per* Weldon, J., that the payment of the fee is a question peculiarly for the judge to deal with at the trial. *Briggs v. McBride*, vol. 19, 202.

JUSTICE OF THE PEACE.

1—Return of conviction—Should be to County Court—Action to recover penalty for not returning—In what court to be brought—Notice of action—Act, 32 and 33 Vic. cap. 31, sec. 78—Not ultra vires.

The 78th section of the Statutes of Canada, 32 & 33 Vic. cap. 31, which declares that in case the justice of the peace before whom any conviction takes place neglects or refuses to make a return of such conviction, as required by the 76th section of the Act, he shall forfeit and pay the sum of $80, with costs of suit, to be recovered by any person suing for the same by action of debt in any court of record in the province in which such return ought to have been made, is not *ultra vires*, and such penalty may be recovered in the County Court, this section over-riding the provision in the Con. Stat., cap. 51, sec. 7, that the County Courts shall not have jurisdiction over actions against justices of the peace.

Held, also, that in this province convictions should be returned to the County Court of the county in which they are made.

No notice of action is necessary before suing a justice for recovery of the penalty provided by the 78th section for not making such return. *Ward* v. *Reed*, vol. 22, 279.

2—Selling spirituous liquors on Sunday—Licensed tavern-keeper—Necessity of proof of being—Admissions of defendant—Purchaser of liquor, competent witness to prove selling.

In proceedings for the recovery of a penalty for selling liquors on Sunday contrary to the provisions of 38 Vic. cap. 71, it must be made to appear that the defendant is a licensed tavern-keeper; and where the defendant pleaded not guilty, but admitted that he was a licensed tavern-keeper, and the only other evidence was that of a witness who stated that he knew where defendant's licensed tavern was, it was

Held, that this was sufficient evidence of the fact—persons purchasing liquor are competent witnesses to prove the selling. *Ex parte Birmingham*, vol. 18, 504.

3—Disqualification from interest—Relationship.

To disqualify a justice from acting in a prosecution before him he should have either a pecuniary or such other substantial interest in the result as to make it likely that he would be biased in favor of one of the parties.

It is not a ground of disqualification that the justice and the counsel who conducted the prosecution are partners in business as attorneys, provided they have no joint interest in the fees earned by the counsel on the prosecution, or in any fees payable to the justice on the trial of the information. Neither is it any disqualification that the justice was appointed and paid by the town council at whose instance the complaint was made and the prosecution carried on—his salary being a fixed sum, not dependent on the amount of fines collected. *Regina* v. *Grimmer*, vol. 25, 424.

—Opposing discharge from prison of person illegally arrested under warrant. See False Imprisonment 1.

—When notice of action against, for false imprisonment contains two grounds of action, proof of either will be sufficient, if there be a count in the declaration to which such proof will apply. See False Imprisonment 6.

—Action against for false imprisonment—Where warrant put in evidence by plaintiff—Necessity of defendant proving conviction—Whether recitals in warrant sufficient—Whether question for jury. See False Imprisonment 2.

—*Nisi prius* record sufficient proof of the commencement of the action against. See Practice 8.

—Information under The Canada Temperance Act—Whether must be before two justices. See Canada Temperance Act 7.

—The local government of this province has power to appoint justices of the peace. *Ex parte Williamson*, vol. 24, 64.

—Incapacity to hear cause—Other justices called in jurisdiction—Right to issue summons—Absence. See Canada Temperance Act, 19.

—Title to land—Jurisdiction. See Title to Land.

JUSTICES' COURT.

Whether filing of particulars is the commencement of action.

In a suit brought in a justice's court, the filing of the particulars of the plaintiff's claim with the justice is not the commencement of the action. *McPherson v. McKinnon*, vol. 19, 3.

Costs of review—When not in discretion of judge—Judgment "wholly reversed." See Damages 2.

JUSTIFICATION.

Plea of—In an action for false imprisonment, under an attachment for non-payment of costs on review from justice's court, did not set forth suit in justice's court, nor the making of the proper affidavit to give the judge jurisdiction—Bad on demurrer. See False Imprisonment 5.

—Plea of—In trespass. See Trespass 1.

Writ of—Attachment gives on its face sufficient justification to officer. See Affidavit 2.

—Conviction good on its face, justices having jurisdiction over subject matter. See Canada Temperance Act 19.

LAND DAMAGES.

1—Assessment for, when land taken for railway purposes.

An assessment of damages against a railway company under the Act, 40 Vic. cap. 17, for land taken by the company for railway purposes, was sought to be quashed on the grounds, 1st, that no demand was made on the company before warrant issued; 2nd, that the assessment was not laid before the company before the annual meeting, but

Held, by Allen, C.J., and Duff and Palmer, JJ., that it was sufficient that the persons, whose land was taken, and the company had not agreed in order to authorise issue of warrant; also, that the failure to lay the assessment before the company before the annual meeting could not affect the assessment. *Ex parte, The Albert Railway Co.*, vol. 19, 48.

LANDLORD AND TENANT.

1—Evidence of continuing tenancy—Notice to quit.

In an action of ejectment no title to the land was proved in the lessor of the plaintiff, but it appeared on the trial that in April, 1845, L. H., the defendant's father went into possession of the land under a lease for three years at a rent of £5 per annum, the lease purporting to be made by the lessor of the plaintiff and T. by one S., their attorney. L. H. occupied the land from the time of his entry under above lease until his death, about fifteen years afterwards; and after his death his family, of whom the defendant was one, continued to occupy it. There was no evidence of any payment of rent by any person, nor of any communication or dealings between L. H. and the lessor of plaintiff and T. or S., after the expiration of the lease until April, 1864, when the defendant and his brother J. H. signed a letter written by him and addressed to S. "for Messrs. T. and H. (the lessors or plaintiff) offering to buy the land in question, which was described as then occupied by L. H., for the sum of £237 payable in instalments in four years, and the letter concluded as follows: "In the meantime we agree to become answerable for the payment of the rent at the rate of £5 per year from the 1st May next, in the event of the offer not being accepted by the owners of the estate." It did not appear whether this letter had been communicated by S. to Messrs. T. and H. except so far as might be inferred from its production on the trial by plaintiff's counsel; neither did it appear whether the year's rent mentioned in the letter had been paid. S. died in May, 1866, and the extent of his authority to act for T. and H. was not shewn. Defendant and several others of the children of L. H. continued in possession of the land without any recognition of right in T. and H. except the letter of 1864. No notice to quit or demand of possession was proved before bringing this action.

Held, that there was evidence to be left to the jury of a continuing tenancy in L. H. after the expiration of the lease which could not be put an end to without a notice to quit. *Heathcote* v. *Hughes*, vol. 19, 308.

2—Lease of an unfurnished house—No implied contract that it is tenantable—Rent payable in advance—Action for use and occupation—Evidence, letter written by party seeking to put in.

On the demise of an unfurnished house there is no implied contract that the premises are in a tenantable condition.

Where, on the demise of premises, the rent is made payable in advance, an action for use and occupation will lie as in other cases after the term is up. *Gilles* v. *Morrison*, vol. 22, 207.

3—Privilege from distress—Logs delivered to mill owner to be sawn into deals—Mill owner jointly interested in the logs—Pleadings—Evidence of persons comprising company.

Logs delivered to a mill owner in the way of his trade to be sawn into deals, for remuneration, are privileged from distress for rent.

Held, by Allen C.J., Weldon and King, JJ., that such privilege is destroyed if the tenant is a joint owner with other persons of the logs; by Palmer, J., that the tenant's undivided interest can be distrained upon in such case.

When in replevin the defendant waived the taking as a distress for rent due from R. for a saw mill, to which the defendant pleaded that R. was a manufacturer of deals and carried on that business in the mill; that before the distress the P. Lumber Company delivered logs to R. to be manufactured into deals at the mill, and to be delivered to them or to any person to whom they might sell; that the lumber company sold the deals to the plaintiff, and that a reasonable time to remove them had not elapsed before the distress. Replication—that by agreement between the P. Lumber Company and R. they were to purchase logs which were to be sawn by R. at the mill on joint account, and that he was to be jointly interested with the company in the deals so sawn; that the deals replevied were sawn from logs so purchased, and that R. was a joint owner with the company of the said deals.

Held, that this sufficiently shewed a joint ownership of the deals between the plaintiff and R.

Quære, whether an allegation that R. was jointly interested with other persons in the deals or that he was jointly interested in the profits to arise from the manufacture and sale of the deals, was sufficient to shew that he was a joint owner.

Plaintiff claimed the logs from which the deals in question were cut, through the P. Lumber Company;

Held, that the declarations of members of that company made at the time of a purchase of the logs by them for the company were admissible to shew who were the persons composing the company. *Guy* v. *Rankin*, vol. 23, 49.

4—Agreement for a lease—Demise—Right to distrain.

Plaintiff being in possession of land belonging to the defendant, and negotiating for a lease, signed a memorandum, which, after describing the property, stated as follows—"twenty-five years $50 a year, commencing from 1st September, 1880." The plaintiff remained in possession more than a year after this; but the parties having disputed about the terms of the lease, it was not executed and no rent was paid.

Held, that the agreement amounted to an actual demise at a fixed rent; and that the defendant could distrain. *Buckley, et al.*, appellant, v. *Russell*, respondent, vol. 24, 305.

5—Landlord and tenant—Consol. Stat., cap. 83, sec. 8-11—Seizure of tenant's goods under execution—Landlord's claim for rent—Notice to sheriff—Evidence of value of goods seized.

In an action against a sheriff for selling goods under execution without paying a year's rent to the judgment debtor's landlord, evidence that the value of the goods seized exceeded the amount of the rent due is sufficient, in the absence of evidence by the defendant of the amount which the goods realized on sale. *Sheriff* v. *Vye*, vol. 24, 572.

6—Distress—Breaking outer door of building—Distress after sunset—Irregularity.

Breaking open a tenant's building or house in order to distrain for rent, renders the distress illegal and not merely irregular.

A distress made after sunset is illegal. Where a distress is illegal in its inception, trespass lies, and sec. 7, of cap. 83, Con. Stat., respecting "irregularity" in distraining is not applicable. *Myers* v. *Smith* (4 Allen 207), not followed. *Russell*, appellant, v. *Buckley*, respondent, vol. 25, 264.

7—Agreement that landlord might occupy premises for a certain time to make improvements—Eviction—Evidence of.

Plaintiff demised a building to S. for a term of years—the lease containing a provision that the plaintiff might enter and occupy the building up to a certain day, in order to make repairs and improvements, and that he should not enter after that day without the consent of S. The repairs not having been completed within the time fixed, the plaintiff continued to occupy—claiming the right to do so—and to make repairs without the consent of S., who objected that he was deprived of the possession of the property, and notified the plaintiff that he should claim damages therefor.

Held, that this was evidence of an eviction, and was not a mere trespass upon S.

Where there has been an intentional interference by the landlord with the tenant's beneficial enjoyment of the demised premises so as to prevent him from occupying any part of them for any considerable time, this amounts to an eviction, and operates as a suspension of the rent. *Ferguson* v. *Troop*, vol. 25, 440.

—Summary ejectment by landlord. See Summary Ejectment.

Lands—Agreement for sale of—Mistake in description—Specific performance. See Agreement 6.

Land owners—Adjoining—Line agreed upon. See Possession 1.

Larceny — Unstamped promissory note — Whether "valuable security." See Criminal Law 3.

Lease—Entire rent reserved—Consideration illegal in part. See Railway Company 1.

—When assignee may terminate. See Insolvent Act of 1875.

—An agreement for a conditional sale of chattels under a lease, not bill of sale. See Contract 6.

—Of unfurnished house—No implied contract that it is tenantable. See Landlord and Tenant 9.

—Right of widow to lease where income and profits of estate devised to her during widowhood. See Will 9.

—Agreement that landlord might occupy premises to make improvements. See Landlord and Tenant 7.

Letter—Evidence—Written by party—Seeking to put in. See Evidence 9.

Leave—Not reserved at trial to move for nonsuit. See Amendment 2.

Leave and license—Bidding at sheriff's sale—After having forbidden sale, not evidence of. See Sheriff's Sale 1.

Legacy—Payment of. See Will 3.

Library fees—Whether each member of a firm of attorneys must pay. See Attorneys 4.

License—Business—Power of city of St. John to compel commercial travellers to pay for. See Business License 1.

—Coachman in Portland. See Hackney Coaches 1.

LIEN.

Timber driver—Where entitled to take charge of timber drive. Con. Stat. cap. 109.

In order to give a timber driver a lien on timber for services performed under the Con. Stat. cap. 109; it is necessary that the timber should be within the limits of the parish for which he was appointed, at the time he first takes charge of it. *Sinclair* v. *Holland*, vol. 24, 529.

—Persons entitled to hold goods for refusal to deliver until other charges were paid—Waiver. See Trover 3.

—Not applicable as plea in trover. See Pleading 1.

—Of Judgment creditor of a mortgagor. See Mortgage 2.

Life insurance—There being no binding contract—An acknowledgment in the policy that the advance premium had been paid amounts to nothing. See Insurance 1.

Life Estate—Reservation of, in land conveyed by deed—Whether good. See Conveyance 1.

Lights—Carrying as required by 31 Vic. cap. 58—Onus of proof. See Collision 1.

LIMITATIONS.

1—Statute of—Abatement for matter of form—Section 13 of cap. 85, Consol. Stat.

An action was begun in a justice's court by the title of "the estate of the late R. K." against the defendant, and a nonsuit was granted because the name of the executrix was not stated in the summons.

Held, that the suit abated for a matter of form, and prevented the plaintiff's claim being barred by the statute of limitations under sec. 13, of cap. 85, Consol. Stat. *Kerr* v. *Squires*, vol. 22, 448.

2—Statute of—Tenant by curtesy—Right of entry in heir—When it accrues.

A son has no right of entry in land of which his mother died seized, during the life time of his father, who has the right to possession as tenant by the curtesy, and the statute of limitations will not run against him until his father's death. *Doe dem Budreau v. Budreau*, vol. 22, 553.

3—Statute of—Mortgage—Extinguishment of right—Recovery of mortgage in ejectment by default and obtaining possession after right extinguished—Effect of.

In ejectment, it appeared that the land in question had belonged to defendant's grandfather, who mortgaged it to one H., and afterwards remained in possession for twenty years without paying rent or interest, or making any written acknowledgment of H.'s right, and died in possession leaving eleven children. After his death, H. recovered in ejectment against two of the children and heirs and took possession.

Held, 1. That H.'s right under the mortgage was extinguished by the lapse of the twenty years.

2. That the previous recovery in ejectment, neither displaced the title so acquired by the mortgagor, nor estopped his heirs from setting up their rights; such judgment being at most *prima facie* evidence of title in H. which could be disproved. *Doe dem Hazen v. Laskey*, vol. 23, 481.

4—Statute of.

The plaintiff advanced money to his father at different times between the years 1860 and 1867, on a promise by the father to devise the plaintiff a farm.

The father died, but did not devise the farm as agreed.

Held, per Fisher and Wetmore, JJ., in an action to recover the money to which the statute of limitations was pleaded, that the plaintiff could only recover the money advanced within six years before the commencement of the action.

Per Weldon, J., that, as by the Probate Act the plaintiff had a year after the testator's death to file his account against the estate, he could recover for the money advanced within six years preceding his father's death. *Prior v. Wilmot, et al.*, executors, vol. 19, 520.

5—Payment by one joint maker of a note.

Payment of interest for several years on a joint and several note, by one maker, will not prevent the statute from operating in favor of the other makers. *Price v. Whiting*, vol. 19, 620.

—Statute of—In first action, part of claim barred by—Action for same disallowed alleging special agreement *res adjudicata*. See Former Recovery 2.

—Acts of possession of unreclaimed land—Sufficiency of. See Possession 2.

—Limitation of actions—Partition by agreement of land owned by tenants in common. See Adverse Possession 1.

—Of time within which to bring action under insurance policy. See Insurance 9.

—Covenant in mortgage deed—Payment by co-obligor, cap. 81, sec. 40, and cap. 85, sec. 126, Con. Stat., N. B.—Liability of personal representatives and heirs and devisees. See Addenda 27.

LIMIT BOND.

1—Action on, order of commissioner for debtor's discharge—What it should set out.

In an action on a limit bond the defendant put in evidence an order of a commissioner granted under the Consol. Stat., cap. 38, sec. 15, discharging the principal defendant from the limits.

Held, that the order was bad in not setting forth the preliminary circumstances which were necessary to justify the commissioner in making it, and that the general statement that the debtor "had in all respects conformed himself to the provisions of the chapter" was insufficient. *Cowell*, assignee v. *Treze*, vol. 19, 537.

Line — Adjoining properties. See Acquiescence 1.

Liquor Licenses—Expiration of. See Canada Temperance Act 5.

Liquor License Act, 1883 — Sale of liquors without license in counties where the Canada Temperance Act, 1878, is in force—Prosecutions for—Procedure. See Canada Temperance Act 17.

Liquor License Act, 1883 — Seizure of liquors under sec. 82 of that Act—Dismissal of complaint for unlawfully keeping liquor for sale—Right of defendant to have liquors restored to him—Replevin.

Held, that, upon dismissal of complaint, the inspector's right to retain possession of the liquor ceased, and plaintiff was entitled to have it restored to him without an order from the magistrate. See *Tennant v. Bulyea*, vol. 24, 248.

Locus in quo—Insufficient description of — In an action of trespass — Not ground of demurrer. See Trespass 3.

Logs—Delivered to mill-owner to be sawn into deals—Privileged from distress. See Landlord and Tenant 3.

Lunatic—Service of summons upon. See Writ, *ex parte McKnight*.

Magistrate—Police of Portland—Jurisdiction of. See Portland Civil Court 1.

—Town of Milltown—Appointment of. See Milltown, Town of, 1.

Maker of note—Liability where payee has been discharged. See Accommodation Note 1.

Malice—Demand of assignment under. See Insolvent Act 1.

MANDAMUS.

1—Where rule for, unnecessary, the officer acting under Act of Parliament which has not been declared invalid.

The local license law of F. having provided that licenses to sell liquor should be granted on the certificate of the Police Magistrate, the Canada Temperance Act of 1878 having passed, the Magistrate refused to grant the certificate on the ground that he had no power under that Act to do so; he told the applicant's attorney that if the Act was declared *ultra vires* he would be willing to grant the certificate at any time. The applicant having obtained a rule *nisi* to quash a conviction thus raising the question of the validity of the Act, also obtained a rule *nisi* for the magistrate to show cause why a mandamus should not issue to compel him to grant the certificate.

Held, that the proceeding was quite unnecessary, and the rule was discharged with costs. *Ex parte*, Grieves, vol. 19, 4.

2—Affidavit on which granted—When objection to, can be taken—Municipality—Mandamus issued to—Who to make return.

When a mandamus has been issued and returned, and a rule *nisi* has been granted to quash the return, it is too late, on showing cause against such rule, to object to the sufficiency of the affidavits on which the mandamus was granted.

Where a mandamus issued directed to the municipality of a county, the return should be made by the municipality under its seal and not by the warden, and it is no excuse to say that there had been no meeting of the municipality. *The Queen v. The Municipality of Charlotte*, vol. 22, 636.

—To compel County Court Judge to certify proceedings—When granted by the court. See Appeal 3.

—To compel City of Fredericton to grant license to sell spirituous liquors. See Spirituous Liquors.

To compel County Court Judge to hear cause on review, defective affidavit. See Affidavit 5.

Mandatory Injunction—To compel secretary of Board of School Trustees to give up property of the corporation. See Injunction 1.

MARRIAGE.

Evidence of—Presumption—Where a marriage ceremony was performed by a Protestant clergyman in Ireland in 1860, between two persons who intended to be married, but who for the purpose of concealment used false names, and they afterwards lived together in Ireland as man and wife for two years, when they came to this province and continued so to live together.

Held, (Palmer J, dissenting), that in the absence of any evidence as to the law of marriage in Ireland, it would be presumed that the marriage there was lawful, although the parties themselves had doubts about its legality, in consequence of their having used false names, and went through another marriage ceremony here in 1865.

Per Palmer, J., that the evidence did not show any intention by the parties to contract a legal marriage in Ireland, nor any belief that they had done so. *In re James Tierney*, vol. 25, 286.

—In foreign country—Adultery—necessity of proving marriage—Law of such country. See Adultery.

—May be proved by a person present at the ceremony—Not necessary to produce certificate of registry. See Slander 6.

MARRIED WOMAN.

1—Separate property—Evidence of.

Where property, apparently in the husband's possession, is claimed to belong to the wife as her separate property, so as to exempt it from seizure under execution against the husband, the evidence of the separate property of the wife ought to be clear and satisfactory, and in order to justify such claims being sustained, there ought to be no reasonable doubt of their correctness.

Per Allen, C.J., and Wetmore, J., who decided that a new trial should be granted, although the jury had found the property to be the separate property of the wife—Weldon and Fisher, JJ., dissenting. *Seery* v. *Temple*, vol. 19, 362.

2—Separate property—Disposal by husband—Substitution of other property—Evidence—Conversation between husband and wife—Trover—Joint conversion.

A cow, the separate property of a married woman, was exchanged by her husband, with her consent, for a heifer. The heifer was afterwards sold, and the husband used the money with the understanding that he was to purchase a cow for his wife at a future time to replace the first cow. The husband afterwards bought a horse, which was exchanged for another, and that was exchanged for a cow, with the consent of the wife.

Held, that this cow was not liable to seizure under an execution against the husband.

The directions of the wife to the husband respecting the several sales and exchanges are evidence. *Ford et al.*, appellants, and Bowser and wife, respondents, vol. 21, 410.

Husband executing trust deed—Releasing debt. See Deed 4.

—Non-abatement of suit by marriage. See County Court 5.

MARKET.

Public—Grant of public market place—Whether authorizes establishment of

market, 11 Vic. 61; 14 Vic. cap. 15; 22 Vic. cap. 8; 30 Vic. cap. 37, considered—Whether York County Council or City Council of Fredericton have control of the Queen's ward market—Imposing tolls or closing market without express authority—Repeal of Acts.

The grant of a piece of land for a public market place authorizes the grantee to establish a market there.

—Control and management of the market under construction of Act, held to lie in city council of the city of Fredericton.

In the absence of express authority to do so, the city council of the city of Fredericton has no power to close the market, or to impose tolls on the sale of articles in the market house; the market, by the grant, being a free market. *Edwards* v. *Burgoyne*, vol. 21, 228.

Marksman—Affidavit made by—*Jurat*. See Affidavit 5.

Marsh-land—When unreclaimed—Acts of possession. See Possession 2.

Master—Of government steam dredge, liable for negligence of his fellow servants. See Negligence 2.

—Of ship—Wages of—How recovered. See Ship 1.

MASTER AND SERVANT.

1—Injury to servant—Death of master—Survival of action—Declaration alleging contract.

A declaration against executors of S. alleged that plaintiff entered into the service of testator as a workman in his mill upon the terms and conditions, amongst others that he (S.) should take proper means and precautions to prevent damage happening to him and not to expose him to unreasonable and unnecessary risk or danger; that while plaintiff was in such employ upon said terms, he was employed by S. to work in said mill, in a place where it was dangerous, etc., after dark, which was unknown to plaintiff, and in consequence thereof was struck by a piece of timber and his leg broken, etc. It being objected on demurrer that this being an action of tort, did not survive against the representatives of deceased.

Held, by Wetmore and Duff, JJ., (Weldon J., dissenting), that as the declaration alleged in terms a contract and breach of it, it shewed a cause of action which survived against the defendants. *Connolly* v. *Skives, et al., Executors, etc.*, vol. 18, 606.

2—Master and servant—Employment of surgeon by an agent to attend a servant of his principal—Admission of counsel—How far client bound by.

Defendant residing in England, and having a general agent in this province, carried on a milling business here, which was managed by A., there being also a bookkeeper, B., at the mill. A workman in the defendant's employ at the mill having been injured, A. and B. employed the plaintiff, a surgeon, to attend him.

Held, *per* Allen, C.J., Fraser and Tuck, JJ., (Wetmore, J., dissenting), 1. That such engagement was beyond the scope of their duties as agents, and that the defendant was not bound by it.

2. That an admission made by the defendant's counsel in an interlocutory proceeding, that A. and B. had employed the plaintiff, was not an admission that they had any authority to bind the defendant. *Guy, et al*, Appellants, and *Brady*, Respondents, vol. 24, 563.

Negligence—Injury to servant—Fellow servant's sub-contractor. See Negligence 5.

MEDIXNIKIKS BOOM COMPANY.

Duties of boom master—Who liable for services in sorting lumber—Construction of Acts, 8 Vic. cap. 49, and 27 Vic. cap. 61.

Held, 1. That the Act, 27 Vic. cap. 61, imposed no liability on the owners of lumber passing through the booms, except to furnish men to assist in sorting the lumber in the boom and passing it through to the river St. John.

2. That the boom-master could not maintain an action against an owner of such lumber for boomage under sec. 6, of the Act, 8 Vic. cap. 49; but that his remedy was against the company.

Semble, that the toll imposed for boomage by sec. 6 of the Act of incorporation, applies only to lumber intended for the use of the mills. *Medixnikiks Boom Co.*, Appellants, and *Dalton*, Respondent, vol. 25, 28.

Mill-owner—Logs delivered to be sawn into deals—Privileged from distress. See Landlord and Tenant 3.

Mill privilege—Right for flowage. See Easement 2.

MILLTOWN.

1—Town of—Police magistrate—Appointment of—Continuance in office.

The Act incorporating the town of Milltown authorized the town council at the first meeting after every annual election, or at any subsequent meeting, to appoint a justice of the peace, to act as police magistrate, or to recommend any other person to the government to be appointed. The government had, on the recommendation of the council, appointed G., who was not a justice of the peace, to be police magistrate, and the following year after the annual election of councillors, the council appointed G. for another year.

Held, (Weldon, J., dissenting), that whether the appointment by the town council was valid or not, G.'s appointment by the government would continue in force until a new appointment was legally made. *Ex parte Coughlin*, vol. 24, 308.

—Whether a "city" or county within meaning of Canada Temperance Act. See Canada Temperance Act 10.

Minors—Warrant against estate of non-resident, under assessment without order of county court judge is bad. See *Certiorari* 5.

Misappropriation—Of money by one partner of firm of attorneys—Liability of co-partner. See Attorneys 6.

Misconduct—Neglect to attend a trial when subpœnaed. See Attorney 3.

Misdirection — Slander — New trial. See Slander 5.

—As to passing of property. See Sale 5.

—Infringement of patent. See Patent.

Misfeasance — Liability of railway conductor for. See Railway Conductor 1.

Misjoinder—Of counts in indictment. See Criminal Law 5.

Misnomer—Trial postponed in order to allow name of defendant to be changed. See Practice 2.

Misrepresentation—Policy of insurance —Must be material. See Insurance 5.

Moncton—Town of—Civil court—Review from—Affidavit for—Before whom to be sworn. See Review 1.

MONEY HAD AND RECEIVED.

Where plaintiff was suspected of having taken money from a bank, and it was afterwards proved, and the defendant, a police officer, represented to plaintiff's wife, that her husband was in prison for the taking, and she paid over a sum of money to the defendant, plaintiff can recover on count for money had and received, there being no evidence that the money so paid over was the specific money taken from the bank. See False Imprisonment 4, *Ellis* v. *Power*, vol. 20, 40.

When action may lie for. See Contract 16.

—Proceeds of sale. See Bankruptcy 2.

—Action for—Waiver of tort. See Conversion 1.

—Evidence of admission to auditors of correctness of entries showing balance against official where cash book kept by himself. See Evidence 11.

—Recovery of advances made in part payment of goods ordered to be manufactured. See Contract 16.

Money lent—Barred by statute of limitations. See Limitations, Statute of, 4.

Money paid—Illegal contract. See Contract 8.

MORTGAGE.

1—Alleged payment—Where mortgagor and mortgagee dead — Evidence — Onus of proof.

In a suit brought for the foreclosure and sale of mortgaged premises, it appeared that both the mortgagor and mortgagee were dead and that the mortgagor and mortgagee's books were destroyed. A reference was made to a barrister to take accounts of the payments made on the mortgage, and although there was some slight evidence of an additional payment beyond the amount credited by the plaintiff, the barrister disallowed it.

Held, that the burthen was on the defendant to discharge themselves from their liability on the mortgage, and that the barrister properly disallowed the defendant's claim, as the evidence of payment was entirely insufficient, particularly after the mortgagee's death. *Colwell* v. *Robinson*, vol. 23, 69.

2—Consolidation of — Registry Act—Judgment creditor—Tender of interest and costs after commencement of foreclosure suit—Amendment of Bill on Appeal.

Plaintiff agreed with D., as agent of the defendants, to lend them $25,000, to be secured by mortgage on two adjoining lots of land. The defendants required the money for the purpose of erecting a warehouse, which was to cover the principal part of both lots. At the time of the agreement the title to one of the lots was in the defendants, and they executed a mortgage to the plaintiff of that lot, to secure the payment of $15,000 and interest. The title to the other lot was in D., who held it as trustee of the defendants, and he, in pursuance of the arrangement, also executed a mortgage of it to the plaintiff for $10,000—the balance of the sum agreed to be loaned—and gave the plaintiff his bond for $10,000 and interest. Immediately after giving the mortgage, D. conveyed to the defendants his equity of redemption in the lot. The interest on both mortgages being in arrear, the plaintiff brought a suit for their foreclosure, after which the defendants tendered the interest due on $15,000 mortgage, and the costs of the suit, and claimed that the mortgage should not be foreclosed.

Held, that as the whole sum secured was the debt of the defendants, the mortgage given by D. was in effect their mortgage, and they could not redeem their own mortgage without also paying the mortgage given by D.

When a mortgage becomes forfeited by non-payment of the interest, and a suit for foreclosure is brought, the suit can only be terminated by payment of the principal, interest and costs, under Con. Stat., cap. 39, sec. 111; and in such a case, a tender of the interest due and costs of the suit is of no avail.

The lien of a judgment creditor of a mortgagor, subsequent to the mortgage, is subject to the pre-existing security of the mortgagee, and can only attach upon any surplus that may remain after the mortgage is satisfied.

In a suit to foreclose two mortgages given to the plaintiff, one by the defendant and the other by D., who afterwards conveyed his equity of redemption to the defendant, it was objected by the answer that the plaintiff could not consolidate the mortgages, because they were given by different persons. Evidence was then received on the part of the plaintiff to shew that the two mortgages were one transaction, and were given to secure a loan to the defendant for whose benefit D. held the property mortgaged by him in trust.

Held, on appeal, that such evidence should not have been received, without amending the bill, and alleging facts to warrant its admission; but that such amendment might be made on hearing the appeal. *Maritime Warehousing and Dock Co.* and *The Maritime Bank of the Dominion of Canada*, appellants, and *Nicholson*, respondent, vol. 21. 170.

3—Foreclosure of mortgage—Staying proceedings—Whether defendant entitled to statement of the amount due before appearance—Con. Stat. cap. 49, secs. 40 & 111.

Where a suit has been commenced for foreclosure of a mortgage, the defendant offering to pay the amount due, is entitled under the Con. Stat. cap. 49, sec. 111, to be furnished with a detailed statement of the amount of principal, interest and costs; and on payment of the amount, to have the suit stayed without entering an appearance.

Where a plaintiff refuses to give such statement, or to produce the bond and mortgage to the judge in equity, he has the right to refer the matter to a barrister to ascertain the amount due. *Smith et al., Exrs., etc., v. Cormier*, vol. 25, 487.

—Statute of Limitations, cap. 84, sec. 1, and cap. 85, secs. 1 & 6 Con. Stat. N. B.—Covenant in mortgage deed—Payment by co-obligor. See Addenda 27.

— Extinguishment of mortgagor's right—Recovery by mortgagee in ejectment by default—Effect of. See Limitations 3.

—Whether right in judgment passes to assignee of mortgage. See Ejectment 2.

—Not a due execution of a trust for sale and conversion. See Will 3.

— Chattels — Mortgage of, not an assignment under condition in fire policy. See Addenda 45.

Mortmain—See British Statutes.

MOTION PAPER.

1—Notice of Motion. A notice under Rule 2, Hilary Term, 6 Wm. IV., that a rule *nisi* would be moved for, is irregular, and the court will not hear the motion though the affidavits have been served, and notice of motion given and the cause entered on the motion paper. *Shelton v. Milliken*, vol. 22, 53.

—Cause directed to be entered on—Stay of proceedings—Whether can give notice of motion for new trial pending stay. See Judge's Order.

—Affidavit used on motion—Application for time to answer. See Practice 20.

Multifariousness—Bill in equity—Demurrer. See Equity. *Franks v. McGrath*.

MUNICIPALITY.

1—Liability of, for debts of sessions—Estoppel—Debentures issued under seal of the general sessions of the peace by Sessions of Albert, under 38 Vic. cap. 85—County estopped from disputing its liability—Con. Stat. cap. 99, sec. 106—Plea alleging conclusions of law, bad.

To an action of debt brought to recover interest on debentures, bearing the seal of the General Session of Albert County, and issued under the Act, 38 Vic. cap. 85, passed "to facilitate the construction of the Petticodiac and Elgin Branch Railway, the defendant corporation pleaded several pleas setting up that certain proceedings required by the Act to be taken before the debentures could be issued, had not been taken. The General Sessions of the County of Albert was not a corporate body, but the Act incorporating that county with others, declared that all debts due by the county or session should be paid by the municipality. Con. Stat. cap. 99, sec. 106. By the 10th section of the Act, 38 Vic. cap. 85, it was enacted that upon the issuing of the debentures, or any part of them, it should be taken and considered that everything required by the Act, in order to the issuing of such debentures, had been done, according to the terms of the Act.

Held, that the defendant corporation was liable on the debentures, that the liability of the sessions devolved upon it; that it could not be allowed to defeat the action by showing the facts alleged in the plea; that the County of Albert was estopped from disputing its liability to pay, and in like manner the defendant corporation, which stood in the place of the county, was estopped also.

A plea stating only conclusions of law, without any facts to support them is bad. *Jones* v. *The Municipality of County of Albert*, vol. 20, 78.

MUNICIPALITY OF ST. JOHN.

1—Court house—Injury to person falling down stairway leading to Court-room owing to want of light—Where fee vested in the Mayor, etc. of the city of St. John, in trust for holding of courts and city and county offices—Where municipality has partial control of building — Whether bound to keep building and approaches safe—Principle governing liability in such case—Circular stairway—Whether want of light is proof of negligence.

The corporation of St. John being the owners in fee of the court house, executed a deed in 1826, by which they declared that they held it (*inter alia*) for the sitting of the courts of justice, and for the public city and county offices, and that it should not be used for any other purposes than those expressed, without the consent of the justices in session of the city and county. The contingent expenses of the court house, such as fuel, light, and the care of the building, were paid by the sessions out of the assessments on the county under the Municipalities Act, 40 Vic. cap. 3, by which all the powers theretofore vested in the sessions to impose rates and do any other things were to be exercised by the municipality; and since that time the meetings of the municipal council have been held in the court house. The rooms appropriated for the sittings of the courts were in the second story of the building, and were reached by a spiral staircase of twenty-four steps. The plaintiff had gone into the court room late in the afternoon, while the court was sitting, to see a person there, and remained till after dark, and in coming down the stairs he fell and was injured. There was no light on the stairs, nor in the hall between the court room and the stairs, though there were brackets for gas jets in both places, and also a gaselier near the foot of the stairs.

Held, by Weldon, Wetmore and King, JJ., in an action against the defendants for negligence in not lighting the stairs, that there was no duty imposed on the defendants by law to light the stairs, and that the plaintiff could not recover against them.

Held, also, *per* Weldon and Wetmore, JJ., that the plaintiff could not recover because the title to the court house was in the corporation of St. John.

Per King, J., that though the plaintiff had a right to be in the court house, he was not there on any business in which the defendants were interested, and they were not bound to protect him against ordinary risks, and that the non-lighting of the stairs was not evidence of negligence.

Per Allen, C.J., and Palmer, J., that it was the duty of the defendants to keep the approach of the court room in a reasonably safe condition for persons attending there, and that as the plaintiff had a right to go there he was entitled to recover for the injury sustained by the defendants, omitting to light the stairs. *Beach v. The Municipality of St. John*, vol. 21, 243.

—Mandamus issued to—Who to make return. See Mandamus 2.

Murder—An indictment for, in short form, prisoner cannot be convicted of assault. See Indictment 1.

Naturalization—Who must sign certificate of. See Aliens 1.

NEGLIGENCE.

1—Of contractor—Liability of employer.

S. contracted to erect a building for W. on his (W.'s) land. W. engaged B. to superintend the erection; his duty being to enforce the conditions of the contract, furnish drawings, etc., make estimates of the amount due, and when the building was completed to issue a certificate, which, if unconditional, would be an acceptance of the contract. W. also reserved the right to alter or modify the plans and specifications and to make any deviation in the construction, detail or execution of the work without avoiding the contract, and in case of unnecessary delay or of the inability of S. to perform the work within a given time, W. might, on giving notice in writing, take possession and carry on the work to completion, charging the same to S. The building to be at the risk of S. until accepted by W.

Held, by Weldon, J., that by the terms of the contract, W. retained control over the work, and was liable for an injury to the plaintiff's building which was the result of S.'s improper and careless execution of the contract.

Per Wetmore, J., that W. was not by the terms of the contract liable for the injury, and if it was sought to make him liable on the ground that he interfered and controlled S. in the execution of the work, that was a question for the jury. *McMillan v. Walker*, vol. 21, 31.

Appeal to Supreme Court of Canada dismissed. See Addenda No. 8.

2—Placing anchor of dredge in channel of public harbor—Master must place buoys or signals—When dredge the property of the Crown and being used in improving navigation—Liability of master for acts of fellow servants of the Crown.

By the first count of the declaration, it was alleged that the master of a government dredge placed the anchor of the dredge in the main channel of a public harbor, with the fluke of the anchor sticking up and so left it for an unreasonable length of time without placing any proper buoy or signal to mark the place of the anchor, and without taking any proper means to guard against accidents to vessels navigating the harbor, and that the plaintiff's mariners having occasion to pass out of the said harbor with the plaintiff's vessel, without any default on their part, ran upon the anchor and injured the vessel.

Held, that the count described a good cause of action, that the master of the dredge should have placed a buoy to the anchor to warn vessels navigating the harbor.

By the third count it was alleged that the master of a dredge placed the anchor of the dredge in a part of the channel of a public harbor usually navigated by vessels in a dangerous and improper position, and permitted the same to remain in such dangerous and improper position and that the plaintiff's vessel in passing out of the said harbor in charge of their mariners, without any knowledge on the part of the latter of the improper and dangerous position of the anchor, and without any default on their part, ran on the anchor and was injured, etc.

Held, that the count disclosed a good cause of action. By the plea the defendant, the master of the dredge, alleged that the dredge was the property of Her Majesty, and was being used in dredging out and improving a public harbor, that for this purpose, dredging, it was necessary to anchor it, and that he directed A. M. and others to put the anchor out and that they placed it in the manner alleged in declaration, without any knowledge on his part that it was carelessly and improperly put out, and that A. M. and the others were not employed by him but were his fellow servants in the employ of Her Majesty.

Held, that the plea did not afford an answer to the declaration, that the master of the dredge having directed the men to put out the anchor in a place where it might be dangerous to navigation, could not excuse himself by saying the men were his fellow servants in Her Majesty's employ, and that he did not know it was negligently or improperly placed there. *Lunt* v. *Lloyd*, vol. 21, 202.

3—Where plaintiff offers no evidence to connect defendant with act of negligence—Effect of such evidence on cross-examination—How far plaintiff entitled to benefit of.

Where in an action for negligence the plaintiff offered no evidence to connect one of several defendants with the negligent act complained of, and the only evidence of such connection, and that very slight, was elicited from the defendant himself in cross-examination.

Held, that there should be a new trial unless the plaintiff consented that a verdict should be entered for such defendant. *Keenan* v. *The Trustees of Leinster Baptist Church*, vol. 21, 211.

4—Ferry boat—Injury to passenger—Contributory negligence—Acts shewing invitation to land.

Plaintiff was a passenger in defendant's steam ferry boat plying across the harbor of St. John. A movable chain was placed across the end of the boat to prevent passengers and teams from going beyond it while the boat was in motion. When the boat arrived at the wharf or landing place it stopped and the passengers began to go on shore though the boat had not been moored to the wharf, but a gangway, or platform, on which teams were accustomed to pass to and from the boat, was in the course of being placed in its position for that purpose. The plaintiff was a stranger, and while following the other passengers, and while in the act of stepping from the boat to the wharf in the dark—the guard chain having been let down—fell into an open space between the end of the boat and the wharf, and was injured.

Held, *Per* Palmer, King, and Fraser, JJ., (Weldon, J., dissenting), that the taking down the guard chain, and putting out the gangway, were facts from which it might be inferred that the defendants had led the plaintiff to believe that the trip of the boat had ended, and that he might safely go ashore; and, therefore, that there was evidence of negligence to leave to the jury. *McDonald* v. *Mayor, etc., of St. John*, vol. 24, 370. See same case, Railway Company No. 6, vol. 25, 318.

5—Master and servant—Injury to servant of sub-contractor—Negligence by servant of principal contractor—Fellow servants—Contributory negligence.

Defendants having agreed with the town of W. to construct waterworks for the town, sub-let to P. the digging of the trenches for the water pipes and re-filling them after the pipes were laid. P. employed the plaintiff in that work, part of his duty being to see that the earth was clear from the end of each pipe so that the joints could be caulked, and while he was in the trench attending to his duty, an iron pipe, which was being put into the trench by the defendants' servants, fell upon him and injured him. The usual mode of lowering the pipes into the trench was by means of ropes at each end, whereby the pipes were let down gradually; but on this occasion only one rope was used, the other end of the pipe being pried in with a handspike, in consequence of which it fell into the trench suddenly and struck the plaintiff. The men in charge of the pipe knew, or ought to have known, that the workmen were in the trench at the time.

Held, 1. That the plaintiff, having been employed and paid by P., was his servant, and not the fellow-servant of the men who caused the injury; 2. That there was negligence on the part of the defendants' servants in the manner of putting the pipe into the trench; 3. That there was no evidence of contributory negligence on the part of the plaintiff, and that he was entitled to recover. *Delong* v. *Burrell-Johnson County Iron Co.*, vol. 25, 140.

Railway Company—Liability to fence. See Railway Company 2.

—Contributory negligence. See Railway Company 5.

—Negligence—Injury to passengers while landing from ferry owned by another company. See Railway Company 6.

Railway conductor—Accident to passenger—Right of action—Contributory negligence. See Railway Conductor 1.

Negligence—Want of light at staircase in public building. See Municipality of St. John 1.

—Loss of goods—Whether necessary to give affirmative evidence of negligence in action against carriers. See Carrier 2.

—Loss of sense—Evidence of expert. See Evidence 19.

—Question for jury. See Evidence 11.

Newcastle civil court—Commissioner of—Jurisdiction to try offences against the Canada Temperance Act. See Canada Temperance Act 13.

NEW TRIAL.

1—Agreement to leave all matters to jury—Binding effect of—No cause of action shewn.

Where both parties on the trial of a cause, by their counsel agreed that the claims which they were putting forward on both sides should all be left to the jury without any objection being made as to the legal liability upon such claims, and the jury found for plaintiff;

Held, that defendant could not afterward move for a new trial on the ground that plaintiff failed to show any cause of action. *Foxwell* v. *Smith*, vol. 18, 431.

2—Trespass — Joint and several—Election and abandonment — Damages not plainly appearing to be confined to one act of trespass—Evidence of separate trespass —Effect of time of election—Judges discretion.

In an action of trespass, *qu. cl. fr.*, against several defendants, a joint act of trespass was proved against C. and his co-defendants, by C. entering on the land with the other defendants and making a survey and running the lines, after which several distinct trespasses were committed by the other defendants, in which, however, C. took no part. Plaintiff being required to elect, stated that he would go for the trespass of entering on the land and running the lines and the consequence which would follow therefrom; and in addressing the jury he urged that defendant C. was liable for the necessary consequences of his survey, and that plaintiff's land had been damaged to the extent of £300.

The jury found a verdict for plaintiff for $250. On motion for a new trial, the court granted the application, not being satisfied that the jury had confined the damages to the one act of entering on the land and running the lines, or that they had not taken into consideration the subsequent acts of the other defendants cutting down the wood, etc., imposing, however, on defendant terms of payment of costs.

Held, also, that plaintiff by giving evidence of separate trespasses by some or one of the defendants did not thereby abandon the joint trespass previously proved against all.

It must be in the judges discretion whether he will require plaintiff's counsel to elect at close of his case or at a later period of the trial. *Gagson* v. *Chapman, et al*, vol. 18, 440.

3—Opinion expressed by judge—Question left to jury.

In an action where the question being tried is the competency of the testatrix to make a will, it is no misdirection for the judge to state as his opinion that the party contesting the will has failed to establish that the testatrix was subject to delusions, provided the evidence relied on as showing delusions, and the question of sanity or insanity are left to the jury. *Doe dem, Hu..n* v. *Rector, etc., St. James Church*, vol. 18, 479.

4—Cause tried out of its turn—Costs.

Where a cause was tried out of its order in the absence of the defendant, on the statement of the plaintiff's counsel that it was undefended, the court granted a new trial without costs, on an affidavit of the defendant's attorney that the defendant had a good defence and intended to defend the action. *McIntosh* v. *Hamilton*, vol. 18, 654.

5—Action on account stated—Where jury only allowed half the amount—Quantum meruit—Evidence.

Where plaintiff claimed $1,000 as the amount of an account stated between himself and a deceased person as due plaintiff's wife for board and lodging for a number of years, and the jury allowed $500; there being nothing to warrant a verdict for that amount, a new trial was granted on application of defendant, plaintiff having sued on the *quantum meruit* for nursing the intestate in his last illness, put in evidence, subject to objection, the inventory of the estate.

Held, improperly received, the only question for the jury being, what were the services worth? not, what was the intestate worth? *Powell v. Ward*, vol. 19, 57.

6—Where party applying for, kn[illegible] at the time that he was related to the j[illegible]ge and did not disclose the fact—Application refused—Certiorari to bring up the proceedings before county court judge.

On a trial before a county court judge the defendant knowing that he was related to the judge, did not disclose the fact of this relationship, but took the chances of the trial. The judge was not aware of the relationship. The verdict having gone against the defendant, he obtained a stay of judgment, and made application for a new trial. At the hearing, the defendant produced an affidavit in which he deposed to the relationship, and asked for a new trial on that ground. The judge refused to allow the affidavit to be read, and declined to hear the application on that ground.

Held, that defendant under these circumstances was not entitled to a new trial, but that the judge ought to have received the affidavit.

Quære, whether the court would in any case grant a *certiorari* to bring up proceedings had before a county court judge. *Ex parte Ferguson*, vol. 19, 117.

7—Evidence where improperly received and afterwards withdrawn by judge from jury.

Held, under authority of *Wilmot v. Vanwart*, 1 P. & B. 436, that where evidence which has been improperly received has been withdrawn by the judge from the consideration of the jury, such improper admission of evidence is not a ground for a new trial. *Stewart v. Snowball*, vol. 19, 597. See Addenda 49.

8—On verdict being against evidence—Rule as to granting.

In an action on a policy of insurance where the defence set up was fraud in the assured. On the first trial a verdict was found for the plaintiffs, but a new trial was granted on the ground of the question of fraud not having been submitted to the jury. On the next two trials the juries disagreed. On the last trial a verdict was again found for the plaintiffs, the issue of fraud being fairly and properly left to the jury.

Allen, C.J., and Duff, J., being of opinion that the evidence established the fraud of the plaintiff 's without any moral doubt, thought that the case should be submitted to another jury, but Weldon, Fisher, and Wetmore, JJ., being of opinion that there was evidence to sustain the finding, and the case being one peculiarly for a jury, and having been already before four juries, thought that there ought not to be another trial, and the rule was discharged. *Gibson v. The North British & Mercantile Ins. Co.*, vol. 19, 632.

9—Appeal—On question of fact—Bills of Sale Act—Verbal defeasance.

Appeal from an order of a county court judge refusing a rule for a new trial on the ground of the verdict being against evidence, the court will not interfere with the finding of the court below.

Quære, whether a bill of sale absolute in its terms but subject to a defeasance, which is not reduced to writing and filed, is void against the persons named in section 1, of the Bills of Sale Act, Con. Stat., cap. 75, secs. 1 & 2. *Sherman v. Whipley*, vol. 20, 76.

10—Verdict against evidence.

Where there is a contrariety of evidence the court will not grant a new trial, though they may be of opinion that the strength and weight of evidence were against the verdict. *Fleming* v. *The North British & Mercantile Ins. Co.*, vol. 20, 153.

11—Perverse verdict

Where the judge on a trial of a cause told the jury there was no evidence on which they could find for the defendant, and they found a verdict for the defendant, the court ordered a new trial without inquiring into the correctness of the verdict. *Doe dem. Estabrooks* v. *Towse*, vol. 22, 10.

12—Summons for, not disposed of—Judgment—Irregularity.

A judgment signed, while a summons for a new trial which did not contain a stay of proceedings, and on which no action had been taken for a long time after the return, but which had not been argued or disposed of, will not be set aside as irregular. *Stephenson* v. *Hayward*, vol. 22, 104.

13—Refusal to interfere with verdict.

When the evidence is such that the jury might have found for either party, the Court will not interfere with their verdict unless there is some substantial objection either to the admission of evidence, or to the judge's charge; these being the only grounds taken for a new trial. *Belyea* v. *Merrett*, vol. 23, 223.

14—Verdict against weight of evidence.

In an action by an endorsee against maker of note, in which the making of note was denied — Contradictory evidence given—Court equally divided as to granting new trial. See *Russel* v. *Legere*; *Russel* v. *Bishop*, vol. 21, 238, 322.

15—Whether, under a notice of motion for a new trial, that the verdict is "against evidence"—it is open to the party to argue that it is against "the weight of evidence." See *Stephenson* v. *Fraser*, vol. 24, 462. See Addenda 50.

16 — Surprise — Omission to subpœna witness.

A new trial on the ground of surprise refused, where the defendant had omitted to subpœna a material witness because he understood the plaintiff had subpœnaed him; the witness not having attended. *Smith* v. *Chapman*, vol. 25, 206.

—Motion for, refused—When defendant had reserved right to move for non-suit, or a verdict. See Amendment 2.

—Challenge to juror after hand is on the book. See Challenge 2.

—Juror an alien. See Juror.

—Court has no power to extend time for giving the notice of motion for. See Notice of Motion.

—On motion for, party who objected to any testimony that witness might give cannot claim that evidence was improperly received, no specific evidence having been objected to. See Evidence 4.

—Not granted to Crown in criminal action. See Evidence 16.

—Court will not grant when defect relied on as ground for, is apparent on the face of the declaration. See Husband and Wife 2.

—Not granted in County Court where cause is tried in County Court without a jury. See Husband and Wife 2.

—Reading judgment in former suit to jury on second trial, and commenting thereon, improper, but not ground for new trial. See Settled Accounts 1.

—Court will hear only one counsel on motion for. See Trespass 7.

—A judge has no power to order in review cases under Con. Stat., cap. 60, sec. 43. See *Certiorari* 6, 7.

—Refused where evidence improperly admitted is unimportant. See Sale 4.

—Slander—Misdirection. See Slander 3.

—Notice of motion for—No one appearing to support motion. See Practice 11.

—The fact of one of the jurors being in debt to the defendant, who obtained the verdict, is not of itself a ground for a new trial. See Will 10.

—Excessive damages—Where jury must have acted under influence of undue motives. See Trespass 11.

—Commission for examination of witnesses—Return—Where inadmissible on account of omission to retain interrogatories through no fault of the plaintiff. See Practice 13.

—Feigned issue sent down for trial—Motion for a new trial on a feigned issue sent down by Supreme Court in Equity must be made before a Judge in Equity. *Pomeroy v. Minas Marine Ins. Co.*, vol. 18, 654.

—Negligence—Not having evidence of corporation exercising powers carelessly. See Action on the Case.

—Evidence—Voluntary conveyance—Question for jury as to *bona fides*. See Deed.

—Ordered unless plaintiff would allow verdict to be reduced. See Collision 1.

—What entitles to. See Practice 4.

—Should not be granted when plaintiff could only have received nominal damages. See Replevin 1.

—Evidence received on trial and not objected to. See Carrier 2, Agreement 7.

—Where plaintiff would have been entitled to nominal damages for non-delivery of mill machinery at the time agreed upon.

—Actual damage not having been proved; verdict for defendant. New trial refused. See Contract 11.

—Case tried on its merits after improper plea, judgment should not be reversed. See Plea 1.

—Excessive damage—Action of tort, court will not try case on affidavits. See Practice 25.

—Action of tort—Actual damage necessary to be shown. See County Court 6.

NEXT OF KINDRED.

Person dying since 6th April, 1858, intestate, and without children, leaving a mother and uncles and aunts—Who entitled to real estate.

If a person dies intestate and without children, between the 6th April, 1858, and the passing of the Consolidated Statutes, leaving a mother and uncles and aunts, his mother as his next of kindred, is entitled under cap. 78 of those statutes, to the real estate of which he died seised. *Doe dem. Wood v. DeForest* vol. 23, 200.

Non assumpsit—Plea of—Right to dispute consideration under. See Agreement 5.

Nominal damages—Refusal of court to grant a new trial where plaintiff entitled to; no actual damage having been proved. See Contract 11.

Non-Resident—Where defendant became, before cause of action accrued. See Attachment 3.

NON-SUIT.

1—Judgment as in case of—When defendant entitled to.

Held, that where a cause was once entered for trial, but the trial was postponed, though the cause was not made a remanet, and a new notice of trial was subsequently given, but the plaintiff did not proceed to trial pursuant to the notice, defendant was entitled to judgment as in case of non-suit. *Cyr* v. *Ouillette*, vol 20, 264.

2—Practice — Judgment as in case of — When defendant may move for.

Defendant having moved for judgment as in case of non-suit after plaintiff had after issue joined, allowed two terms and one circuit court at which the cause might have been tried, to elapse without proceeding to trial.

Held, by Weldon, Wetmore, Duff and King, JJ., (Palmer, J. dissenting), that the rule of practice of the court as settled by *Oliver* v. *Campbell*, is that it is not sufficient that two terms and one circuit at which the plaintiff might have proceeded to trial should have elapsed, but that two circuits, at either of which the plaintiff might have proceeded to trial, must have passed before the plaintiff can be held to be in default, and the defendant entitled to judgment as in case of non-suit. *Randolph* v. *Taylor*, vol. 29, 585.

—No ground for, that declaration on replevin bond, alleged bond to have been executed by sureties only, when it had been executed by plaintiff. See Replevin 5.

—Justice's court—Where improperly granted—No evidence having been given by the defendant—Power of judge on review to order judgment to be entered for the plaintiff for the amount proved on the trial. See *Certiorari* 8.

—Whether should be granted—Where title to land brought in question in county court — Remitting cause to supreme court. See Trespass 10.

—Agreement of counsel at trial that verdict should be entered for defendant if the court should be of opinion that plaintiff had failed to make out a case —Whether court has power to enter a non-suit. See Practice.

—**Notice**—Where notice given under 12 Vic., cap. 8, sec. 10, stated that defendant would move to enter non-suit and leave to enter non-suit had not been reserved at trial, the court refused to allow the defendant to amend notice. See Amendment 2.

—Plaintiff not giving evidence of negligence in carrier, defendant disproving, not competent to move for non-suit. See Carrier 2.

—Where plaintiff entitled to nominal damage—no actual damage proved New trial refused. See Contract 15.

Notice of action—Act done in pursuance of statute—School Act, Con. Stat cap. 65.

In an action for seizing plaintiff's property under an execution issued for school rates, the defendant is entitled to notice of action under the Con. Stat. cap. 65, sec 81, if he, acting as secretary of the trustees of schools, honestly believed that the plaintiff was liable to pay the tax, and that in issuing the execution he (defendant) was discharging his duty under the law; and there are facts existing which might give rise to such belief.

The words in section 81—"anything done by virtue of the office of secretary" —mean anything done by the defendant in the reasonable belief that he was pursuing the directions of the Act; even though the validity of his appointment as secretary was doubtful. *Mickeen*, appellant, and *Finnigan*, respondent, vol. 24, 327.

—A fishery officer who wrongfully prevented a riparian owner from exercising his right of fishing, not entitled to. See Fisheries Act 2.

—Not necessary before suing a justice of the peace for recovery of penalty for not making return of a conviction before him. See Justice of Peace 1.

NOTICE.

—Two grounds of action—Proof of either one or the other would be sufficient. See False Imprisonment 6.

—**Notice of appeal**—Equity—Serving. See Equity Appeal.

—**Equity**—Statement of grounds. See Equity Appeal 1.

—**Notice of hearing**—If plaintiff gives—In suit in equity, but does not attend, cost of day allowed. See Practice 5.

—Notice of intended examination, sufficient time. See Debtor 1.

NOTICE OF MOTION.

Under Act, 42 Vic. cap. 8, sec. 10—Time for giving—Power of court to extend—Practise.

The court has no power to extend the time for giving the notice of motion, the statements of the grounds of motion and the authorities relied upon by Act, 42 Vic. cap. 8, sec. 10, beyond the term next after the term following the circuit at which the cause was tried. *Woodman v. Town of Moncton*, vol. 20, 12.

—Under Rule 2, Hilary Term, 6 Wm. IV. irregular. See Motion Paper.

Notice to quit—Necessity of—Where evidence of continuing tenancy exists. See Landlord and Tenant 1.

Nominal damages—Where plaintiff could only have recovered—A new trial should not be granted. See Replevin 1.

Novation — See Agreement 4; Contract 1.

Nuisance—Erection of fence on street. See Addenda 40.

Objection—General, to admission of evidence not ground for new trial. See Evidence 4.

—To juror—Should be such as judge or clerk can properly hear at time. See Challenge 4.

Offer to suffer judgment—See County Court 2.

Official — Of corporation cash book kept by entries showing balances against—Admission of correctness. See Evidence 14.

—Public—Appointment by Government—Continuance in office until successor legally appointed. See Milltown, Town of.

—**Opinion of experts**—Involving truth of evidence of other witnesses. See Evidence 8.

—Of witnesses—Collision—Questions for jury. See Evidence 13.

Order of commissioners—For debtors' discharge—What it should set out. See Limit Bond.

Original order — For review — Served instead of copy—Judge granting second order. See Review 6.

ON VIEW.

Fishery officer—What constitutes on view materials unlawfully in use for the purpose of drifting for salmon.

The defendant was a fishery officer under the Fishery Act, 31 Vic., cap. 60. Seeing plaintiff's boat coming ashore at river Charlo, in the county of Restigouche, with wet nets in it, and plaintiff's servants admitting that they had been drifting for salmon in the Bay of Chaleurs, the defendant seized the boat and nets, and during the same day served plaintiff with a paper, whereby defendant purported to confiscate plaintiff's boat and nets on view. The Bay of Chaleurs was outside the limits for which defendant was appointed Fishery Officer.

Held, that under the Fisheries Act, defendant was not justified in seizing and confiscating the boat and nets unless the offence was committed on his own view, which, in this case, it was not. *McFee* v. *Mowat*, vol. 19, 252.

Appeal to Supreme Court of Canada dismissed. See Addenda 4.

OVERSEER OF POOR.

Town of Upper Mills—Proper parties to action for support of illegitimate child.

Held, that the overseer of poor for the town was a corporation sole and for the breach of any contract made with him for the support of the poor of the town, the action should have been against the corporation and not against the town. *Ross & Wife* v. *Town of Upper Mills*, vol. 22, 168.

PARISH COURT COMMISSIONERS.

Jurisdiction to try offences under the Canada Temperance Act, 1878.

The parish court commissioners have jurisdiction to try offences under the Canada Temperance Act, 1878.

The local government has the right to appoint parish court commissioners and justices of the peace. *Ex parte, Perkins*, vol. 21, 66. *Ex parte, Williamson* vol. 24, 64.

PARISH OFFICER.

Appointment by parish councillors.

The mere absence from the parish of a parish officer appointed by the county council under section 66, cap. 99, of the Con. Stat. does not create such a vacancy as will authorise the appointment of a person to fill the office by the councillors of the parish. *The Queen* v. *Close*, vol. 19, 302.

Parish court—Right of plaintiff by abandoning the excess upon the particulars filed to bring the action within the jurisdiction of. See *Certiorari* 8.

Parol agreement — Whether circumstances shew that there had been a substitution of, for written contract is question for jury. See Contract 3.

Sale of logs—Ownership. See Statute of Frauds 1.

—Parol evidence—When admissible. See Agreement 2.

—Not admissible to shew variation in contract required to be in writing by Statute of Frauds. See Sale 2.

PARTICULARS.

1—Of demand—Sufficient if particulars refer to accounts rendered without giving items for same.

Particulars of demand which refer to an account rendered without re-stating the items of the account, are sufficient to entitle the plaintiff to prove the items on the trial. *Palmer* v. *Harding*, vol. 19, 281.

—Filing of — Whether commencement of action in justice's courts. See Justice's Court 1.

—Demand of—Effect on application for order for inspection of books. See Books.

—Of claim—Sufficiency of. See Conversion 1.

—Demand of, in ejectment—Stay of proceedings. See Ejectment 6.

PARTITION.

1—Mutual deeds of—Reservation of common right to quarry in one moiety—Words of inheritance—Opening new quarries.

A. and B. being tenants in common in fee of a lot of land under the surface of which was plaster rock, made partition thereof by deed; A. releasing to B.

all his right in the western half of the lot, and granting to him the right of digging and carrying off plaster from the quarries, on the eastern half; and B. releasing to A. all his right in the eastern half, except the plaster therein, which was to continue in common as before, B. retaining and reserving his original right of digging and carrying away the same. In trespass by the plaintiff, claiming through A. against the defendant, claiming through B.,

Held, 1. That B. never parted with his right as owner in fee of the plaster in the eastern half of the lot; and that such right on his death vested in his heirs, though there were no words of inheritance in the exception.

2. That B.'s right to dig and carry away plaster was not a mere license expiring at his death, but an absolute reservation of ownership with the same legal incidents as if the partition had not been made.

3. That the right of B.'s grantee to dig for plaster was not confined to quarries opened at the time of the partition.

4. That it was not essential to B.'s reservation of the right to enter and dig that he should have given A. any specific compensation for said right. *Prince of Wales Coal Co. v. Gesner*, vol. 22, 115.

—By agreement—Tenants in common. See Adverse Possession 1.

—Suit for—Procedure—See Court—Rules of.

Parties in possession—To compel to come in and defend—Where lessor of plaintiff and defendant both die pending suit. See Ejectment 3.

Partners—Where one partner purchases from assignee the estate of insolvent firm *en bloc*. Right to sue for debts due firm in his own name. See Insolvent Act. *Leonard v. Griffin*.

—Firm of attorneys—Misappropriation of money by one—Liability of co-partner. See Attorney 6.

—Confession given by one for himself and his co-partner with his consent—Effect of. See Execution 1.

—One acknowledging—Service by summons. See Execution 1.

—Joint conviction—Penalty must be several. See Canada Temperance Act 21.

PARTNERSHIP.

1—Refusal of judge to allow defendants to add new plea—Cannot be proved by declaration of one alleged partner—Right of opposite counsel to interpose and cross-examine.

Held, by Weldon, J., that sec. 161 of cap. 37 of Con. Stat., leaves no discretion in a judge at *nisi prius* to refuse an amendment, unless the proposed new pleading would be demurrable.

Held, also, by Allen, C.J., and Fisher, Wetmore and Duff, JJ., that in an action against two defendants, when it is sought to charge them as partners, a declaration made by one is inadmissible to prove the partnership, and at all events before such evidence is admissible at all, defendant's counsel has a right to interpose and cross-examine the witness called to prove the declaration. *Harper v. Smith and Mann*, vol. 20, 408.

—Money borrowed by one partner—Liability of firm for. See Co-partners 1.

—Filing bill in equity to obtain decree of. See Injunction 2.

—English Bankruptcy Act—One partner doing business in this province—Property vesting in trustee. See Bankruptcy.

Passengers—Duty of, as to getting on trains. See Railway Conductor 1.

—Ferry boat—Invitation to go ashore. See Negligence 4.

—Injury to intermediate ferry owned by another company than one issuing through ticket. See Railway Company 6.

PATENT.

Infringement—Pleading—Articles made by order of patentee before patent issued, but sold afterwards—Misdirection.

It is no defence to an action for infringement of a patent granted to the plaintiff, that before the patent was obtained the plaintiff had employed the defendant to manufacture a certain number of the articles, if the defendant, after he had notice of the patent, sold the articles without the authority of the plaintiff. *Clark*, appellant, and *Griffiths*, respondent, vol. 24, 567.

Payment—Appropriation. See Contract 7.

—Alleged to have been made on mortgage—Mortgagor and mortgagee both dead—Onus of proof. See Mortgage 1.

Penalty—Action against justice of the peace to recover penalty for not returning conviction had before him. See Justice of the Peace 1.

—Under Canada Temperance Act, where greater than Act authorizes. See Canada Temperance Act 9.

—Under section 110, Canada Temperance Act—How recoverable. See Canada Temperance Act 6.

Penal statutes—Construction of. See Inspection.

Penitentiary. See Dominion Penitentiary.

Pending of suit—Application to set aside judgment not affected thereby. See Deed 2.

Percentage—Of price agreed to be paid as work progresses can be recovered where work is destroyed by fire. See Contract 8.

Perils of the sea—Loss of freight by vessel being frozen in—Whether peril insured against. See Insurance 18.

Personal property—A person cannot by affixing personal property to the land of another, where he has no right to affix it, alter its character as a chattel. See Replevin 3.

Perverse verdict—New trial. See New Trial 11.

Petroleum—Conviction for storage of. See Police Magistrate of St. John.

PLEA.

1—Professing to answer the whole cause of action—Answering only part—Bad on general demurrer.

If a plea professes in its commencement to answer the whole cause of action, and afterwards answers only a part, the whole plea is bad, and the plaintiff may demur generally. It must answer the whole, or be limited in its commencement to that part to which it is an answer. *Willett* v. *Lockhart*, vol. 19, 637.

2—Assault and battery—Plea of son assault demesne—Replication justifying assault only.

In an action for assault and battery, defendant pleaded *son assault demesne*.

Replication, setting out acts of defendant which justified an assault, but not a battery.

Held, bad, because it professed to answer the whole of the plea, but only answered a part. *Purdee* v. *Snider*, vol. 23, 271.

3—Where false or embarrassing—Setting aside summary application.

Declaration stated that defendant was one of the part owners of a ship, and as such was, with the other part owners, indebted to plaintiff in a bill of exchange drawn by W. S., the master of the ship, for £753 on S. V. & Co., of Liverpool, payable to plaintiff's order sixty days after sight; that plaintiff had placed said bill of exchange in the hands of his attorney for collection from defendant and the other owners of the ship; that afterwards defendant requested said attorney to delay proceedings on the bill until the vessel's arrival at St. John; and, in consideration that the attorney did so delay, defendant promised plaintiff to make immediate payment to him of said bill of exchange on the arrival of the ship at St. John; and did, also, for the consideration and on the conditions aforesaid, promise to pay him another bill of exchange for £173, drawn by said W. S. on S. V. & Co., payable to plaintiff's order; that the said attorney, with plaintiff's consent, did delay proceedings on the first mentioned bill of exchange till the arrival of the ship, and all things happened, etc., necessary to entitle plaintiff to be paid the last mentioned bill of exchange, yet defendant had not paid the same.

Defendant pleaded, 1st, that he did not promise as alleged; 2nd, payment before action brought; 3rd, that before action brought he satisfied and discharged plaintiff's claim with respect to the first mentioned bill of exchange; 4th, that said W. S. was induced by plaintiff to draw the second mentioned bill of exchange to defraud defendant and the other owners of the ship, and plaintiff concealed this fraud from defendant, etc., and that before action, defendant paid the residue of plaintiff's claim in the first count mentioned.

On application to a judge at Chambers on an affidavit of the plaintiff's attorney stating that the defendant had paid him the amount of the £753 bill, but had not paid the £173, and he believed it was not paid to the plaintiff (who resided in Savannah), there being no affidavit of the defendant that he had paid it, but merely that the plea was true in fact. The second plea was set aside as false, under the authority of the Con. Stat., cap. 37, sec. 88; the third as embarrassing; and that part of the fifth plea which alleged payment of the residue of the plaintiff's claim, as false and embarrassing.

Held, that the fifth plea was good, and that so much of the judge's order as set it aside in part should be rescinded. But (Palmer, J., dissenting), that the order to set aside the second and third pleas was properly made. *Richardson, et al.*, v. *Vaughan*, vol. 24, 75.

4—Assumpsit—plea of "never indebted"—Whether applicable to county courts—Appeal after merits tried on improper plea—Accord and satisfaction.

In an action of assumpsit in a county court, defendant pleaded "never indebted." The case was tried without objection to the plea and a verdict given for the plaintiff.

Held, on appeal that whether such a plea is applicable to suits in the county courts or not, the judgment ought not to be reversed after the case had been tried on its merits.

Where the plaintiff's demand is for a liquidated amount, the payment of a smaller sum will not amount to a satisfaction of the larger sum, even though the plaintiff agreed to accept it in full. *Pitfield*, appellant, and *Kimball*, respondent, vol. 25, 198.

—In an action on promissory note—Accommodation. See Accommodation 1.

—Should set out some fact and not only a matter of law. See Bankruptcy.

—**Puis darreign continuance**—Discharge under Insolvent Act. See Attorney 2.

—Of *non-cepit*, entitled to succeed under. See Replevin 3.

—Justifying an imprisonment under warrant issued by receiver of taxes, St John.

Held, bad for that the proceedings taken were not set out in detail. See Arrest 5.

—Of accord and satisfaction by promissory note, when note has been returned. See Accord and Satisfaction 1.

—What evidence of. See Agreement 7.

—That alleged indorsement of bill of exchange was made without knowledge or consent of the assignee—Held good. See Bill of Exchange 1.

—Not guilty in trover, plaintiff having property need not prove right of present possession. See Bill of Sale 2.

—Of justification under an attachment for costs in case of review from justice's court—What plea must set out. See False Imprisonment 5.

—In Abatement. See Replevin 5; County Court 5.

—Of misrepresentation, must allege that it is material. See Insurance 5.

—Of false swearing, must allege that it was done wilfully. See Insurance 5.

—Stating only conclusions of law is bad. See Municipality.

—Power of judge to refuse new plea by way of amendment. See Partnership 1.

—Of property in lumber, by sheriff, supported by possession under writ of replevin. See Replevin 4.

—Leave and license. See Sheriff's Sale.

—That action was not brought within time limited by condition of insurance policy—Good defence. See Insurance 10.

—Where false—Setting aside. See False Pleas 1.

—Non-assumpsit—Right to dispute consideration of. See Agreement 5.

—Time allowed for filing and service of plea. See Court 7.

—Abatement—County Court. See County Court 5.

—No affidavit of debt against estate if necessary must be pleaded. See Executors 1.

—Action for infringement of patent. See Patent.

—Time of filing and serving after demand of. See Court General Rules 7.

—*Autre fois* convict—Onus of proof. See Summary Convictions Act 12.

—Additional plea—Supreme Court of Canada no power to allow. See Addenda 31-9.

—County court — General issue — Sufficiency of. See County Court 7.

PLEADING.

1—Trover — Claim of lien for commission charges, etc., plea not traversing right of property—Evidence of lien, when may be given and to what plea applicable.

To a declaration "for that defendants converted to their own use, or wrongfully deprived plaintiff of the use and possession of plaintiff's corn," defendants pleaded that they were brokers and commission merchants, and that said corn was placed in their hands as such brokers and commission merchants by plaintiff for sale or return, and defendants had necessarily incurred costs, charges and expenses in the storing and safe custody thereof whilst so in their hands, wherefore they claimed a lien upon the corn therefor until such lien should be satisfied, and that defendants refused to return said corn until such costs, etc., were paid, which was the grievance complained of.

Held, that the plea was clearly bad; that it was applicable to an action of detinue only, and was no answer to an action for wrongful conversion. *Nevins v. Schofield*, vol. 18, 135.

2—Insolvent Act of 1879—Charging fraud under section 136.

Not necessary to allege that defendants have gone into insolvency. *Barry v. Hogan*, vol. 18, 465.

3—Departure.

To an action on a policy of insurance defendants did not traverse the allegation in the declaration, and thereby admitted the signing of the policy by defendants, and the sending it to their agent for delivery, and also that it contained an acknowledgment of payment of the premium; but they avoided the effect of the admissions by setting out the conditions that the policy was not to operate as a contract until the premium was paid, and the policy delivered, and alleging that neither of these conditions were performed.

Held, that this was a proper mode of denying the performance of conditions precedent.

A declaration in an action on a policy of insurance having alleged a general performance of all conditions necessary to entitle plaintiff to recover, defendants pleaded that certain conditions of the policy were not performed by the assured, viz., that the advance premium was not paid, nor the policy delivered; and plaintiff replied to this, that defendant's agent waived performance of these conditions.

Held, a departure from the declaration, and therefore bad.

Another count alleged a waiver by defendant's agent of the pre-payment of premiums, and his agreement to give assured time for payment thereof till demand. Defendants answered this by stating the conditions of the policy that no agent of the company except the president or secretary had power to waive performance of any of the conditions, and that the alleged waiver was not made by the president or secretary. The replication alleged that the assured tendered the premium to the agent, and that it thereupon became his duty to receive it, and to deliver the policy.

Held, bad for departure.

Plaintiff also replied generally to defendants' pleas that they were estopped from denying payment of the advanced premium in consequence of the admission of the receipt of it in the policy.

Held, bad for departure, being inconsistent with the averment in declaration that assured tendered the premium to the agent, who did not receive it, but waived performance of that condition, and agreed to give time. *Calhoun v. Union Mutual Ins. Co.*, vol. 19, 13.

4 — Covenant — Necessity of setting out agreement sued on.

A declaration alleging that R., of whom defendants were executors, in his life time represented to plaintiffs that he had an arrangement with a railway company by which the company was bound to carry all lumber cut, or to be cut by R. or his assigns from a certain described tract of land, at a certain rate, which R. agreed to assign to plaintiffs if they purchased the property. It then averred that plaintiffs were induced by this representation to purchase said lands, etc., but R. had not transferred his interest in said arrangement to plaintiffs, who now sued for breach of covenant. Plaintiffs were ordered by a judge at chambers to amend their declaration by stating what the arrangement was between R. and the railway company.

Held, on motion to rescind the order that it was rightly made.

Held, also, that allegations of H.'s object in making the agreement with plaintiffs, and of their entering into the agreement confiding in his representation, were quite immaterial in an action for breach of covenant, and as they might tend to embarrass defendants in their pleading were properly ordered to be struck out. *Vose* v. *Huff*, vol. 19, 59.

5—Departure—Replication.

By the second count of the declaration the plaintiff alleged that C. A. F., on the 19th January, 1875, by his promissory note then over due, promised to pay J. B., or order $600 with eight per cent. interest twelve months after date, and the said J. B. indorsed the same to the defendant who endorsed the same to the plaintiff, etc.

To a plea by the defendant that he did not indorse the said promissory note to the plaintiff, the plaintiff replied that the said J. B. to whose order the said promissory note was payable, was the plaintiff, and that the plaintiff after making the said promissory note endorsed the same in blank without recourse upon him, the said plaintiff to one R. H. H., who endorsed the same to the defendant, who endorsed the same to the plaintiff as alleged.

Held, that the replication was bad for departure. *Bell* v. *Moffat*, vol. 16, 241.

6—Assignment of debt—Suit by assignee in equity.

The assignee of a debt brought a suit in equity for the recovery of it against the debtor and the assignor, alleging as the reason for not proceeding at law that he had requested the assignors to have an action at law brought in his (the assignor's) name, for the recovery of the debt for the benefit of the plaintiff, and that the assignor had refused to have such action brought. A demurrer to the bill for want of equity having been overruled;

Held, on appeal by Palmer and King, JJ., (Allen, C.J., doubting), that the allegation in the bill was sufficient, as it was capable of the meaning, that the plaintiff had requested the assignor of the debt to allow an action to be brought in his name for the recovery of it, and the assignor had refused to allow it. *Kerr* v. *Steeves*, vol. 22, 124.

7—Assault and battery—Plea of son assault demesne—Replication justifying assault only.

In an action for assault and battery defendant pleaded *son assault demesne*; replication, setting out acts of defendant which justified an assault, but not a battery.

Held, bad, because it professed to answer the whole of the plea, but only answered a part. *Parker* v. *Snider*, vol. 23, 271.

8—Action by company on foreign judgment—Pleading whether declaration must state incorporation.

In an action brought by a company on a foreign judgment, where the declaration stated that the defendant had appeared in the original suit.

Held, by Allen, C.J., Weldon, King and Fraser, JJ., (Wetmore and Palmer, JJ., dissenting), that the incorporation of the plaintiff's need not be alleged in the declaration. *The Waterous Engine Works Co.* v. *Campbell*, 22 N. B. R. 503, distinguished. *Star Kidney Pad Co.* v. *McCarthy*, vol. 24, 93.

9—Surety—Bond for faithful discharge of agent's duties—Discharge of surety by alteration of agent's duties—Continuing agency—Pleading.

Declaration on a bond, after reciting that D. had been appointed plaintiff's agent, and that defendant had become surety for the faithful performance of D.'s duties, stated the condition of the bond to be that D. should from time to time, and at all times thereafter faithfully execute the office of agent, and pay over all monies—Breach that he had not accounted, etc. Pleas 1. That by agreement between plaintiff and D. before making the bond, D.'s appointment was to be for a year, and that he had faithfully discharged all his duties as agent while he was so employed. 2. That after the execution of the bond, and before breach, the agreement mentioned in the first plea was cancelled, and a new agreement made with D. imposing different, and more onerous duties on him, without the defendant's consent.

Held, 1st. That the second plea was good, as it showed a material alteration in the original contract whereby D.'s duties were different from those for the performance of which the defendant became liable, and that he was thereby discharged. 2nd. (Allen, C.J., dissenting), that the first plea was good, that the words of the bond that D. should from time to time, etc., faithfully execute the office of agent had no fixed meaning as to the continuance of the agency, and were not inconsistent with his appointment for a limited time—Which defendant had a right to prove.

Per Allen, C.J., that the bond showed a continuing agency till terminated by the parties, and that the verbal agreement that it was to be for a year, was at variance with the construction of the bond. *The Canada Life Assurance Co.* v. *Calkins*, vol. 21, 276.

—If one of several pleas was irregularly pleaded, the plaintiff's attorney might apply to have it struck out; but he could not accept part of the pleas, and treat the other as a nullity. See Attorney 2.

—Duplicity in, not ground for general demurrer. See Accord and Satisfaction 1.

—Sheriff having seised goods under execution against H. cannot set up that H. had no property in the goods. See Bill of Sale 1.

—If the obtaining of an affidavit were a condition precedent to the right to sue for a debt against an estate to be available as a defence, it would have to be specially pleaded. See Executions 1.

—Slander—Necessity of setting out all the material words constituting. See Slander 1.

—The master of a dredge having directed the men to put an anchor in a place where it might be dangerous to navigation could not excuse himself by saying the men were his fellow servants in Her Majesty's employ. See Negligence 2.

—Action by a company incorporated by letters patent under the Canada Joint Stock Companies Act, 1877—Declaration—Necessity of alleging incorporation. See Joint Stock Companies Act 1.

—Action of trespass to property of infant under fourteen years of age—Who entitled to maintain—Plea. See Infant 1.

—Equity—Setting out documents at full length. See Will 9.

—Equity—Bill—Multifariousness. See Equity.

—Executors—Excuse for not proving will. See Will 7.

—Demurrer to replication. See Insurance 11.

—Bill of exchange—Whether defence of insufficient stamping should be pleaded. See Bill of Exchange.

— Judgment—Action on—Release—Where obtained before judgment—Whether plea of release available. See Judgment 3.

—Professing to answer the whole plea and only answering a part. See Trespass 9.

—Replevin—Showing joint ownership in deals seized under distress. See Landlord and Tenant 3.

—Whether objection that policy of insurance was not countersigned by agent available under the plea of *non est factum*. See Insurance 15.

— *Plene administravit* — Under plea of—Evidence of probable expense of present and other suits not admissible. See Evidence 15.

—Insolvent Act of 1875—Charging fraud under sec. 136, not necessary to allege that defendants have gone into insolvency. See Insolvent Act of 1875 ; 1.

—Injunction order—Allegation that defendant falsely procured same—Whether sufficient. See Action on the Case.

—Tort—Proper mode of denying existence of duty. See Action on the Case 2.

—Joint owners—Joint ownership no answer to action for misfeasance and misuse of property. See Action on the Case.

—Abatement—Marriage of plaintiff—County Court. See County Court 5.

—County Court—Pleading general issue only. See County Court 7.

—Set-off, of judgment, pleading. See Set-off 1.

POLICEMAN.

1—St. John—Power of common council to reduce pay—Month's notice required.

Act 19 Vic. cap. 52—imposes on the corporation of St. John a statutory duty to pay the policemen their wages, and an action will lie for the recovery thereof—month's notice requisite to reduce previous rate of wages. *Mayor, etc., of St. John v. Patchell*, vol. 22, 173.

Police Magistrate—Town of Woodstock—Whether being deputy collector of Inland Revenue disqualifies from trying officers against the Canada Temperance Act. See Canada Temperance Act 11.

POLICE MAGISTRATE OF ST. JOHN.

1—Conviction by—Review—Petroleum—Storage of.

There is a right of review to a judge from a conviction by the police magistrate of St. John.

The Act, 34 Vic. cap. 33, by sec. 1, declares that "no person shall have, keep or sell in any place, or building, within the limits of the city of St. John . . . any crude or refined petroleum, etc., in any larger quantity than 200 gallons in the aggregate, to be contained in not more than five barrels."

Held, that the Act does not prevent a person having more than the stated quantity of petroleum in different parts of the city, provided he has not more than 200 gallons or five barrels in any one place. *The Mayor of St. John v. Masters*, vol. 19, 585.

Policy of Insurance—Where loss, if any, payable to a person other than the assured—The assured the proper person to bring action for loss. See Insurance 1.

Poor, overseer of—Town of Upper Mills—Action for support of illegitimate child. See Overseer of Poor.

PORTLAND.

Town of, liability to keep sidewalks in repair.

Town bound to keep sidewalks in repair and reasonably safe condition for persons using same, this applicable to sidewalks built before town incorporated and which had been continued to be kept in repair by town—Action for negligence. See *Griffiths* v. *Town of Portland*, vol. 23, 559.

See same case appealed to Supreme Court of Canada, and appeal allowed. See Addenda, No. 21.

Police Magistrate — Jurisdiction of. See Costs 3.

Power of town council to exact license fee from coachmen. See Hackney Coaches.

—Street, injuries arising from non-repair of. See Streets.

PORTLAND CIVIL COURT.

Whether magistrate has jurisdiction under $20 where parties reside outside of Portland.

In an action of debt in the Portland civil court, the plaintiff lived in the city of St. John and the defendant in the parish of Lancaster, the amount claimed being under $20.

Held, that the magistrate had jurisdiction. *Purchase* v. *Seely*, vol. 19, 549.

Police magistrate—Conviction before—Certiorari taken away—Proceedings on review.

Where there is a proper information upon oath, before the police magistrate of the town of Portland, charging an offence within his jurisdiction, the party desiring to impugn the correctness of the magistrate's decision must proceed under 11 Vic. cap. 12, sec. 27, (Acts of N. Brunswick), and 33 Vic. cap. 33, Acts of Canada, the remedy by *certiorari* being taken away. *Ex parte Abel*, vol. 18, 600.

POSSESSION.

1—Acts of—Adjoining land owners—Line agreed upon—Possessio Pedis.

The lessor of the plaintiff and the defendant were owners of adjoining land and they and those through whom they respectively claimed, had occupied on either side of a line that had been agreed upon more than twenty years before, and along which a fence had been erected and continued for over twenty years. The *locus in quo* was a portion of the land adjoining this fence and on defendant's side of it.

Held, that acts of possession by the defendant and those through whom he claimed, on any part of the land on his side of the fence, would extend his possession up to the agreed line, and that a *possessio pedis* up to the line was not necessary to support his title by possession. *Doe dem Appleby* v. *Secord*, vol. 22, 377.

2—Discontinuance of possession—Acts of possession of unreclaimed marsh land—Evidence—Ancient documents—Declaration against interest—Effect of assessment on land as an act of ownership.

A., the grantee of a tract of 100 acres of land, died intestate in 1805. In 1809 his administrator obtained a license under the Act, George III, cap. 11, to sell the land for payment of debts, and gave a power of attorney to B. authorizing him to sell the land, and settle all claims against A.'s estate. There was no evidence of any sale under the license, except a statement upon the grant to A. in the handwriting of B., who had since died, that he had sold the land to C. on the 10th January, 1809, for £30; the grant, with this writing upon it, being in C.'s possession at the time of his death.

The land, at the time of granting the license, and for some years afterwards, was of little value, being low and boggy and partly covered with lakes and swamps. In 1812, C. went upon the land, claiming it as his, and agreed with the owner of the adjoining land upon the dividing line between the two tracts—setting stakes to mark the line; and afterwards, at different times between that year and 1858, allowed several persons to cut wild grass and fence stakes upon the land, and prevented other persons from cutting wood upon it. In 1858 C. caused the land to be surveyed, and the lines of it to be traced out, and at that time he had the grant to A. in his possession. Afterwards, about the year 1860, C. cut a ditch between two of the lakes upon the land, the effect of which was partially to drain the water from the land into a ditch upon the adjoining land, which connected with a canal cut by the commissioners of sewers for the purpose of draining and improving the marsh lands in the district. C. died in 1865, having devised the land to his son, who erected a fence upon a part of it, throwing down a fence which had been erected without his permission, and authorized persons to cut wood upon it; and in 1874 sold it to the defendant, who took possession, and soon afterwards dug a ditch upon it, and continued it through the adjoining land, by means of which the tide flowed in though a canal which had been cut by the commissioners of sewers on other land. The effect of the salt water upon the bog land was to destroy its natural vegetation of moss and wild grass, and by the deposit of mud left by the tide, to improve the land, and gradually to produce a good quality of grass.

The land was within the jurisdiction of the commissioners of sewers for the parish of Sackville, appointed under the Revised Statutes cap. 67, who, during C.'s lifetime, had caused a canal or ditch to be cut on other land between the shore of the Bay of Fundy and the land in dispute, for the purpose of draining and improving the marsh land in the district, and, as was alleged, had assessed C. for the amount which, in their opinion, the land in dispute was benefitted by their operations.

In ejectment brought for the land in 1879 by the heirs of A.,

Held, *per* Palmer, King and Fraser, JJ., (Wetmore, J., dissenting). 1. That there was evidence that the heirs of A. had discontinued their possession of the land, and considering the nature of it, and the occupation of which it was capable, that the acts of possession by C., and those claiming under him, for upwards of twenty years, were so open, continuous and exclusive as to bar the right of A.'s heirs.

2. That C.'s entry on the land was not wrongful, but under color of right, referrable to a sale to him by B., and therefore his possession extended to the hole tract.

3. *Per* Palmer and Fraser, JJ., that the writing on the grant to B. that he had sold the land to C., being in C.'s possession at the time of his death, was admissible in evidence as an ancient document, and that a sale and conveyance by B. might be presumed in favor of C.'s possession. *Per* King, J., that the writing was admissible, either as a declaration by B. against his pecuniary interest, or as a declaration by him explanatory of his delivery of the grant to C. *Per* Wetmore, J., that the writing not being such a document as would pass a title to land, should not have been received in evidence.

4. *Per* Palmer and Fraser, JJ., (Wetmore, J., dissenting, and King, J., doubting), that the acts of the commissioners of sewers in cutting ditches on other land, which had the effect to some extent of draining the land in dispute and allowing the tide to flow in upon it, were the same in effect as if done by C. himself, and were acts of possession by him, though not done upon the land in dispute. Also, that evidence of assess-

ments made by the commissioners upon C. for a portion of the expense of cutting such ditches, should have been admitted. *Per* King, J., that such evidence was inadmissible, the assessment bills not stating that the assessments related to the land in question. *Estabrooks* v. *Towse*, vol. 24, 387.

—License to grantee of bill of sale, to take. See Bill of Sale 1.

Postea—Where stayed—Judge's order necessary to obtain from clerk. See Practice 13.

Pound—Public—Erected on private property by permission—Necessity of continuous use to establish title. See Statutory Title.

POWER OF ATTORNEY.

Authority to convey land for money consideration—Conveyance by agent for other consideration—Whether void—Ratification.

Where a power of attorney authorizes an agent to do a particular act, and this is followed by general words, these general words are not to be extended beyond what is necessary for doing the particular act.

A. and B., tenants of land residing abroad, executed powers of attorney, authorizing the sale of their interests for such sums of money as their respective agents should think reasonable. The defendants, wishing to open a street through the land, applied to the agents, who conveyed to them by deed of gift, the piece of land required, believing that the opening of the street would increase the value of the adjoining land of their principals.

After this, partition was made between A. and B. by mutual deeds of release, and the land through which the proposed street was to be laid out, became the sole property of A., and in the deed thereof executed by B. to A., and on a plan annexed thereto, the land released to A. was described as bounded by the proposed street. A similar plan was annexed to the deed given by A. to B. The defendants afterwards entered on the land and opened the street, for which A. brought trespass.

Held, 1. That A.'s agent had exceeded his authority in conveying the land to the defendants, without any pecuniary consideration, and that no title passed by the deed.

2. That A. had not ratified the deed by accepting the conveyance from B., describing the land as bounded by the street, because it did not appear that when A. accepted the deed from B., she knew that her agent had exceeded his authority in conveying the land to the defendants; and because the reference to the line of the street in the deed from B., was not the act of A., and the acceptance of the deed conveying B.'s interest in a part only of the land, did not preclude A., from relying on her original title to the whole lot. *Hazen* v. *Town of Portland*, vol. 21, 332. See Addenda 31 *Fawcett* v. *Anderson*.

PRACTICE.

1—In ejectment—Vacant possession—Service—Affidavit.

Held, in an action of ejectment for recovery of a vacant possession, where the sheriff's affidavit stated he had affixed a copy of the declaration and notice upon the outer door of the dwelling house, the lessor was entitled to judgment *nisi* against the casual ejector. *Crothers* v. *Roe*, vol. 19, 138.

2—Amendment—Misnomer—Costs.

When a judge at *nisi prius* being satisfied there had been a mistake in the name of defendants, allowed the name of "The Town of M.," to be substituted for the "the Town Council of M.," and postponed the trial.

Held, that the amendment was rightly made, but that the judge, in granting the order, should have allowed costs to the defendants. *Woodman* v. *Town Council of Moncton*, vol. 19, 338.

3—Argument of summons—Where point not taken in obtaining summons—Promissory note—Where payable at particular place—In affidavit for attachment on—What necessary to allege as to presentment.

On the argument for a summons to set aside an attachment, the party applying to set it aside cannot avail himself of any grounds, except those on which he obtained the summons.

Held, that an affidavit for an attachment against the maker of a note payable at a particular place, which alleged that the note was duly presented for payment at, etc., but was refused payment, and was dishonored, and has not been paid, and there is now due to me (plaintiff) for principal money thereon the sum of, etc., was sufficient. *McLellan* v. *Barnes*, vol. 19, 374.

4—Motion for new trial.

Where a counsel moving for a new trial under Act, 42 Vic. cap. 8, fails to make out such a case as would have entitled him to a rule *nisi* under the former practice, the motion will be refused without hearing the counsel for the opposite party. *Peabody* v. *North-West Boom Co.*, vol. 19, 495.

5—Costs of day—Where plaintiff gives notice of hearing but does not attend.

In a suit in equity where plaintiff's solicitor gave notice of hearing, but did not attend, or proceed to the hearing, and the defendant's solicitor attended, and applied for costs of the day, which the judge ordered.

Held, that the order was rightly made. *Melbee* v. *Jones*, vol. 19, 536.

6—Reading to witness statements previously sworn to by other—Separate counsel for defendant—Right to cross-examine.

On the trial of the cause the judge refused to allow defendant's counsel to read to witness B. what S. had sworn was said by him, B., about making a mistake, in order to ask B. whether such statement was true or not.

Held, *per* Weldon, J., that the judge was right, and B. could only be asked to give his version of the conversation.

Per Weldon, J., that the statement which the counsel wished to read not being in themselves evidence, the judge should have allowed them to be read to the witness for the purpose of contradiction.

The defendants appeared by the same attorney, but were represented at the trial by separate counsel.

Held, *per* Weldon, J., that only one counsel had a right to cross-examine and address the jury.

Per Wetmore, J., that at all events the judge should have satisfied himself that defendants' interests were identical before refusing to allow the counsel for both to cross-examine and address the jury. *McMillan* v. *Walker*, vol. 21, 31. See Addenda 9.

7—Rule nisi—Where not entered on crown paper—When applicant entitled to have made absolute.

A rule *nisi* having been taken out and served, requiring defendants to show cause at this time why a certain conviction made by them as justices should not be quashed, they did not enter the case on the crown paper.

Held, that the second motion day of the term was the proper time for moving to make the rule absolute. *Ernest* v. *Ingram*, vol. 21, 195.

8—Commencement of action—Contents nisi prius record.

In an action against a justice of the peace.

Held, that the statement of the time of issuing the summons contained in the *nisi prius* record was sufficient proof of the commencement of the action. *Lyon v. Barnes*, vol. 22, 55.

9—Entry of cause—Entry docket—Where wrongly entitled—Interlocutory judment—Memorandum of judgment docket—Date of filing—Whether necessary to contain—Where more than a year has elapsed since last proceeding—Terms notice—Not necessary when plaintiff delayed at defendant's request.

Held, by Weldon, Palmer, King and Fraser, JJ., (Allen, C.J., and Wetmore, J., dissenting), that the entry by the clerk is what constitutes the entry of a cause and not the filing of the entry docket by the attorney, therefore where the writ and affidavit of service were filed with the clerk, with an entry docket describing one of the plaintiffs by a wrong name, but the clerk received the fees and entered the cause properly in his books, defendant was not entitled to have judgment set aside for the defect in the entry docket.

The statement of the date of entry of the cause required by the 4th Rule of Hilary Term 1875, to be written on the memorandum of interlocutory judgment is for the convenience of the clerk, and its omission is not a ground for setting aside the judgment.

It is not necessary to state on the judgment docket the day of filing.

Although where more than a year has elapsed since the signing of the interlocutory judgment, a term's notice of the intention to proceed must ordinarily be given before signing final judgment, such notice is not necessary where the plaintiff has delayed proceeding at the defendant's request. *Ross v. Miller*, vol. 22, 191.

10—Judgment—Setting aside—Assessment of damages—Affidavit for—Credits—Power of single judge to assess in term—Affidavit—Swearing before the attorney who prepares the affidavit, but is not the attorney on the record.

Affidavits used on a motion to set aside a judgment may be sworn before the attorney who prepares the affidavits, he not being the attorney on the record.

A single judge has power to assess damages during term as well as in vacation.

On motion to set aside a judgment, the court has power to order a reduction. *Maritime Bank v. McKean*, vol. 22, 526.

11—Notice of motion for new trial—Not appearing to support motion.

If a party gives notice of motion for a new trial, and does not appear to support it when reached on the paper, it will be dismissed with costs on application of the opposite party. *Harris v. Fowle*, vol. 22, 572.

12—Writ signed and sealed by Clerk of the court, but issued after appointment of his successor—Wrong form of capias—Irregularity—Filing affidavits to hold to bail.

Blank writs duly signed and sealed, and delivered by the clerk of the court to attorneys, are not affected by the subsequent resignation of the clerk, but may be issued by the attorney without being re-signed.

A *capias* issued as a first process, but in form a *capias* issued after the commencement of an action is irregular only, and may be amended.

Affidavits to hold to bail need not be filed before the entry of the cause. *Mecker v. Peters*, vol 23, 95.

13—Postea—Where stayed—Judge's order necessary to obtain from clerk.

Where a *postea* had been stayed, and the cause entered on the paper by the defendant to move for a new trial, but, on being reached, was allowed by the court to stand over—no counsel appearing for the plaintiff—the plaintiff's attorney has no right afterward without a judge's order to obtain the *postea* from the clerk, and sign judgment on the verdict. *Ford* v. *Reid*, vol. 23, 220.

14—Agreement of counsel at trial—Power of court to depart from.

A verdict was entered for the plaintiff at *nisi prius* pursuant to an agreement that the verdict should be entered for the defendant if the courts should be of opinion that the plaintiff had failed to make out a case.

Held, (Weldon and Wetmore, JJ., dissenting), that the court had no power to enter a nonsuit. *Purdee* v. *Snider*, vol. 23, 221.

15—Commission to examine witnesses—Interrogatories not returned with depositions—Nonsuit—Discharging jury.

A commission issued to examine witnesses abroad upon interrogatories and *viva voce*, but was returned without the interrogatories, in consequence of which the judge on the trial refused to allow either the deposition or the *viva voce* examinations of the witness to be read and the plaintiff was nonsuited.

Held, *per* Allen, C.J., Weldon, Palmer, King, and Fraser, JJ., that the evidence was properly rejected, but as the omission to return the interrogatories was not the fault of the plaintiff, a new trial should be granted on payment of costs.

Per Wetmore, J., that it was not clear that the *viva voce* examination could not have been read; therefore,

Quære, whether the plaintiff ought to pay costs.

Quære, whether a judge has power to discharge the jury from giving a verdict in such a case, without the defendant's consent. *Moran* v. *Taylor*, vol. 23, 224.

16—Counsel—Argument of—Whether parties bound by—Judgment—Setting aside or altering.

Parties are bound by the views presented by their counsel in arguing cases, and the court will not entertain a motion to set aside or alter their judgment on the ground that counsel had misrepresented the point to be argued, or was not sufficiently instructed. *Towee* v. *Outhouse and Knapp*, vol. 23, 334.

17—Rule—Service of, on party outside the jurisdiction of the court.

Where one of the parties in a cause was out of the jurisdiction of the court, it was ordered that the service of a rule *nisi* on him should be deemed sufficient service. *Ex parte Hyneman*, vol. 23, 480.

18—Judge's order—Making same a rule of court.

A judge's order can be made a rule of court, on production of the order with counsel's signature, but only during term. *McLeod* v. *James*, vol. 18, 139.

19—Motion for a new trial.

On a feigned issue sent down by Supreme Court in Equity, must be made before a judge in equity. *Powers* v. *Mines Ins. Co.*, vol. 18, 654.

20—Affidavits—Argument upon, or application for time to answer.

Held, (Wetmore, J., dissenting), on a motion heard on affidavits, the party moving must elect at the time the affidavits in opposition are read whether he will then argue the case, or apply for time to answer these affidavits. Their should be but one argument, and that when all the facts are before the court. *McCully v. Noonan*, vol. 24, 142.

Time to answer will be granted. *Ib.*

21—Affidavits used on obtaining rule nisi—Defect in—When may be objected to.

If an affidavit on which a rule *nisi* was granted is defective in not stating the deponent's addition, it may be objected to by the opposite party on shewing cause. *Ex parte Bain*, vol. 24, 159.

22—Rule nisi granted by judge at chambers—Filing of papers.

It is the duty of a party obtaining a rule *nisi* for a *certiorari* from a judge at chambers to file in the clerk's office the affidavits on which the rule was granted. *Ex parte Ryan*, vol. 24, 528.

23—Issue in law and fact—Ex parte order directing trial of—Rule nisi—Statement of grounds—Counsel confined to.

Plaintiff obtained a judge's order *ex parte* under Con. Stat., cap. 37, sec. 76, to reply and demur to defendant's pleas, and that the issue in law should be tried first;

Held (Wetmore, J., dissenting), that as the plaintiff had the option (subject to the direction of the court) of determining which issue he would try first, the defendant could not object to the order as having been granted *ex parte*. *Bell v. Moffat*, 2 P. B. 151, distinguished.

In supporting a rule *nisi* counsel will be confined to the grounds stated on obtaining the rule. *Grey v. Chapman*, vol. 24, 542.

24—Con. Stat., cap. 38—Bail Bond—One surety—Sufficiency of—Time of giving bond—Assignment of.

A bail bond given by a debtor under Con. Stat., cap. 38, sec. 5, is valid, though only signed by one surety, and may be assigned by the sheriff to the plaintiff in the suit. *Taylor v. Harper*, 5 Allen, 191, followed.

Such bond need not be given contemporaneously with the arrest, but may be given after the defendant has been imprisoned. *O'Brien*, appellant, and *Burchill*, respondent, vol. 24, 560.

25—Affidavits—Excessive damages—Action of tort.

Affidavits will not be received to shew that the damages are excessive in an action of tort. *Smith v. Chapman*, vol. 25, 296.

When plaintiff in person argues his own cause before the court, he cannot also be heard by counsel. See Bankruptcy.

—An order to arrest one of several defendants may be made. See Arrest 1.

—The defendant may be allowed to withdraw a demurrer, and plead without notice to plaintiff. See Trespass 5.

—A second attachment might issue, the first having been set aside. See Attachment 4.

—Refusal to hear a second application for a *certiorari*. See *Certiorari* 2.

—When respondent is entitled to have appeal dismissed with costs. See County Court Appeal 1.

—A plea professing to answer the whole cause of action, and in fact answering only a part, is bad. See Plea 1.

—Second application, where on first, facts were known. See Ejectment 3.

—Inquisition of sheriff's jury set aside by the court, if contrary to law and evidence. See Replevin 2.

—In trespass where declaration does not set out premises, the defendant may apply to court or a judge for an order to compel plaintiff to amend or give particulars. See Trespass 6.

—Filing of the particulars of the plaintiff's claim with the justice is not commencement of the action in a justice's court. See Justice's Court 1.

—Setting aside of judgment in ejectment for irregularity. See Ejectment 1.

—Whether the court would in any case grant a *certiorari* to bring up proceedings had before a county court judge. See New Trial 6.

—Discovery of new evidence, but such as only cumulative is no ground for a new trial. See Sale 2.

—There cannot be judgment of non-suit, and also a judgment for plaintiff on some of the issues. See Insurance 3.

—The obligors, on a bond given under Attachment Act, cannot, in an action on the bond, raise any question as to defendant's ownership of the property attached. See Attachment 2.

—The court will not interfere to aid attorneys in carrying out loose understandings. See Attorney 2.

—The fact of plaintiff having denied on cross-examination a fact afterward testified to by the defendant, will not prevent plaintiff calling witnesses to rebut defendant's testimony on the point as to which plaintiff had been cross-examined. See Ejectment 1.

—An irregularity in writ or *capias* which does not mislead the defendant is not sufficient to justify the setting aside of the arrest. See Arrest 2.

—Not to allow appeal on question of costs. See Costs 10.

—On an appeal from an order from a county court judge refusing a new trial on the ground of the verdict being against evidence, the court will not interfere with the finding of the court below. See New Trial 9.

—Extension of time for giving notice of motion as required by 42 Vic. cap. 8, sec. 10. See Notice of Motion.

—Where cause was entered for trial, but trial was postponed without being made a remanet, and new notice of trial having been given, plaintiff did not proceed to trial pursuant thereto, defendant is entitled to judgment as in case of a nonsuit. See Nonsuit 1.

—County court, not necessary to issue *ca. sa.* to fix bail. See Bail.

—Court has no power to grant attachment for non-payment of costs where non-suit was set aside with costs. See Costs 8.

—Where defendant gives notice of motion for leave to enter non-suit or a verdict, motion for new trial refused. See Amendment 2.

—Court will hear only one counsel on motion for new trial. See Trespass 7.

—As to construction of term "shilling." See Slander 8.

—Challenge to array—Where prisoner's husband has an action pending against sheriff. See Challenge 3.

—When defendant may move for judgment as in case of a non-suit. See Non-suit 1, 2.

—Court cannot give execution against a corporation for non-payment of costs. See Costs 7.

—Where cause has been noticed for trial and entered at the circuit—Court will presume cause was at issue. See Costs 16.

—Writ of *habeas corpus*—Proceedings—When issues by common law. See *Habeas Corpus* 2.

—When a judge who tries a cause dies without giving the plaintiff a certificate for costs, he is without remedy, as another judge cannot grant the certificate. See Costs 16.

—If in an action for negligence against a number of defendants, no evidence is produced against one of them, he is entitled to have a verdict of acquittal entered for him at the end of the plaintiff's case. See Negligence 3.

—Appeal under 11 Vic. cap. 12, court refused to interfere with decision of the justice where the evidence was conflicting. See Appeal 6.

Although return of gaoler shewed that a prisoner was properly in custody under the sentence of a court of competent jurisdiction, the court has power to enquire into the facts of the case. See Criminal Law 1.

—Attachment—Contempt of court—Interrogatories—When to be filed—Costs. See Attachment 7.

—A single judge has power to assess damages during term as well as in vacation. See Practice 10.

—A motion under Rule 2, Hilary Term 6, Wm. 4, that a rule *nisi* would be moved for, is irregular. See Motion Paper 1.

—A copy of judge's order made a rule of court. See Judge's Order 2.

Court of Equity—Amendment of title in bill—Describing defendant in his official character—Objection to jurisdiction—When to be taken. See Equity.

—County court appeal—Rule—When appeal allowed. See County Court Appeal 3.

—Delay in filing affidavit for bail and entry docket. See Bail Bond 1.

—Joint action of tort—Costs of acquitted defendant—Time of taxing. See Costs 19.

—Irregularity—Where notice of bail by firm of attorneys, one of whom has not paid his library fees. See Attorneys 4.

—Necessity of alleging in declaration the incorporation of company. See Joint Stock Companies Act 1.

—On a motion to set aside a judgment—Power of court to order a reduction. See Practice 10.

—Order of discharge under cap. 41, Con. Stat.—Whether court has power to set aside. See *Habeas Corpus* 3.

—Right of counsel to re-examine witness on matters brought out on cross-examination. See Ship's Husband 1.

—Review from justice's court—County court judge remitting cause to justice to enter up judgment. See Review 3.

—Review from justice's court—Time for granting summons. See Review 6.

—Appeal—To support the judgment appealed from—Right of respondent to avail himself of other grounds than those on which it was decided below. See Ship 1.

—When judgment signed before summons for a new trial, which did not contain a stay of proceedings has been disposed of. See New Trial 12.

—Amendment of trial—When proposed amendment would make count demurrable. See False Imprisonment 7.

—Canada Temperance Act—Prosecution before two justices—Information. See Canada Temperance Act 14.

—County court appeal—Omission to enter cause on appeal paper. See County Court Appeal 4.

—Equity appeal—Serving notice of. See Equity Appeal 1.

—Whether same should lie. See Costs 22.

—Equity appeal—Notice of—Statement of grounds. See Equity Appeal 2.

—Ejectment—Service of declaration—House locked—Refusal to open door. See Ejectment 5.

—Misappropriation of money by one partner of firm of attorneys—Summary application to court. See Attorneys 6.

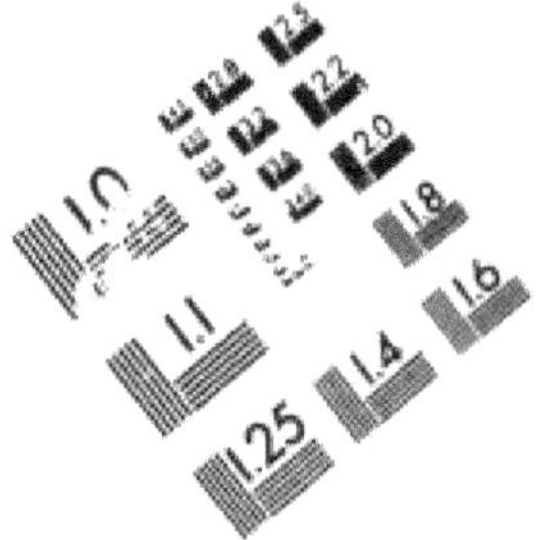

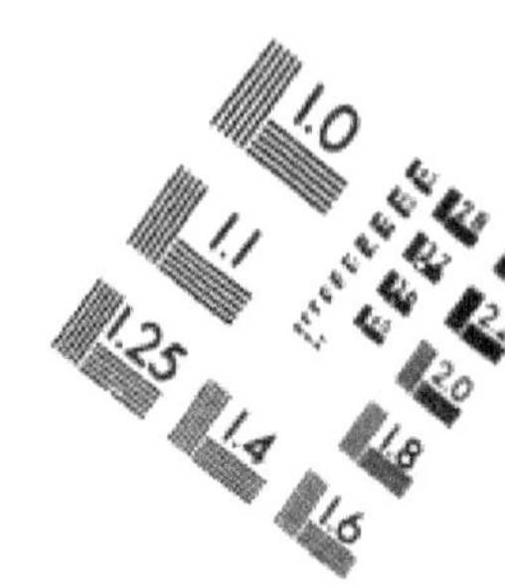

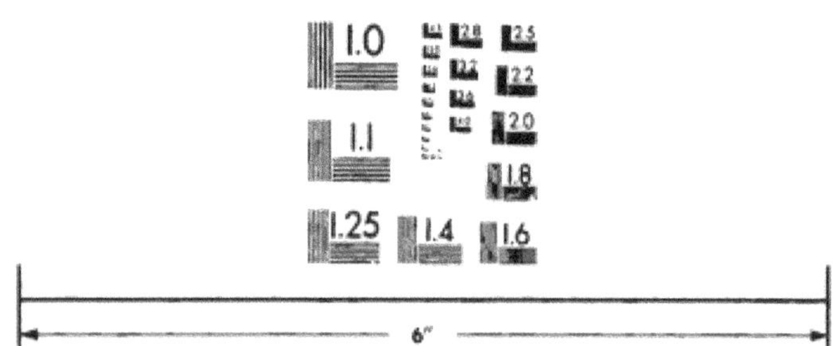

—Equity—Amending bill—Prayer—General relief—Where inconsistent with specific prayer. See Equity 1.

—Judgment — Setting aside — Taxation of costs without notice. See Costs 21.

—Special questions left to jury—Where not unanimous in answering—Whether verdict can be entered within two hours. See Verdict.

—Stay of proceedings—Cause ordered to be entered on motion paper—Whether notice of motion for new trial can be given pending stay. See Judge's Order 4.

—Where defendant pleads to one count only of declaration. See Costs 21.

—Where agreement before action to give credit of receipt found—Refusal of plaintiff to credit—Defendant's remedy. See Judgment 2.

—*Procedendo.* See *Procedendo.*

—Summons—Service of—Where defendant a lunatic. See Writ.

Presentment — In affidavit for attachment on promissory note, what must be alleged as to. See Practice 3.

Prescription. See Easement.

Primary creditor—Where estate is put in liquidation — Property vests in assignee subject to charges. See Garnishee Act.

Prisoners — *Habeas corpus* — Whether order to bring in again can be made without issuing new writ. See *Habeas Corpus* 1.

—In custody under a warrant of commitment made by a magistrate in due form of law, judge cannot make an *ex parte* order for his discharge. See Judge's Order 1.

Privileged communication — What constitutes—Publication of. See Slander 1.

—Reasons given by husband to wife for travelling under assumed name. See False Imprisonment 4.

—County court appeal—Judge certifying proceedings—Bond—Perfecting of. See County Court Appeal 7.

—Defective return. See County Court Appeal 8.

—Arbitration—Refusal to make submission to arbitration a rule of court where action pending on the award. See Award 3.

—Replevin—Claim of property—Setting aside defective claim. See Replevin 6.

—Setting aside pleas—Summary application. See Pleas 3.

—Staying proceedings until costs of former suit paid. See Stay of Action 2.

PRINCIPAL AND AGENT.

1—Attorney—Retainer—What constitutes.

The question of agency is for the jury. When W., a student at law, was in the habit of receiving, whilst a student in the office of defendant, letters for defendant from the post office, his agency after he is admitted an attorney is not necessarily continued, although he occupies by permission of defendant a portion of his office, and had access to the defendants post office box whenever he wished, it being no longer his duty to bring to defendant his letters, and W. never having had any authority to open defendant's letters, and never having opened them to defendant's knowledge, and defendant cannot be made liable for money received by W. on collection of a note, there being no evidence of a retainer by defendant.

Neither could the defendant be liable for a conversion until after the money came into his hands. *Eastern Township Bank v. Harrington*, vol. 18, 631.

2—Principal and agent—Municipal corporation—Committee appointed with specific duties—Extent of authority.

The B. Co. contracted with the town of Woodstock to construct in the town a system of waterworks, and furnish all materials, and to do everything necessary for their complete construction, and for placing them in readiness to be used. The town council appointed a committee to superintend the performance of the work under the contract.

Held, that the power of the committee was limited to superintending the work, and that they had no authority to bind the town by ordering extra work. *Boyer* appellant, and *Town of Woodstock*, respondent, vol. 24, 521.

—The agent of plaintiff having means of knowledge of conditions endorsed on a way bill, plaintiff bound by them. See Carrier 1.

—Right of agent to sue. See Agreement 5.

—Agent exceeding authority. See Power of Attorney. See *Fawcett* v. *Anderson*, Addenda 34.

Principal and surety—Bond given by surety — Alteration in duties. See Pleading 9.

PROBATE COURT.

1—Whether heir-at-law who is not entitled to any of the personal estate can cite executor to prove will in solemn form.

Held, that the heir-at-law, though he may not be entitled to any of the personal estate of a deceased person, may, under Con. Stat., cap. 55, sec. 44, file a petition to have an alleged will of the deceased proved in solemn form. *In re Annie B. Fox*, vol. 20, 301.

2—Proof of will in solemn form—Statement in petition for—Preliminary objections to petition—Appeal from decision thereon.

A petition to prove a will in solemn form under the Con. Stat., cap. 52, sec. 53, must state the names, ages, occupations, and places of residence of the heirs, etc., whether such petition is by a person interested in supporting the will, or in defeating it.

The citation must contain similar statements.

The words, "*and all others interested*," in the form of citation (C) are not a part of the form; but a direction to the judge of probates to name in the citation all the persons who are interested.

The decision of a judge of probates on the sufficiency of a petition to prove a will in solemn form, may be appealed from, though it may not be the final decision of a contested case, (Weldon, J., dissenting). *In re Charles McMullen*, vol. 23, 382.

—Questions of fact decided from the evidence sent up on appeal irrespective of the finding of the judge of probates. See Appeal 7.

—Proceedings, ministerial, may not be removed by *certiorari*. See *Certiorari* 5.

PROCEDENDO.

1—Conviction removed and confirmed, enforcement of conviction.

Where a conviction under the second part of the Canada Temperance Act has been removed by *certiorari* and afterwards confirmed, a *procedendo* will issue to carry back the record of the proceedings to the magistrate, in order that he may enforce the conviction. *Regina* v. *Grimmer*, vol. 25, 480.

2—Rule to take return off file when not necessary—Validity of conviction.

Where proceedings have been removed into this court by *certiorari* and affirmed, it is not necessary to take out a rule to take the return off file before applying for a *procedendo*, it being sufficient that leave has been granted to remove the return from the files.

Where a conviction has been removed by *certiorari* and affirmed, the court will not, on an application for a *procedendo* to the convicting justice, examine into the validity of the conviction on grounds not taken on the motion to quash it. *Regina* v. *White & Perry*, vol. 25, 483.

Proclamation—Under Canada Temperance Act—Declaring second part of the Act in force—Evidence. See Canada Temperance Act 7.

Progeny—Of mare, conveyed by bill of sale, passes with mare. See Bill of Sale 2.

Prohibition—Writ of—Application for—To restrain county court judge from proceeding with scrutiny of votes in election under Canada Temperance Act. See Canada Temperance Act 8.

PROMISSORY NOTE.

1—Payment—Usury.

Defendant purchased property from an administrator under an agreement that the amount of a joint note, which he held against the intestate and one of the administrators for money lent, should be deducted from the purchase money.

Held, in an action for the purchase money, that the defendant was only entitled to deduct the amount which he had actually loaned, that a sum retained by him as usurious interest at the time of the loan, could not be included in such amount. *Trueman*, administrator v. *Wood*, vol. 19, 522.

2—Endorsement before delivery by one not payee.

When one not a payee of a promissory note, payable to B. or order, puts his name on it before it is delivered to the payee to take effect as a note, with intent to give it credit, he will be held liable as a maker. *Bell* v. *Moffat*, vol. 20, 721.

3—Original consideration — Unstamped — Presumption.

R. being indebted to S. in $30, gave him an unstamped note for the amount.

Held, that S. might sue R. on the original consideration without shewing that the note was not outstanding, and could not be made available against him; and that the note being *prima facie* of no value when delivered, would in the absence of evidence, be presumed to continue so. *Richard* v. *Simpson*, vol. 20, 118.

4—Note payable in bankable currency—whether payable "otherwise than in money," within Act, 30 Vic. cap. 34. See *Dunn* v. *Allen*, vol. 24, 1.

5—Indorsement in blank—Transfer by widow of indorsee—Title of transferee—Executor de son tort.

The indorsee of a promissory note indorsed in blank, died intestate, and his widow without administering, sold and delivered the note, the plaintiff applying the proceeds in payment of the funeral expenses and debts of the deceased.

Held, that no property in the note passed to the plaintiff and that he could not sue the maker. *Green*, appellant, and *Holt*, respondent, vol. 25, 412.

6—Accommodation paper—Liability of indorsee to pay under agreement with payee—Extinguishment of debt.

A., being indebted to plaintiff and other persons, gave plaintiff a bill of sale of his goods, plaintiff agreeing to pay A.'s borrowed money and accommodation notes. Among the accommodation notes was one made by the defendant in favour of A., who endorsed it to the plaintiff without notice that it was an accommodation note. The note was discounted by a bank, and the proceeds received by A., and the plaintiff was obliged to pay it at maturity. In an action by the plaintiff to recover the amount of the note,

Held, 1 That as it was one of the conditions on which A. gave the bill of sale, that the plaintiff should pay his (A.'s) accommodation notes, he could not recover in the action, as his payment of the note in pursuance of his agreement was an extinguishment of the debt, though he did not know that it was an accommodation note.

2. That though the plaintiff's agreement to pay the accommodation notes was made with A., the defendant could avail himself of it as a defence to an action on the notes. *Peters v. Waterbury, et al.*, vol. 24, 154.

— Accommodation — Liability of maker where payee has been discharged. See Accommodation Note 1.

—Refusal of court to receive in evidence, note on which action was brought as the stamp was not cancelled See Evidence 3.

—Given for debt, and afterwards returned. See Accord and Satisfaction 1.

—Trover — Executor — Action by — Measure of damages where executor the maker of note. See Trover 4.

—Unstamped—Stealing of—Whether "valuable security" within meaning of Act of Canada, 32 & 33 Vic. cap. 21. See Criminal Law 3.

—Right to affix double stamps. See Bill of Exchange.

—Initials—Affidavit to hold to bail. See Affidavit 6.

—Of third party, given in settlement of bill of exchange—whether accepted in satisfaction and discharge of bill. See Agreement 7.

Proof of former trial. See Evidence 6.

PROPERTY, PASSING OF — VESTING OF.

1—Sale—Acts to be performed by seller—Trover.

Plaintiffs contracted with P. to put up 30,000 cans of lobsters for them during the fishing season of 1879, he to paint, label, and prepare the cans ready for shipment before delivery; the plaintiffs to pay 5½ cents per can, and furnish the cans, paint, etc., property in the fish to be the plaintiffs' from the time the cans were filled.

Held, in an action of trover against B., a purchaser at a sale under an execution against P. of 33 cases of cans put up by P., which at the time of seizure, and sale were not ready for delivery, that the fact that something remained to be done by P. before they would be ready for delivery did not prevent the property vesting in the plaintiff. *Murray, et al. v. Bourgeois*, vol. 20, 143.

2—Contract of sale—Goods not specified—Pretension to pass property in—Appropriation.

T. a brick maker sold 50,000 bricks out of a kiln containing 100,000 to the plaintiff, who paid the contract price, and hauled away about 16,000. The balance remained in the kiln in T.'s yard, and were never in any way separated from the rest of the kiln, or appropriated to the plaintiff. The defendant (the sheriff) subsequently sold them under an execution at the suit of W. against J. Plaintiff brought trover against defendant, claiming property in 34,000 of the bricks.

Held, per Weldon and Fisher, JJ., that the contract was executed, and the property in the bricks passed to the plaintiff at the time of sale.

Per Wetmore, J., that there being no specific identification or appropriation of the bricks, the contract was executory, and the property did not pass to the plaintiff. *Close v. Temple*, vol. 20, 231.

Appeal to Supreme Court of Canada allowed. See Addenda 53.

—Vesting of. See Replevin 4.

—To be acquired—Passing of bill of sale. See Bill of Sale 1.

—Property in lumber, ownership and control of lumber until payment of draft given for stampage under the agreement—Construction of agreement. See Addenda 28.

Prospective damages—Husband and wife—Injury to wife. See Husband and Wife 4.

Provincial Legislature. See *Ultra Vires*.

Quashing conviction — Judgment — Crown has no appeal from. See Indictment.

Quantum meruit—Improper admission of evidence to influence jury as to. See New Trial 5.

—Work done under a written agreement—Action for. See Assumpsit 4.

Quarries—Right to open new ones where right to quarry reserved in mutual deeds of partition. See Partition 1.

Questions tending to criminate—Witness not bound to state his reasons for refusing to answer. See False Imprisonment 4.

Quit—Where a continuing tenancy exists—The tenant must receive notice to. See Landlord and Tenant 1.

RAILWAY.

1—Meaning of centre line of—Description of lands—Evidence. See Ejectment 4.

RAILWAY COMPANY.

Right to grant running powers over its line to another company—Power of, to contract after the time limited by Act of Incorporation — Specific performance of contract—When equity will enforce—Lease—Entire rent reserved—Consideration illegal in part.

The Grand Southern Railway Company was incorporated by 35 Vic. cap. 47, passed 11th April, 1872, for the purpose of constructing a railroad from the city of St. John to St. Stephen, the capital stock to consist of at least $2,000,000, and the liability of the stockholders restricted to the amount of stock they held; $50,000 of the stock subscribed to be paid in before the operations of the company commenced; and that to entitle the company to the privileges of their charter, the construction of the road should commence within three years, and should be *bona fide* continued from year to year, so that the whole be completed within eight years from the passing of this Act. No stock having been paid in under this Act, the time for commencing the construction of the road was extended by 37 Vic. cap. 85; but the time for completion remained as before, and the company was authorized to commence the construction of the road as soon as $20,000 of the stock was "subscribed" for, $24,000 was subscribed for, but only $1,240 was paid in. The company did not complete the road within the time limited (11th April, 1880), and the legislature refused to extend the time.

On the 20th January, 1876, the company contracted with the government to construct the railway mentioned in the Act of Incorporation, to commence work by the 31st December following, and to complete the road by the 11th April, 1880, the government having power to terminate the contract by a six month's notice, unless the company gave satisfactory proof that the work was proceeding so as to be completed within the time limited. In January, 1879, the government gave the company a notice under the terms of the agreement.

By Act, 33 Vic. cap. 59, the Carleton Branch Railway Company was incorporated for the purpose of constructing a railway from the west side of the harbour of St. John to the European and North American Railway, near Fairville, with power to take and hold land etc., and provided that lands taken by the company should be held as lands taken and appropriated for highways On the 30th April, 1880, the Grand Southern Railway Company (respondents), entered into an agreement with the Carleton Branch Railroad Company (appellants), whereby the appellants granted to the respondents for a term of fifteen years the right to connect their railway with the appellant's railway, and to run their train over it, and to lay down sidings, etc., and also demised to the respondents certain lots of lands with the right to build station houses and freight houses on one of the lots, reserving to the appellants for the lands demised, and the rights and privileges granted, an annual rent. It was also agreed that if during the fifteen years the respondent could not use the track on the Carleton Branch Railroad for certain specified causes, they (respondents) might built a track for their own use alonside of the appellant's railway, with necessary earthworks, etc., and in case such track was constructed, the respondents should pay the appellants a certain specified rent per annum for so long thereafter as they should use the land for that purpose, and that they should have the right to use and maintain the second track at the special rents for 999 years.

The respondents filed a bill, alleging that on the 2nd June, 1880, they commenced to grade their line of railway so as to connect with the Carleton Branch road, but were prevented by the appellants. The bill prayed that it might be declared that the Carleton Branch Railway Company was bound to perform and execute the agreement entered into with the respondents, and should be enjoined from preventing or obstructing the respondents from uniting their railway with the appellants' line, and from interfering with or hindering the respondents from passing with their locomotives, etc., over the appellants' road in accordance with the agreement of the 30th April, 1880. An injunction order having been granted in the terms of the prayer:

Held, on appeal, by Allen, C.J., and Duff, J., (Weldon, J., dissenting.)

1. That the bill was in effect a bill for specific performance of an agreement, and before the court would enforce it, it must be satisfied that there was no reasonable ground to contend that the agreement was illegal, or against the policy of the law.

2. That the agreement of the 30th April, 1880, having been entered into after the time limited by the Act incorporating the Grand Southern Railway Company for the completion of the road, was *ultra vires* and void.

3. That the agreement was not such a one as a court of equity would attempt to enforce; and whether it was valid or invalid, in view of the financial condition of the Grand Southern Railway Company, it was not an agreement which the court ought to be active in enforcing.

4. *Semble*, that though the Carleton Branch Railway Company might grant to another company a right to connect with their railway, and have running power over it, it had no power to grant to another company a right to construct a separate track alongside its own line, or to make such a demise of its lands as purported to be made by the agreement of 30th April, 1880.

5. That if the demise of the lands to the Grand Southern Railway Company was illegal, it vitiated the grant of the easement or running powers over the Carleton Branch Railway, because one entire rent was reserved in respect of

both; and the legal part of the consideration could not be severed from the illegal part.

Held, per Weldon, J., that as the effect of the injunction order was merely to preserve the *status quo*, until the rights of the parties could be determined on the hearing, the appeal should be dismissed. *The Carleton Branch Railway Co. v. The Grand Southern Railway Co.*, vol. 21, 339.

2—Liability to fence—Occupier of adjoining land—41 Vic. cap. 97, sec. 22.

By Act, 41 Vic. cap. 97, sec. 22, a railway company were bound to erect and maintain sufficient fences on each side of their line where it passed through enclosed or improved land, and were made liable for all damages sustained by reason of neglect to maintain such fences. Plaintiff's cow strayed from his land into the highway, and thence into land belonging to H., adjoining the railway, and from thence out upon the railway track through a defective fence, and was killed by a train, but without any negligence in the management of the train.

Held, that the obligation to fence was general, and not merely as against the occupiers of land adjoining the railway; and that the company were liable for killing the cow. *St. John Railway Co. v. Montgomery*, vol. 21, 441.

3—Freight—Reasonable charge—Common carriers' implied promise—Action to recover back excessive charges.

By Act, 27 Vic. cap. 48, and 41 Vic. cap. 92, the Legislature gave power to the defendant company to construct and maintain a railway from St. John to the main boundary for the purpose of transportation of persons, goods and property of all descriptions, giving them all powers and privileges necessary to carry into effect such purposes and objects, and empowering them to purchase and hold engines, cars, and other necessary things for the transportation of persons, goods and property of all descriptions, and granting to them a toll upon all passengers and property of all descriptions, which may be conveyed or transported by them upon such road, at such rate as may be established from time to time by the directors of the company. Defendants having their line of railway in operation, plaintiff's builder at St. John delivered to them for transportation six platform cars. Nothing was said about the rate of freight previous to the six cars being carried, and no rate of transportation had been established by the directors for such description of property. Defendants refused to deliver the cars unless plaintiff paid at the rate of $23 a car, which he did under protest. Afterwards the builder at St. John sent seventeen more cars to the defendant's line, and they were by them received and transported in the same manner, nothing being said about the rate of freight. The like sum of $23 a car was demanded before delivery and paid under protest, and plaintiff thereupon brought action to recover the amount paid in excess of a reasonable charge.

Held, 1. That *prima facie*, and in the absence of proof of a more limited provision, the defendants must be taken to hold themselves out as carriers of all descriptions of property capable of being reasonably and conveniently transported over rails by a locomotive engine, to the extent to which they have the means and accommodation for such traffic;

2. That as to the six cars first sent, the defendants were entitled only to a reasonable compensation, as there was no established toll and no special agreement;

3. As to the remaining seventeen cars, that the defendants were bound to transport them for a reasonable remuneration at least, in the absence of a rate of freight established according to statute; that there was no implied promise on plaintiff's part to pay the same freight as on the six cars previously sent, the proper inference to be drawn from the transaction being, that the plaintiff relied on his right to have the goods carried at such rate as the law should declare to be the proper rate. *Green v. The St. John and Maine Railway Co.*, vol. 22, 252.

4—Action against for killing horse—Act 33 Vic. cap. 49 — Evidence — Sufficiency of—Fencing railway—Necessity of company shewing that lands were unimproved—Where fences had been erected by company.

In an action against a railway company for negligently killing the plaintiff's mare, he proved that on the night of the 13th October, the train was stopped while passing through or near his land, and that a passenger on the train saw the conductor, and some of the other men employed on the train, examining a mare which was lying at the foot of an embankment near the railway, and unable to rise without assistance: that early the next morning the plaintiff's mare was found dead near the same place, with several of her ribs broken, and that she had been grazing about there the previous evening, and was then uninjured.

Held, that there was sufficient evidence to leave to the jury that the mare which the conductor of the train was examining the previous night was the plaintiff's mare.

By Act, 33 Vic. cap. 49, a railway company was required to fence the sides of their road where it passed through enclosed or improved land; they put up a fence but allowed it to get out of repair, in consequence of which a horse strayed on the railway and was killed by the engine;

Held, in an action for killing the horse, that the defendants were bound to shew that the land where the horse was killed was not improved, so as to bring themselves within the exception in the Act. *New Brunswick Railway Co. v. Armstrong*, vol. 23, 193.

5—Fire set by sparks from defendant's locomotive—Coal or wood—Whether bound to burn coal, being less dangerous—Where property insured — Contributory negligence—Evidence.

Railway companies are bound to use care, as well in the kind of fuel which they burn as in the construction and appliances of their engines; and it is a proper direction to leave to the jury to find whether under the circumstances, it is or is not, negligence to use wood as fuel for their engines, the evidence shewing that there is more danger from the use of wood than from coal.

Where plaintiff's property has been burned through defendant's negligence, it is no answer to defendant's liability for damages that the property was insured.

Where plaintiff's barn was burned by the negligence of the defendants, although plaintiff was guilty of negligence in constructing his barn in such a way that hay in it would be exposed to sparks blown against, or falling upon, the barn, that will not disentitle him to recover if defendants might, by the exercise of ordinary care and caution on their part, have avoided the consequences of plaintiff's carelessness or neglect.

Evidence that fires frequently occurred along defendants' line of railway after the passing of their trains, is admissible in an action against the defendants for injury resulting from sparks from their locomotive.

Evidence offered by defendants to show what kind of fuel was used on other railways in the province, is irrelevant. *Robinson v. New Brunswick Railway Co.*, vol. 23, 323.

Appeal to Supreme Court of Canada allowed. See Addenda No. 24.

6—Through ticket—Injury to passenger on ferry boat owned by another company—Negligence of latter company—Contributory negligence.

Plaintiff purchased a through railway ticket from Boston, U. S., to Cape Breton, in the course of which journey he was obliged to cross the harbour of St. John by a ferry owned by the defendants.

On reaching the ferry he produced his ticket to the collector of fares, who tore off and retained a portion of it, returning the remainder of the ticket to plaintiff, and then allowing him to go on board the ferry boat and cross the harbour.

Held, 1. That this was evidence that the ticket was issued in Boston by the defendant's authority, and amounted to a contract by them with the plaintiff to convey him safely across the harbour.

2. That even if there was no contract between plaintiff and defendants, they having received him as a passenger were liable to an action if he sustained injury through their negligence while crossing the ferry.

Plaintiff was a passenger in defendants' steam ferry boat plying across the harbour of St. John.

A movable chain was placed across the end of the boat to prevent passengers and teams from going beyond it while the boat was in motion. When the boat arrived at the wharf or landing place it stopped and the passengers began to go on shore, though the boat had not been moored to the wharf, but a gangway or platform on which teams were accustomed to pass to and from the boat, was in the course of being placed in its position for that purpose. The plaintiff was a stranger, and while following the other passengers, and while in the act of stepping from the boat to the wharf, in the dark—the guard chain having been let down—fell into an open space between the end of the boat and the wharf, and was injured. The jury found that the guard chain was let down for the purpose of more conveniently mooring the boat to the wharf, but that it was not necessary to let it down for that purpose; and that it might reasonably be taken by the passengers to be an intimation that they might land.

Held, that the taking down of the guard chain was an intimation to the passengers that they might safely land, and that the plaintiff—not having heard any caution to the contrary—was justified in supposing that he had a right to do so, and that his attempting to land was not, under the circumstances, evidence of contributory negligence, though the boat had not been moored to the wharf at the time. *Macdonald v. The Mayor, etc., of St. John*, vol. 25, 318.

RAILWAY CONDUCTOR.

1—Employed by the government—Whether liable for nonfeasance—For misfeasance Evidence of misfeasance—Duty of conductor as to starting of trains—Call "all on board"—Conductor's duty as to waiting for passengers to get on board after call—Passenger's duty as to getting on the train—Affording opportunity to passengers to get on from the platform.

The defendant was conductor of a railway owned by the crown. While at a station he was by the regulations of the railway under the orders of the station master as regards the time of starting the train. But it was his duty to give the signal to the engine driver to go ahead. It was also his duty not to give the signal while passengers were getting on board, and in order that he might be in a position to see whether there was any getting on board he should stand when making the signal "near the front end of the first passenger car." The defendant in this case left the platform, passed across the train to a platform on the opposite side of the track, and there gave the signal to start, the time for starting having already expired. After the signal and while the cars were in motion, the plaintiff, who was waiting on the platform, in attempting to get on board, was thrown down and injured. On motion to enter a non-suit it was contended that the action would not lie as the defendant was an employee of the crown, and would not be liable except for misfeasance, and that while at the station he was under the control of the station master.

Held, that, even if it were necessary to show misfeasance in order to sustain the action against the defendant, the giving of the signal to start under such circumstances was evidence of a wrongful act done by him.

The judge directed the jury that it was the duty of the conductor to wait a reasonable time after the call was given for the passengers to get on board, and to see if there was any in the waiting room or elsewhere.

Held, by Allen, C.J., Weldon and Duff, JJ., (Wetmore, J., dissenting), that this direction went too far and was wrong.

Per Weldon and Duff, JJ., it is the duty of persons who propose to travel by any railway train to ascertain and know the time of its departure, and to get on board before the time has elapsed.

Per Allen, C.J., passengers are not bound to get on board until the call "all on board" is given, and it is the conductor's duty after the call to give the passengers a reasonable opportunity of getting into the cars and not to start the train until a reasonable time has elapsed.

Per Wetmore, J., it is the duty of the conductor after the call "all on board" to give the passengers in the waiting rooms of the station, as well as those on the platform a reasonable opportunity of getting on board the train.

Quære, *per* Allen, C.J., whether the words "while passengers are getting on board" in No. 124 of the Intercolonial Regulations, which forbids conductors starting the train while passengers are getting on board, applies or not to passengers who are on the platform ready to go into the cars as soon as those immediately in front of them, and who may be in the act of stepping in, have entered?

Passengers by railway should be afforded an opportunity of getting into the cars from the platform of the station, and where, under the evidence, it was doubtful whether the plaintiff had had such an opportunity afforded her, and further evidence on that point was thought desirable for an intelligent direction to the jury on the question of contributory negligence a majority of the court, (Wetmore, J., dissenting), granted a new trial. *Hall* v. *McFadden*, vol. 19, 340.

Appeal to Supreme Court of Canada, dismissed. See Addenda 51.

2—Intercolonial railway — Negligence of conductor—Accident to passenger—Right of action—Contributory negligence.

Plaintiff having a first-class ticket from Sussex to Penobsquis by the Intercolonial Railway, intended going to Penobsquis (her home) by the mixed freight and passenger train, which was due to leave Sussex at 1:47 p.m. The train on that day was an unusually long one, and when the passenger cars were brought to the platform the engine was across the highway. When the train came in, it was brought up so that the forward part of the first-class car was opposite the platform. It was then about ten minutes after the advertised time of departure. Plaintiff was standing on the platform when the train came in, but did not get on board. The conductor of the train (the defendant) got off the train and went to an hotel for dinner. While he was absent, without his knowledge, the train was backed down so that only the second-class car remained opposite the platform. The jury found that the first-class car did not remain at the platform long enough to enable plaintiff to get on board. The defendant, after finishing his dinner, came over hastily (being behind time and therefore somewhat in a hurry) called "all aboard," glanced down the platform, saw no person attempting to get on board, crossed the train between two box cars to signal the driver to start (it being necessary to cross the train in order to be seen by the driver, owing to a curve in the track), and almost immediately the train started. The 12th regulation for government of the Intercolonial Railway, prescribes that conductors must not start the train while passengers are getting on board, and that they should stand at the front end of the first passenger car when giving the signal to the driver to start, which he did not do in this instance. Plaintiff and a lady friend who was going by the same train were standing on the platform, and when they heard the call "all aboard" they went towards the cars as quickly as they could. F. got on all right, but plaintiff (who had a paper box in her hands), in attempting to get on board caught the hand rail of the car, when she slipped owing to the motion of the train, and was seriously injured. The jury found that the call "all aboard" was a notice to passengers to get on board.

Held, by Allen, C.J., and Wetmore and King, JJ., that although the plaintiff's contract was with the crown, the defendant owed to her as a passenger a duty to exercise reasonable care, and that there was ample evidence of negligence to leave to the jury.

But, *per* Weldon, J., that the defendant having brought the first-class passenger car to the platform, it then became (by the regulations) under the control of the station master, and defendant was not liable for starting the train from the position it had afterwards been placed in, also that it was plaintiff's duty to have gone on board as soon as the train came to the station. *Hall v. McFadden*, vol. 21, 586.

RAILWAY PASSENGERS.

1—Refusing to pay fare—Conductor's Right to eject from car—After having waited a reasonable time, and having then rang the bell, the conductor need not accept any tender of fare — Consolidated Railway Act—Orders in Council of August, 1885, for regulation of government railways.

The defendant, a railway conductor, asked the plaintiff for his ticket, to which the latter replied that he was travelling on public business, that he had no ticket or pass, and no money to pay his fare. The conductor thereupon told the plaintiff that he would have to put him off, and rang the bell and stopped the train for that purpose. Before plaintiff was actually put off the train, but before the bell was rung, the plaintiff tendered his fare, which the conductor refused to accept.

Held, in an action for assault, that there was no necessity for the conductor to wait a reasonable time after demanding the fare for the plaintiff to pay it, as the latter had said that he had no money: that the offer or tender of the fare, not accepted by the conductor, made after the bell had been rung, was too late; and that the conductor had a right to put the plaintiff off the train at a proper place, using no unnecessary force. *Thomas* v. *Gelbert*, vol. 20, 95.

RATES AND TAXES.

1—St. John—Act 31 Vic. cap. 85, secs. 6 & 7—Creating lien on land for two years—Whether can be recovered from tenant after that time.

Sec. 6 of the Act, 31 Vic. cap. 36, relating to the assessment and levying of taxes in the city of St. John, declares that the taxes to accrue on any property termed "real estate" under the Assessment Act of 1859, shall be a special lien on such property for two years after such taxes accrue. The 7th section declares that the taxes on such real estate may be levied and recovered from the owner of the property so assessed, or from any other person occupying the same as a tenant—a demand of payment being first made upon him—and if paid by the tenant, he may deduct the amount from the rent payable by him, or recover it from his landlord by action.

Held, that sec. 7. only provided a mode of enforcing the lien given by the 6th section, and that such taxes could not be recovered from the tenant after two years.

Quære, where even during the two years the tax can be enforced under sec. 7, against any person in possession of the land where the person assessed has parted with the title. *Armstrong* v. *Mayor, etc., of St. John*, vol. 20, 388.

Ratification—Writ issued without authority—Subsequent adoption and ratification. See Writs.

—If agents acts, what not. See Power of Attorney 1.

Raw hides—Exporting of. See Statute of Canada 1.

Reading to witness—Paper not in evidence not permissible. See Evidence 16.

—Refusing to allow defendant's counsel to read to witness B., what S. had sworn was said by him, B., about making a mistake, in order to ask B. whether such statement was true or not. See Practice 7.

Rebutting—Evidence—Where plaintiff has been cross-examined as to facts sought to be rebutted. See Ejectment 4.

Receipt, where mislaid—After credit for. See Judgment 2.

Recognisance—Ambiguous—Defective. See Controverted Elections Act 1.

Registered deed, effect of, where grantee had notice of a prior unregistered deed. See Trespass 3.

—Relation to date when not registered till after death of grantor. See *Doe dem* v. *Flanagan*, vol. 24, 154.

Registered owner of ship—Liability for wages, may be explained. See Ship.

Registry—Bill of sale—Absolute—Grantor continuing in possession. See Bill of Sale 3.

—Debtor and creditor account—Whether statement requires to be registered. See Bill of Sale 4.

Registrar—Sec 10 cap. 136, Revised Statutes—Whether of probates or deeds. See Will 7.

REGISTRATION OF VESSEL.

1—Ferry boat, effect of registration where bill of sale previously given—When boat subsequently rebuilt since bill of sale—Replevin — Inquisition — Whether can be set aside when contrary to law and evidence.

Defendant being owner of an unregistered ferry boat, gave plaintiff a bill of sale of it, by way of mortgage. Subsequently defendant from time to time made repairs to the boat, and finally substantially rebuilt her, when he registered her at the port of St. John under a new name, declaring himself to be the sole owner.

Held, that plaintiff's title under the bill of sale was good. *Gibson* v. *Gill*, vol. 19, 565.

RELATION.

Deed recorded after death of grantee—No rights intervening—Relation back to date of deed. See *Doe dem Flanagan*, vol. 25, 151.

Relationship to judge, when ground for new trial. See New Trial 6.

—Wife of judge related to wife of party in the cause. See False Pleas 1.

Relief of Bail—County court judge has no power to relieve bail who render their principal after expiration of thirty days after service upon them of writ in action on bond. See Bail 1.

Release, when obtained before judgment—Action on judgment—Whether plea of release available. See Judgment 3.

—By husband—Separate property of wife. See Deed 4.

REMANDING PRISONER.

1—Circuit court—No written order or warrant necessary—Return of habeas corpus.

Where a prisoner is committed to be held until discharged by due course of law, the warrant continues in force until the prisoner is discharged or sent to the penitentiary. It is sufficient, if at the circuit the judge remands a prisoner into the custody of the proper officer in court, no written order of commitment is necessary.

The sheriff, although he cannot return a warrant in *hæc verba*, must return the truth of the whole matter. *Regina* v. *Mulholland*, vol. 20, 476.

Remanet—Costs of making cause a remanet part of general costs in the cause. See Costs 18.

Rent—Where payable in advance—Action for use and occupation. See Landlord and Tenant 2.

REPLEVIN.

1—New trial—Nominal damages.

In replevin for wood the defendant pleaded *non cepit*. The jury found for the defendant contrary to the evidence.

On motion for a new trial,

Held, *per* Weldon and Fisher, JJ., (Wetmore, J., dissenting), that as the plaintiff could only have recovered nominal damages, a new trial should not be granted. *Hamilton* v. *Simpson*, vol. 19, 457.

2—Inquisition.

Held, in an action of replevin, by Allen, C.J., and Palmer, J., (Duff, J., dissenting), that where the inquisition of a sheriff's jury on a writ of *de pro. prob.* is contrary to law and evidence, the court has power over it, and will set the inquisition aside. *Gibson* v. *Gill*, vol. 19, 565.

3—Pleadings—Defence that property replevied has become part of freehold—Where defendant merely has mortgage on property—Entitled to succeed on non-cepit.

In an action of replevin for a quantity of mill machinery, defendant pleaded *non cepit*, and property in himself.

Held, that a defence that the machinery was part of the freehold and could not be replevied, was not available under the pleadings; and *per* Allen, C.J., and Duff, J., that defendant should either have pleaded that the machinery was affixed to the freehold, or have applied to the court to set aside the writ. *Per* Palmer, J., that the sheriff's return to the writ was a record which the parties to the suit were estopped from disputing, and that defendant's only remedy would be to apply to set aside the writ, and compel the sheriff to restore the property and amend the return.

Held, also, that on the plea of *non cepit* a defendant who never had possession of the machinery, but had merely taken a mortgage on the mill in which it was placed and also on the machinery, was entitled to succeed. *Alexander* v. *Cowie*, vol. 19, 509.

4—Contract to cut lumber—Vesting of property—Writ of replevin—Sheriff's possession under—Trespass—Pleading.

In November, 1874, A. agreed in writing with B. to get logs off land under B.'s control, and that they should be B.'s property as cut down. In December following, C. agreed with A. to cut and haul logs for him from the land specified in the agreement between A. and B., which logs were to be A.'s property at the landing. A. agreed to furnish C. with supplies to get the logs. C. cut logs under this agreement and hauled them to the landing. In November, 1873, the logs not having been driven and A. not having furnished sufficient supplies, he and C. rescinded their agreement, C. giving his note to A. for the supplies delivered. The logs remained on the landing, and in February, 1876, they were seized as the property of A., who had become insolvent, under a writ of attachment issued under the Insolvent Act of 1875. In May, 1876, C. sold the logs to the plaintiff, who drove them to the boom of the South-west Miramichi, where they were replevied by the assignee of A.'s estate. The plaintiff put in a claim of property in them, and the sheriff returned the writ of replevin, with such claim to the attorney who issued the writ. No writ *de pro. prob.* having been issued, the sheriff kept possession of the logs, and the plaintiff in this action brought trespass against him for taking them, to which he pleaded property in himself.

Held, *per* Weldon and Fisher, JJ., (Palmer, J., dissenting), that the sheriff's possession of the logs under the writ of replevin gave him such a special property in them as would support the plea of property.

Per Palmer, J., that by the seizure the sheriff acquired a mere possession of the logs and property, either general or special; and that to avail himself of this justification of taking them under the writ, the facts should have been pleaded.

Per Weldon, J., that the logs having been cut on B.'s land by C., as the servant of A., the property vested in B., under his agreement with A.

Per Palmer, J., that the cutting of the logs by C. under his agreement with A. was not a performance of A.'s agreement with B. to cut the logs for him, and did not vest the property in them in B. At most it was a question for the jury. That when the logs were hauled to the landing by C. they became the property of A. and were re vested in C. on the cancellation of the agreement, no act having been done by A. in the meantime to transfer the property to B. *Swim* v. *Sheriff*—*Hutchison* v. *Sheriff* vol. 20, 25.

Appeal to Supreme Court of Canada dismissed. See Addenda 39.

5—Bond—Execution by sole plaintiff (a feme covert) and two sureties sufficient—Plea in abatement—Non-suit.

A *feme covert* sued out a writ of replevin, and the bond required by the Con. Stat. cap. 37, sec. 202, was executed by her, and by her husband and another as sureties.

Held, 1st, that the bond was sufficient and might be assigned under the Act. 2nd, that it was no ground of non-suit on the plea of *non est factum*, that the declaration in an action on the bond alleged it to be the bond of the sureties only. *Vernon et al.* v. *Thompson et al.*, vol. 20, 116.

6—Claim of property—Setting aside defective claims.

Where a writ of replevin issued against five persons, and the property was found in the possession of one of them, who only was served with the writ; a claim of property put in by him and others is irregular, and will be set aside as to all but the defendant served with the writ. *Douthrite* v. *Sterres*, vol. 24, 545.

—Action in county court—Necessary to state value of goods in declaration. See County Court 1.

Return of sheriff to writ of—Estoppel. See Sheriff 1.

—Promise to indemnify sheriff—Action on. See Sheriff 2.

—Seizure of liquors — Dismissal of complaint—Right of defendant to have liquors restored to him. See Liquor License Act.

Representation—Sale of lumber—Estimated quantity—Survey bills. See Agreement 6.

Res Judicata—Con. Stats. cap. 38, sec. 7—Disclosure by debtor—Second application for disclosure. See Debtor 1.

Replication—In an action on promissory note—Bad by departure. See Pleading 7.

—Action for assault and battery—Plea of *son assault demesne*—Justifying assault only. See Pleading 5.

Representation as to quantity of lumber sold. See Agreement 6.

Request to leave—Necessity of, to justify assault, where one enters the house of another quietly. See Assault 1.

Reasonable and probable cause—Order of judge annulling demand not evidence of. See Addenda 41.

Reservation—Of life estate in portion of land conveyed by deed—Whether good. See Conveyance 1.

—Of common right to quarry in one moiety, where property divided by mutual deeds of partition. See Partition 1.

Residuary estate—When annuity to wife changeable on—Division of, by agreement of legatees. See Will 5.

—Whether certain property specified, belonged to. See Will 1.

Restitution—Writ of. See Summary Ejectment 2.

Return to habeas corpus—Must contain the whole truth of the matter. See Remanding Prisoner.

REVIEW.

1—Certificate that there was reasonable cause for joining a defendant—Con. Stat. cap. 37, sec. 209—Reviewing judge's exercise of discretion.

When the judge who tried the cause had certified that there was reasonable cause for joining a defendant, who had a verdict of *non cepit*, the court refused to review the exercise of the judge's discretion. *Alexander* v. *Currie and Tamie*, vol. 20, 476.

2—Civil court—Woodstock town of.

The proceedings by review under Con. Stat., cap. 60, do not apply to a judgment in the civil court of the town of Woodstock, under Act, 43 Vic. cap 48, sec. 10. *Lighton* v. *Dearing*, vol. 21, 440.

3—From justice's court—Remitting cause to justice to enter up judgment.

On review from a justice's court, the county court judge is not required to enter up judgment, but may remit the cause to the justice before whom it was tried to do so. *Ex parte Cook*, vol. 22, 557.

4—Civil court of the town of Moncton——Affidavit for—Before whom sworn.

An affidavit for review from a judgment in the civil court of the town of Moncton should be sworn before one of the parties mentioned in sec. 7, cap. 58, Con. Stat. *Ex parte Steves*, vol. 22, 558.

5—Jurisdiction—Court not legally constituted.

A judge has no power under sec. 43, cap. 60, of the Con. Stat. to review a judgment, when the person before whom the proceedings were had, had no authority to hold any court. *Worrall* v. *Brideau*, vol. 22, 562.

6—Time for granting—Second order where first not properly served.

Under cap. 60, sec. 43, of the Con. Stat., a judge may grant an order for review within thirty days after the party seeking the review obtained from the justice a copy of the proceedings; the time is not limited to thirty days after the judgment.

Where by mistake, the original order for review had been served, instead of a copy, the judge may grant a second order within the time limited by section 43. *Tower* v. *Outhouse*, vol. 22, 570.

—In action for false imprisonment defendant pleaded attachment granted by county court judge for non-payment of costs in case of review from justice's court, but plea did not set forth suit in justice's court, nor the making of the affidavit to give judge jurisdiction.

Held, bad on demurrer. See False Imprisonment 5.

—Refusal of magistrate to certify proceedings for. See Assault 3.

—Right of, to a judge from a conviction by the police magistrate of St. John. See Police Magistrate 1.

—Under Con. Stat., cap. 60—Judge has no right to grant a new trial. See *Certiorari* 6, 7.

—County court judge—When judge does not exceed his jurisdiction—Whether *certiorari* will lie. See *Certiorari* 8.

—Right of judge to order judgment to be entered for plaintiff, when improperly non-suited. See *Certiorari* 1.

—Whether order of a judge of county court in a case of review is final. See *Certiorari* 1.

—From justice's court—Costs of—When not in discretion of judge. See Damages 2.

—Whether right of, exists—Whether *certiorari* will be granted. See *Certiorari* 10.

—Of taxation when clerk refuses to tax costs claimed by plaintiff — no motion to review necessary. See Costs 6.

—Taxation of costs of arbitration. See Arbitration 1.

—Affidavit to obtain order for review—Entitling of. See Affidavit 5.

Revocation—Of will—Defendant relative revocation. See Will 8.

—**Executed parol license**—Easement. See Easement 2.

Riparian owner — Action against a fishery officer for seizing rods and lines. See Trespass 11.

—Tenant at will—Right of fishing. See Fisheries' Act 2.

Riparian proprietors—Whether Act. 31 Vic. cap. 60, sec. 7, sub-sec. 7, applies to riparian proprietors in New Brunswick, who acquired titles prior to July 1st, 1867. See Fisheries' Act 3.

Rivers—Tidal—Right to obstruct. See Addenda 29.

Rules. See Court general rules.

Rule nisi. A motion under Rule 2 Hilary Term 6, Wm. 4, that a rule *nisi* would be moved for, is irregular. See Motion Paper 1.

—For new trial—Costs of—Where plaintiff reduced his verdict to nominal damages rather than submit to new trial. See Costs 6.

—Where not entered on crown paper—Second motion day proper time for moving to make the rule absolute. See Practice 7.

—In supporting a rule *nisi*, counsel confined to the grounds stated on obtaining the rule. See Practice 23.

—Statement of grounds on which moved for. See Practice 23.

—Granted by judge at chambers—Filing of papers. See Practice 22.

St. John—Party complaining of assessments made in St. John is entitled to rule *nisi* for *certiorari*, without giving bond. See Assessment 2.

—Receiver of taxes of—Necessity of setting out in detail proceedings taken. See Arrest 5.

—Police magistrate of—Right of review to a judge from conviction by. See Police Magistrate of St. John.

—Rates and taxes—Creating lien on land for two years—Whether can be recovered from tenant after that time. See Rates and Taxes 1.

—City of — By-law — Retrospective operation of. See Contract 4.

—By-law respecting buildings. See Addenda 32.

—City of — Non-residents—Whether trustees of estate residing out of the city, but employing agents there to collect and pay moneys, co. See Assessment 4.

—Power of common council to reduce pay of policemen—Month's notice. See Policeman 1.

—What constitutes an inhabitant for purposes of taxation. See Inhabitant 1.

St. John City Court—Bailable action—Execution delivered to sheriff to fix bail—Effect of. See Bail 2.

—Costs—Taxation of—Want of affidavit. See Costs 25.

—Right of Dominion Parliament to make fishery regulations—Harbor of St. John. See Fisheries Act 4.

—Streets—Power of mayor, etc., to raise level of, and erect fence. See Addenda 40.

SALE.

1—Contract—Novation—Sale of land—Delivery of deed for inspection—Receipt for—Action on.

A new contract by novation cannot be created without the consent of the original creditor.

Land was sold at auction by plaintiff under power of sale in a mortgage to W., and defendant became the purchaser, the terms of sale being ten per cent. cash and balance in one and two years, with interest, secured by joint notes of defendant and some other responsible person. Defendant paid the ten per cent., and a conveyance was prepared and executed by W. in favor of defendant, and was given to plaintiff for the purpose of having sale completed. Plaintiff took the deed to defendant and said that he wished to show it to his attorney; but plaintiff objecting to part with the deed without something to show that the purchase money had not been paid, defendant signed and gave to plaintiff a receipt as follows: "Received from E. A. (plaintiff) a deed given by W. for a piece of land bought, etc. The above-mentioned deed I receive only to be examined, and if lawfully and properly executed, to be kept; if not lawfully and properly executed, to be returned to E. A. When the deed is lawfully and properly executed to the satisfaction of my attorney I will pay the amount of balance due on the said deed, provided I am given a good warrantee deed, and the mortgage, which is on record, is properly cancelled, if required."

In an action brought by plaintiff on this agreement,

Held, that there was no new contract created between defendant and plaintiff, and the action was not maintainable.

Held, also, that the defendant was not bound by the receipt to pay the remainder of the purchase money in cash, but only in the manner agreed to at the time of sale. *Anderson* v. *Fawcett*, vol. 19, 34.

2—Specific article—Contract reduced to writing—Evidence adding to or varying not admissible—Warranty that article sold is fit for the purpose for which it is bought—Not implied on sale of specific article which purchaser may examine—Statute of Frauds.

Where a contract, which required to be in writing by the Statute of Frauds, for the sale of a quantity of hemlock bark, was reduced to writing, and contained in a bill of parcels which clearly showed that the bark was then at Shediac, and the parties were contracting in reference to that particular bark; and evidence was received of alleged statements by one of the defendants in regard to the delivery, which statements were altogether immaterial, or the effect of which was to add or to vary the terms of the written contract; the court

Held, that the evidence was improperly admitted, and granted a new trial.

There is this distinction between written contracts at common law and written contracts under the Statute of Frauds, that parol evidence will not be admitted to show a subsequent variation of the latter.

Where the buyer had an opportunity before the purchase of examining a specific quantity of hemlock bark purchased by him, the court

Held, that there was no implied warranty on the part of the seller that it was merchantable hemlock bark. *Peters* v. *Hamilton*, vol. 19, 281.

Appeal to Supreme Court of Canada allowed. See Addenda 52.

3—Molasses—Agreement as to determination of quantity—Dispute as to whether by guage inscribed on casks, or by that guage, if correct according to the system of the place where guaged—Where guage erroneous—Evidence—Admissibility of paper spoken of between parties where conversation admissible—Discovery of cumulative evidence—No ground for a new trial.

The plaintiffs alleged that they purchased a quantity of molasses from defendants under the agreement that the quantity was to be determined by the St. John guage, which had already been made, provided that the guaging had been done correctly according to the St. John system. The defendants, on the other hand, alleged that the agreement was that the quantity was to be ascertained by the guage inscribed upon the casks by the St. John guager, whether the same was more or less than the correct quantity. The evidence on this point was contradictory. The rod with which the St. John guager had guaged the molasses was too short, and had, without his knowledge, been tampered with, and the actual quantity of molasses was considerably less than what the plaintiffs paid for, and the plaintiffs brought this action to recover back the amount so overpaid. The judge left the questions to the jury in the following manner: Did the plaintiffs purchase on the St. John guage as inscribed on the casks, and was the bargain that such inscribed guage should be taken as the correct quantity, whether the same showed more or less than the correct quantities? If so, inasmuch as both parties apparently acted on the *bona fide* belief that the guaging had been done correctly in the ordinary way, the plaintiffs would be precluded from opening up the matter and claiming for any deficiency. Secondly, If such was not the bargain, was it that plaintiffs should accept the molasses by the St. John guage made in the ordinary way? If so, then if the guage had been regularly done by the St. John guager with a lawful instrument, and the quantities should not be satisfactory to the purchasers, they would, notwithstanding, be barred by the measurement, and could not recover for any deficiency; but if the guaging was not done with a lawful instrument, but with a rod of imperfect dimensions, it would not be a guaging by the St. John system. In fact, it amounted to no guaging at all, and the guaging upon which the defendants sold had not taken place, and plaintiffs would be entitled to recover back any money overpaid on account of such short delivery.

Held, on motion for a new trial, that this direction was correct.

S., a gauger at St. John, sent defendant a certificate of a quantity of molasses contained in a number of casks by them sold to the plaintiffs, as ascertained by a regauging.

The certificate he afterwards saw in defendant's possession, and conversed with one of them about it. The conversation between S. and the defendant, having been received in evidence, the certificate was offered in evidence, and received subject to objection.

Held, that as the conversation was admissible, the certificate, concerning which they were conversing, was also admissible.

The discovery of new evidence, but such as is only cumulative, is no ground for a new trial. *Carr* v. *McNama*, vol. 19, 121.

4—Sale of goods—Statute of Frauds—Guarantee—New trial—Unimportant evidence admitted.

A. agreed to get out logs for plaintiff, who was to furnish the supplies. A. employed defendant to haul the supplies to his camp, and so informed the plaintiff; but when the defendant went for them the plaintiff refused to give them without a written order from A., but, (as he stated) told the defendant he would give them to him, and hold him responsible if A. did not pay for them. The defendant's account of what took place was that when the plaintiff was getting the goods ready he told the defendant he should charge [illegible] him, to which the defendant [illegible] that he need not do so; the[illegible] not for him, but for A., and [illegible] the defendant, did not want them, and that plaintiff afterwards delivered him the goods, and he took them away. The plaintiff had charged the goods to A., but altered the entry and charged them to the defendant as got for A. The question left to the jury was, whether the goods were sold and the credit given to the defendant, or to A., and they found the former.

Held, on appeal, by Allen, C.J., and Weldon, Wetmore and Palmer, JJ., (King, J., dubitante), that the direction was proper; that if the sale was made to the defendant it was immaterial whether he accepted the goods as his own, or as the agent of A., that his liability was original, and not a collateral engagement to answer for the debt or default of A.

Per King, J. That the inference to be drawn from the evidence was that the plaintiff delivered the goods on account of A.

Where evidence improperly admitted was unimportant, and could not have influenced the jury, a new trial was refused. *Black* v. *Doherty*, vol. 22, 215.

5—Passing of property — Defendant on agreement between parties—Security to be given.

G., residing in this province, ordered goods from the plaintiff at Quebec, promising to give a note for the price indorsed by the defendant. The plaintiffs sent the goods to G. with the invoice, and wrote requesting him to send a note for the amount with the defendant's indorsement. G. received the goods, but did not obtain the defendant's indorsement, and shortly afterwards the defendant got possession of the goods under a bill of sale from G. In trover for the goods, the jury were directed that if the plaintiff forwarded the goods to G. fairly expecting he was to receive a note indorsed by the defendant, the property in the goods would remain in the plaintiff and he would be entitled to recover.

Held, a misdirection; that, if in the opinion of the judge, there was evidence of it, it should have been left to the jury to find whether the agreement was that the property should not vest in G. unless the note indorsed by the defendant was received. *McCall et al.* v. *Gillespie*, vol. 21, 98.

—Payment—Appropriation. See Contract 7.

—Passing of property. See Property, passing of, 2.

—Of goods—Offer by letter—Acceptance—Statute of Frauds. See Contract 17.

—Of lumber—Estimated quantity—Representation. See Agreement 6.

—Of two descriptions of goods—Entire contract—Acceptance. See Contract 13.

—Conditional sale—Representation—Estoppel. See Trover 6.

SALE OF LAND.

1—Leasehold property—Execution—Notice o' sale.

Quære—Whether the sheriff should advertise leasehold property for three months previous to sale under execution. *Munroe* v. *Griffith*, vol. 20, 113.

2—Contract—Conditions of sale—Performance of.

Where the terms of sale require twenty-five per cent. of the purchase money to be paid at the time of sale, the purchaser must perform the condition strictly, a tender of the instalment on the afternoon of the day of sale is not a compliance with the condition. *Macdonald* v. *Mayor, etc., St. John*, vol. 20, 114.

3—Tender of conveyance — Recovery of deposit—Waiver.

It is the duty of the vendor of lands to prepare and tender the conveyance.

B. purchased land at an auction sale and paid a deposit, under an agreement that he was to receive a clear title. The land was incumbered, and the incumbrance was not removed at the time limited for the giving of the deed.

Held, that B. could treat the contract as rescinded and sue for the purchase money even though he knew of the incumbrance at the time of the sale. *Taylor v. Executors of Wetmore, etc.*, vol. 20, 165.

—Property may vest in purchasers, although something remains to be done. See Property—Passage of.

—By sheriff—Bidding by one who had forbidden the sale not evidence of leave and license. See Sheriff's Sale 1.

—Sale of land—Description—Mistake. See Agreement 6.

—Deed handed to purchaser for examination. See Agreement 5.

Sale under warrant for taxes—Judicial Act in granting order for reversal of, before disputing validity of sale. See Assessment 8.

Schools—Common—Remedy against secretary of school trustees for refusing to hand over property of corporation. See Injunction 1.

Schools Act—Sec. 81, meaning of words in. See Notice of Action.

Scrutiny—Parties to—Election under Can. Temp. Act—Inquiry by judge. See Canada Temperance Act, 8, 20.

Scuffling—Captain of vessel charged with. See Evidence 16.

Seal—Cutting off from will. See Will 8.

Seaman's Act, 1873—Conviction for harbouring foreign sailors—Written consent of consul to prosecute—Certiorari—When return may be amended.

A conviction under the Dom. Stat., 36 Vic., cap. 129, for unlawfully harbouring foreign sailors—deserters from a foreign ship—should show on the face of the proceedings, either the consent of both parties, or the written consent of the foreign consul, that the justice should proceed, as required by section 127 of this Act: and where such consent did not so appear, an affidavit stating that the justice had the consent, was not allowed to be read on shewing cause against a rule *nisi* to quash the conviction.

Where in such a prosecution both parties had treated the vessel as a foreign vessel, and the master and sailors as foreigners, although there was no direct proof that they were so; it is too late, on shewing cause against a rule *nisi* to quash a conviction based on the vessel and crew being foreign, to object that there was not evidence of these facts. *Regina v. Blair, etc.*, vol. 24, 245.

Jurisdiction of county court judge. See Ship 1.

Search warrant—When copy may be demanded—Reasonable search for goods. See False Imprisonment 1.

—Where goods stolen—Information. See Trespass 9.

Second trial—Reading of and commenting on judgment in former trial to jury is improper, but not ground for a new trial. See Settled Accounts 1.

Secretary of school trustees—Remedy against, for retaining property of corporation. See Injunction 1.

—Whether entitled to notice of action. See Notice of Action.

Secular calling—See Slander 6.

Security for costs—Bond considered defective—Duty of defendant's attorney. See Judgment 1.

—Where plaintiff insolvent, action brought for benefit of third person. See Costs 23.

Separate property—See Married Woman. See Husband and Wife.

Session, county—Liability of municipality for debts contracted by. See Municipality 1.

SETTLED ACCOUNTS.

1—With deceased person—Conclusiveness of—Account stated—Improper admission of irrelevant evidence—New trial.

In an action on a special agreement for board and lodging, and to pay an extra sum for additional accommodation, evidence of circumstances shewing the reasonableness of the plaintiff's claim is proper.

Where accounts including the plaintiff's charge for the board of a person since deceased, had been settled between them, annually, for eighteen years, but after such person's death, an action was brought against his administrator, for an extra sum claimed to have been agreed to be paid by the deceased for additional accommodation during that period, it is not misdirection to tell the jury that the settlement, though strong evidence against the claim, was not conclusive; without also pointing out the danger of disturbing settled accounts, after the death of one of the parties.

Asking a witness if he wrote a letter containing certain statements, which were read to him, is improper, and a ground for a new trial if the letter is material.

Reading to the jury on the second trial of a cause, the judgment of the court setting aside a former verdict, for the improper admission of evidence, and commenting on such evidence and on the judgment, though improper, is not a ground for a new trial. *Powell v. Wark*, vol. 20, 15.

SET-OFF.

Equitable set-off—Judgment—Cross-claims and damages arising out of the same contract—Assignment of claim after verdict—Pleading set-off.

G. brought an action against H. for breach of an agreement to construct railway cars, and for money had and received. On the same day H. brought an action against G. on the same agreement for refusing to accept the cars, and also to recover a balance due on other transactions between them. G. obtained a verdict for $160 in March, 1884, on the special count with leave to move to enter a verdict, also on the count for money had and received which was granted, and in June, 1885, judgment was signed for $5,025. In April, 1884, G. assigned to L. all his interest in his claim against H., and in the judgment that might be signed, and notice of this assignment was given to H. in May, 1884. In February, 1885, G. gave a confession to H. for the amount of the account due by him to H., and judgment was then signed by H. against G. for $2,214.

On an application by H. to set off the amount of his judgment against the judgment recovered against him by G., (the difference between the two judgments having been paid by H. to G.'s attorney with consent of G. and L.),

Held, by Allen, C.J., Palmer, King, and Fraser, JJ., (Wetmore, J., dissenting), that under the circumstances H. was entitled, notwithstanding the notice of assignment, to have his judgment set off against the judgment of G. *Harris v. Greene*, vol. 25, 451.

Reversed on appeal to Supreme Court of Canada.

—Promissory note—Amount not recoverable under pleadings in former action by present defendant. See Former Recovery 1.

Servant—May sue for wages for the time he has worked. See Assumpsit 3.

Several defendants—An order to arrest one may be made. See Arrest 1.

Shareholders— Where certificate evidence of, under 37 Vic. cap. 94, Acts of Parliament. See Evidence 16.

SHERIFF.

1—Writ of replevin—False return—Estoppel Actual damages.

The plaintiff delivered to the sheriff a writ of replevin against S., under which the sheriff seized the goods mentioned in the writ. No claim of property was made within forty-eight hours after the seizure, but a warrant under the Absconding Debtors' Act was lodged with the sheriff, under which he attached the goods as the property of C. The plaintiff then applied to the sheriff for the goods, and he offered to deliver them if the plaintiff would attend at a warehouse where they were locked up, but the plaintiff refused to do so, claiming to have the key of the warehouse which the sheriff refused to give him. The sheriff considering that his offer to deliver and the plaintiff's refusal amounted to a delivery of the goods, made a return to the writ of replevin, that he had delivered the goods to the plaintiff.

In an action against the sheriff for a false return, in which a verdict was given against him for the value of the goods.

Held, (Wetmore, J., dissenting), that the sheriff was not estopped by his return from shewing that the goods were not the property of the plaintiff, but were the property of C., the absconding debtor.

Per Wetmore, J., that, as no claim of property had been put in, it was the sheriff's duty to deliver the goods to the plaintiff, and having failed to do so, he was liable for the value of the goods.

Per Fraser, J., that, if the goods were the property of C., the plaintiff had sustained no damage by the non-delivery of them to him, and could not maintain the action against the sheriff. *Robinson* v. *Shirreff*, vol. 25, 58.

2—Seizure of property by, under execution—Promise by attorney of judgment creditors to indemnify—Adoption by client of attorney's acts—Exemplification of judgment—Evidence—Several claimants of property replevied—Delivery by sheriff to one claimant—Agreement to indemnify sheriff—Action on agreement.

A promise by the attorney of a judgment creditor to indemnify a sheriff for seizing goods under an execution issued on the judgment is binding upon his client where the attorney has the management of the business, and the subsequent acts of the client shew that he had adopted the proceedings which his attorney had taken in reference to the execution.

An exemplification of a judgment in an action brought by the judgment debtor against the sheriff for seizing the goods, is evidence in an action by the sheriff against the judgment creditor on the promise to indemnify.

A sheriff having taken logs under a writ of replevin issued by A. against B. claims of property were put in by H. M. and S. respectively, but no writ de pro. pro. was issued. Part of the logs having got into the possession of M., he afterwards requested the sheriff to deliver the remainder of them to him. The sheriff objected to doing so—S., having brought action against him for detaining them—but on M. stating to him that he would be kept harmless if he delivered up the logs to him, the sheriff delivered the logs to M., who sawed them in his mill. S. recovered in his action against the sheriff for a part of the logs delivered to M. at whose expense the suit was defended.

Held, that the sheriff was entitled to recover against M. on his promise to indemnify, the amount of the judgment recovered by S. against the sheriff. *Shirreff* v. *Muirhead*, vol. 25, 126.

—Action against for seizing property. See Judgment Creditor.

—Seizing of tenants goods under execution — Landlord's claim for rent —Evidence of value of goods seized. See Landlord and Tenant 5.

—Sale of chattels not seen by sheriff at time of levy, and not mentioned in notice of sale. See *Woods*, appellant, and *McCann*, respondent, vol. 25, 253.

Sheriff's return—He is estopped from returning *nulla bona* to execution issued on plaintiff's judgment, where he holds property under writ of attachment issued by plaintiff. See Attachment.

—Possession of—Under writ of replevin. See Replevin 4.

Sheriff's fees—On executions — Liability of attorney for. See Particulars 1.

Shilling—Meaning of—In rule of court. See Slander 3.

SHERIFF'S SALE.

1—Bidding by plaintiff who had forbidden sale, not evidence of leave and license—Measure of damages—Evidence.

In an action of trespass by the husband and wife against the defendant, sheriff of Queens, for taking the property of the wife under an execution against the husband, the defendant, on the trial was allowed to add a plea of leave and license. The evidence offered to support the plea was the fact of the female plaintiff having attended the sheriff's sale and bid in some of the goods. She had previously forbidden the sale, and the defendant in his evidence stated that he took the goods and sold them under the execution. It also appeared that she purchased the goods at a low price, no one bidding against her.

The judge directed the jury that there was no evidence to support the plea, and that the fact of the wife buying the goods at a low price did not affect the question of damages; the defendant would be liable for the value of the goods.

Held, that the direction was good.

Application to add a plea of leave and license was made after evidence that the female plaintiff had bid at the sale was given, and on the ground that this supported the plea. The defendant in his evidence claimed to sell adversely to the plaintiffs under an execution against the husband. Subsequently the defendants' counsel, without stating by whom he would prove it, offered evidence to shew the plaintiff's assent to the sale, which was refused.

Held, rightly so. *Scott* v. *Palmer*, vol. 21, 304.

SHIP.

1—Master—Wages of—How recovered—Registered owner—Liability for wages—May be explained—Appeal—Practise—County court jurisdiction.

R. B., plaintiff's brother, having a vessel partly built, entered into an agreement with defendant, by which the latter was to supply a certain amount to complete her. The agreement provided that the vessel when completed should be registered in defendant's name as security; that R. B. should take her to Liverpool on his own account and pay all disbursements, for which defendant was to advance R. B. a further sum. She was to be sold at Liverpool, the defendant paid, and the balance given to R. B.

Under this agreement R. B. finished the vessel and she was registered in the name of the defendant. R. B. employed plaintiff as captain, without any other authority from defendant to do so, and he did not interfere. The vessel proceeded to Liverpool under the directions of R. B., he going in the ship himself, but instead of selling her and paying the defendant, he chartered the vessel and carried out to America against the defendant's protest, and on her voyage back to Europe she was wrecked and put into Nassau, abandoned the voyage, and went from thence to Pictou for Pictou, where R. B. discharged plaintiff and settled with him, a balance of £32 2s. 8d. sterling, being found due plaintiff for wages for which this action was brought. On the trial, which took place in the county court of Kent, it was proved that defendant resided at St. John (being more than twenty miles from Pictou) at time of plaintiff's discharge and ever since.

The county court judge left the case to the jury, who found a verdict for the plaintiff, but the judge afterwards nonsuited him on the ground that by the 56th section of the "The Seaman's Act, 1873," the court had no jurisdiction to try the case.

Held, 1st, that the county court had jurisdiction, and the judge was wrong in ordering a non-suit on that ground; but

Held by Allen, C.J., and Palmer and King, JJ., that under the facts proved, R. B. and not the defendant was liable for plaintiff's wages, and the non-suit was upheld on that ground. And also that it is open to the respondents in order to support the judgment of the court appealed from, to avail himself of other grounds than those on which it was decided below.

Held, by Weldon, J., that there was evidence of defendant's liability to go to the jury, and that there should be a new trial.

By Wetmore, J., that there was evidence of defendant's liability to go to the jury, and that the verdict should be restored. *Brown* v. *Vaughan*, vol. 21, 238.

2—Mortgagee of ship—Agreement not to charter without consent of mortgagor—Notice of charter by telegram—Construction of port of loading—Acquiescence by mortgagor.

Plaintiff, the managing owner of a vessel, residing in this Province, mortgaged her to defendant, a broker in England, who covenanted that if the vessel should be consigned to him, he would not charter her without the plaintiff's consent. Afterwards, while the vessel was on a voyage to King's Lynn, in England, the plaintiff wrote to defendant telling him if he had not already chartered the vessel, not to do so, but to send her in ballast to Sydney, C. B., for coal. On the 29th of May, 1880, a few days after the receipt of this letter, the defendant agreed to charter her to carry a load of coal from North Shields in England, to Salem, Massachusetts; but in consequence of the master refusing to sign the charter-party unless the plaintiff was communicated with, the defendant telegraphed to plaintiff as follows: "Fixed Kersten (vessel's name) coal—Salem, 12 offered 67/6, dry deals, Saguenay to St. Malo,"—to which plaintiff answered by by telegraph, "Take coals, don't take deals." Immediately on receipt of this the charter-party was signed, and the vessel proceeded to Shields, about 170 miles from King's Lynn, took in cargo and sailed for Salem about the end June, and early in July ran ashore and was injured. She was got off and repaired, sailed again, and arrived at Salem. The plaintiff received a copy of the charter-party from the defendant on the 20th June, which was the first knowledge he had that the vessel had gone to Shields to load, but he made no objection on that account, and when he was afterwards in July informed of the damage to the vessel, he requested the defendant to do the best for his (plaintiff's) interest in looking after the repairs, insurance, etc. The defendant continued to act as the plaintiff's agent in reference to the vessel and other matters for about two years after this, making advances to the plaintiff without any complaint by him of the vessel having been sent to Shields until the defendant pressed for payment of the amount due him, when the plaintiff brought this action for breach of agreement.

Held, per Wetmore, Palmer and Fraser, JJ., 1. That the telegrams did not necessarily mean that the vessel should load at Kings Lynn, but authorized the defendant to charter her to load at any port where a prudent merchant would send a vessel for such purpose.

2. That as by the telegrams it could not be known what port of loading was intended, that must be ascertained by extrinsic evidence, and the court had a right to look to what was written and done by the parties after the telegrams were sent, to assist in interpreting them, and to show what port of loading was intended.

3. That the plaintiff by his conduct and dealings with defendant after knowing that the vessel had been chartered to load at Shields, and not making any objection, was estopped from saying that the defendant had not put the proper interpretation on the telegrams.

Per King, J. 1. That the meaning of the telegrams was that the vessel was to load at King's Lynn, where she then was; or, if that was not a coal shipping port, from such a port reasonably near; and according to the construction of the telegrams there was a breach of covenant by defendant in chartering the vessel without the plaintiff's consent.

2. But that the plaintiff's conduct after knowing of the charter, and not making any objection, had ratified the defendant's act, or treated it as an immaterial variance fr[illegible] his instructions.

3. That the word "fixed" in defendant's telegram implied a completed transaction; but the defendant's telegram and the plaintiff's answer shewed that that was not the meaning intended, and that it was conditional on the plaintiff's assent. *Appleby v. Black et al.*, vol. 24, 598.

—Notice of abandonment—Whether owner entitled to reasonable time to make enquiries after hearing of loss. See Insurance 16.

—Freight—Whether owner of vessel *prima facie* entitled to. See Insurance 3.

— Registered owners — Equitable owner. See Insurance 14.

—Sale by master—When allowable. See Insurance 16.

—Notice of abandonment—Waiver of. See Insurance 16.

—Repairs—Where should be made. See Insurance 17.

SHIP'S HUSBAND.

1—Part owner of vessel—Agent of other part owners—Settlement of accounts by him, sufficient account stated to entitle others to bring an action at law—Crediting agent not payment of money to principal—Right of counsel to re-examine witness on matters brought out on cross-examination.

The plaintiff and defendant with others were part owners of a vessel of which the defendant acted as ship's husband. The course of business was for the defendant to make up the accounts of each voyage at its close, and to apportion the earnings of the vessel amongst the part owners according to their respective shares, and the amounts so apportioned were then carried to the credit of each part owner in account with the ship's husband, and held subject to his order. The earnings of the several voyages so credited were entered separately in the books of the ship's husband, and the balances were not carried forward as a continuous account.

In an action by the plaintiff against the defendant for his share of the earnings,

Held, by Weldon, Wetmore, and King, JJ., (Palmer, J., dissenting), that each voyage was a separate adventure, and that the balances so credited were sufficient account stated to entitle the plaintiff to bring an action at law.

Where A. employs an agent to receive money for him from B., and the agent instead of receiving money consents that the amount shall be credited by B in his own account with him, B. is not thereby discharged.

In an action by A. against B. for the amount credited the agent, A.'s counsel on the cross-examination of B. questioned him without objection with a view of shewing that the amount of the agent's indebtedness was disputed, and when B.'s counsel objected and the judge sustained the objection and ruled out the evidence as irrelevant.

Held, (Weldon, J., dissenting), that the evidence was improperly rejected. *Turner* v. *McMann*, vol. 22, 391.

Ship owners—Action against charterers for refusal to load vessel—Unavoidable delay. See Charter Party 1.

Signature—To invoice properly proved by comparing with signature purporting to be of same person as indorser of bill of exchange. See Evidence 16.

SLANDER.

1—Privileged communication—Malice—Publication—Evidence—Damages—Whether excessive or not.

The defendant having been appointed chief postoffice inspector for Canada with station at Ottawa, was engaged under directions from the Deputy Postmaster General in making enquiries into certain irregularities which had been discovered at the St. John postoffice. Mr. John McMillan was the postoffice inspector for the district in which St. John was situated. Believing that the plaintiff was guilty, the defendant had the latter before him, and in the course of a conversation charged him with abstracting the missing letters, which the plaintiff stoutly denied. Thereupon the defendant, calling Mr. Woodrow the assistant postmaster into the room, told the latter to suspend the plaintiff that he, defendant, had charged him with abstracting the letters. The plaintiff having brought an action for slander was allowed to give evidence of the conversation between defendant and himself when no one was present, and in which, according to the plaintiff, the defendant had said among other things that if plaintiff was not guilty "the experience of a lifetime was wrong, that his whole past experience was thrown away," and also that "his, defendant's, reputation was at stake, these things must be ferreted out, the stigma must be taken off the office." There was no other evidence of any malice on the part of the defendant, who said that he had none, and that he had no acquaintance with plaintiff except from seeing him in the office, and had no knowledge of him whatever. The jury found that the defendant was actuated by ill-feeling in his communication to Woodrow, but not in that to plaintiff himself.

Leave being reserved to enter a nonsuit or a verdict for the defendant, the verdict was for the plaintiff, the jury assessing the damages at $5,000.

Held, by Fisher and Wetmore, JJ.,

(Weldon, J., dissenting), that the words addressed by the defendant to Woodrow were not privileged, as the defendant was not properly holding the investigation, there being no authority in the Postoffice Act for his appointment; that the communication was a publication of the slander, and that there was ample evidence on which the jury could find malice.

Held, that the damages were not excessive. *Waterbury* v. *Dewe*, vol. 19, 225.

Appeal to the Supreme Court allowed. See Addenda 8.

2—Charging the plaintiff with the use of false weights and measures—Evidence of the loss of customers—Customers must be called—Plaintiff cannot state their allegations—Charging plaintiff with an indictable offence.

In an action of slander for charging the plaintiff with using false weights and measures, whereby he had been injured in his business of a trader, the evidence of special damage was that given by the plaintiff himself, who said that in consequence of the speaking of the words, several of his former customers refused to deal with him, giving as their reasons for such refusal, the charge which the defendant had made against him of using false weights and measures.

Held, that this evidence was improperly admitted.

The proper way to prove that fact was to call the persons who made the declarations and let them testify, under oath, that they had refused to deal with the plaintiff in consequence of the defendant's charge. But as the only effect of the evidence was to increase the damages, a new trial was refused on condition that the plaintiff would consent to reduce the verdict on that branch of the case to nominal damages.

The test whether an action of slander will lie without proof of special damage is, whether the words imputed an indictable offence.

The defendant spoke of the plaintiff, the following words: "He tore the robes off the priest at Woodstock, and as a judgment for such has a withered hand," meaning thereby that the plaintiff had been guilty of an assault upon the Roman Catholic priest at Woodstock, and had torn the clerical vestments off the priest, and for such assault had been visited with a withering of the hand.

Held, that the words were actionable without proof of special damage. *McCann* v. *Kearney*, vol. 20, 84.

3—Action for—Costs—Where plaintiff recovered $8.

Held, in an action for slander, that a verdict for $8, or 40 shillings currency, will entitle a plaintiff to costs, the Statute 21 Jac. 1 cap. 16, having been adopted in this province on its establishment as a part of the practice of the court, and the universal practice having been to read it as meaning 40 shillings currency and not sterling. *Wood* v. *Mackay*, vol. 20, 262.

4—Pleadings—Evidence—Setting out all the material words constituting the slander—Variance.

In the first count of the declaration it was alleged that the defendant spoke, the following words about the plaintiff: "Go and get a search warrant and you will get your pork there," meaning thereby that the plaintiff had feloniously stolen pork. The words proved were, "Go and get your warrant and you will get your pork." These words were spoken by the defendant in the course of a conversation with one B., who stated that his pork had been stolen, and that he thought of taking out a search warrant to search the plaintiff's place. The judge directed the jury that the words as laid were not proved, and withdrew that count from their consideration.

Held, by Allen, C.J., and Duff and King, JJ., (Weldon and Wetmore, JJ., dissenting), that the words as laid were capable of the defamatory meaning attributed to them when read in connection with the facts in evidence, and that the words were sufficiently proved, and the count should have been left to the jury.

By the fifth count of the declaration, the plaintiff alleged that the defendant falsely spoke and published of him the words following: "Judson Harris in there," meaning thereby that the plaintiff had feloniously stolen pork. Some pork had been stolen from B. According to the evidence of one of the plaintiff's witnesses, the defendant, during the forenoon of the day on which it was said these words had been used, said he knew where the pork was, stating where, and intimating that he knew who stole it. Being asked by the witness during the afternoon what he meant, he said, "Judson Harris in there."

Held, that the count was bad in not setting out all the material words constituting the slander. *Harris* v. *Clayton*, vol. 21, 237.

5—Misdirection—New trial.

In an action of slander, where there is undisputed evidence that the words complained of applied to the plaintiff, it is misdirection to leave to the jury to find whether the defendant, when he spoke the words, intended the plaintiff, without pointing out such evidence to them. *Good* v. *Good*, vol. 22, 439.

6—Where meaning of words ambiguous—Evidence of what a witness understood by the words—Whether ground for new trial—Marriage—Proof of by witness—Authority to solemnize—Secular calling—1st Rev. Stat., cap. 106—Pedigree—Entries in family Bible—Secondary evidence.

In an action of slander for saying of the plaintiff—a married man—"He is as big a whore-dog as ever run," and "To go and ask M. (a married woman) what he done to her," the witness to whom the words were spoken cannot be asked what he understood by the words, without first proving that the word "whore-dog" has some local or technical meaning, or something different from its ordinary and natural meaning.

Semble, that there was no ambiguity about the meaning of the word, and therefore, though the witness should not have been asked what he understood by it, it was not a ground for setting aside a verdict for the plaintiff, the witness' answer being in accordance with the meaning ascribed to the word in the declaration.

A marriage may be proved by a person who was present at the ceremony. It is not necessary to produce the certificate of registry.

The Revised Statutes, cap. 106, authorizes any christian minister, duly ordained according to the rites and ceremonies of the denomination to which he belongs, being a British subject, not engaged in any secular calling, and having charge of a congregation, to solemnize marriage.

Held, (the other requisites of the statute being proved), that evidence that a person belonging to the denomination of Free Christian Baptists claiming the right to solemnize marriage, was the son of a British subject residing in the province, and that he himself also resided here at the time of his ordination, and was not shown ever to have resided elsewhere, was evidence that he was a British subject.

Proof that at the time of his ordination, the minister lived upon his farm, and that he afterwards farmed part of his time and preached part of his time, is not evidence that he was engaged in a secular calling within the meaning of the statute.

Entries in a Bible, or other family record, by deceased members of a family, are not evidence to prove where a member of a family was born. *Currie v. Staies*, vol. 25, 4.

7—Words actionable per se—Innuendo—Crime committed in a foreign country—Extraditable offence under Treaty of Washington.

A declaration in slander charged defendant with having spoken of the plaintiff, an unmarried woman, the following words:—"*J.* had a bastard child at the factory, and done away with it; and I can prove it." The factory was in the State of Maine: and the *innuendo* in the declaration stated the meaning of the words "done away with it" to be, that the plaintiff had destroyed the child's life.

Held, that the words "done away with it" imputed a criminal offence, and were actionable *per se* without any *innuendo*.

Murder being an extraditable offence under the Treaty of Washington (1842) the courts of this country will take notice that it is punishable as a crime in the United States. *Porter v. McMahon*, vol. 25, 211.

—Publication of. See False Imprisonment.

—Special damage—Test whether slander will lie for words without proof of. See Slander 2.

Socage—Guardian in—Trespass to property of infant. See Infant 1.

Special Bail—Where defendant had entered and been rendered—Discharge from custody—Delay in signing judgment. See Discharge 1.

Specific Performance—Sale of land and remuneration for deficiency in logs. See Agreement 6.

SPIRITUOUS LIQUORS.

Mandamus—To compel the City of Fredericton to grant license to applicant to sell spirituous liquors by retail—Canada Temperance Act of 1878, ultra vires.

Held, by Allen, C.J., Weldon, Fisher, and Wetmore, (Palmer, J., dissenting), that the Canada Temperance Act of 1878, which prohibits the sale of spirituous liquors in those counties or cities where the Act is brought in force is *ultra vires*. *Regina v. Mayor of Fredericton*, vol. 19, 139.

Appeal to Supreme Court of Canada allowed. See Addenda No. 1.

—**Intoxicating**—Whether synonymous terms. See Summary Conviction Act 8.

Stamp—Note not properly stamped having been given, pleaded in accord and satisfaction. See Accord and Satisfaction 1.

—Promissory note being without, where required by law plaintiff may sue on the original consideration without shewing that the note cannot be made available against defendant. See Original Consideration.

Stamp Act, 42 Vic. cap. 17—Double stamping under sections 13 and 25—Holder—Reasonable time—Insolvent Act, sec. 136—Liability under. See *Bank of Nova Scotia v. Cushing*, vol. 21, 198.

—Cancelling stamps. See *Binns v. Allen*, vol. 21, 1.

—Bill of exchange—Double stamping by payee—Pleading. See Bill of exchange.

—Right to affix double stamps—Knowledge of defect—What constitutes. See Bill of Exchange.

Statute—Repeal by implication. See Canada Temperance Act 17.

STATUTE OF CANADA, 37 VIC. CAP. 45.

Exporting raw hides.

Lading raw hides on board a vessel in an inspectoral district, without being inspected and marked, and sending them to another part of the province, is not "exporting" them within the Act, 37 Vic. cap. 45, sec. 96. *Ex parte Shannahan*, vol. 19, 499.

STATUTE OF FRAUDS.

1—Parol agreement for sale of logs—That a contra account be allowed in payment—Part payment—Acceptance—Sale under execution before acceptance—Account stated—Evidence of—New trial.

A. being indebted to B. for supplies used by A. in getting out a quantity of logs and timber, a parol agreement was made between A. and B.'s agent for the sale of the logs and timber to B., and the amount to be paid by B. was settled at $1,450. After allowing the amount of B.'s claim against A. neither party did anything further with the logs and timber, although B. claimed them, and they were seized and sold under an execution issued by J., one of A.'s creditors. B. forbade the sale; but subsequently made arrangements with J., and took the logs and timber and drove them to his mill where they were sawed up. A. contended that the sale to B. was completed, and that as A. subsequently got possession, that would amount to an acceptance and take the case out of the Statute of Frauds; also that there was an actual settlement of accounts at the time of the sale, and that the allowance of B.'s contra account was such a part payment as would take the case out of the statute; B. on the other hand contended that the agreement was parol; that nothing was done under it; that A. was to drive the logs and timber, which he did not do; and that he, B., purchased the logs and timber from the purchaser under J.'s execution, and that he did nothing previous to the sale under the execution amounting to an acceptance.

The jury found for A. and against B. on all the matters in dispute.

Held, by Weldon, Fisher and Wetmore, JJ., (Allen, C.J., dissenting), that as the jury had found that B. took possession under the parol agreement to purchase, and they could not say there was no evidence to support such a finding, the property in the logs and timber passed to B., and a new trial was refused.

Allen, C.J., was of opinion that as B. had done nothing amounting to an acceptance prior to the sale under J.'s execution, the property in the logs and timber passed by that sale to the purchaser, and that the questions as to whether B. took possession under the parol agreement with A., or under the purchase from the purchaser under J.'s execution, ought not to have been left to the jury.

Held, by Weldon, Fisher and Wetmore, JJ., (Allen, C.J., dissenting), that the jury were justified in finding that the allowance of B.'s contra account amounted to a part payment, and that the case was thereby taken out of the statute; but by Allen, C.J., that it was only a verbal agreement to allow A.'s indebtedness to B. to go as part payment, and that there was no evidence of part payment to be left to the jury, and that their finding amounted to nothing.

By Allen, C.J., in order to recover upon an account stated, it ought to appear that the account was stated with reference to former transactions between the parties. In the present case the parol agreement between the parties was executory; there was no debt then due from B. to A., and there could be no stating of accounts upon which A. could recover; for, if so, he would recover indirectly in another form of action the price of goods verbally agreed to be sold, which he could not recover in an action brought for the price of the goods, because there had been no sale, the requirements of the statute not having been complied with.

Weldon, J., thought the amount of the verdict should be reduced. *Murray v. Moffat*, vol. 19, 481.

2—Verbal promise—Whether primary or collateral—Hiring—Agency.

This action was brought to recover four and a half months' wages on an alleged verbal hiring by one H. as agent for defendant. At the trial, which took place in the Victoria County Court, the judge ordered a non-suit on the ground that the contract disclosed by plaintiff was a contract of guarantee, and so within the Statute of Frauds, and also that the agency of H. was not made out. The evidence showed that one M. was carrying on lumbering operations on the Tobique under a contract with defendant, who was to supply him, and he, M., was to receive so much per thousand. Defendant was also carrying on an operation on his own account in the neighborhood, and H. had charge of the latter operation for defendant. He also attended to getting in the supplies to M. which defendant had contracted to give. It appeared that both M. and defendant's operations were to be promoted by the construction of a portage road from the Tobique through to the Nepisiquit Lake, and it was in connection with the laying out of this road that the first hiring of plaintiff took place. Plaintiff said his first interview was with H., who asked him if he would go with him, H., and look out a portage road to Nipisiquit Lake, that plaintiff said he would go, and shortly after this conversation, on the same day, he met M. and H., when the former asked him if he would go with them to look out the road. Plaintiff said he did not know, whereupon H. said, "If you go up I will do what is right with you." He then agreed to go, and the next morning he went with M. and his crew and laid out the road, after which, at M.'s request, he built a camp and cut out some hauling roads for M.'s lumbering operations, being employed altogether at this work, including the laying out of the road, about twenty days. After this plaintiff left and went home and remained ten days, but before going he told M. he had business at home and would be back in eight or ten days. On his way home plaintiff met H. with teams coming up, when he asked H. if he would pay him his wages if he went back to M. and worked for the concern, to which H. replied that he would. Plaintiff remained home ten days, and went back and worked (in all) four months and fifteen days. More than a year after the work was done plaintiff applied to defendant for payment, which the latter refused, saying that if H. had agreed to pay the wages, he, defendant, would pay, but that H. had denied making any such promise.

Held, on appeal, by Weldon, Wetmore and King, JJ., that the alleged contract between plaintiff and H. was collateral to the contract of hiring that existed between plaintiff and M., and therefore within the Statute of Frauds; but by Allen, C.J., and Palmer, J., that it should have been left to the jury to say whether H.'s promise was primary or collateral.

Held, by Allen, C.J., and Palmer and King, JJ., (Wetmore, J., dissenting), that there was evidence for the jury of H.'s authority to employ plaintiff on defendant's behalf. *Forbes* v. *Temple*, vol. 22, 511.

—Contracts under — Parol evidence will not be admitted to show a subsequent variation. See Sale 2.

—Guarantee. See Sale 4.

—Substitution of third party. See Agreement 4.

—Voidable contract — Repudiation — Recovery under common count. See Contract 12.

—Contract for sale of goods—Offer by letter to sell—Acceptance. See Contract 17.

STATUTE OF LIMITATIONS. (See Limitations.)

STATUTORY TITLE.

Adverse possession—Public pound.

The sessions of Kent county having in 1852 appropriated money for the erection of a pound in the parish of Kent, it was by the verbal permission of the then owner erected on land, the documentary title to which was now in defendant, the understanding being that it was to be occupied as long as it was kept up, and was necessary, and used as a public pound. The pound was used continuously from 1852 down to 1862, when it was allowed to get out of repair, and was not used again until 1872, when the sessions repaired it, and continued to use it for several years, until defendant took possession, when plaintiffs (claiming through the sessions) brought trespass.

Held, that plaintiffs had failed to make out a statutory title by twenty years possession. *Municipality of Kent* v. *McArthur*, vol. 22, 111.

STAY OF ACTION.

1—Executor—Separate actions for penalty for not proving will.

Where separate actions for not proving a will were brought against two executors under the Rev. Stat., cap. 136, sec. 10, Con. Stat., cap. 32, sec. 11, the proceedings in one action were stayed till after judgment in the other, (Wetmore, J., dissenting). *Wagner* v. *Hutchinson*; *Snow* v. *Sullivan*, vol. 21, 537.

2—Second suit for same matter—Staying proceedings.

A. died, having effected a policy of insurance on his life for the benefit of his wife, and payable to her. The widow brought an action in her own name to recover the amount of the policy, and was non-suited on the ground that the action should have been brought by A.'s representative. She then brought an action as administratrix. On an application to stay proceedings until the costs of the former suit were paid;

Held, following *Pashley* v. *Poole*, 2 D. & R. 52, that the second action was not vexatious, and the application was refused. *Abbinett, admx., etc.,* v. *The North Western Mutual Life Ins. Co.*, vol. 24, 1.

Stay of proceedings—Caused by demand of particulars must be set aside before plaintiff can get order for inspection of defendant's books. See Books.

—Cause directed to be entered on motion papers — Whether notice of motion for new trial can be given pending stay. See Judge's Order 1.

—Demand of particulars in ejectment. See Ejectment 6.

—Rule *nisi* for *certiorari* containing. See Attachment 7.

—**Steamboat**—Action for loss of goods—Evidence. See Carrier 2.

Stock—Devised by will and afterwards sold—How paid to devisee. See Will 3.

STREETS.

1—Liability of town to keep in repair—Where town raises level of street and neglects to fence.

Held, in an action against the town of Portland, that whether their Act of Incorporation imposes on them an absolute duty to keep all the streets of the town in proper repair or not, at all events, if they assume the duty of constructing or repairing a street, they must take care and leave the work which they do upon it in such a condition as not to be dangerous to any one who may use it.

Therefore defendants having raised a street some four feet above the level of the adjoining land and left it unfenced, so that it was dangerous and unsafe for travellers in the night, and plaintiff while travelling over it in the night time having accidentally walked off and been injured, she was entitled to recover damages for the injuries sustained.

Held, also, that the section of the Act of Incorporation giving power to the town to make by-laws compelling the owners of land lying along and below the level of streets to be fenced, was not intended to provide for cases where it was the street and not the land of the adjoining owner that required to be fenced; and where the necessity for fencing was created by the Act of the town in raising the street. *Clarke* v. *Town of Portland*, vol. 19, 189.

2—Non-repair—Action for injuries resulting from—Where no misfeasance.

The intention of the Legislature in passing the Act incorporating the Town of Portland was simply to transfer to the town council the exercise of the power and authority over the streets of the town which had been previously exercised by the sessions and by the commissioners of highways, under 25 Vic. cap. 16, and the Act of Incorporation did not create any more extensive obligation on the part of the town with respect to highways than had previously existed; therefore,

Held, that no action will lie against the town for injuries resulting from the non-repair of a street, there being no acts of misfeasance on the part of the town. *Dwyer* v. *Town of Portland*, vol. 20, 423.

—Liability to keep streets in repair—Town of Portland. See Portland, Town of.

—Power of Mayor, etc., St. John, to raise level of streets — Erecting fence. See Addenda 40.

Student at law—Rules as to examination for—Easter Term, 1881.

SUMMARY CONVICTIONS ACT.

1—Where Act requires particular person to prosecute—Information.

Where an Act requires a particular person to prosecute for an offence, the information must be laid by him, or at least by his authority, and in his name; and if it is laid in the name of another person the justice has no jurisdiction to proceed. *Mayor of St. John* v. *Masters et al.*, vol. 19, 587.

2—Prosecution for selling liquor without license—When informant does not appear—Conviction—Not stating time of offence.

In a prosecution against a person for selling liquor without license, the informant did not appear, but no objection was taken, and witnesses were examined and defendant convicted.

Held, that he could not afterwards object to the conviction on that ground.

The Legislature having prescribed a form of conviction, it is not necessary that the time when the offence was committed should be set out. *Ex parte Gidding*, vol. 19, 47.

3—Conviction — Canada Temperance Act, 1878 — Where uncertain as to time of offence—Amendment—Section 118.

To sustain a conviction the evidence must be reasonably sufficient to show that the offence existed and was committed at the time of the information, and the facts necessary to support the charge must be stated expressly and not left to be gathered from inference or intendment.

Therefore, where a conviction under the Canada Temperance Act, 1878, made on the 4th August, stated that the defendant had sold spirituous liquors "within three months now last past," and the evidence of one witness proved a sale in May previous to the information (which was laid on the 25th July), and another witness proved a sale "since the 22nd June then last;"

Held, that the conviction was uncertain, as it was consistent with the evidence that the magistrate may have convicted on the testimony of the witness who proved a sale "since the 22nd June," which sale may have been after the date of the information.

Held, also, that the conviction could not be amended under the 118th section of the Act. *Regina* v. *Blair*; *in re Hickey*, vol. 24, 72.

4—Conviction uncertain — Amendment — Canada Temperance Act, 1878—Section 118.

Where a conviction under Canada Temperance Act stated that the defendant had sold "spirituous or other intoxicating liquors," and the proof was a sale of brandy, the conviction was amended under section 118 of the Act by striking out the words "spirituous or other."

Quære, Whether "spirituous" and "intoxicating" are not synonymous expressions, and the conviction not therefore uncertain. *Regina* v. *Blair*; *in re McCarthy*, vol. 24, 71.

5—Conviction uncertain — Amendment — Section 118 — Canada Temperance Act, 1878.

An information under the Canada Temperance Act, 1878, was laid on the 25th July, charging defendant with having sold spirituous liquors within three months then last past. The hearing took place on the 4th August, and the conviction, dated that day, found defendant guilty of selling intoxicating liquors "within three months last past." One witness proved a sale "about two weeks" before his examination, and others respectively proved sales "within a month" and "sometime last month."

Held, that the conviction was bad for uncertainty, as it was quite consistent with the evidence of some of the witnesses that the sales of liquor which they testified to might have been after the 25th July (the date of the information), and that the conviction could not be amended. *Regina* v. *Blair*; *in re Kearney*, vol. 24, 74.

6—Previous conviction—Whether defendant must be present at hearing—Canada Temperance Act, 1878.

A defendant may be convicted of a second offence under the Canada Temperance Act, 1878, sec. 122, though he is not present at the trial to be asked as to a previous conviction (Weldon and Wetmore, JJ., dissenting). *Ex parte Graves*; *ex parte McDonald*, vol. 24, 57.

7—Canada Temperance Act, 1878—Conviction for first offence—When wrong form used—Power of court to amend.

In a conviction for a first offence under the Canada Temperance Act, 1878, the form (I1) given by the Summary Convictions Act, 32 & 33 Vic. cap. 31, awarding distress for non-payment of the fine, and in default thereof imprisonment, must be adopted, and not the form (I2).

Where, in such a case, the form (12) is adopted, it is not amendable under the 117th and 118th sections of the Canada Temperance Act. *Regina* v. *Sullivan ; In re Dwyer*, vol. 24, 149.

8—Certificate of dismissal—Where informant does not appear—Right to grant—Subsequent complaint for same offence—Whether bona fides of justice in granting certificate can be inquired into—Canada Temperance Act, 1878.

Held, by Allen, C.J., Weldon, Wetmore, King and Fraser, JJ., that the certificate of dismissal provided for by the 43rd section of the Summary Convictions Act may be granted as well where the informant neglects to appear and the complaint is dismissed on that ground, as where he does appear and the information is dismissed on the merits.

By Palmer, J., that such certificate can only be granted where the information is dismissed after hearing.

Held, also, (Weldon and Wetmore, JJ., dissenting), that the magistrate or other officers before whom an information for an offence against the Canada Temperance Act is being heard, if a certificate of dismissal of a prosecution for the same alleged offence is relied on as a bar to his proceeding, has a right to inquire whether the previous prosecution was real and *bona fide*, or was instituted fraudulently and collusively. *Ex parte Phillips*, vol. 24, 119.

9—Minute of judgment—Variance from formal conviction.

The minute of a conviction made under the Summary Convictions Act, 32 & 33 Vic. cap. 31, sec. 42, should state the adjudication of the justices both as to the amount of the fine and the mode of enforcing it, whether by distress or imprisonment, so as to be a complete judgment in substance. Therefore, where the minute of conviction under the Canada Temperance Act, 1878, stated only that the justices adjudged the defendant to pay a fine of $50 and costs, a conviction which was subsequently drawn up, after the parties had separated, awarding distress in default of payment of the fine, and for want of distress imprisonment for a certain time, was quashed, the justices having no power after their adjudication to add to or vary their judgment *Regina* v. *Perley and Hurtt ; In re White*, vol. 25, 43.

10—Warrant to arrest—Information—Belief of complainant—Substantiation of.

A sworn information stating that the complainant has just cause to suspect and believe, and does suspect and believe, that the party charged has committed a specified offence triable under the Summary Convictions Act, 32 & 33 Vic. cap. 31., will not authorize a justice to arrest in the first instance. It is the duty of the justice before issuing a warrant to examine upon oath the complainant, or his witnesses, as to the facts upon which such suspicion and belief are founded, and to exercise his own judgment thereon. *Ex parte Bogee*, vol. 24, 345.

11—Indian Act 1880—Conviction—Liquor sold to Indians—Whether imprisonment can be adjudged for non-payment of fine—Certiorari.

Imprisonment in case of immediate non-payment of a fine imposed under sec. 90, of the Indian Act 1880, can only be adjudged when the offence is selling liquor to Indians on board a vessel.

In other cases the conviction must follow the form, (I1), in the Summary Convictions Act, 32 & 33 Vic. cap 31, and award a distress in default of payment of the fine.

When a justice exceeds his jurisdiction in prosecutions under the Indian Act, a *certiorari* is not taken away by sec. 97, or by the Act, 47 Vic. cap. 27, sec. 15. *Ex parte Goodine*, vol. 25. 151.

12—Selling and keeping liquor for sale—Identity—Of offence—Onus of proof.

J. was convicted on the 16th May for selling liquor between the 21st January and the 18th April preceding, contrary to the Canada Temperance Act. He was subsequently convicted for unlawfully keeping liquor for sale between the 14th February and the 24th March, in the same year.

Held, that the onus was on him to prove that the two charges were identical—that the keeping for sale with which he was charged, was in fact the selling of which he had been convicted—and that the mere fact that the days between which he was charged with keeping liquor for sale, was included within the times stated in the conviction for selling, did not sustain a defence of *autrefois convict*. *Regina v. Marsh*, vol. 25, 371.

—Prosecution for assault under—Defendant's right to show that assault was committed in defence of his own land. See Assault 2.

—Whether provisions of the 57th and 62nd sections, are applicable to convictions under the Can. Tem. Act, sec. 100. See Canada Temperance Act 16.

—Dismissal of complaint—Right of defendant to have liquors returned. See Liquor License Act.

—Summons for witness—Where conviction made by justice without jurisdiction. See Canada Temperance Act 19.

—Partners—Joint conviction—Penalty must be several. See Canada Temperance Act 21.

—Amendment of conviction under Can. Tem. Act. See Canada Temperance Act 22.

SUMMARY EJECTMENT.

1—Con. Stat. cap. 83—Mortgagor and Mortgagee—Summary Ejectment.

There is not such a tenancy existing between a mortgagor and mortgagee as will render the former liable to proceedings by summary ejectment under the Con. Stat., cap. 84, and the Act, 13 Vic. cap 12. *Ex parte McBean*, vol. 24, 312.

2—Expiration of tenancy—Writ of restitution.

The Summary Ejectment Act, Con. Stat., cap. 84, sec. 22, does not apply where the landlord relies upon a surrender of the lease by the tenant, and not on an expiration of the tenancy.

Where the tenant has been turned out of possession, and the proceedings are afterwards quashed on appeal, the court has no discretion as to awarding a writ of restitution. *Philip*, appellant, and *McLaughlin*, respondent, vol. 24, 532.

Summary proceedings—Setting aside pleas as false. See Plea 3.

—Where right of action—Refusal of court to interfere. See Bankruptcy 2.

Summons—One partner acknowledging service for self and co-partner. See Execution 1.

—Service of—Where defendant is insane. See Writ.

—Not moved with costs. See Costs 28.

—To witness, issue of, by justice called in by other justice. See Canada Temperance Act 19.

SUPERSEDEAS.

Section 52, cap. 37, Con. Stat.—Rules of Hilary Term 2nd Victoria—Declaring—

Within what time—What included in word as used in the 52nd section—Computation of time.

The defendant was arrested on the 11th July, 1879. Application was made for an order of supersedeas on an affidavit of defendant sworn on September 11th, 1879, and a certificate of the sheriff bearing the same date, showing that no declaration had been served; an affidavit sworn on the 13th September, had been filed in the clerk's office, was also used.

Held by Allen, C.J., and Duff, J., (Wetmore, J., dissenting), that defendant had not shewn enough to entitle him to the order.

Held, that the day of the arrest should be excluded in the computation of the two months within which time the plaintiff must declare by section 52 of Con. Stat., cap. 37.

Held, by Allen, C.J., and Duff, J., (Wetmore, J., dissenting), that the word "declare" in the 52nd section, read in connection with the Rules of Hilary Term 2nd Victoria, does not require the declaration to be filed as well as served within the two months. *Weldon* v. *O'Sullivan*, vol. 19, 402.

—Absconding, concealed or absent Debtor's Act. See Absconding Debtor.

SUPREME COURT OF CANADA.

1—Preparation of cases for—What control this court has over the case—What case should not contain—Judge's notes of trial—Must be taken as reported by him.

Where an appeal is had from this court to the Supreme Court of Canada, this court has power to see that copies of the records of the court and of all documents and affidavits on file are correctly certified, and, if necessary, to require the clerk to correct any errors that may be made to appear, and the judges have power to see that correct copies of their judgments are transmitted, but the court has no power over the judge's notes of the trial and cannot alter or interfere with them in any way. It must be assumed that they are correct as reported by him.

Semble, The court has power to see that the case on appeal is presented on the grounds taken in this court. The court has no power to order that an affidavit used in an application to set aside or vary an order allowing an appeal to the Supreme Court of Canada, and settling the case, be made part of the case on appeal.

Per Allen, C.J., no more of the proceedings than is necessary to raise the question in dispute for the consideration of the court of appeal ought to be made part of the case. It is unnecessary to transmit a copy of the affidavit verifying the execution of the bond, or of the affidavit of justification, or of the judgment roll. The substance of the Pleadings instead of the *verbatim* copy might properly be stated, and when it can be avoided no more of the evidence than bears upon the question at issue, should be transcribed and transmitted. *Copp* v. *Read*, vol. 19, 435.

Time of appeal to, should not be extended by an *ex parte* order. See Appeal 11.

—A judge has power to extend the time for perfecting an appeal to. See Appeal 9.

—No power to allow additional plea. See Addenda 31 & 39.

Surety—Defective affidavit of justification—On petition under Controverted Elections Act. See Controverted Elections Act 1.

—Bond given as. See Pleading 1.

Surplus—Will—Whether it refers to personal estate alone, or real estate also. See Will 2.

Surplusage — Entitling of affidavit. See Affidavit 5.

—When words may be treated as. See Canada Temperance Act 22.

Surveyor—mutually chosen—dividing line. See Acquiescence 1.

Survey bills, how far conclusive. See Estoppel 5.

Taxation of costs—When costs are taxed on different day from that appointed—Whether sufficient to entitle plaintiff to an execution. See Costs 4.

—Of costs on demurrer while other issues are pending, may be set aside. See Costs 11.

—On day other than that appointed—Review of. See Costs 17.

—City of St. John—What constitutes an inhabitant for purposes of. See Inhabitant 1.

—Without notice. See Costs 21.

Taxes—Statute requiring bond to be given before a party complaining of an assessment should be entitled to a rule *nisi* for *certiorari* is not applicable to assessments made in city of St. John. See Assessment 2.

—Receiver of, of the city of St. John —Necessity of setting out in detail proceedings taken. See Arrest 5.

—Income of Dominion official resident in St. John not subject to taxation for municipal purposes. See Dominion Official 1.

Municipal taxation of Dominion official. See Assessment 7.

—Creating lien on land in city of St. John for two years cannot be recovered from tenant after that time. See Rates and Taxes 1.

—Costs of execution—Arrest for, under execution. See False Imprisonment, 8.

Owner of land dead — Assessment against widow. See Assessment 8.

Telegraph company—Erection of line—Right to cut trees—Company bound to shew necessity. See Trespass 6.

—Doing damage to shade and ornamental trees. See Trespass 7.

Telegram—Construction of. See Ship 2.

Temperance—Act of Canada of 1878. See Mandamus 1.

—Act *ultra vires*. See Spirituous Liquors.

Temperance Act of 1878. See Canada Temperance Act.

Tenant—Mill owner—Logs delivered to be sawn into deals—Privilege from distress. See Landlord and Tenant.

Tenants in common — One co-tenant cannot legally authorize another person to do what he himself could not do. See Trespass 1.

—Partition by agreement of land owned by. See Adverse Possession 1.

Tenant by curtesy—Right of entry in heir-at-law, when it accrues. See Limitations 2.

Tender—It is the duty of the vendors of lands to prepare and tender the conveyance. See Sale of Land 3.

—For charges—When necessity of, to prove conversion, where property held for proper charges, and also for charges which were not a lien upon the property. See Trover 3.

—Of price before action. See Contract 6.

—Of interest and costs on foreclosure of mortgage. See Mortgage 2.

Testator—Will— Cutting off seal—Whether "tearing" within meaning of Wills Act. See Will 8.

—Whether witness to previous will can prove capacity of. See Will 10.

Third parties—Declaration of—Admission of, as evidence. See Trespass 4.

—Contract—Policy of Insurance—Beneficiary not entitled to bring action in his own name. See Contract 5.

—Previous settlement with—Accounts—Effect of, as an admission of correctness. See Evidence 10.

Timber driver—Right to lien. See Lien.

Title to land—In prosecution for assault, defendant may show that assault was committed in defence of. See Assault 2.

—Action in county court—Judge should not non-suit the plaintiff but remit the cause to the Supreme Court under Con. Stat., cap. 51, sec. 45. See Trespass 10.

—When may or not be considered in question. See Costs 24.

—Justice of the peace—Jurisdiction—Title to land—Easement.

In order to oust the civil jurisdiction of a justice of the peace, on the ground that the title to land came in question, it is not enough for the defendant to make such objection: the justice must enquire into the matter sufficiently to ascertain whether the title really is in question.

Plaintiff and defendant owned adjoining lots of land, defendant having a right of way over plaintiff's land, from the street;

Held, that the defendant had no right to deposit snow upon the way, hauled from his own land; and that his claim to do so did not raise the question of title to land. *Doohan* v. *LaForest*, vol. 24, 553.

Tolls and rates—Power of city council of Fredericton to impose, on the sale of articles in the public market. See Market 1.

Tort—Joint action—Costs of acquitted defendant—Time of taxing. See Costs 19.

Total loss—Covenant in insurance policy that amount of claim shall be fixed by arbitration does not apply where there is a total loss. See Insurance 8.

Town of Portland—Non-repair of streets. See Streets 2.

—Power to exact license fee from coachman holding license in city of St. John. See Hackney Coaches 1.

Town of Upper Mills—Overseers of the poor—Proper parties to bring action for support of illegitimate child. See Overseer of Poor.

Transfer—Chattels—Evidence of date when made. See Evidence 18.

Trees—Ornamental trees—Right of Telegraph Company to cut. See Trespass 6.

TRESPASS.

1—Building overhanging land of adjoining owner—Entry to prevent falling—Justification—Tenants in common—License by one—Pleading.

A declaration contained three counts.

1st. That plaintiffs were seised and possessed of a lot of land in the city of S. and that defendants erected a building on land adjoining which did then and for a long time before the commencement of this action, overhang plaintiffs' said land, whereby plaintiffs have been utterly hindered and prevented from using and enjoying their land.

2nd. That defendants broke and entered said land and placed thereon divers buildings, bricks and other materials, and dug up the soil of plaintiffs' land, and have ever since kept and continued said building upon plaintiffs' said land, whereby they have been hindered and prevented from using and enjoying their said land.

3rd. That plaintiffs were seised and possessed of said land which was then and ever since had been vacant; that defendants being owners of the adjoining lot of land erected a building thereon, which building was so carelessly and negligently constructed that it sagged over and overhung plaintiffs' land, and had ever since continued to overhang the same, whereby plaintiffs had been altogether prevented from erecting a building upon their land and using and occupying the same.

Defendants pleaded (3rd and 4th) that they did what was complained of by leave of two of the plaintiffs.

(5th to the 1st count) that the wall and foundation of defendants' building was supported by the soil of plaintiff's land; that before the said time when, etc., the plaintiffs had wrongfully, carelessly and improperly kept and continued the soil of said close to be dug out and excavated, and also wrongfully, illegally and carelessly kept and continued large quantities of water collected and being in and upon plaintiffs' said land, so as to flow to, against and into the earth and soil of defendants under their said foundation wall, so as to soften and undermine the same, and carelessly and negligently cause the foundation of the said wall to give way and settle, and thereby cause the top of the defendants' building to move over and overhang plaintiffs' close, where the same remained in danger of falling and being destroyed, whereupon defendants, in order to prevent the same from falling, entered plaintiffs' said land for the purpose of repairing and maintaining said building and doing all other things necessary to prevent said building from falling by reason of said wrongful act of plaintiffs, doing no unnecessary damage, and that such necessary work could not have been done without such entry, which are the supposed trespasses in the first count mentioned.

(6th to the 1st count). That plaintiffs wrongfully and illegally caused the earth and soil of defendants under said foundation wall to give way and sink, so that the said building sagged over and overhung plaintiffs' land, and was in great danger of falling and doing damage, and in order to prevent such injury and damage, it became necessary to enter upon plaintiffs' land to maintain and repair such foundation, whereupon defendants did enter upon plaintiffs' land to maintain and repair the same, doing no unnecessary damage, which are the trespasses in the first count mentioned.

To the 2nd count defendant pleaded pleas similar to the fifth and sixth pleas to 1st count.

To the 3rd count they pleaded that their said building was not so carelessly and negligently constructed that it sagged over and overhung plaintiffs' land; but, on the contrary, that such sagging and overhanging was caused by the improper, illegal and careless way in which plaintiffs had allowed their lands to be excavated and dug out, and the water that they had improperly allowed to collect upon said land and premises, and flow against and under the foundation wall of defendants' building.

To these pleas plaintiffs demurred.

Held, that all the pleas were bad as constituting no defence to the action. *Hutchinson v. Trustees Y. M. C. Ass.*, vol. 19, 65.

2—Declaration, where only one trespass laid, whether more can be proved.

In an action of trespass *quare clausum fregit*, only one trespass was laid in the declaration, but on the trial, plaintiff proved, subject to objection, several trespasses, and obtained a verdict on them all, though the amounts were found separately. A rule *nisi* for a new trial having been obtained, plaintiff, on shewing cause was allowed to abandon all but one trespass, and the rule was discharged. *Ingraham v. Parks*, vol. 19, 101.

3—To land—Grantee under registered deed having notice of prior unregistered deed—Registration—Way—Obstruction of.

In a court of law the legal title to land must prevail, and the fact that a subsequent purchaser under a registered deed had notice of the existence of a prior unregistered deed, does not affect the title.

Plaintiff, in order to obtain access to his ship yard, obtained a deed from M. of a strip of land wide enough for road way, describing it by metes and bounds. Between the strip so deeded, however, and the ship yard, there was another piece of land not owned by M., but belonging to defendant. On the same day that plaintiff obtained his deed, but subsequent to it, defendant also obtained from M. a deed of the same land, containing in the *habendum* the following words, "except the right of road way to Archibald Park's (plaintiff) ship yard deeded to him." Defendant got his deed on record first, defendant having made an obstruction on the land so deeded to plaintiff, the latter sued him for such obstruction, claiming in the declaration "a way for his horses, cattle and carriages to and from his ship yard."

Held, that plaintiff was not entitled to the right of way claimed. *Parks* v. *Ingraham*, vol. 19, 195.

4—Grant—Construction of—Evidence—Declarations of third parties—Admissible as part of res gestæ—Jury fee—Payment of.

When the description of the lines in a grant is free from ambiguity, its bounds cannot be extended beyond the lines described therein, either by reference to a plan annexed or any other grant.

On the trial of an action of trespass, *qu. cl. fr.*, plaintiff stated that he had frequently seen a cedar tree, which the plan annexed to the grant of his land showed, stood in one angle of the grant, while it was standing; that it was cut down about twenty years before the trial; that there was a cedar stump on the side of the road about eight feet to the west of the cedar tree, and about two feet to the north of it, that in 1859 he employed H., a surveyor (since dead), to run out the southern line of his grant; that H. started from this cedar stump and ran the line out to the rear, and that M., defendant's brother, who owned the land which adjoined plaintiff's land on the south side and conterminous with defendant's land, pointed out the stump as the boundary between the two tracts, and that it was marked as such by the surveyor. The defendant objected to this evidence: but

Held, admissible as part of the *res gestæ*. *Boggs* v. *McBride*, vol. 19, 222.

5—Insufficient description of locus in quo—Demurrer—Leave to withdraw.

It is not a ground of demurrer that the declaration in trespass does not sufficiently describe the *locus in quo*. Application to compel plaintiff to amend the declaration should be made under Con. Stat., cap., 37, sec. 93.

The defendant may be allowed to withdraw his demurrer and plead without notice to the plaintiff. *Parsons* v. *Barnet, et al.*, vol. 19, 497.

6—Declaration—Where premises not set out—Defendant's Remedy—Telegraph company—Erection of line—Right to cut trees—Company bound to shew necessity.

A declaration alleging that defendant cut down and destroyed trees standing upon plaintiff's land, sets out a clear cause of action.

The objection that in trespass to real estate the declaration does not set out the particulars of the premises is not available, on a general demurrer, but defendant's proper course is to apply to the court or a judge for an order to compel plaintiff to amend or give particulars.

The Act, 34 Vic. cap. 52, incorporating the Dominion Telegraph Company, declares in the 4th section that the company may enter upon lands or places, and survey, set off and take such parts thereof, as may be necessary for such line, etc.; and in case of disagreement between the company and the owners of lands so taken, or in respect of any damage done to the same, it may be settled by arbitration in the mode therein described.

By section 20 the company are authorized and empowered to enter upon the lands of any person or persons and survey and take levels, and to set out and ascertain such parts thereof as *they shall think* necessary and proper for making the said intended telegraph, and all such other works, matters and conveniences as they shall think proper and necessary for the making, preserving, etc., the said telegraph, and to build and set up on such lands, such station-houses and observatories, watch-houses and other works, etc., *as and where the said company shall think requisite and convenient, etc., "provided always that the said company shall not cut down or mutilate any tree planted or left standing for shade or ornament, or any fruit tree, unless it be necessary to do so for the erection, use or safety of any of its lines."*

In an action against the company to recover damages for cutting down ornamental trees, the defendants pleaded that the trees were standing by the side of a public highway and the defendants were erecting their line of telegraph along the highway, and because the trees were in the way and obstructed the passage of the line of telegraph, and because they deemed it necessary and advisable so to do, they committed the acts complained of by virtue of the statute and not otherwise.

Held, 1st., that the arbitration clause in the 4th section, did not apply to a case like this, where the complaint was that the defendants had wrongfully destroyed plaintiff's trees.

2nd. That the proviso in the 20th section imposed on the defendants, if the ornamental trees would obstruct their line on the side of the highway where they located it, the burden of shewing that it was necessary for them to take it on that side, and that the defendant's pleas were bad for want of an averment that it was necessary to cut the trees, not merely that they deemed it necessary. *Gilchrist* v. *Dominion Telegraph Co.*, vol. 19, 553.

Appeal to Supreme Court of Canada dismissed. See Addenda, 55.

7—Arbitration as to damages—Evidence—Telegraph company—New trial—Counsel moving for—Act 41 Vic. cap. 8.

The court will only hear one counsel on moving for a new trial under 41 Vic. cap. 8.

The plaintiff sued the defendants, a company empowered by Act, 34 Vic. cap 52, to control lines of telegraph in the Dominion of Canada, for cutting and destroying shade and ornamental trees in his land while building their line. The Act, after giving the company power to enter on and take lands, etc., for constructing the line, provides that in case of any disagreement between the company and the occupier of any lands which they may take in respect to any damage done, the amount of such damage shall be determined by arbitrators, to be chosen in the manner therein pointed out. The 20th section contains a proviso that shade, ornamental or fruit trees, shall not be cut or destroyed unless it be necessary to do so for the erection, use, or safety of the lines.

Held, that the arbitration clause did not apply to damage done to shade trees, etc., unless it was necessary for the erection, use, or safety of the line, and that the burden of showing the necessity for such damage was on the defendants.

On the trial there was no positive evidence that the line was constructed by the defendants, but it appeared that they were the company authorized to build, and that they operated the line when completed.

Held, that under this evidence the jury were justified in finding that the defendants constructed the line. *Gilchrist* v. *The Dominion Telegraph Co.*, vol. 20, 241.

8—To land—Wrongful entry by defendant—Abandonment of possession by plaintiff—Whether trespass can afterwards be maintained.

A person in possession of land upon which another enters and commits a trespass, does not, by allowing the trespasser to continue in the exclusive possession of the land for a period of nine months, thereby lose his right to maintain an action of trespass for the original wrongful entry.

Quære, per Allen, C.J., Weldon, King and Fraser, JJ., whether the plaintiff could recover for a distinct act of trespass committed by the defendant on a part of the land about three months after his first entry, and while he continued in the exclusive possession of the land.

Per Wetmore, J., that the acts of trespass were continuous, and the plaintiff could recover for all the trespasses committed while the defendant remained in possession. *Appleby* v. *Devine*, vol. 22, 198.

9—When goods illegally placed on land of another—Right of owner to enter and retake—Search warrant—Where goods stolen—Information—What should allege—Right to arrest person on whose land goods are found—Pleading.

When A.'s goods have been wrongfully taken by another and placed on the land of B., and the latter, although requested by A. to allow him to remove them, does not permit him to do so;

Held, that A. may then lawfully enter and remove his goods.

In order to obtain a search warrant under the Act, 32 & 33 Vic. cap. 30, it is not necessary that the information should allege that the goods have been stolen by the party whose premises are sought to be searched, and it is sufficient if it allege that they have been feloniously stolen.

Under a search warrant, the goods alleged to have been stolen, having upon the search made under the warrant, been found in the store and warehouses of a party who, though not the party charged in the information with having stolen them, had refused to allow the owner to see them or to give him any satisfaction regarding them, the constable is justified not only in taking the goods so found, but also the body of the party on whose premises they were found, before the justice who issued the warrant, to give an account of how he came by them.

In an action for taking goods under a search warrant, the defendant pleaded that the goods were feloniously stolen by one G., or some person or persons unknown to defendant, to which plaintiff replied "that the said goods were not feloniously stolen by the said G. as alleged."

Held, bad, because while professing to answer the whole plea, it did not do so. *Hamilton* v. *Calder*, vol. 23, 373.

10 — Purchaser under registered deed — Whether actual entry necessary to maintain trespass—Title to land—County Court —Remitting cause to Supreme Court.

In an action of trespass *quare clausum fregit* by A. and wife, it was shown that the *locus in quo* consisted of a vacant lot of land in St. John formerly owned by one H. Sometime in March, 1878, H. gave defendant permission to pile stone on the lot, and he fenced it and used it for that purpose. H. stated on the trial that he told defendant he could have the use of the lot till he wanted it to build on, while defendant swore that he took it by the year. On cross examination, he said he was to have it for not less than a year.

H. having become insolvent, this property was purchased from his assignee by the female plaintiff by deed, dated 10th April, 1879, registered 15th of the same month. A. being desirous of building, requested defendant to remove the stone, a large quantity of which was still there. Defendant at first promised to do so, but subsequently refused and continued in possession, whereupon the present action was brought. On the trial in the St. John County Court, A. stated that he went into possession after buying the property, but he did not state the nature or acts of possession, nor was he cross-examined on this point. At the close of the plaintiff's case, defendant's counsel moved for a non-suit on the grounds:

1. That the action should not have been brought in the County Court, the title to land being in question.

2. That defendant was tenant from year to year, and there was no notice to quit.

3. Even if defendant's holding was for a year certain, which had expired, plaintiff could not maintain trespass against him without actual entry and demand of possession.

Leave was thereupon reserved to enter a non-suit, and a verdict for plaintiff taken by consent. Subsequently at chambers the County Court judge granted a non-suit on the third ground, and against this order the plaintiff appealed.

Held, by Weldon and Wetmore, JJ., that under the Con. Stat., cap. 74, sec. 12, a purchaser under a registered deed is not to make an actual entry in order to maintain trespass, but even if so, there was evidence for the jury of an entry in this case.

Held, by Weldon, Wetmore, Palmer and King, JJ., that the title to land was brought in question, and that the judge should not have non-suited plaintiff, but should have remitted the cause to the Supreme Court under Con. Stat., cap. 51, sec. 45; but,

Held, by Duff, J., that the title to land did not come in question, and that the non-suit was right. *Armstrong* v. *McGourty*, vol. 22, 29.

11—Damages—Excessive—Where jury must have acted under influence of undue motives—New trial.

Three several actions for trespass and assault were brought by A., B. and C. respectively, riparian proprietors of land fronting on rivers above the ebb and flow of the tide, for forcibly seizing and taking away their fishing rods and lines while they were engaged in fly fishing for salmon in front of their respective lots. The defendant was a fishery officer, appointed under The Fisheries Act, 31 Vic. cap. 60, and justified the seizure on the ground that the plaintiffs were fishing without license, in violation of an order in council of June, 1879. Some force was used towards the plaintiffs to compel them to give up their rods, etc., though there was no actual injury, the defendant presenting a pistol, and threatening to use it, if resistance was made. Each of the plaintiffs obtained a verdict; A., (who was a county court judge), recovering $3,000 damages; B., $1,200, and C., $1,000.

Held, by Allen, C.J., Palmer and King, JJ., (Weldon and Wetmore, JJ., dissenting), that the damages in each case were excessive, but in the cases of B. and C. not so excessive as to justify the interference of the court.

In A.'s case a new trial was granted unless the plaintiff consented to reduce the damages to $1,500. *Steadman* v. *Fanning*; *Hanson* v. *Same*; *Spurr* v. *Same*, vol. 22, 630.

Appeal to Supreme Court of Canada allowed. See Addenda No. 15.

—Damages—Joint and several trespasses—When doubtful as to what trespass damage is given. See New Trial 2.

—Execution against husband—Levy on wife's property—No removal or touching of goods—Nominal sale—Effect of. See Trover 1.

—Abandonment—Election of trespass, time for, in discretion of judge. See New Trial 2.

—Against sheriff for holding goods under writ of replevin, no writ *de pro. pro.* having issued. See Replevin 4.

—One of several defendants offering to suffer judgment by default. See Costs 18.

—To land—Action in Supreme Court—Offer to suffer judgment by default for $8—Whether plaintiff entitled to full costs. See Costs 20.

—To property of infant under fourteen years of age—Guardian in socage—Who entitled to maintain action. See Infant 1.

—Dividing line—Adjoining properties—Surveyor mutually agreed upon—Acquiescence. See Acquiescence 1.

—Notice of action—Schools Act. See Notice of Action.

—Trespass to land—Cutting trees—Telegraph company. See Costs 21.

—Illegal distress—Trespass lies for. See Landlord and Tenant 6.

TRIAL.

Right to begin—Right of reply—Ejectment by heir-at-law—Admission of heirship and ancestor being seised.

On the trial of an action of ejectment brought by the heir-at-law, where defendant's counsel admits the heirship of the lessor of the plaintiff, and that his ancestor died seised of the property sought to be recovered, but sets up a will in his, defendant's favor, defendant is entitled to begin and to have the general reply. *Doe dem. Hasen* v. *Rector, etc., St. James' Church*, vol. 18, 479.

—Second, reading former judgment to jury and commenting thereon. See Settled Accounts 1.

—Without jury in county court cannot have new trial in same court. See Husband and Wife 2.

—In action—Whether jury should be allowed to view the *locus in quo* after the judge had charged them. See Jury View.

—Evidence received without objection, judge not bound to withdraw it from jury. See Carrier 2.

TROVER.

1—Levy and sale of wife's property under execution against husband—No touching or removal of goods from plaintiff's possession.

Where a sheriff having in his hands an execution against S. made a levy upon goods belonging to the wife of S., and went through the form of a sale, but took no possession of the property, which was neither removed or touched, the husband and wife afterwards brought an action of trespass and trover against the sheriff.

Held, that as the goods were the wife's, the levy and sale did not affect her property, and as they were neither removed or touched there was neither trespass or conversion. *Smith and wife* v. *White, sheriff, etc.*, vol. 18, 443.

2—Conversion—Evidence of.

Where B. delivered goods to S. under a verbal agreement that he should take them and pay certain bills against B., but S. d[illegible]pay the bill, and some eight [illegible]wards B. demanded the goods back, but S., as he swore, gave him no satisfaction regarding them.

Held, sufficient evidence of a conversion to support an action of trover. *Stockton* v. *Beatty*, vol. 19, 104.

3—Lien—Persons entitled to hold goods for—Claiming to hold for other charges—Tender—Waiver—Conversion.

The defendants, merchants in St. John, instructed plaintiffs, commission merchants in New York, to purchase for them a quantity of corn and ship to St. John. On arriving in St. John, the corn was found to be heated and musty, and defendants refused to receive it, and notified plaintiffs they held it subject to their order. Plaintiffs consented to assume the invoice and directed defendants to sell for them to best advantage. Defendants undertook to sell, but were unable to find a purchaser, and it remained in their hands for a long time. A dispute having arisen concerning it, plaintiffs demanded it and defendants refused to give it up until various charges and expenses for which they claimed a lien, and of which they had given plaintiffs a memorandum, were paid. The goods were not subject to a lien for some of the charges for which defendants claimed to hold.

Held, by Weldon, J., that the defendants having furnished plaintiffs with a memorandum of the items of the different charges for which they claimed a lien, there was no waiver of their lien for proper charges, and in the absence of a tender of these charges their refusal was no evidence of a conversion.

Held, by Wetmore, J., that defendants having claimed to hold for charges which were not a lien upon the property, their refusal to deliver until those charges were paid was a waiver of their lien for proper charges and dispensed with the necessity of a tender of them. *Nevins* v. *Schoefield*, vol. 21, 124; also, vol. 18, 435.

4—Promissory note—Executor—Action by—Measure of damages—When executor maker of note.

A., who was the maker of a note in favor of F., was appointed by the latter executor of his will. Defendant took possession of the note at F.'s death and refused to give it up to A. on request. In an action of trover brought by A., as executor for the conversion of the note, verdict was received for the amount of the note, leave being reserved to defendant to reduce it to nominal damages.

Held, by Weldon, Wetmore, King and Fraser, JJ., that the amount of the note was not the proper measure of damages, and that the verdict should be reduced to nominal damages.

Per Allen, C.J., that the verdict should stand subject to be reduced to nominal damages in case defendant delivered up the note. *Robinson* v. *Ferguson*, vol. 23, 332.

5—Joint Conversion.

The sale of property by one defendant, and the purchase by another, is evidence of a joint conversion. *Ford et al.*, appellants; and *Bower and wife*, respondents; vol. 24, 510.

6—Conditional sale of goods—Payment by instalments—Agreement that title shall not pass till payment—Estoppel—Shipment—Bill of lading—Possession of conversion—Bills of Sale Act.

Plaintiff, a manufacturer of safes at Toronto, agreed to sell a safe to T., paint his name upon it, and send it to him at St. John by railway; that it was to be paid for by instalments in two years, but that no title to it was to pass to T. till the whole price was paid, until which time the safe was to be on hire; and on default of any of the payments, plaintiff was to be at liberty to retake possession of the safe. T. gave his notes for the price of the safe according to agreement; his name was painted on the door of it, and the plaintiff sent it to St. John by railway addressed to T., with a bill of lading or way bill. There was a covering over the safe, which prevented T.'s name upon it from being seen until the covering was taken off. While the safe remained in the railway warehouse, T. transferred it to the defendant, to whom he was indebted, delivering to him the bill of lading or way bill, and he thereupon paid the freight upon it from Toronto and took possession of it, not knowing that T.'s name was painted on it. The first note given by T. not having been paid, the plaintiff demanded the safe from the defendant, who refused to give it up, claiming to own it.

Held, (Palmer, J., dissenting), 1. That even if the painting of T.'s name on the safe and sending it to him would amount to a representation that it was his property, on which a purchaser from him might act, the defendant, when he took possession of the safe, did not know that T.'s name was on it, and therefore was not induced to purchase it by any representation of the plaintiff (the bill of lading not being in evidence), and that the plaintiff was not estopped from showing that T. had no right to sell it.

2. That the agreement between the plaintiff and T. was not a bill of sale requiring registration. *Trueman*, appellant, and *Bain*, respondent, vol. 25, 298.

—Assignee of bill of lading is entitled to an action for—To recover the value of goods sold by consignee. See Bill of Lading 1.

—To receive from sheriff goods taken in execution against a party in possession where property had been previously transferred by bill of sale. See Bill of Sale 2.

—Conversion—Third party having property. See Agreement 1.

—Married woman—Joint conversion. See Married Woman 2.

TRUSTEE AND CESTUI QUE TRUST.

Necessity of assent of creditors to constitute relation of. See Deed 3.

Trust deed—Fraudulent. See Deed 2, 3, 4.

Further assurance, consideration. See Deed 2.

Trustees—Under will—Their powers. See Will 5.

Two cents—Whether provisions of statute restricting damages to apply in case justice has gone beyond his judicial duty. See False Imprisonment 1.

Ultra Vires.—Whether sec. 78, cap. 31 of Act 32 & 33 Vic. is. See Justice of the Peace 1.

—Bills of Sales Act not. See Bills of Sale Act 1, 2.

—Canada Temperance Act. See Spirituous Liquors.

—**Incorporating company—Obstructions in tidal and navigable rivers**—45 Vic. cap. 100, N. B.

Understanding, between attorneys—Court will not aid in carrying out. See Attorney 2.

—Attorneys should carry on their business according to the established rules of practice. See Attorney 2.

Underwriters—Notice of abandonment of vessel—Waiver. See Insurance 16.

Use and occupation—Action for—Where rent payable in advance. See Landlord and Tenant 2.

Usury—Usurious interest not allowed as part payment. See Promissory Note 1.

Vacant possession—In ejectment—Action for recovery of—Practise. See Practise 1.

Value—Need not be stated in indictment for taking and appropriating with intent to defraud. See Intent to defraud.

Valuable security—Whether insufficiently or defectively stamped promissory note is. See Criminal Law 3.

Vendor—Acts to be performed by, do not prevent property from vesting in vendee. See Property, passing of, 1.

Venire—To coroner may be issued on a suggestion on the record that the sheriff, for the reason stated, is not impartial. See Challenge 2.

Venue—Change of—Object of rule of Trinity Term, 1873.

The object of the rule of Trinity Term, which declares that "no venue shall be changed, unless by consent of parties without the special order of the court or a judge, founded upon a rule nisi or summons," was to prevent the venue from being changed by an order of course; but it does not necessarily require any special circumstances to be stated in defendant's affidavit, beyond what would previously have been required to be stated in the common affidavit. *Friar v. McGowan*, vol. 19, 25.

VERDICT.

1—Special questions left to jury—Where not unanimous in answering—Whether verdict can be entered within two hours.

In an action to recover damages sustained by plaintiff in consequence of being knocked down upon a public highway by a runaway horse belonging to defendant, the defence was, that the horse had been left tied to a post by a strap from the bridle and that he also was secured by a strap from the foot to a part of the waggon; and that a sudden noise caused him to take fright and break loose.

On the trial the judge directed the jury that if they found that the horse was sufficiently fastened, either by the head or by the foot, the defendant was entitled to a verdict; and he asked them if they gave a verdict for the plaintiff, to state how they found both as to the head fastening and foot fastening of the horse. Cap. 45, sec. 10, of the Consol. Stat., provides that if a jury cannot agree within two hours, any five of the seven may return a verdict. The jury returned into court within two hours and the foreman in answer to the usual question by the clerk, stated that they found a verdict for the plaintiff, and on being asked by the judge how they found on the two questions left to them, it appeared that they were unanimous as to the head fastening being insufficient; and that five of them thought the foot fastening also insufficient.

The verdict was thereupon entered for the plaintiff.

The counsel for both parties were present when the verdict was returned, but no one drew attention to the circumstance of the finding by five only as to the foot fastening.

Held, by Allen, C.J., Wetmore and King, JJ., that the verdict could not be treated as a general verdict for the plaintiff, but that the verdict and answers to the special questions must be taken together, and that the jury not being unanimous in their answer to one of the questions (the same being essential to the finding) the verdict should not have been received within the two hours.

2. That in order to constitute a waiver of the irregularity there must be either an express assent by the counsel, or circumstances from which an assent might be fairly inferred.

Held, by Weldon and Palmer, JJ., 1. That as the general verdict was found by all the jurors, that was sufficient, as they were not bound to answer questions specially.

2. That the counsel for defendant having allowed the verdict to be entered without objection, it was now too late to avail himself of it as a ground for a new trial. *Cheesman* v. *Hathaway*, vol. 23, 415.

—Reducing—Where jury allowed interest as part of damages. See Collision 1.

Power of court to change where some counts in indictment allege intent to prejudice, and others simply charge the crime. See Evidence 15.

—Against evidence—Where evidence is conflicting, is not a ground for a new trial. See New Trial 10.

Verbal promise—Whether primary or collateral — Hiring. See Statute of Frauds 2.

Vexatious Proceedings—Attaching order set aside. See Garnishee Act 2.

—Refusal of court to stay proceedings until costs of a former suit paid. See Stay of Action 2.

Vexing or harrassing—Affidavit to obtain judge's order to hold to bail in an action of tort need not state that arrest not made for purpose of. See Arrest 2.

View—See Jury.

Void proceeding — *Certiorari* will be granted to remove. See *Certiorari*.

VOLUNTARY CONVEYANCE.

Whether avoided by subsequent deed under Insolvent Confined Debtor's Act.

A deed given by a debtor under the Insolvent Confined Debtor's Act can have no greater effect than a deed from the sheriff when he sells under an execution; neither the one nor the other will, in the absence of fraud, defeat a previous voluntary deed executed by the debtor. *Black* v. *Cogswell*, vol. 19, 44.

—Husband to wife through medium of third party—Whether can support by proof of parol ante-nuptial agreement. See Husband and Wife 5.

Voidable contract—Repudiation by one party—Recovery under common counts. See Contract 12.

Wages—Where servant leaves before time expires—When may sue for, at once. See Assumpsit 3.

—Of policeman of city of St. John—Power of common council to reduce—Month's notice. See Police 1.

—Of master of ship—How recovered — Registered owner — Liability for — See Ship 1.

Waiver—If land is incumbered and the incumbrance was not removed at the time limited for giving the deed. See Sale of Land 3.

—Of conditions in insurance policy—To what confined. See Insurance 6.

—Of requirements of proof—What constitutes. See Insurance 6.

—Refusal to deliver property held for proper charges until other changes are paid, whether is waiver of lien for proper charges. See Trover 3.

—Tort—Action for goods sold and delivered and for money had and received. See Conversion 1.

— Preliminary proofs — Insurance policy—What constitutes. See Insurance 10.

—Delay in moving to set aside a judgment for irregularity. See Judgment 1.

—Loss of vessel—Notice of abandonment. See Insurance 16.

—Policy of Marine Insurance—Countersigning by agent See Insurance 15.

—Where jury not unanimous—Verdict entered within two hours—Counsel for both parties present whether constitutes waiver. See Verdict.

WARRANT.

Dominion penitentiary — Conviction by Supreme Court of Nova Scotia—Warrant to commit prisoner— Statement of date of sentence—Habeas corpus.

The judges of the Supreme Court of this province have the exclusive right to issue writs of *habeas corpus* to inquire into the legality of the imprisonment of a person confined in the Dominion penitentiary at Dorchester, though he was committed there by the court of another province (Tuck, J., dissenting).

S. was tried by the Supreme Court of Nova Scotia in March, 1884, upon an indictment containing counts at common law, charging him as a public officer with making false and fraudulent entries and returns, and with fraudulently destroying public papers, and also containing counts charging similar acts as an offence under 41 Vic. cap. 7, sec. 67 He was found guilty, and upon the 14th April, 1884, sentenced to four years' imprisonment in the Dorchester penitentiary upon the counts, charging the offence as at common law, judgment being respited upon the other counts.

The warrant under which he was committed to the penitentiary was in the following words;

Province of Nova Scotia.
Halifax, S. S.

Supreme Court, 188

To the Warden and Governor of the Penitentiary at Dorchester, in the Province of New Brunswick :

Whereas, Robert Strather was, during the March sitting of the Supreme Court at Halifax, indicted for making fraudulent entries and fraudulent returns, and was found guilty upon said indictment, and thereupon sentenced by the court to be imprisoned at hard labor in the penitentiary at Dorchester for the space of four years ;

Now, therefore, these are to require and command you to receive the said Robert Strather into your custody, and him to detain in the said penitentiary for the said period of four years in conformity with the terms of his said sentence, and for which this shall be your sufficient warrant.

Dated at Halifax this 14th day of April, A. D. 1884.

S. H. Holmes,
[L.S.] Clerk Court.

The Penitentiary Act, 46 Vic. cap. 37, directs that a copy of the sentence taken from the minutes of the court by which the prisoner was tried, certified by the judge or clerk of the court, shall be delivered to the warden of the penitentiary with any prisoner committed to his custody.

Held, per Allen, C.J., Wetmore, Palmer and Fraser, JJ., that the warrant under which S. was committed to the penitentiary was not a compliance with the statute, and did not authorize the warden of the penitentiary to detain S.

Per Allen, C.J., Wetmore and Fraser, JJ., that as the warrant did not state the day the prisoner was sentenced, the time when his term of imprisonment commenced and would expire was uncertain, and the warrant therefore defective.

Per Palmer, J., that the warrant did not show that S. was convicted of any crime, the mere "making of fraudulent entries and fraudulent returns," as alleged in the warrant, being no offence at common law or by statute, and that his imprisonment was therefore illegal.

Per King, J., 1. That as the Penitentiary Act did not require the offence to be mentioned in the warrant to commit the prisoner, the omission of such a statement did not render it void, it being the warrant of a superior court.

2. That it should be presumed, in the absence of anything to the contrary, that the facts existed which made the acts charged a criminal offence.

3. That the omission to state the date of the sentence in the warrant of commitment was only an irregularity, and did not render the warrant void. *Ex parte Strather*, vol. 25, 374.

—Assessments—Wrong inclusion of—Vitiates whole. See Assessment 8.

—Under Con. Stat. cap. 100, sec. 77, against real estate of non-resident minors under assessment made against their guardian. See *Certiorari* 5.

—Where prisoner is committed to be held till discharged in due course of law, the warrant continues in force till he is discharged or sent to penitentiary. See Remanding Prisoner 1.

—Irregular—Whether a justification to the officer arresting a party under it. See Criminal Law 7.

—Reciting conviction—*Prima facie* evidence of. See False Imprisonment 2.

—Warrant to arrest in first instance when improper. See Summary Conviction Act 9.

Warrant and defence—Construction of words in deed. See Estoppel 4.

WARRANTY.

Fitness of article for purpose intended.

Where a person orders an ascertained article, there is no implied warranty that it is fit for the purpose for which he ordered it. The rule however is otherwise where the article is not ascertained; and where plaintiff ordered machinery from defendants.

Held, that the latter was bound to supply such machinery as was reasonably fit for the purpose for which they knew it was intended. *Morrow* v. *The Waterous Engine Co.*, vol. 18, 509.

—Whether phosphate rock is stone or ore—Question of fact. See Insurance 2.

—Not implied on sale of specific article which purchasers may examine. See Sale 2.

Insurance—Meaning of. See Insurance 17.

Way—Obstruction of. See Trespass 2.

Wharves—Harbour of St. John—Power of corporation to erect. See Easement 2.

Widow—Devise of revenue and income of estate to—Right to lease. See Will 9.

—Estate of, in lands of deceased husband before assignment of dower. See Dower 1.

Wife—Separate property of—Evidence of, must be clear and satisfactory. See Married Woman 1.

—Where part of the purchase money belonged to the husband, if the property was bought by or for the wife, it vests in her. See Husband and Wife 1.

Wife's separate property—How far husband liable for taxes on, in city of St. John. See Inhabitant 1.

WILL.

1—Construction of—Direction that the proceeds of certain specified property should be conveyed to certain of the devisees to whom testator had said in will he could not give more than their share of the residuary estate—Whether these specified properties formed part of residuary estate or not.

The testator in his will stated that—"whereas the advances in money heretofore made by me to my dear departed son, R. M. H., in his lifetime, and to his widow since his death, amount to far more than I can give to either of my other dear children, I cannot in justice give my dear grandchildren, the daughters of my said dear son, anything beyond a share in the residue of my real estate, as hereinafter provided for," etc.

The testator after providing that the residue of his estate should be divided into six parts, and directing that one of these six parts should be conveyed to his said grandchildren, the children of his son, R. M. H., provided as follows: "I direct that the Lone Water farm in Westfield, and the lot of land on the Black River Road, in the parish of Simonds, both of which were heretofore conveyed by me to my dear son R. M., and re-conveyed by him and his wife to me, form part of the share of my said grandchildren in this partition, and that the same be sold as soon as good and fair prices can be obtained for them, and the proceeds thereof be invested on good security or securities for my said grandchildren"—and then a provision for the payment of the income to their mother for them.

Held, on appeal, reversing the judgment of the court below, that the testator's grandchildren did not take a sixth of the residue, and the Lone Water Farm, and the lot on the Black River Road besides, but that the latter formed part of the residuary estate. *Hazen* v. *Hazen*, vol. 20, 70.

2—Surplus—Whether of both real and personal estate, or either—Intestacy as to part.

The testator after making certain specific bequests concluded his will as follows:—"Should there be any surplus or deficiency, a *pro rata* addition or deduction, as may be, to be made to the following bequests, namely "Worn out preacher's and widow's fund—Wesleyan Missionary Society; Bible Society."

By the will he gave his executors power to dispose of certain lands at Sussex, but there was nothing in the will concerning four lots of lands in St. John, of which he was possessed, at the time the will was made and at the time of his death.

Held, by Allen, C.J., an[illegible]ore, J., (Palmer, J., dissenting), varying the judgment of the court below that the "surplus" had reference to the testator's personal estate, and the land of Sussex only, and that there was an intestacy in regard to the four lots in St. John. *Lockhart* v. *Ray*, vol. 20, 129.

3—Annuities—Sale of corpus to pay—Legacy, payment of—Where stock devised was sold by testator after making will—Substitution.

R. died on 3rd August, 1876, leaving a will dated 6th August, 1875, and a codicil dated 21st July, 1876. By the will he devised to his wife S. in lieu of her dower, during her life the annuity or clear yearly sum of $10,000, "which should be a charge on his general estate." His executors and trustees were also to permit her during her life to occupy the dwelling-house she then resided in, in the city of London. He devised to his executors and trustees "all the lands, tenements, and hereditaments mentioned and described in the schedules annexed to the will, marked A. B. C. D. and E., upon trust during the life of his wife, to collect and receive the rents, issues and profits thereof, which should be and be taken to form a portion of his general estate," and from and out of the said general estate, during the life of his said wife to pay to each of his daughters M. A., E., M. S., A. L., and L. C., the clear yearly sum of $1,600, and after his wife's death to collect and receive the rents, issues, dividends, and profits of the several lands, etc., mentioned in the said several schedules, and to pay to his daughter M. A. the rents, etc., of the lands apportioned to her and mentioned in Schedule A.; to his daughter E. of those mentioned in Schedule B.; to his daughter M. S. of those mentioned in Schedule C.; to his daughter A. L. of those mentioned in Schedule D.; and to his daughter L. C. of those mentioned in Schedule E.; each of his said daughters being charged with the insurance, ground rents, (if any), rates and taxes, repairs and other expenses connected with or incidental to the management and upholding of the property apportioned to her, and the same being from time to time deducted from such quarterly payments." The will then directed the executors to keep the properties mentioned in the schedules insured against loss by fire, and in case of total loss that it should be optional with the parties to whom the property was apportioned by the schedules, either to direct the insurance money to be applied in rebuilding, or to lease the property. It then declared what was to be done with the share of each of his daughters in case of her death.

The rents and profits of the whole estate left by the testator proved insufficient, after paying the annuity of $10,000 to the widow and the rent of and taxes upon his house in London, to pay the several sums of $1,600 a year to each of his daughters during the life of their mother, and the first question raised in this suit was whether the executors and trustees had power to sell or mortgage any part of the *corpus* of the property to make up the deficiency.

Allen, C.J., in the court below, decided this question in the negative; and

Held, on appeal, by Weldon and Wetmore, JJ., (Fisher, J., expressing no opinion), that the conclusion of the chief justice was correct; but Palmer, J., that while the scheduled property could not be touched to pay the annuities of $1,600, yet that the whole of the rest of the testator's estate was charged with the payment of these legacies, and that the executors and trustees were bound to pay them at the times mentioned in the will, so long as there was enough to pay the annuity to the widow, the other legacies and these annuities, without touching the *corpus* of the scheduled property.

In the residuary clause of the will there were the following words: "The rest, residue and remainder of my estate, both real and personal, and wheresoever situated, I give, etc., to my executors and trustees—upon the trust after paying my brother D. R., to whom I bequeath the sum and legacy of $4,000, to sell and dispose of the same, etc., and apportion the proceeds equally" among his, the testator's children, upon the same trusts as were declared with reference to the scheduled property.

Held, by Weldon, Fisher and Wetmore, JJ., that D. R. was entitled to be paid his legacy of $4,000 regardless of whether there was sufficient to pay the annuities to the daughters or not; and by Palmer, J., that he was entitled to be paid it out of the same fund as the daughters, and that both were entitled to and should be paid in full.

The testator, at the time he made the will, had 100 shares of the capital stock of the Maritime Bank, the par value of each share being $100. Fifty per cent. had been paid up, though the testator had purchased the stock for $3,342.74. After making the will, and before any further call was made, the testator sold the stock. By the will, however, he devised $3,000 of the paid up stock of the said bank to one daughter, in schedule A, and $5,000 to another in schedule E. The executors were directed, in case any of the stocks, etc., devised should be disposed of during the testator's life, to substitute therefor money or other property of equal value.

Held, by Weldon and Fisher, JJ., that the legatees were entitled to be paid the amount actually paid by the testator for the stock, and the 50 per cent. remaining unpaid.

Held, by Wetmore and Palmer, JJ., that they were entitled to have this stock replaced by a sum equal in value to the amount of the paid up stock immediately after the death of the testator. *Almon v. Lewis*, vol. 20, 284.

Appeal allowed to Supreme Court of Canada. See Addenda, No. 6.

4—Execution—Signature by testator—Presumptions where no positive evidence of signature being to will when attested by witnesses—What a sufficient acknowledgment in the presence of witnesses—Evidence—How far attestation clause may be—Witnesses signing in each other's presence.

If a testator produces a paper and asks persons to sign it, giving them to understand that it is his will, it is not necessary to have direct evidence that his signature was on the paper when he asked them to sign it; but the court is at liberty to judge from all the circumstances of the case whether his signature was there at the time or not.

To a will written in the testator's handwriting and concluding with the following testimonium clause: "In witness whereof I have hereunto set my hand and seal," etc., was an attestation clause, also in the testator's handwriting as follows: "The [illegible]d Alexander Ferguson" (the testator) "this, etc., sealed and delivered this instrument as and for his last will and testament, and we, at his request and in his presence, and in the presence of each other, have hereunto written our names as subscribing witnesses." Signed, "Charles McKeen, William McKeen." When produced, the will bore the testator's signature in the usual place. It was not signed in the presence of the witnesses, and there was no evidence that either of them saw his signature to the paper when they subscribed it as witnesses.

The testator brought the will to the witnesses' shop and told C. McK., one of them, it was his will, and asked him to sign it. The other, W. McK., a brother of the first, coming in at the time, the testator said, "Let your brother sign also," which the latter did, without knowing what the paper was. He did not remember seeing his brother sign it. He did not know what the paper was, and no one told him.

Held, by Allen, C.J., and Palmer, J., (Duff, J., dubitante), that it might be presumed that the testator signed it before he went to the shop, and that it was then a complete instrument, so far as he himself could complete it.

Held, by Allen, C.J., and Duff, J., (Palmer, J., dissenting), that there was not an acknowledgment by the testator of the will in the presence of the witnesses, as required by the Act, Con. Stat., cap. 77, sec. 5.

By Duff, J., that there was not a

proper attestation by the witnesses in the presence of each other.

By Palmer, J., that, looking at the attestation clause, there was sufficient evidence of the witnesses having signed the will in the presence of the testator, and in the presence of each other, to justify the court in upholding the will. *In re the goods of Alexander Ferguson*, vol. 21, 71.

5—Construction of—Authority to rebuild buildings destroyed by fire—Where buildings destroyed in testator's lifetime—Description of new buildings—Effect of change in the building laws—Power to sell—A mortgage not as a general rule a due execution of a trust for sale and conversion—Insurance—Whether trustees can increase insurance when directed to insure in about the amount in which testator insured—Annuity—When chargeable on a particular fund—When on corpus of estate—Division of annual income of residuary estate—Parties consenting to a decree bound by it—Costs—Appeal.

The testator devised his house and other buildings on Charlotte street, St. John, to trustees upon trust during the life of his wife, to permit her to have the use and occupation of them, and of any buildings which, in case of fire, might be substituted in lieu of, or to replace the same, and to receive the rents and profits thereof to her own use and benefit.

After his death the property was to be conveyed to the rector of Trinity Church, St. John. He devised his real estate in Queen's Ward, and certain stock and bonds to them upon certain trusts, and charged the real estate stocks and bonds with the payment of an annuity of $5,000 to his wife.

The will then continued:—"Which annuity shall commence from my decease and be paid quarterly without deduction. And I direct that my said trustees shall stand seised and possessed of this last mentioned real estate, stocks and bonds, and the annual rents, profits, dividends and interest thereof upon trust, by and out of the said rents and profits, dividends and interests, to pay to my said wife the said annuity, or clear yearly sum of $5,000 during her life by even and equally quarterly payments in each year; the first quarterly payment thereof to fall due and be payable at the expiration of three months from and after my decease, and as to the surplus of the said rents, profits, dividends, and interests, which shall remain in each year during the life of my said wife, after the payment of the said annuity to her, I direct my said trustees to pay and apply said surplus in like manner as is directed as to the annual income of my residuary estate." The testator also directed the trustees generally to manage the real estate, to keep the house and other buildings on Charlotte street, and the buildings on the Queen's Ward properties in tenantable repair, and insured against loss by fire in about the amounts the testator had them insured upon them, and in case of loss to apply the insurance money towards repairing the damage, or in erecting new buildings in lieu of those destroyed; giving them power to erect buildings of a like or of a different character on the same site. In case the insurance money should prove insufficient for the purpose, power was given to use and apply such a portion of the capital of the residuary, real and personal estate, not charged with the widow's annuity, as the trustees should deem necessary. All matters and things done in reference to the Charlotte street buildings were to be done with the widow's consent and subject to her approval.

The trustees were authorized after the expiration of one year from the testator's death, and at such times thereafter as they should deem most advantageous, to sell the property not charged with the widow's annuity and to stand possessed of the proceeds upon the trust therein declared.

The buildings were burned in the testator's life time, and he collected the insurance moneys with the exception of $700, a balance due in respect of part of the Queen's Ward properties. This amount was paid to the trustees. The Queen's Ward properties were in the business centre of the city, and without the buildings would bring in little, if any, rental. The testator had commenced to rebuild on one of these properties, all of which continued to belong to him up to the time of his death, and vested in his trustees under the devise to them.

Held, affirming the judgment of the court below, that as the clear intention of the testator was to provide a residence for his wife during her life, the trustees were authorized to rebuild the house and other buildings on Charlotte street.

Held, that the order of the court below that "the trustees were bound to rebuild the dwelling house and such other buildings as were necessary for the comfortable enjoyment of the premises by the widow, of the character, dimensions and capacity, with such offices and appliances as were standing thereon before the fire, as near as might be, consulting the wishes and desires of the widow, and conforming thereto in regard to the dwelling house and appurtenances, and to such changes and alterations therein as she might desire for her personal comfort, so as there should be no material or substantial change therein in any respect, to the injury of the inheritance or otherwise, did not go beyond the powers given to the trustees by the will. Also that the trustees must build such buildings as the law at the time of building allowed.

Held, affirming the judgment of the court below, that the trustees were authorised to rebuild the buildings on the properties in Queen's ward.

Held, varying the judgment of the court below, that the trustees were not authorized to raise the money necessary for rebuilding by mortgaging some part of the real estate not charged with the annuity to the wife.

Held, affirming the judgment of the court below, that the trustees might insure any new buildings which they might erect, in such sums as they thought necessary to protect the interests of the estate.

Held, affirming the judgment of the court below, that the testator intended to bequeath to his wife an annuity of $5,000, and that in case the particular property upon which it was made a charge should prove insufficient for that purpose, the amount should be paid in full out of the residuary estate.

After giving a number of general and specific legacies the will directed the trustees to convert the residuary personal estate not consisting of moneys invested in stocks, funds, or securities yielding income, and at their discretion either to get in the moneys so invested, or to allow them so to continue, and after paying the testator's debts and testamentary expenses and the several legacies, to invest the surplus produce thereof, pursuant to general directions for investment thereinafter declared. After certain directions as to how sales of real estate should be made, the will proceeds as follows:—"And I direct that my said trustees shall stand possessed of the real estate charged with the said annuity" (to the widow) "subject thereto, and of the proceeds thereof when sold, and of all other residuary estate, and of the proceeds thereof when sold, the investments thereof, and the residue of my personal estate remaining after payment of my debts, funeral expenses and legacies. And the investment of said residue of my said personal estate, and also after the decease of my said wife, of the said 100 shares of capital stock of the Bank of New Brunswick, and the said £2,000 in bonds of the mayor, etc., of the city of St. John, subject, however, to any deduction therefrom directed or authorized to be made by this my will upon trust as to one-third part thereof for my nephews, John A. Wright, Charles H. Wright, Alexander W. Wright and Octavius Wright, share and share alike. And as to one-third part of such residuary estate as aforesaid upon trust to pay unto my brother Nehemiah the net interest and dividends and annual income thereof during his life, for his own absolute use and benefit, and after the decease of my said brother Nehemiah to pay the said one-third part to and among the children of my said brother Nehemiah share and share alike. And as to one other equal third part thereof, to pay the same to Jane Elizabeth, the wife of my late brother George, for her own absolute use and benefit forever." The taxes on the property charged with the annuity to the wife were directed to be paid out of the residuary estate, and directions were given for the investment of the residuary estate in certain specified securities.

Held, that the will gave no authority to the trustees to pay over the income of any portion of the residuary estate to the Misses Wright or to Mrs. Jane Elizabeth Merritt during the widow's life time. But as all parties interested in the residuary estate had consented to the court below making a decree allowing this to be done, the appellant, who was one of the assenting parties, must be bound by it.

Held, that the trustees were not authorized to divide the residuary estate during the widow's life time, and that the residuary legatees had no right to claim a division on giving security for the payment of the widow's annuity. *Merritt v. Wright*, vol. 21, 135.

6—Construction of—Word "Heirs" construed same as "Children" or "Issue"—Where such was clear intention of testator.

Wills ought to be so interpreted as not to defeat the intention of the testator by technical rules of construction, but by considering the language in a free, liberal and common-sense spirit, to give effect to the manifest intention.

Therefore the word "heirs" was construed as a word of substitution, and held to have the same effect as the words "children" or "issue," such being the manifest intention of the testator. *Otty v. Cruikshank*, vol. 21, 169.

7—Executors—Penalty for not proving—Excuse—Pleading.

In an action under the Rev. Stat., cap. 136, sec. 10, to recover the penalty for not proving a will in the Probate Court, the declaration stated the making of the will by M., and appointing the defendant the executor, of which he had notice; that he did not prove it in the Probate Court, or register it in any office of the Registrar of Probates for the county of N., where the deceased dwelt, or renounce the executorship within thirty days, though he had no just excuse for the delay.

Pleas.—1. That the defendant did prove and record the will in the Registrar's office of the county of N., where the deceased had last dwelt.

2. That after the death of M. the plaintiff with the defendant's consent took possession of all the personal property of M., and still had the use and enjoyment thereof; and that all the debts and funeral expenses being paid, the will was proved and recorded in the office of the Registrar of deeds and wills for the county of N., wherein all M.'s

real estate was situated, and that the plaintiff entered into the possession of and still possessed such real estate; wherefore the defendant did not prove the will in the Probate Court, or renounce the executorship thereof.

Held, on demurrer, *per* Allen, C.J., Wetmore, Palmer, and King, JJ., (Weldon, J., dissenting), that the pleas were bad; that the registrar mentioned in cap. 136, sec. 10, was the Registrar of Probates, and not the Registrar of Deeds.

Per Weldon, J., that the registry of the will in the office of the Registrar of Deeds was sufficient. *Wagner* v. *Hutchinson*, vol. 22, 1.

8—Cutting off seal—Execution of new will—Invalid by reason of improper attestation—Dependent relative revocation.

Deceased having duly executed a will in 1874, and the will having been found amongst his papers at his death in 1881, in a mutilated state, along with another insufficiently executed will, the two questions arising in this case were, first, Whether the mutilation amounted to a tearing or other destruction of the will within the meaning of the Wills Act, and if so, whether it was done by the testator, and with the intention of revoking the will. The facts proved before the Judge of Probates bearing on the act of mutilation were these: The testator at the time of executing the will affixed his seal to it in the presence of the attesting witnesses, but the instrument was not expressed to be under seal, nor did the attestation clause refer to the sealing of it. After the testator's death the will was found with the seal cut out, leaving a hole in the paper where the seal had been; several pencil marks were also drawn through the signature.

The facts bearing on the question of the testator's intention in mutilating the will were as follows: Deceased who was a deaf mute made his will when he was sick in 1874. In this will he left the bulk of his property to his eldest brother, C. and in case of C.'s death to another brother, appointing the last named to be the executor of the will.

Upon the death of the elder brother in 1880, the testator became very much dissatisfied apparently because he thought he should exercise more control as the oldest surviving member of the family. The testator in conversation with one of the witnesses to the last will, referred to the first will, (the one in question), as having been obtained from him by false pretenses, and as having been executed by him under circumstances which he dwelt upon as shewing that he never intended to make such a will.

Held, by Palmer and King, JJ., (Weldon, J. dissenting), that the testator meant the revocation of this will to depend upon the efficiency of the new disposition, or that he meant to revoke this will, simply because he had, as he thought, made another in its place, and that there was a tearing of the will within the meaning of the Wills Act, with the intention of revoking the will, and not merely a dependent relative revocation. *In re Drury's Will*, vol. 22, 318.

9—Estate during widowhood—Devise of income and profits—Right to lease—Equity pleadings—Setting out documents at full length.

A testator made the following devise: "After paying all my just debts and funeral expenses, I devise and bequeath all my property, real and personal, to be equally divided among my children without any distinction whatsoever, as soon as the youngest shall attain the age of twenty-one years, reserving to my dear wife, so long as she shall remain my widow, the revenues and incomes to be derived therefrom for her own support and the education and maintenance of my children.

Held, that the widow took an estate in the land during her widowhood, and that her right to lease it while her estate continued, would not be affected by a mortgage given by the owners of the estate in remainder. *King v. Murray*, vol. 22, 342.

10—Certified copy under sec. 15, cap. 74, Consol. Stat.—Prima facie proof of validity—Evidence — Cumulative — Right to rebut—Testator—Witness to previous will —Whether can prove capacity of testator —Juror. —Disqualification.

On the trial of an action of ejectment where the lessors of the plaintiff claimed as heirs-at-law of one R. S. After the plaintiff's counsel had opened the case the defendant's counsel admitted that the lessors of the plaintiff were the heirs-at-law of R. S., who died, seised of the land in dispute, leaving a will under which the defendant claimed as devisee. Upon this statement defendant's counsel claimed the right to begin, which being allowed, he gave in evidence (subject to objection) a copy of the will of R. S., certified by the Registrar of the deeds and wills of St. John, as having been admitted to probate before the judge of probates of St. John, and registered in the records of deeds and wills for the county. This evidence was offered and received under sec. 15, of cap. 74, Consol. Stat. Defendant's counsel then stopped relying on that as *prima facie* evidence. The lessors of the plaintiff then went into evidence attacking the will on the ground of the testator's incapacity, and the defendant then (subject to objection) produced the original will and gave evidence to shew the capacity of the testator.

Held, 1. That the certified copy of the will was properly admitted and was *prima facie* evidence of its validity.

2. That the lessors of the plaintiff having called evidence to shew the incapacity of the testator to make a will, the defendant had a right to rebut the case so set up by the lessors of the plaintiff.

The will in question was made in 1866, but the testator had made a previous will in 1863, and Mr. Justice Duff, who was then an attorney and barrister, and had prepared and witnessed the will of 1863, gave evidence in which he stated (subject to objection) that when R. S. made that will, he was, in his opinion, of sound disposing mind, memory and understanding.

Held, by 'Allen, C.J., and Wetmore, and King, JJ., (Wetmore, J., dissenting), that the evidence was improperly admitted.

Held, also, by Allen, C.J., and Wetmore and King, JJ., that although the evidence was not material to the issue which the jury had to try, namely, as to the testator's capacity in 1866, when the will in question was made, it was impossible to say the jury were not influenced by it, and there should be a new trial.

Held, that the fact of one of the jurors being in debt to the defendant (who obtained the verdict), was not of itself a ground for a new trial. *Doe dem Simonds v. Gilbert*, vol. 22, 576.

11—A will made by the husband in 1884, not revoked by the marriage ceremony performed in 1885, where marriage ceremony in 1884 valid. See *in re James Tiernay*, vol. 25, 286.

—When heir-at-law is entitled to have alleged will proved in solemn form. See Probate Court 1.

—Separate actions against executors for penalty for not proving—One stayed. See Stay of Action 1.

Proof of, in solemn form—Petition for —Citation— Preliminary objections — Appeal. See Probate Court 2.

—Surplus—Whether residuary personal estate of the testator passed—Construction of will. See Addenda 20.

Witness—Not bound to state reasons for refusing to answer questions that he believes will tend to criminate him. See False Imprisonment 4.

—Medical witness—Stating conclusions. See *Doe dem Hazen* v. *St. James Church*, vol. 18, 479.

—Expert. See Contract 15. Evidence 19.

—Recall of—General objection to admission of his evidence does not enable the defendants on a motion for a new trial to claim that a part of the evidence was improperly received. See Evidence 4.

—Recalling to rebut defendant's testimony on the point as to which plaintiff had been cross-examined. See Ejectment 4.

—Abroad—Commission for examination of—Return. See Insurance 16.

—Interrogatories—Return of. See Practice 15. See also Rules of Court, vol. 24, 515.

—Reading to witness, paper not in evidence, not permissible. See Evidence 16.

—Refusing to allow defendant's counsel to read to witness B. what S. had sworn was said by him, B., about making a mistake in order to ask B. whether such statement was true or not. See Practice 7.

—Summons to, issue of, by justice called in by other justice. See Canada Temperance Act 19.

Right of separate counsel to examine. See Practice 6.

Witness's fees may be taxed for same person in each suit where several suits by same plaintiff. See Costs 3.

—Refunding, when party does not attend. See Attorney 3.

—Affidavit for taxation of. See Costs 18.

—Allowance of—St. John City Court. See Costs 25.

Woodstock Civil Court—No appeal provided for. See Review 2.

Woodstock, town of—Power of magistrate to try offences against Canada Temperance Act committed outside of Town. See Canada Temperance Act, 1878, 11.

—Whether town council has power to assess inhabitants of town for expenses of carrying on prosecutions under the Canada Temperance Act. See Canada Temperance Act, 1878, 12.

—Whether a city within meaning of the Canada Temperance Act. See Canada Temperance Act, 1878, 12.

Words—"Next." See Execution 1.

—"Valuable security." See Criminal Law, 3.

—"Heirs." See Will 6.

—"Warrant and defend." See Estoppel 4.

—"City" and "county." See Canada Temperance Act 10.

—"Anything done by virtue of office of secretary." See Notice of Action.

—"Absence." See Canada Temperance Act 19.

—"Fixed." See Ship 2.

—"Spirituous" and "intoxicating." See Summary Conviction Act 8.

WRITS.

Issue of, without authority—Confirmation of, by party having no authority at time of issuing writ, but having subsequent authority—Held good. *Albert Mining Co.* v. *Spurr*, vol. 18, 665.

—Writ good on its face—A justification to offer. See Justification.

Capias—Issuing wrong form—Irregularity. See Practise 12.

—Signed and sealed by clerk of the court, but issued after appointment of his successor. See Practice 12.

—Affidavit to obtain order for arrest need not state plaintiff's belief that defendant is about to quit the province. See Arrest 1.

—Time of filing. See Court General Rule 3.

Writ of error—Prisoner not bound to proceed by. See Criminal Law 4.

Writ of prohibition—Scrutiny. See Canada Temperance Act 8.

Writ of restitution — See Summary Ejectment 2.

WRIT.

Service on lunatic—Service of—Where defendant is insane—Whether service good.

It appearing by the sheriff's affidavit of service of a writ issued out of the county court, that at the time of service the defendant was insane, and was confined in the provincial lunatic asylum, the county court judge refused to assess the damages (the defendant not having appeared), and on application to this court for a *mandamus* to compel him to do so, a rule *nisi* was granted. *Ex parte McKnight*, vol. 23, 272.

REMAINDER OF CASES CONTAINED IN VOLUME 25, AND OMITTED IN DIGEST.

Affidavit to hold to bail made by an agent—statement of means of knowledge—Negativing intention to vex and harass defendant—Waiver—Appointment of commissioner to take affidavits—Presumption of appointment.

An affidavit to arrest a debtor made by the managing agent in this province of a foreign banking corporation, stated that he was such agent, that the defendant was indebted to the company in a certain amount, and that the arrest was not made by himself, nor the company, for the purpose of vexing or harassing the defendant.

Held, 1. That it was not necessary that the agent should state his means of knowing the existence of the debt.

2. That, without stating that the suit was brought by his direction, the affidavit did not sufficiently negative that the arrest was made for the purpose of vexing and harassing the debtor as required by Con. Stat. cap. 38. The omission to make such a statement in the affidavit is an irregularity only, and is waived by putting in special bail, if the bail might have known of the irregularity by examining the affidavit in the clerk's office.

Where an affidavit purported to have been sworn before a commissioner for taking affidavits,

Held, (Wetmore, J., dissenting), that it would be presumed that he had been appointed a commissioner unless the contrary was clearly shown.

Per Wetmore, J., that where the application made by the bail to set aside the proceedings, raised a doubt as to the authority of the person to take affidavits, the *onus* was on the plaintiff to prove his authority; and in the absence of such proof, the affidavit was a nullity, and the objection was not waived by entering special bail. *Halifax Banking Co.*, v. *Smith*, vol. 25, 610.

Arbitration—Award—Uncertainty.

An award ought to be so certain that no reasonable doubt can arise on the face of it as to the arbitrators' meaning, or as to the nature and extent of the duties imposed by it on the parties; and if it be doubtful whether the award has decided the questions referred, it will be set aside for uncertainty.

Two partners being possessed of a considerable quantity of real and personal estate, and having a large amount of debts due them, desired to dissolve the partnership, but being unable to agree upon terms, submitted all matters in difference between them to arbitration. The arbitrators awarded that one of the partners should pay the other a certain sum in full payment, discharge and satisfaction of all moneys, debts and demands due or owing by him to his copartner upon any account whatsoever.

Held, that the award was bad for uncertainty, there being no decision respecting the partnership property. *In re Fairley* and *Wilson*, vol. 25, 568.

County courts—Practice—Change of venue—Non-resident plaintiff—Appeal—Certiorari.

Where the plaintiff in an action in the county court resides out of the province, and the defendant applies to change the venue, the plaintiff on opposing such application, may shew that the cause can be more conveniently tried in the county in which he had laid it; and if he omits to do so, and an order is made to change the venue, he cannot afterwards make a separate application to bring it back to the original county.

Quære, Whether an appeal will lie under the County Court Act, sec. 51, from the order of a judge to change the venue. *Ex parte Brown*, vol. 25, 598.

Crown grant—Bed of tidal river—Riparian owner—Public right of navigation—Injury to piers in the tide way—Injunction to protect rights of riparian owners—Assessment of damages by consent—Right to appeal from.

A grant by the crown of a tract of land fronting on the shore of the Bay of Fundy described it as commencing at the bay shore and running a certain course and distance inland, thence along the exterior lines of the tract till it again met the bay shore at a different point, and thence following the bay shore to the place of beginning, conveys to the grantee the bed of a tidal river which runs through the land, and discharges into the bay between the starting point of the grant and the place where the line again strikes the bay shore.

The Provincial Act, 45 Vic., cap. 100, passed since the British North America Act came into force, is *ultra vires* so far as it professes to authorize the erection of piers and booms in a tidal river.

Piers erected in the river under the supposed authority of the Act become the property of the owner of the bed of the river; but may be used by persons navigating the river, for the purpose of protecting and securing lumber floating down the river, and to prevent its loss by floating out to sea.

What will be a reasonable use of the piers for that purpose, will depend upon the quantity of lumber in the river, and the state of the tides, winds and currents at the time.

Where lumber floating down a river in the course of navigation, is left by the tide on the shore between high and low water mark, without any negligence on the part of the owner of lumber, it is not an improper interference with the right of the riparian owner, if it is removed within a reasonable time.

Where, on an application for an injunction to restrain the erection of piers and booms in a tidal river, the bed of which belongs to the plaintiff, and to prohibit interference with his riparian rights, it was agreed that the judge should assess the damage which the plaintiff had sustained by the acts of the defendant; the amount assessed is not the subject of appeal, it being mere matter of agreement and no part of the duty of the judge under the Equity Act. *Quiddy River Boom Co. v. Davidson*, vol. 25, 580.

False imprisonment—Liability of informant for arrest under warrant—Omission in warrant to state information on oath—Irregularity—Malicious injury to property—Act 32 & 33 Vic., cap. 22, secs. 49, 50—Statement of value.

A party applying to a magistrate for a warrant to arrest another for an alleged offence, is deemed only to appeal to the magistrate to exercise his jurisdiction, and is not liable in trespass for an arrest under the warrant; but if he goes beyond this, and interferes in the exercise of the ministerial powers under the warrant, he will be liable.

Where an information is on oath, the omission to state that fact in a warrant to arrest is an irregularity only.

Neither an information against a person for malicious injury to property under the 32 & 33 Vic., cap. 22, secs. 49, 50, nor the warrant issued thereon, stated the value of the property injured.

Held, an irregularity only, as the magistrate had jurisdiction over the offence, either by way of preliminary examination, if the value exceeded $20, or summarily, if it was within that sum. *Kingston v. Wallace, et al.*, vol. 25, 573.

Municipal taxation—Employees of Federal Government—Assessment on income—Principle governing.

Persons in the employ of the Intercolonial Railway department at Moncton were divided into five classes:

1. Members of the civil service of the Dominion, under the Civil Service Act of 1882, who received a yearly salary, and contributed to the superannuation fund of the civil service.

2. Persons who receive a yearly salary, but were not appointed to the civil service as provided by the Act of 1882, but held an office created by a Dominion statute, or were appointed by the Governor-General under authority of a statute, and who did not contribute to the superannuation fund.

3. Persons paid monthly, at a certain rate per year, and were liable to be dismissed at any time, and who were not appointed under the Civil Service Act, nor as mentioned in class 2, and did not contribute to the superannuation fund.

4. Engine drivers and conductors, employed in running trains, and paid by the mileage run, who received their pay monthly, and were subject to dismissal at any time.

5. Carpenters and other mechanics and workmen, who were paid monthly according to the time employed, and were subject to dismissal at any time in same manner as class 4.

Held, 1, *per tot curiam*, that the persons in classes 1 and 2 were not liable to be assessed for municipal purposes on their incomes received from the Government, (following *Ackman v. Town of Moncton*, 24 N. B. Rep. 103).

2. *Per* Allen, C.J., Wetmore, King, and Fraser, JJ., (Palmer, J., dissenting), that the persons belonging to the third class were also exempt.

Slander—Justification—Malice—Privileged communication—Evidence in mitigation of damages—Amendment—Adding new count.

Plaintiff having held the office of trustee, and also of secretary of the trustees in a school district, was succeeded in the office of secretary by the defendant, who was also the auditor of the trustees' accounts. At a meeting of the ratepayers of the district, at which the accounts of the school district, while the plaintiff was a trustee, were discussed, the plaintiff swore that the defendant charged him of having stolen the school funds. The defendant denied using the words charged, and swore that he only stated at the meeting that as he understood the plaintiff's book, he had received more money than he had paid out, and that he (defendant) had received a letter from the Chief Superintendent of Education, stating that the trustees had paid a teacher a certain sum out of the school funds. Neither the letter nor the book was read before the meeting. In an action for slander in charging the plaintiff with stealing and embezzling the monies, in which the defendant pleaded "not guilty," only,

Held, per Allen, C.J., Fraser and Tuck, JJ., (Wetmore, J., dissenting), that the letter and book were admissible in evidence in mitigation of damages, and to rebut any presumption of malice—no objection having been made that such evidence was not admissible under the plea.

If language, which would otherwise be privileged, be unnecessarily violent and excessive, and used in a manner not suited to the occasion, it loses its protection as a privileged communication. Where, in an action for slander, a count was added at the trial, charging the defendant with speaking other slanderous words of the same character, but at a different time and place from those charged in the existing declaration, and there was no affidavit by the defendant that he would be prejudiced in his defence by the amendment;

Held, per Allen, C.J., Fraser and Tuck, JJ., (Wetmore, J., dissenting), that the amendment was properly allowed, the defence on the trial being a denial only of the speaking of the words charged. *Bolser* v. *Crossman*, vol. 25, 556.

ADDENDA.

List of Cases in Addenda.

NOTE.

The following List of Cases appealed to Supreme Court of Canada and referred to in the Digest by Numbers, should have been numbered in consecutive order in the following addenda, but by an oversight in revision of proof sheets, the numbers have been omitted, but appear in following list as referred to in the Digest.

No.	Name of Case.	Page.
1	The Mayor, Aldermen and commonalty of the City of Fredericton, *appellants*, and The Queen, on the prosecution of Thomas Barker, *respondent*	247
2	Charles Russell, *appellant*, and The Queen, on the information of John Woodward, *respondent*	247
3	James Clark, *appellant*, and The Scottish Imperial Insurance Company, *respondent*	248
4	Charles W. Weldon, *appellant*, and James Vaughan and David Maurice Vaughan, *respondents*	248
5	John Mowat, *appellant*, and William McFee, *respondent*	249
6	Henri Jonas, *appellant*, and Humphrey T. Gilbert, *respondent*	250
7	Louis J. Alnon, *et al.*, *appellants*, and James D. Lewin, *et al.*, *respondents*	250
8	Nicholas Power, *appellant*, and Thomas Ellis, *respondent*	251
9	John Dewe, *appellant*, and David H. Waterbury, *respondent*	252
10	John Walker and William Spears, *appellants*, and James McMillan, *respondent*	253

No.	Name of Case.	Page.
11	—James McSorley, *appellant*, and The Mayor, etc., of the City of St. John, and William Sandall, *respondents*	251
12	—Tertullus Theal, *appellant*, and The Queen, *respondent*	251
13	—Dennis Commean, *appellant*, and Kennedy Burns, *respondent*	252
14	—J. H. Chapman, *appellant*, and Francis and James A. Teits *respondents*	253
15	—James DeWolf Spurr and John N. Moore, *appellants*, and The Albert Mining Company, *respondents*	256
16	—William H. Venning, *appellant*, and James Steadman *respondent*, do. do. Edgar Hanson do. do. do. James DeWolf Spurr, do.	257
17	—Patrick George Carvill, George McKean and George T. Carvill, (defendants) *appellants*, and George A. Schofield, Thomas Gilbert and James Nevis, (plaintiffs) *respondents*...........	258
18	—Galeon Vernon and Mary E. Vernon, (plaintiffs) *appellants*, and Warren Oliver, (defendant) *respondent*	259
19	—The Millville Mutual Marine and Fire Insurance Co., (defendants) *appellants*, and Bartholomew J. Driscoll and John M. Driscoll, (plaintiffs) *respondents*..........................	259
20	—Thomas R. Jones, Robert T. A. Scott and Norman Robertson, (plaintiffs) *appellants*, and William H. Tuck, (defendant) *respondent*	260
21	—Austin J. Roberts, (defendant) *appellant*, and Lorenzo H. Vaughan, Thomas A. Vaughan, Robert M. Vaughan, (plaintiffs) *respondents*	261
22	—The Town of Portland, (defendants) *appellants*, and William Griffiths, (plaintiff) *respondent*	262
23	—John Taylor, (defendant) *appellant*, and Robert G. Moran, Benjamin Wishart, Robert Galloway and David Smith (plaintiffs), *respondents*	262
24	—*Ex parte* James D. Lewin	263
25	—The New Brunswick Railway Company (defendants), *appellants*, and Issachar N. Robinson (plaintiff) *respondent*............	263
26	—Robert A. Chapman and W. J. Robinson, *appellants*, and Silas W. Hand, *respondent*..	264
27	—John P. Lawless, *appellant*, and James Sullivan *et al.*, *respondents*	264

No.	Name of Case.	Page.
28	James D. Lewin and G. Sidney Smith, surviving trustees under the marriage settlement of Martha M. S. Robertson, *appellants*, and Georgina Wilson, Benjamin Lawton and James Harris, *respondents*	265
29	Ezekiel McLeod (assignee of Jewett & Co.), *appellant*, and The New Brunswick Railway Co., *respondents*	266
30	The Quoddy River Driving Boom Co., and Hugh R. Robertson and Lambert L. L. Bevan, *appellants*, and William Davidson, *respondent*	267
31	James H. Ray, *et al.*, *appellants*, and The Annual Conference of New Brunswick and Prince Edward Island, in connection with the Methodist Church of Canada, *et al.*, *respondents*	268
32	The South West Boom Co., *appellants*, and David McMillan, *respondent*	268
33	Joshua Spears and William C. Spears (plaintiffs), *appellants*, and James Walker, *respondent*	269
34	James Flanagan and Johanna, his wife, *defendants*, and John Doe, on the demise of Gilbert R. Elliott, *et al.*, *plaintiffs*	269
35	Fawcett *v.* Anderson	270
36	Edwards *v.* The Mayor, etc., of St. John	270-1
37	Byrne *v.* Arnold	271
38	Temple *v.* Nicholson	271-2
39	Waterous *v.* Morrow	272-3
40	Swim *v.* Sheriff	273-4
41	The Mayor, etc., of St. John *v.* Pattison	274-5-6
42	Collins *v.* Everitt	276
43	The Trustees of the St. John Young Men's Christian Association *v.* Hutchinson, *et al.*	276-7
44	Pugsley *v.* Ring	277-8
45	Domville *v.* Gleeson	279-80
46	Sovereign Fire Ins. Co. of Can. *v.* Peters	281
47	Providence Washington Insurance Co. *v.* Chapman	281-2

No.	Name of Case.	Page.
48	—The Delaware Mutual Insurance Co. *v.* Chapman	282
49	—Domville *v.* Cameron	282-3
50	—Snowball *v.* Stewart	283
51	—Fraser *v.* Stephenson	283-4
52	—Hall *v.* McFadden	284-5
53	—Peters *v.* Hamilton	285-6
54	—Temple *v.* Close	286-7
55	—Jones *v.* DeWolf	287-8
56	—The Dominion Telegraph Co. *v.* Gilchrist	288-9

ADDENDA.

CONTAINING CASES SUSTAINED, MODIFIED, OR OVERRULED—REPORTED AND UNREPORTED.

ON

APPEAL TO THE SUPREME COURT OF CANADA,

AND

TO WHICH REFERENCE IS MADE IN THE FOREGOING DIGEST OF CASES.

THE MAYOR, ALDERMEN, and Commonalty of the City of Fredericton, *Appellants*,

and

THE QUEEN, on the prosecution of Thomas Barker, *Respondent*.

On appeal from the Supreme Court of New Brunswick.

Canada Temperance Act, 1878—Constitutionality of—Powers of Dominion Parliament—Secs. 91 and 92, B. N. A. Act, 1867—Power to prohibit sale of intoxicating liquors—Distribution of legislative power.

Held, 1. That the Act of the Parliament of Canada, 41 Vic., cap. 16, "An Act respecting the traffic in intoxicating liquors," cited as "The Canada Temperance Act, 1878," is within the legislative capacity of that body.

2. That by the British North America Act, 1867, plenary powers of legislation are given to the Parliament of Canada over all matters within the scope of its jurisdiction, and that they may be exercised either absolutely or conditionally; in the latter case the legislation may be made to depend upon some subsequent event, and be brought into force in one part of the Dominion and not in the other.

3. That under sub-sec. 2, of sec. 91, B. N. A. Act, 1867, "regulation of trade and commerce," the Parliament of Canada alone has the power of prohibiting the traffic in intoxicating liquors in the Dominion, or in any part of it, and the court has no right whatever to enquire what motive induced parliament to exercise its powers. (Henry, J., dissenting).

Appeal allowed with costs.

Supreme Court of Canada Reports, vol. 3, 505, 19 N. B. R. 139. See next case.

PRIVY COUNCIL.

CHARLES RUSSELL, *Appellant*.

and

THE QUEEN, on the information of John Woodward, *Respondent*.

On appeal from the Supreme Court of the Province of New Brunswick.

British North America Act, ss. 91, 92, sub ss. 9, 13, 16—Legislative powers of the Dominion Parliament—Validity of Canada Temperance Act, 1878.

Held, that the Canada Temperance Act, 1878, which in effect, wherever throughout the Dominion it is put in force, uniformly prohibits the sale of intoxicating liquors, except in wholesale quantities, or for certain specified purposes, regulates the traffic in the excepted cases, makes sales of liquors in violation of the prohibitions and regulations contained in the Act, criminal offences, punishable by fine, and for the third or subsequent offence by imprisonment, is within the legislative competence of the Dominion Parliament.

The objects and scope of the Act are general, viz., to promote temperance by means of a uniform law throughout the Dominion. They relate to the peace, order and good government of Canada, and not to the class of subjects, "property and civil rights." Provision for the special application of the Act to particular places does not alter its character as general legislation. 7 App. cas. 829, L. R.

JAMES CLARK, *Appellant.*

and

THE SCOTTISH IMPERIAL INSURANCE COMPANY, *Respondents.*

On appeal from the Supreme Court of New Brunswick.

Fire insurance—Advance made to build a vessel—Insurable interest.

C. made advances to B. upon a vessel, then in course of construction, upon the faith of a verbal agreement with B. that after the vessel should be launched she should be placed in his hands for sale, and that out of the proceeds the advances so made should be paid. When vessel was well advanced C. disclosed the facts and nature of his interest to the agent of the respondents' company, and the company issued a policy of insurance against loss by fire to C. in the sum of $3,000. The vessel was still unfinished and in B.'s possession when she was burned.

Held, reversing the judgment of the court below, that C.'s interest, relating as it did to a specific chattel, was an equitable interest which was insurable, and therefore C. was entitled to recover.

Appeal allowed with costs.

Supreme Court of Canada Reports, vol 4, 192, 18 N. B. R. 240.

CHARLES W. WELDON, *Appellant.*

and

JAMES VAUGHAN and DAVID MAURICE VAUGHAN, *Respondents.*

On appeal from the Supreme Court of New Brunswick.

Assumpsit—Contract—Damages—Construction of contract—"Accord and satisfaction."

Appellant, part owner of a vessel, brought an action against respondents, merchants and ship brokers in England, alleging in his declaration that while he had entire charge of said vessel as ship's husband, they, being his agents, refused to obey and follow his directions in regard to said vessel, and committed a breach of an agreement by which they undertook not to charter nor send the vessel on any voyage except as ordered by appellant, or with his consent.

On the trial it appeared that E. V., a brother of respondents, had obtained from appellant a fourth share in the vessel, the purchase being effected by one of the respondents; and it was also shewn that the agreement between the parties was as alleged in the declaration. On the arrival of the vessel at Liverpool, respondents went to a large expense in coppering her, contrary to directions, and sent her on a voyage to Liverpool, of which he disapproved.

Appellant wrote to respondents complaining of their conduct, and protesting against the expense incurred. They replied that appellant could have no cause of complaint against them in their management of the vessel, and alleged that they would not have purchased a fourth interest in the vessel if they had not understood that they were to have the management and control of the vessel when on the other side of the Atlantic. A correspondence ensued, and finally, on the 17th November, 1869, appellant wrote to them, referring to the fact that respondents complained of the "eternal bickerings," and that it was not their fault. He then re-asserted his right to control the vessel, stated in detail his grounds of complaint against them, and closed with the words, "To end the matter, if your brother will dispose of his quarter, I will purchase it, say for $4,200 in cash." This amount was about the same price for the share as appellant had sold it for some years before. Respondents accepted the offer, and the transfer was made to appellant.

Held, on appeal, reversing the judgment of the Supreme Court of New Brunswick, that the expression "to end the matter" should be construed as applying to the bickerings referred to, and there had not been an accord and satisfaction.

The contract having been made between appellant and respondents only, and being a contract of agency apart from any question of ownership, the action was properly brought by appellant in his own name.

(Taschereau and Gwynne, JJ., dissenting).

Appeal allowed with costs.

Supreme Court of Canada Reports, vol. 5, 35, 18 N. B. R. 70.

JOHN MOWAT, *Appellant*,

and

WILLIAM MCFEE, *Respondent*.

On appeal from the Supreme Court of New Brunswick.

The Fisheries Act, 31 Vic., cap. 60—Jurisdiction of Dominion Parliament over Bay of Chaleurs—14 and 15 Vic., cap. 63, (Imp.)—Justification, plea of—Fishery officer, right of, to seize "on view."

Under the Imperial Statute, 14 and 15 Vic., cap. 63, regulating the boundary line between Old Canada and New Brunswick, the whole of the Bay of Chaleurs is within the present boundaries of the Provinces of Quebec and New Brunswick, and within the Dominion of Canada and the operations of the Fisheries Act, 31 Vic., cap. 60. Therefore the Act of drifting for salmon in the Bay of Chaleurs, although that drifting may have been more than three miles from either shore of New Brunswick or of Quebec, abutting on the Bay, is a drifting in Canadian waters and within the prohibition of the last mentioned Act and of the regulations made in virtue thereof.

2. The term "on view" in sub-sec. 4 of sec. 16 of the Fisheries Act (1), is not to be limited to seeing the net in the water while in the very act of drifting. If the party acting "on view" sees what, if testified to by him, would be sufficient to convict of the offence charged, that is sufficient for the purposes of the Act.

(1) "All materials, implements or appliances used, and all fish had in contravention to this Act or any regulation or regulations under it, shall be confiscated to Her Majesty, and may be

seized and confiscated on view by any fishery officer, or taken and removed by any person for delivery to any magistrate, and the proceeds of disposal thereof may be applied towards defraying expenses under this Act."

Appeal dismissed with costs.

Supreme Court of Canada Reports, vol. 5, 66, 19 N. B. R. 252.

HENRI JONAS, *Appellant*,

and

HUMPHREY T. GILBERT, *Respondent*.

On appeal from the Supreme Court of New Brunswick.

By-law—Power to impose license tax—Discrimination between residents and non-residents—33 Vic., cap. 4. (N. B.)

J. brought an action against G., the Police Magistrate of the City of St. John, for wrongfully causing the plaintiff, a commercial traveller, to be arrested and imprisoned on a warrant issued on a conviction by the police magistrate, for violation of a by-law made by the common council of the City of St. John, under an alleged authority conferred on that body by 33 Vic., cap. 4, passed by the Legislature of New Brunswick. Sec. 3 of the Act authorized the Mayor of the City of St. John to license persons to use any art, trade, etc., within the City of St. John, on payment of such sum or sums as may from time to time be fixed and determined by the common council of St. John, etc.; and sec. 4 empowered the mayor, etc., by any by-law or ordinance to fix and determine what sum or sums of money should be from time to time paid for license to use any art, trade or occupation, etc.; and to declare how fees should be recoverable; and to impose penalties for any breach of the same, etc. The by-law or ordinance in question discriminated between resident and non-resident merchants, traders, etc., by imposing a license tax of $20 on the former and $40 on the latter.

Held, that assuming the Act, 33 Vic., cap. 4, to be *intra vires* of the Legislature of New Brunswick, the by-law made under it was invalid, because the Act in question gave no power to the common council of St. John, of discriminating between residents and non-residents, such as they had exercised in this by-law.

Appeal allowed with costs.

Supreme Court of Canada Reports, vol. 5, 356, 20 N. B. R. 64.

LOUIS J. ALMON, *et al.* *Appellants*,

and

JAMES D. LEWIN, *et al.*, *Respondents*.

On Appeal from the Supreme Court of New Brunswick.

Will—Annuities, sale of corpus to pay.

J. R. died on the 3rd August, 1876, leaving a will dated 6th August, 1875, and a codicil dated 21st July, 1876. By the will he devised to his widow an annuity of $10,000 for her life, which he declared to be in lieu of her dower. This annuity the testator directed should be chargeable on his general estate. The testator then devised and bequeathed to the executors and trustees of his will, certain real and personal property particularly described in five schedules, marked respectively A, B, C, D, and E, annexed to this will, upon these trusts, viz.: Upon trust, during the life of his wife, to collect and receive the rents, issues, and profits thereof which should be, and be taken to form a portion of his "general estate;" and then from and out of the general estate, during the life of the testator's wife, the executors were to pay to each of his five daughters the clear yearly sum of $1,600 by equal quarterly payments, free from the debts, contracts, and engagements of their respective husbands. Next, resuming the statement of the trusts of the scheduled property specifially given, the testator provided that from and after the death of his wife, the trustees were to collect and receive the rents, issues, dividends, and profits of the lands, etc., mentioned in the said schedules, and to pay to his daughter, M. A. A., the rents, etc., apportioned to her in schedule A; to his daughter, E., of those mentioned in schedule B; to his daughter, M., of those mentioned in schedule C; to his daughter, A., of those mentioned in schedule D; and to his daughter, L., of those mentioned in schedule E; each of said daughters being charged with the insurance, ground rents, rates and taxes, repairs and other expenses with or incidental to the management and upholding of the property apportioned to her, and the same being from time to time deducted from such quarterly payments. The will then directed the executors to keep the properties insured against loss by fire, and in case of total loss, it should be optional with the parties to whom the property was apportioned by the schedules, either to direct the insurance money to be applied in rebuilding, or to lease the property. It then declared what was to be done with the share of each of his daughters in case of her death. In the residuary clause of the will there were the following words: "The rest, residue and remainder of my said estate, both real and personal, and whatsoever and wheresoever situated, I give, devise and bequeath the same to my said executors and trustees, upon the trusts and for the intents and purposes following." He then gave out of the residue a legacy of $4,000 to his brother, D. R., and the ultimate residue he directed to be equally divided among his children upon the same trusts with regard to his daughters, as were thereinbefore declared, with respect to the said estate in the said schedules mentioned.

The rents and profits of the whole estate left by the testator proved insufficient, after paying the annuity of $10,000 to the widow and the rent of and taxes upon his house in L., to pay in full the several sums of $1,600 a year to each of the daughters during the life of their mother, and the question raised on the appeal was whether the executors and trustees had power to sell or mortgage any part of the *corpus*, or apply the funds of the *corpus* of the property to make up the deficiency.

Held, on appeal, that the annuities given to the daughters, and the arrears of their annuities, were chargeable upon the *corpus* of the real and personal estate, subject to the right of the widow to have a sufficient sum set apart to provide for her annuity.

Appeal allowed with costs.

Supreme Court of Canada Reports vol. 5, 514, N. B. R. 284.

NICHOLAS POWER, *Appellant*,

and

THOMAS ELLIS, *Respondent*.

On appeal from the Supreme Court of New Brunswick.

Witness—Refusal to answer questions on cross-examination — Privileged communications—Improper ruling—Misdirection.

Plaintiff (respondent), a teller in a bank in New York, absconded with funds of the bank, and came to St. John, N.B., where he was arrested by the defendant (appellant), a detective residing in Halifax, N.S., and imprisoned in the police station for several hours. No charge having been made against him he was released. While plaintiff was a prisoner at the police station, the defendant went to plaintiff's boarding house and saw his wife, read to her a telegram, and demanded and obtained from her money she had in her possession, telling her that it belonged to the bank and that her husband was in custody.

In an action for assault and false imprisonment and for money had and received, the defendant pleaded, *inter alia*, that the money had been fraudulently stolen by the plaintiff at the city of New York, from the bank, and was not the money of the plaintiff; that defendant, as agent of the bank, received the money to and for the use of the bank, and paid it over to them. Several witnesses were examined, and the plaintiff being examined as a witness on his own behalf did not, on cross-examination answer certain questions, relying, as he said, upon his counsel to advise him; and on being interrogated as to his belief that his doing so would tend to criminate him, he remained silent, and on being pressed he refused to answer whether he apprehended serious consequences if he answered the question proposed. The learned judge then told the jury that there was no identification of the money, and directed them that, if they should be of opinion that the money was obtained by force or duress from plaintiff's wife, they should find for the plaintiff.

Held, (Henry, J., dissenting), that the defendant was entitled to the oath of the party that he objected to answer because he believed his answering would tend to criminate him.

Appeal allowed with costs.

Supreme Court of Canada Reports, vol. 6, 1, 20 N. B. R. 40.

JOHN DEWE, *Appellant*,

and

DAVID H. WATERBURY, *Respondent*.

On appeal from the Supreme Court of New Brunswick.

Slander — Public officer — Privileged communication.

The appellant, D., having been appointed chief post office inspector for Canada, was engaged, under directions from the Postmaster-General, in making enquiries into certain irregularities which had been discovered at the St. John post office. After making enquiries, he had a conversation with the respondent, W., alone in a room in the post office, charging him with abstracting missing letters, which respondent strongly denied. Thereupon the assistant-postmaster was called in, and the appellant said, "I have charged Mr. W. with abstracting the letters. I have charged Mr. W. with the abstractions that have occurred from those money letters, and I have concluded to suspend him." The respondent, having brought an action for slander, was allowed to give evidence of the conversation between himself and appellant. There was no other evidence of malice.

The jury found that appellant was not actuated by ill-feeling towards the respondent in making the observation to him, but found that he was so actuated in the communication he made to the assistant postmaster.

Held, on appeal, 1st. That the appellant was in the due discharge of his duty and acting in accordance with his instructions, and that the words addressed to the assistant postmaster were privileged.

2. That the onus lay upon respondent to prove that the appellant acted under the influence of malicious feelings, and as the jury found that the appellant had not been actuated by ill-feeling, the respondent was not entitled to retain his verdict, and the rule for a non-suit should be made absolute.

Appeal allowed with costs.

Supreme Court of Canada Reports, vol. 6, 143, 19 N. B. R. 225.

JOHN WALKER and WILLIAM SPEARS, *Appellants*,

and

JAMES MCMILLAN, *Respondent*.

Appeal from the Supreme Court of New Brunswick.

41 Vic., caps. 6 and 7 (N. B.)—By-law of city of St. John—Building erected in violation of—Negligence of contractor—Liability of employer—Several defendants appearing by same attorney—Separate counsel at trial—Cross appeal—Rent, loss of—Damages.

On the 20th September, 1877, S. contracted to erect a proper and legal building for W. on his (W.'s) land, in the city of St. John. Two days after, a by-law of the city of St. John, under the Act of the Legislature, 41 Vic., cap. 6, "The St. John Building Act, 1877," was passed, prohibiting the erection of buildings such as the one contracted for, and declaring them to be nuisances. By his contract, W. reserved the right to alter or modify the plans and specifications, and to make any deviation in the construction, detail or execution of the work without avoiding the contract, etc. By the contract it was also declared that W. had engaged H. as superintendent of the erection—his duty being to enforce the conditions of the contract, furnish drawings, etc., make estimates of the amount due, and issue certificates. While W.'s building was in course of erection, the centre wall, having been built on an insufficient foundation, fell, carrying with it the party wall common to W. and McM., his neighbour. On an action by McM. against W. and S. to recover damages for the injury thus sustained, the jury found a verdict for the plaintiff for general damages, $3,952 and $1,375 for loss of rent. This latter amount was found separately, in order that the court might reduce it, if not recoverable. On motion to the Supreme Court of New Brunswick for a non-suit or new trial, the verdict was allowed to stand for $3,952, the amount of the general damages found by the jury. On appeal to the Supreme Court and cross appeal by respondent to have verdict stand for the full amount awarded by the jury—

Held, (Gwynne, J., dissenting), 1. That at the time of the injury complained of, the contract for the erection of W.'s building being in contravention of the provisions of a valid by-law of the city of St. John, the defendant W., his contractor and his agent (S.) were all equally responsible for the consequences of the improper building of the illegal wall which caused the injury to McM., charged in the declaration.

2. That the jury, in the absence of any evidence to the contrary, could adopt the actual loss of rent as a fair criterion by which to establish the actual amount of the damage sustained, and therefore the verdict should stand for the full amount claimed and awarded.

Per Gwynne, J., dissenting, that W. was not, by the terms of the contract, liable for the injury, and, even if the by-law did make the building a nuisance, the plaintiff could not, under the pleadings in the case, have the benefit of it.

The defendants appeared, by the same attorney, pleaded jointly by the same attorney, and their defence was, in substance, precisely the same, but they were represented at the trial by separate counsel. On examination of plaintiff's witness, both counsel claimed the right to cross-examine the witness.

Held, (affirming the ruling of the judge at the trial), that the judge was right in allowing only one counsel to cross-examine the witness.

Appeal dismissed with costs, and cross appeal allowed.

Supreme Court of Canada Reports, vol. 6, 243, 21 N. B. R. 31. See No. 32.

JAMES MCSORLEY, *Appellant*,

and

THE MAYOR, etc., of the city of St. John, and WILLIAM SANDALL, *Respondents*.

On appeal from the Supreme Court of New Brunswick.

False imprisonment — Arrest — Assessment — 41 Vic., cap. 9, N. B. — Execution issued by receiver of taxes for city of St. John — "*Respondeat superior.*"

The 41 Vic., cap. 9, entitled "An Act to widen and extend certain public streets in the city of St. John," authorized commissioners appointed by the Governor in Council to assess the owners of the land who would be benefitted by the widening of the streets, and in their report on the extension of Canterbury street, the commissioners so appointed assessed the benefit to a certain lot at $419.46, and put in their report the name of the appellant, (McS.), as the owner. The amount so assessed was to be paid to the corporation of the city, and, if not, it was the duty of the receiver of taxes, appointed by the city corporation, to issue execution and levy the same. McS., although assessed, was not the owner of the lot. S., the receiver of taxes, in default, issued an execution, and for want of goods McS., was arrested and imprisoned until he paid the amount at the chamberlain's office in the city of St. John. The action was for arrest and false imprisonment, and for money had and received. The jury found a verdict for McS. on the first count against both defendants.

Held, (reversing the judgment of the Supreme Court of New Brunswick), that S., who issued the warrant, founded upon a void assessment, and caused the arrest to be made, was guilty of a trespass, and being at the time a servant of the corporation, under their control, and specially appointed by them to collect and levy the amount so assessed, the maxim of *respondeat superior* applied, and therefore the verdict in favour of McS. for $645.39 against both respondents on the first count should stand. (Ritchie, C.J., and Taschereau, J., dissenting).

Per Gwynne, J., that the corporation had adopted the act of their officer as as their own by receiving and retaining the money paid, and authorizing McS.'s discharge from custody only after such payment.

Appeal allowed with costs.

Supreme Court of Canada Reports vol. 6, 531, 20 N. B. R. 117.

TERRENCE THEAL, *Appellant*,

and

THE QUEEN, *Respondent*.

Criminal appeal — Indictment — Misjoinder of counts — Evidence.

An indictment contained two counts, one charging the prisoner with murdering M. J. T. on the 16th November, 1881; the other with manslaughter of the said M. J. T. on the same day. The grand jury found "a true bill." A motion to quash the indictment for misjoinder was refused, the counsel for the prosecution electing to proceed on the first count only.

Held, (affirming the judgment of the court *a quo*), that the indictment was sufficient.

The prisoner was convicted of manslaughter in killing his wife, who died on the 10th November, 1881. The immediate cause of her death was acute inflammation of the liver, which the medical testimony proved might be occasioned by a blow or a fall against a hard substance. About three weeks before her death, (17th October preceding), the prisoner had knocked his wife down with a bottle; she fell against a door, and remained on the floor insensible for some time; she was confined to her bed soon afterwards and never recovered. Evidence was given of frequent acts of violence committed by the prisoner upon his wife within a year of her death, by knocking her down and kicking her in the side. On the reserved question, viz., whether the evidence of assaults and violence committed by the prisoner upon the deceased, prior to the 10th November or the 17th October, 1881, was properly received, and whether there was any evidence to leave to the jury to sustain the charge in the first count of the indictment?

Held, (affirming the judgment of the Supreme Court of New Brunswick), that the evidence was properly received, and that there was evidence to submit to the jury that the disease which caused her death was produced by the injuries inflicted by the prisoner.

Appeal dismissed.

Supreme Court of Canada Reports, vol. 7, 397, 21 N. B. R. 449.

DOMINION CONTROVERTED ELECTIONS ACT, 1874.

Election Petition for the County of Gloucester, Province of New Brunswick.

DENNIS COMMEAU, *Appellant,*

and

KENNEDY BURNS, *Respondent.*

On appeal from the Supreme Court of New Brunswick.

Appeal on election petition — 42 Vic., cap. 39 (the Supreme and Exchequer Court Amendment Act of 1879), sec. 10—Construction of—Rule absolute by court *in banc* to rescind order of a judge in chambers—Preliminary objection.

A petition was duly filed and presented by appellant on the 5th of August 1883, under the "Dominion Controverted Election Act, 1874," against the return of respondent. Preliminary objections were filed by respondent, and before the same came on for hearing, the attorney and agent of respondent obtained on the 13th October from Mr. Justice Weldon an order authorizing the withdrawal of the deposit money and removal of the petition off the files.

The money was withdrawn, but shortly afterwards, in January, 1883, the appellant, alleging he had had no knowledge of the proceedings taken by his agent and attorney, obtained, upon summons, a second order from Mr. Justice Weldon, rescinding his prior order of 13th October, 1882, and directing that upon the appellant repaying to the clerk of the court the amount of the security, the petition be restored, and that the appellant be at liberty to proceed. Against this order of January, 1883, the respondent appealed to the Supreme Court of New Brunswick, and the court gave judgment rescinding it. Thereupon petitioner appealed to the Supreme Court of Canada.

Held, that the judgment appealed from, is not a judgment on a preliminary objection within the meaning of 42 Vic., cap. 39, sec. 10, (the Supreme Court Amendment Act, 1879), and therefore not appealable.

Bickle v. *Woodfath*, 8 Can. S. C. R. 192, followed.

Appeal quashed with costs.

Supreme Court of Canada Reports, vol. 8, 204, 22 N. B. R. 573.

J. H. CHAPMAN, *Appellant*,

and

FRANCIS and JAMES A. TUFTS, *Respondents*.

Unstamped bill of exchange—42 Vic., cap. 17, sec. 13—Knowledge—Question for judge.

The action was brought by T. *et al.* against C. to recover the amount of a bill of exchange. It appeared that the draft when made, and when received by T. *et al.*, had no stamps; that they knew then that bills and promissory notes required to be stamped, but never gave it a thought, and their first knowledge that the bill was not stamped was when they gave it to their attorney for collection on the 26th February, 1880, and they immediately put on double stamps.

The bill was received in evidence, leave being reserved to the defendant to move for a non-suit; the learned judge stating his opinion that though as a fact the plaintiffs knew the bill was not stamped when they received it, and knew that stamps were necessary, they accidentally and not intentionally omitted to affix them till their attention was called to the omission in February, 1880.

Held, 1. That the question as to whether the holder of a bill or draft has affixed double stamps upon an unstamped bill or draft so soon as the state of the bill was brought to his knowledge, within the terms of 42 Vic., cap. 17, sec. 13, is a question for the judge at the trial, and not for the jury. (Gwynne, J., dissenting).

2. That the "knowledge" referred to in the Act is actual knowledge, and not imputed or presumed knowledge, and that the evidence in this case shewed that T. acquired this knowledge for the first time on the day he affixed stamps for the amount of the double duty, 26th February, 1880.

3. That the want of proper stamps or proper stamping in due time is not a defence which need be pleaded. (Gwynne, J., dissenting.)

Appeal dismissed with costs.

Supreme Court of Canada Reports vol. 8, 543, 22 N. B. R. 195.

JAMES DEWOLFE SPURR and JOHN N. MOORE, *Appellants*,

and

THE ALBERT MINING COMPANY,

Respondents.

On appeal from the Supreme Court of New Brunswick.

Contract—Sale of goods—Payment—Appropriation—Non-suit.

The Albert Mining Co., (respondents), brought this action to recover for coal sold and delivered to appellants during the years 1866, 1867 and 1868.

S. and M. and one McG. were partners carrying on business under the name of the Albertine Oil Company, the defendant S. furnished the capital. The contract for the coal was made by S., who was a large stockholder in the plaintiff company, and entitled to yearly dividends on his stock. The agreement, as proved by plaintiffs, was that S. purchased the coal for the Albertine Oil Company, the members of which he named, that the president of the plaintiff company told S. they would look to him for payment, as the other partners were poor; that the terms of sale were cash on delivery on board the vessels; and that S. agreed that the dividends payable to him on his stock should be applied in payment for the coal; that in consequence of this arrangement the plaintiffs credited the Albertine Oil Company with the amount of S.'s dividends as they were declared from time to time down to August, 1866, leaving a balance of $912 due to S. It also appeared that the coal delivered was charged in the plaintiffs' books to the Albertine Oil Company, and that the the bills of lading on the shipments of the coal were also made out in their name, and that some time afterwards a notice signed by S. and M. was given to the plaintiffs, complaining of the inferior quality of the coal, and claiming damages in consequence. In the latter part of the year 1868, S. repudiated the agreement to appropriate his dividends to the payment of coal, and refused to sign the receipts therefor in the plaintiffs' books. He had signed the receipt for the dividend of 1866. The present action was then brought (in 1873) against S. and M., the surviving partners of the Albertine Oil Company, McG. having died, to recover the value of the coal. S. shortly afterwards brought an action against the plaintiffs for the dividends; the claim was referred to arbitration, and an award was made in favour of S. for upwards of $15,000, which the plaintiffs paid in July, 1874. The receipt given for the payment stated it was in full satisfaction of the judgment in the suit of S. against the Albert Mining Company, and it appeared, (though evidence of this was objected to in the present action), that it included the dividends for the years 1867 and 1868.

The learned judge before whom the action was tried non-suited the plaintiffs, but the Supreme Court of New Brunswick set aside the non-suit.

Held, (reversing the judgment of the court below, Strong, J., dissenting), that there being clear evidence of the appropriation of S.'s dividends in pursuance of agreement made with him, and therefore of the plaintiffs having been paid for the coal in the manner and on the terms agreed on, the plaintiffs were properly non-suited.

Appeal allowed with costs.

Supreme Court of Canada Reports, vol. 9, 35, 22 N. B. R. 346.

William H. Venning, *Appellant*,
and
James Steadman, *Respondent*.

William H. Venning, *Appellant*,
and
Elijah Hanson, *Respondent*.

William H. Venning, *Appellant*,
and
James Dewolfe Spurr, *Respondent*.

On appeal from the Supreme Court of New Brunswick.

Trespass—31 Vic., cap. 60, ss. 2, 19, (D.)—Order-in-council, 11th June, 1879—Construction of—Fishery officer, action against—Notice not necessary—Damages, excessive.

Three several actions for trespass and assault were brought by A. B. & C., respectively, riparian proprietors of land fronting on rivers above the ebb and flow of the tide, against V. for forcibly seizing and taking away their fishing rods and lines, while they were engaged in fly-fishing for salmon in front of their respective lots. The defendant was a fishery officer, appointed under the Fisheries Act, 31 Vic., cap. 60, and justified the seizure on the ground that the plaintiffs were fishing without licenses in violation of an order-in-council of June 11th, 1879, passed in pursuance of section 19 of the Act, which order was in these words:—"Fishing for salmon in the Dominion of Canada, except under the authority of leases or licenses from the Department of Marine and Fisheries is hereby prohibited." The defendant was armed and was in company with several others, a sufficient number to have enforced the seizure if resistance had been made. There was no actual injury. A. recovered $5,000, afterwards reduced to $1,500 damages, B. $1,200, and C. $1,000.

Held, that sections 2 and 19 of the Fisheries Act, and the order-in-council of the 11th June, 1879, did not authorize the defendant in his capacity of Inspector of Fisheries to interfere with A., B. & C.'s exclusive right as riparian proprietors of fishing at the *locus in quo*; but that the damages were in all the cases excessive, and therefore new trials should be granted.

Held, also, (Gwynne J., dissenting) that when the defendant committed the trespasses complained of, he was acting as a Dominion officer, under the instructions of the Department of Marine and Fisheries, and was not entitled to notice of action under C. S. N. B., cap. 89, sec. 1, or cap. 90, sec. 8.

Appeal allowed without costs.

Supreme Court of Canada Reports, vol. 9, 206, 21 N. B. R. 639.

PATRICK GEORGE CARVILL, GEORGE MCKEAN and GEORGE T. CARVILL, (Defendants, *Appellants*,

and

GEORGE A. SCHOFIELD, THOMAS GILBERT and JAMES NEVIS, (Plaintiffs),

Respondents.

On appeal from the Supreme Court of New Brunswick.

Charter party—Damages to ship—Unavoidable delay—Refusal of charterers to load—Action by shipowners.

By a charter party of December 11th, 1878, it was agreed that plaintiff's vessel, then on her way to Shelburne, N.S., should proceed with all possible dispatch, after her arrival in Shelburne, to St. John, and there load from the charterers a cargo of deals for Liverpool; and if the vessel did not arrive at Shelburne on or before 1st January, 1879, the charterers were to be at liberty to cancel the charter party. The vessel arrived at Shelburne in December, and sailed at once for St. John. At the entrance of the harbor of St. John she got upon the rocks and was so badly damaged that it became necessary to put her on the blocks for repairs. Although she was repaired with all possible dispatch, she was not ready to receive her cargo until 21st of April following, prior to which time—on 26th March—the charterers gave the owners notice that they would not furnish a cargo for her. The owners sued for breach of the charter party, and on the trial defendants gave evidence, subject to objection, that freights between St. John and Liverpool were usually much higher in winter than in summer; that lumber would depreciate in value by being wintered over at St. John, and also as to the relative value of lumber during the winter and in the spring in the Liverpool market; and it was contended that the time occupied in repairing the damage was unreasonable and had entirely frustrated the object of the voyage. The judge directed the jury that if the time occupied in getting the vessel off the rocks and repairing her was so long as to put an end, in a commercial sense, to the commercial speculation entered into by the ship-owners and charterers, they should find for the defendants. The verdict being for the defendants, the court below made absolute a rule for a new trial.

On appeal to the Supreme Court of Canada, it was

Held, (affirming the judgment of the court *a quo*) that as there was no condition precedent in the charter that the ship should be at St. John at any fixed date, and as the time taken in repairing the damage was not unreasonable, and the delay did not entirely frustrate the object of the voyage the charterers were not justified in refusing to carry out the contract.

Appeal dismissed with costs.

Supreme Court of Canada Reports, vol. 9, 370, 22 N. B. R. 558.

Gideon Vernon and Mary E. Vernon (Plaintiffs), *Appellants*,

and

Warren Oliver, (Defendant),

Respondent.

On appeal from the Supreme Court of New Brunswick.

Arbitration and award—Misconduct of arbitrators—Bill to rectify award—Prayer for general relief—Jurisdiction of court—Practice—Factum—Scandalous and impertinent.

The bill in this case was filed to rectify an award made under a submission to arbitation between the parties, on the ground that the arbitrators considered matters not included in the submission, and had divided the sums received by the defendant from the plaintiffs, because that defendant's brother and partner was a party to such receipt, although the partnership affairs of the defendant and his brothers were excluded from the submission. The bill prayed that the award might be amended and the defendant decreed to pay the amount due the plaintiffs on the award being rectified, and that, in other respects, the award should stand and be binding on the parties; there was also a prayer for general relief.

Held, (affirming the judgment of the court below), that to grant the relief prayed for, would be to make a new award which the court had no jurisdiction to do, but,

Held, also (reversing the decision of the court below), that under the prayer for general relief the plaintiff was entitled to have the award set aside.

The plaintiffs' factum, containing reflections on the judge in equity and the full court of New Brunswick, was ordered to be taken off the files as scandalous and impertinent.

Appeal allowed without costs. Award ordered to be set aside and plaintiffs' factum to be taken off the files of the court.

Supreme Court of Canada Reports, vol 11. 156. 23 N. B. R. 292.

The Millville Mutual Marine and Fire Insurance Co., (Defendants), *Appellants*,

and

Bartholomew J. Driscoll and John M. Driscoll (Plaintiffs), *Respondents*.

Appeal from the Supreme Court of New Brunswick.

Commission from Supreme Court of N. B.—Con. Stats., cap. 37—Directed to two commissioners—Return signed by one only—Failure to administer interrogatories—Marine Ins.—Total loss—Notice of abandonment—Waiver.

A commission was issued out of the Supreme Court of New Brunswick directed to two commissioners—one named by each of the parties to the suit—to take evidence at St. Thomas, W. I., with liberty to plaintiffs' commissioner to proceed *ex parte* if the other neglected or refused to attend. Both commissioners attended the examination, and defendant's commissioner cross-examined the witnesses but refused to certify to the return which was sent back to the court signed by one commissioner only. Some of the interrogatories and cross-interrogatories were put to the witnesses by the commissioners.

Held, that the failure to administer the interrogatories according to the terms of the commission was a substantial objection and rendered the evidence incapable of being received.

Per Ritchie, C.J., and Strong, Fournier and Henry JJ., that the refusal of one commissioner to sign the return was merely directory and did not vitiate it.

Per Gwynne, J., that the return should have been signed by both commissioners, and not having been so signed was void, and the evidence under it should not have been received.

On a voyage from Porto Rico to New Haven, respondents' vessel sustained damage, and put into St. Thomas. A survey was held by competent persons appointed by the British consul, and according to their report the cost of putting her in good condition would exceed her value. The captain, under instructions from owners, to proceed under best advice, advertised and sold the vessel, and purchaser had her repaired at a cost much less than the report, and sent her to sea.

Held, that there was no evidence to justify the jury in finding that the vessel was a total loss.

Owners of vessel gave notice to agent of underwriters, that they would abandon, which agent refused to accept.

Owners telegraphed to captain that they had abandoned and for him to proceed under the best advice.

Held, that this act of telegraphing to the captain did not constitute a waiver of the notice of abandonment.

Appeal allowed with costs.

Supreme Court of Canada Reports, vol. 11, 183, 23 N. B. R. 169.

THOMAS R. JONES, ROBERT T. A. SCOTT, and NORMAN ROBERTSON, (Plaintiffs), *Appellants.*

and

WILLIAM H. TUCK, (Defendant), *Respondent.*

On appeal from the Supreme Court of New Brunswick.

Arbitration by order of court at nisi prius—To be entered as a verdict—Motion to set aside—Judge's order—Special paper Supreme Court, N. B.—Affidavits in reply—New matter—Discretion of court below.

The cause was referred by court of *nisi prius* to arbitration, the award to be entered on the *postea* as a verdict of a jury. After the award the appellants obtained a judge's order for a stay of proceedings, and for the cause to be entered on the motion paper of the court below, to enable the appellants to move to set aside the award and obtain a new trial, on the ground that the arbitrators had improperly taken evidence af[illegible] case before them was closed. Before the term in which the motion was to be heard, appellants abandoned that portion of the order directing the cause to be placed on the motion paper, and gave the usual notice of motion to set aside the award and *postea*, and for a new trial, which motion, by the practice of the court, would be entered on the special paper. Defendant, in opposing such motion, took the preliminary objection that the judge's order should be rescinded before plaintiffs could proceed on their notice, and presented affidavits on the merits, and plaintiffs requested leave to read affidavits in reply, claiming that defendant's affidavits disclosed new matter. This the court refused, and dismissed the motion, the majority of the judges holding that plaintiffs were bound by the order of the judge, and could not proceed on the special paper until that order was rescinded, the remainder of the court refusing the application on the m[illegible]

On appeal to the Supreme Court [illegible] Canada,

Held, that the cause was rightly [illegible] the special paper, and should have been heard on the merits, and the court should have exercised its discretion a[illegible] to the recention or rejection of affidavits in reply; Strong, J., dissenting, on the ground that such an appeal should not be heard.

Per Ritchie, C.J., a court of appeal ought not to differ from a court below on a matter of discretion, unless it is absolutely clear that such discretion has been wrongly exercised. The statute, (Con. Stats. N. B., cap. 37, sec. 173), applies as well to motions for new trials, where the grounds upon which the motion is made are supported by affidavits, as in other cases. It makes no distinction, but applies to all "motions founded on affidavits."

Appeal allowed.

Supreme Court of Canada Reports, vol. 11, 197, 23 N. B. R., 447.

Austin J. Roberts, Defendant.

Appellant.

and

Lorenzo H. Vaughan, Thomas A. Vaughan, Robert M. Vaughan, (Plaintiffs),

Respondents.

On appeal from the Supreme Court of New Brunswick.

Bill of exchange — Not stamped by drawer—Affixed by drawee before being discounted—Double duty affixed at trial—Knowledge of law relating to stamps—42 Vic., cap. 17—Plea that defendant did not make draft—Con. Stats., N. B. cap. 37, sec. 83, sub-secs. 4 and 5—Evidence of want of stamp—Special plea.

R. remitted by mail to V. a draft on Bay of Fundy Quarrying Co., Boston, Mass., in payment of an account of the Co., of which R. was superintendent. The draft, when received by V., was unstamped, and V. affixed stamps required by the amount of the draft, and initialed them as of the date the draft was drawn, which was at least two days prior to the date on which they were actually fixed. The draft was not paid, and an action was brought against R., who pleaded, according to provisions of Con. Stats. New Brunswick, cap. 37, sec. 83, sub-sec. 4, "that he did not make the draft." On the trial the draft was offered in evidence and objected to on the ground that it was not sufficiently stamped, the plaintiff having previously testified as to the manner in which the stamps were put on, and having also sworn that he knew the law relating to stamps at the time. The draft was admitted, subject to leave reserved to move for a non-suit, and at a later stage of the trial it was again offered with the double duty affixed.

The trial resulted in counsel agreeing that a non-suit should be entered with leave reserved to plaintiffs to move for verdict, court to have power to draw inferences of facts. On motion pursuant to such leave reserved, the Supreme Court of New Brunswick set aside the non-suit and ordered a verdict to be entered for the plaintiffs on the ground that the defect in the draft of want of stamp should have been specially pleaded.

On appeal to the Supreme Court of Canada:—

Held, (Strong and Gwynne, JJ., dissenting), that double duty should have been placed on the note as soon as it came into the hands of the drawee unstamped, and that it was too late at the trial to affix such double duty, the plaintiff having sworn that he knew the law relating to stamps, which precludes the possibility of holding that it was a mere error or mistake.

Held, also, that under the plea that defendant did not make the draft, he was entitled to take advantage of the defect for want of stamps.

Per Strong, J., that the note was sufficiently stamped and plaintiffs were entitled to recover.

Per Gwynne, J., that if the note was not sufficiently stamped the defence should have been specially pleaded.

Appeal allowed with costs.

Supreme Court of Canada Reports, vol. 11, 273, 23 N. B. R. 343.

THE TOWN OF PORTLAND, (Defendants), *Appellants*,

and

WILLIAM GRIFFITHS, (Plaintiff), *Respondent*.

Negligence—Defective sidewalk—Lawful use of streets—Contributory negligence.

In an action against the town of Portland for damages arising from an injury caused by a defective sidewalk, the evidence of the plaintiff shewed that the accident whereby she was injured happened while she was engaged in washing the window of her dwelling from the outside of the house, and that in taking a step backwards her foot went into a hole in the sidewalk, and she was thrown down and hurt; she also swore that she knew the hole was there. There was no evidence as to the nature and extent of the hole, nor was affirmative evidence given of negligence on the part of any officer of the corporation.

The jury awarded the plaintiff $800 damages, and a rule *nisi* for a new trial was discharged.

Held, per Henry, Taschereau, and Gwynne, JJ., that there was no evidence of negligence to justify the verdict of the jury, and there must be a new trial.

Per Ritchie, C.J., and Fournier, J., that the plaintiff was neither walking nor passing over, travelling upon, nor lawfully using the said street as alleged in the declaration, and she was therefore not entitled to recover.

Appeal allowed with costs, and new trial granted.

Supreme Court of Canada Reports, vol. 11, 333, 23 N. B. R., 559.

JOHN TAYLOR (Defendant), *Appellant*.

and

ROBERT G. MORAN, BENJAMIN WISHART, ROBERT GALLAWAY and DAVID SMITH, (Plaintiffs), *Respondents*.

On appeal from the Supreme Court of New Brunswick.

Marine insurance—Voyage policy—Sailing restrictions—Time of entering Gulf of St. Lawrence—Attempt to enter.

In an action on a voyage policy containing this clause, "warranted not to enter or attempt to enter or to use the Gulf of St. Lawrence prior to the 10th day of May, nor after the 30th day of October, (a line drawn from Cape North to Cape Ray, and across the Strait of Canso to the northern entrance thereof, shall be considered the bounds of the Gulf of St. Lawrence,)" the evidence was as follows:—

The captain says: "The voyage was from Liverpool to Quebec, and ship sailed on 2nd April. Nothing happened till we met with ice to the southward of Newfoundland. Shortened sail and dodged about for a few days trying to work our way around it. One night ship was hove to under lower main topsail, and about midnight she drifted into a large field of ice. There was a heavy sea on at the time, and the ship sustained damage. We were in this ice three or four hours. Laid to all the next day, could not get further along on account of the ice. In about twenty-four hours we started to work up towards Quebec."

The log-book showed that the ship got into this ice the 7th of May, and an expert examined at the trial swore that from the entries in the log-book of the 6th, 7th, 8th and 9th of May, the captain was attempting to enter the Gulf of St. Lawrence.

A verdict was taken for the plaintiffs by consent, with leave for the defendants to move to enter a non-suit, or for a new trial; the court to have power to mould the verdict, and also to draw inferences of fact the same as a jury. The Supreme Court of New Brunswick sustained the verdict. On appeal to the Supreme Court of Canada,

Held, reversing the judgment of the court below, Henry, J., dissenting, that the above clause was applicable to a voyage policy, and that there was evidence to go to the jury that the captain was attempting to enter the Gulf contrary to such clause.

Appeal allowed with costs.

Supreme Court of Canada Reports, vol. 11, 347, 24 N. B. R. 39.

Ex parte James D. Lewin.

On appeal from the Supreme Court of New Brunswick.

St. John City Assessment Act, 1882, 45 Vic., cap. 59, N. B.—Chartered bank—Assessment on capital stock of—Par value—Real and personal property of bank—Payment of taxes under protest.

By sec. 25 of the St. John City Assessment Act of 1882, it is provided that "all rates and taxes levied and imposed upon the city of St. John shall be raised by an equal rate upon the value of the real estate situate in the city, and part of the city to be taxed, and upon the personal estate of the inhabitants and of persons

deemed and declared to be inhabitants or residents of the said city. . . . . And upon the capital stock, income or other thing of joint stock companies, corporations, or persons associated in business." And after providing for the levying of a poll tax, such section goes on to say that "the whole residue to be raised shall be levied upon the whole ratable property, real and personal, and ratable income and real value, and amount of the same as nearly as can be ascertained, provided that joint stock shall not be rated above the par value thereof."

Sec. 28 of the same Act provides that "All joint stock companies and corporations shall be assessed, under this Act, in like manner as individuals; and for the purposes of such assessment, the president, or any agent, or manager of such joint stock company or corporation shall be deemed and taken to be the owner of the real and personal estate, capital stock and assets of such company or corporation, and shall be dealt with and may be proceeded against accordingly."

J. D. L., the president of the Bank of New Brunswick, was assessed, under the provisions of the above Act, on real and personal property of the bank valued, in the aggregate, at $1,100,000. The capital stock of the bank at the time of such assessment was only $1,000,000, and he offered to pay the taxes on that amount, which was refused. It is not disputed that the bank was possessed of real and personal property of the assessed value.

On appeal from the Supreme Court of New Brunswick, refusing a *certiorari* to quash the said assessment,

Held (Fournier, J., dissenting), that the real and personal property of the bank are part of its capital stock, and that the assessment could not exceed the par value of such stock, namely, $1,000,000.

The chamberlain of the city of St. John is authorized, without any previous proceedings, to issue execution for taxes, if not paid within a certain time after notice. In order to avoid such execution the bank of New Brunswick paid their taxes under protest.

Held, that such payment did not preclude them from afterwards taking proceedings to have the assessment quashed.

Appeal allowed with costs.

Supreme Court of Canada Reports, vol. 77, 481, 24 N. B. R. 391.

THE NEW BRUNSWICK RAILWAY COMPANY, (Defendants). *Appellants.*

and

ISSACHER N. ROBINSON, (Plaintiff), *Respondent.*

On appeal from the Supreme Court of New Brunswick.

Railway company—Sparks from engine—Proper care to prevent emission of—Use of wood or coal for fuel—Contributory negligence.

R. owned a barn situated about two hundred feet from the New Brunswick Railway Company's line, and such barn was destroyed by fire, caused, as was alleged, by sparks from the defendants' engine. An action was brought to recover damages for the loss of said barn and its contents. On the trial it appeared that the fuel used by the company over this line was wood, and evidence was given to the effect that coal was less apt to throw out sparks. It also appeared that at the place where the fire occurred there was a heavy up-grade, necessitating a full head of steam, and therefore increasing the danger to surrounding property. The jury found that the defendants did not use reasonable care in running the engine, but in what the want of such care consisted did not appear by their finding.

Held, reversing the judgment of the court below, that the company was under no obligation to use coal for fuel, and the use of wood was not in itself evidence of negligence; that the finding of the jury on the question of negligence was not satisfactory, and that therefore there should be a new trial.

Appeal allowed with costs.

Supreme Court of Canada Reports, vol. 11, 688, 24 N. B. R., 323.

ROBERT A. CHAPMAN and W. J. ROBINSON, *Appellants.*

and

SILAS W. RAND, *Respondent.*

On appeal from the Supreme Court of New Brunswick.

Can. Tem. Act—Election under—Scrutiny—Powers of county court judge—Matters affecting the election.

A judge of the county court, in holding a scrutiny of the votes polled at an election under the provision of the Canada Temperance Act, has only to determine the majority of votes cast, on one side or the other, by inspection of the ballots used in the election, and has no power to inquire into offences against the Act, and allow or reject ballots as a result of such inquiry (Henry, J., *dubitante*.)

Appeal allowed with costs.

Supreme Court of Canada Reports, vol. 11, 312. (N. B. R. 374).

JOHN P. LAWLESS, *Appellant.*

and

JAMES SULLIVAN *et al.*, *Respondents.*

On appeal from the Supreme Court of New Brunswick.

Taxes—Foreign corporation—Branch Bank—"Income," as distinguished from "net profits"—31 Vic. cap. 3, sec. 4 (N. B.)

L., manager of the Bank of B. N. A., a foreign banking corporation, having a branch in the city of St. John, derived from such business during the fiscal year of 1875, an income of $40,000, but, during the same period, sustained losses in its business beyond that amount. The bank, having made no gain from said business, disputed the corporation's authority to assess them under 22 Vic. cap. 37, 31 Vic. cap. 36, and 34 Vic. cap. 18, on an income of $40,000.

Held, that under the Acts of Assembly relating to the assessing of rates and taxes in the city of St. John, foreign banking corporations doing business in St. John are liable to be taxed on the gross income received by them during the fiscal year; and that L. had been properly assessed, (Henry, J., dissenting.)

Appeal dismissed with costs.

Supreme Court of Canada Reports, vol. 3, 117, 18 N. B. R. 520.

Above judgment reversed by Privy Council on appeal.

The tax imposed by sec. 4 of New Brunswick Act, 31 Vic. cap. 36, upon "income" is leviable in respect of the balance of gain over loss made in the fiscal year, and where no such balance of gain has been made there is no income or fund which is capable of being assessed. There is nothing in the said section or in the context which should induce a construction of the word "income" when applied to the income of a commercial business for a year, otherwise than its natural and commonly accepted sense as the balance of gain over loss.

6 App. Cas. 373 L. R.

James D. Lewin and G. Sidney Smith, surviving trustees under the marriage settlement of Martha M. S. Robertson, *Appellants.*

and

Georgiana Wilson, Benjamin Lawton, and James Harris, *Respondents.*

On appeal from the Supreme Court in Equity of New Brunswick, without any intermediate appeal to the Supreme Court of New Brunswick.

Statutes of Limitations—Cap. 84, sec. 40, and cap. 85, secs. 1 & 6 Con. Stats. N. B.—Covenant in mortgage deed—Payment by co-obligor.

J. H. borrowed $4,000 from M. C. on the 27th of September, 1850, at which date J. H. and J. W. gave their joint and several bond to M. C. conditioned for the repayment of the money in five years, with interest quarterly in the meantime. At the same time, and to secure the payment of the $4,000, two separate mortgages were given; one by J. H. and wife on H.'s wife's property, and one by J. W. and wife on W.'s property. Neither party executed the mortgage of the other. The mortgage from J. W. contained a provision that upon repayment of the sum of £1,000 and interest, according to the condition of the bond by J. W. and J. H., or either of them, their or either of their heirs, etc., then said mortgage should be void; a similar provision being inserted in the mortgage from J. H. The bond and mortgages were assigned to L., *et al.*, (the (appellants) in 1870, and the principal money has never been paid. J. W. died in 1858, and by his will devised all his residuary real estate, including the lands and premises in the above mentioned mortgage, to J. W., (one of the respondents) and others. J. W., in his lifetime, was, and since his death, the respondents have been in possession of the premises so mortgaged by J. W.

Neither J. W., nor any person claiming by, through, or under him, ever paid any interest on said bond and mortgage, or gave any acknowledgment in writing of the title of M. C. or her assignee. J. H., the co-obligor, paid interest on the bond from its date to 27th March, 1870.

On 20th January, 1881, under Consolidated Statutes of New Brunswick, cap. 40, a suit of foreclosure and sale of the premises mortgaged by J. W. was commenced by the appellants in the Supreme Court of New Brunswick in Equity, and the court gave judgment for the respondents. On appeal to the Supreme Court of Canada,—

Held, affirming the judgment of the court below, (Strong, J., dissenting.)

1st. That all liability of J. W.'s personal representatives, and of his heirs and devisees to any action whatever upon the bond was barred by secs. 1 & 6 of cap. 85, Consolidated Statutes of New Brunswick, although payment by a co-obligor would have maintained the action alive in its integrity under the English Statute 3 & 4 William IV., cap. 42.

2nd. That the right of foreclosure and sale of the lands included in the J. W. mortgage was barred by the Statute of Limitations in real actions, Con. Stats. N. B., cap. 84, sec. 40.

Per Gwynne, J. The only person by whom a payment can be made, or an acknowledgment in writing can be signed, so as to stay the currency of the Statute of Limitations to a point which, being reached, frees the mortgaged lands from all liability under the mortgage, must be either the original party to the mortgage contract, that is to say, the mortgagor, or some person in priority of estate with him, or the agent of one of such persons, and that moneys paid by J. H. in discharge of his own liability had none of the characteristics or quality of a payment made under the liability created by W.'s mortgage.

Appeal dismissed with costs.

Supreme Court of Canada Reports, vol. 9, 637.

EZEKIEL McLEOD, (Assignee of Jewett & Co.,) *Appellant*,

and

THE NEW BRUNSWICK RAILWAY CO., *Respondents*.

On appeal from the Supreme Court of New Brunswick.

Construction of agreement — Property in lumber—Ownership and control of lumber until payment of draft given for stumpage under the agreement.

The respondents, owners of timber lands in New Brunswick, granted to C. & S. a license to cut lumber on 25 square miles. By the license it was agreed *inter alia* :

"Said stumpage to be paid in the following manner : Said company shall first deduct from the amount of stumpage on the timber or lumber cut by grantees on this license as aforesaid, an amount equal to the mileage, paid by them as aforesaid, and the whole of the remainder, if any, shall, not later than the 15th April next, be secured by good endorsed notes, or other sufficient security, to be approved of by the said company, and payable on the 15th July next, and the lumber not to be removed from the booms or landings till the stumpage is secured as aforesaid.

"And said company reserves and retains full and complete ownership and control of all lumber which shall be cut from the aforementioned premises, wherever and however it may be situated, until all matters and things appertaining to or connected with this license shall be settled and adjusted, and all sums due or to become due for stumpage or otherwise, shall be fully paid, and any and all damages for non-performance of this agreement, or stipulation herein expressed, shall be liquidated and paid.

"And if any sum of money shall have become payable by any one of the stipulations or agreements herein expressed, and shall not be paid or secured in some of the modes herein expressed within ten days thereafter, then, in such case, said company shall have full power and authority to take all or any part of said lumber wherever or however situated, and to absolutely sell and dispose of the same either at private or public sale for cash; and after deducting reasonable expenses, commissions, and all sums which may then be due or may become due from any cause whatever, as herein expressed, the balance, if any there may be, they shall pay over on demand to said grantees, after a reasonable time for ascertaining and liquidating all amounts due, or which may become due, either as stumpage or damages."

For securing the stumpage payable to respondents under this license C. & S. gave to the respondents a draft upon J. & Co., which was accepted by J. & Co., and approved of by the respondents, but which was not paid at maturity. After giving the draft C. & S. sold the lumber to J. & Co., who knew the lumber was cut on the plaintiff's land under the said agreement. J. & Co. failed, and appellant, their assignee, took possession of the lumber and sold it.

Held, per Strong, Taschereau and Gwynne, JJ., affirming the judgment of the court below, (Ritchie, C.J., and Fournier and Henry, JJ., dissenting), that upon the case as submitted, and by mere force of the terms of the agreement, the absolute property in the lumber in question did not pass to C. & S. immediately upon the receipt by the company of the accepted draft of C. & S. on J. & Co., and that appellant was liable for the actual payment of the stumpage.

The Court being equally divided the judgment of the court below was affirmed.

Appeal dismissed with costs.

Supreme Court of Canada Reports, vol. 5, 281.

THE QUEDDY RIVER DRIVING BOOM CO. and HUGH R. ROBERTSON and LAMBERT L. L. BEVAN, *Appellants*,

and

WILLIAM DAVIDSON, *Respondent*.

On appeal from the Supreme Court of New Brunswick.

Obstructions in tidal and navigable rivers—45 Vic. cap. 100, (N. B.) *ultra vires*—B. N. A. Act, 1867, sec. 91.

Professing to act under the powers contained in their Act of Incorporation 45 Vic. cap. 100, (N. B.), the Q. R. B. Co. erected booms and piers in the Queddy river which impeded navigation, the booms being in that part of the river which is tidal and navigable.

Held, that the provincial legislature might incorporate a boom company, but could not give it power to obstruct a tidal navigable river, and therefore the Act, 46 cap. 100, N. B., so far as it authorizes the acts done by the company in erecting booms and other works in the Queddy river obstructing its navigation, was *ultra vires* of the New Brunswick legislature; over-ruling to this extent *McMillan* v. *Southwest Boom Co.*, 17 N. B. R. 715.

Appeal dismissed with costs.

Canada Supreme Court Reports, vol. 10, 222. (See post 31.)

James H. Ray, *et al.*, *Appellants.*

and

The Annual Conference of New Brunswick and Prince Edward Island, in connection with the Methodist Church of Canada, *et al.*, *Respondents.*

On appeal from the Supreme Court of New Brunswick.

Will — Construction of — Surplus — Whether residuary personal estate of the testator passed.

Among other bequests the testator declared as follows:—"I bequeath to the worn-out Preachers' and Widows' Fund in connection with the Wesleyan Conference here, the sum of £1,250, to be paid out of the moneys due me by Robert Chestnut, of Fredericton. I bequeath to the Bible Society £150. I bequeath to the Wesleyan Missionary Society in connection with the Conference the sum of £1,500." Then follow other and numerous bequests.

The last clause of the will is:—"Should there be any surplus or deficiency, a *pro rata* addition or deduction, as may be, to be made to the following bequests, namely: the worn-out Preachers, and Widows' Fund; Wesleyan Missionary Society; Bible Society." When the estate came to be wound up, it was found that there was a very large surplus of personal estate, after paying all annuities or bequests. This surplus was claimed, on the one hand, under the will, by these charitable institutions, and on the other hand by the heirs-at-law and next of kin of the testator, as being residuary estate, undisposed of under his will.

Held, affirming the judgment of the Supreme Court of New Brunswick, that the "surplus" had reference to the testator's personal estate out of which the annuities and legacies were payable: and therefore a *pro rata* addition should be made to the three above namel bequests, Statutes of Mortmain not being in force in New Brunswick.

Fournier and Henry, JJ., dissenting.

Appeal dismissed with costs.

Supreme Court of Canada Reports, vol. 6, 308.

The South West Boom Co., *Appellants,*

and

Daniel McMillan, *Respondent.*

On appeal from the Supreme Court of New Brunswick.

Additional plea, Supreme Court no power to allow.

D. McM., the respondent, and S. W. B. Co., the appellants, to recover damages alleged to have been sustained by reason of the obstruction of the River Miramichi by appellants' booms. The pleas were not guilty, and leave and license. On the trial the counsel proposed to add a plea that the wrong complained of was occasioned by an extraordinary freshet. The counsel for the respondent objected on the ground that such plea might have been demurred to. The learned judge refused the application, because he intended to admit the evidence under the plea of not guilty.

On appeal, the counsel for the appellants contended that the obstruction compl ained of was justified under the statute, 17 Vic. cap. 10, N. B., incorporating the South West Boom Co.

Held, that the appellants, not having put in a plea of justification under the statute, or applied to the Supreme Court of New Brunswick in *banco* for leave to amend their pleas, could not rely on that ground before this court to reverse the decision of the court below.

Appeal dismissed with costs.

Supreme Court of Canada Reports, vol. 3, 700. 17 N. B. R. 715. See *ante*, 29; *post*, 30.

JOSHUA SPEARS and WILLIAM C. SPEARS (Plaintiffs), *Appellants*,

and

JAMES WALKER, *Respondent*.

On appeal from the Supreme Court of New Brunswick.

Building contract—Enforcement of—Violation city by-law—Liability of owner—Effect of by-law passed after contract was made.

S. & Co., contractors for the erection of a building for the respondent in the city of St. John, N.B., brought an action claiming to have been prevented by respondent from carrying out their contract. The declaration also contained the common counts, part of the work having been performed. By the terms of the contract the building, when erected, would not have conformed to the provisions of a by-law of the city passed, under authority of an Act of the General Assembly of New Brunswick, 41 Vic. cap. 7, two days after the contract was signed.

On the trial of the action the plaintiffs were non-suited, and an application to the Supreme Court of New Brunswick to set such non-suit aside was refused.

Held, (Henry, J., dissenting), that the by-law of the said city of St. John made the said contract illegal, and therefore the plaintiffs could not recover. *Walker* v. *McMillan*, 6 Can. S. C. R. 241, followed.

Per Henry, J., that the erection of the building would not, so far as the evidence showed, be a violation of the by-law, and therefore the non-suit should be set aside and a new trial ordered.

Appeal dismissed with costs.

Canada Supreme Court Reports, vol. 11, 113. (See *ante* No. 9.)

JAMES FLANAGAN and JOHANNA, his wife, *Defendants*,

and

JOHN DOE, on the demise of GILBERT R. ELLIOTT, *et al.*, *Plaintiffs*.

On Appeal from the Supreme Court of New Brunswick.

Assessment on real estate—In name of occupier—Description as to persons and property—Con. Stat. N. B., cap. 100, sec. 16—Several assessments in one warrant—One illegal assessment—Warrant vitiated by.

Sec. 16, of cap. 100, Con. Stat. New Brunswick, relating to taxes and rates, provides that "real estate, where the assessors cannot obtain the names of any of the owners, shall be rated in the name of the occupier or person having ostensible control, but under such description as to person and property * * as shall be sufficient to indicate the property assessed and the character in which the person is assessed."

T. G., owner of real estate in Westmoreland county, N.B., died leaving a widow, who administered to his estate and resided on the property. The property was assessed for several years in the name of the estate of T. G., and in 1878 it was assessed in the name of "widow G."

Held, affirming the judgment of the court below, that the last named assessment was illegal, as not comprising such descriptions of persons and property as would be sufficient to indicate the property assessed, and the character in which the person was assessed.

Where a warrant for the collection of a single sum for rates for several years

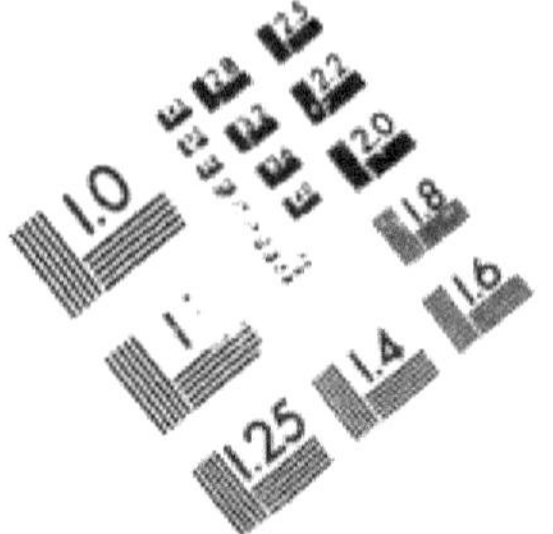

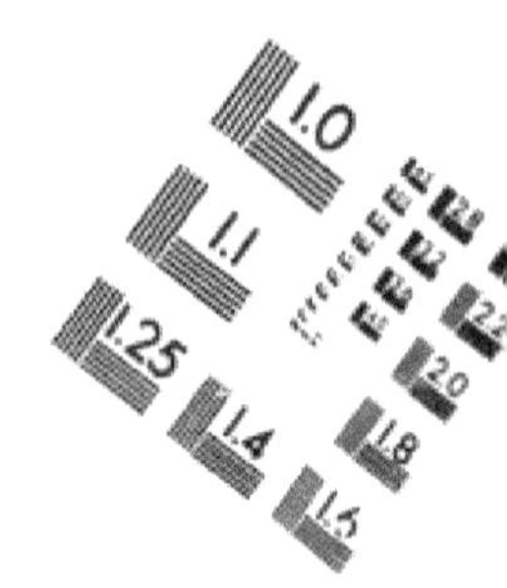

IMAGE EVALUATION
TEST TARGET (MT-3)

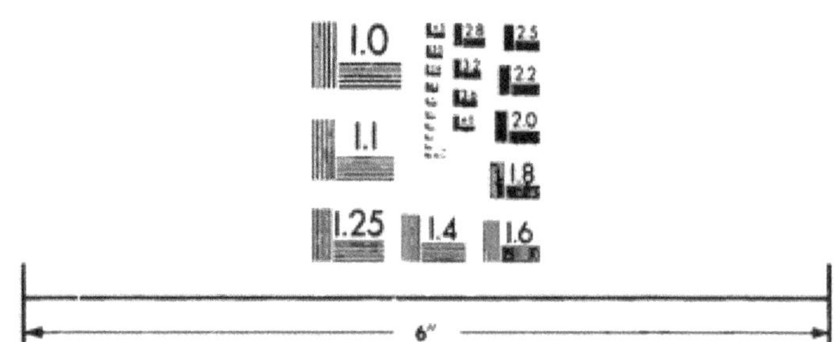

included the amount of an assessment which did not appear to be either against the owner or the occupier of the property:

Held, affirming the judgment of the court below, that the inclusion of such assessment would vitiate the warrant.

Appeal dismissed with costs.

Supreme Court of Canada Reports, vol. 12, 185. N. B. Reports, vol. 25, 154.

Agent—Sale of lands—Authority to deliver deed and receive purchase money—Agent exceeding authority—Memo to agent—New agreement.

One W. sold land under power of sale in a mortgage, and F. became the purchaser, and paid ten per cent. of the purchase money, it being agreed that the balance was to be paid in [illegible]. Shortly after the plaintiff A. brought a deed to F. and demanded the notes. F. wished to show the deed to his attorney, and it was left with him on his delivering to A. a writing as follows: "Received from E. A. a deed given by W. for a certain piece of land bought at auction, Saturday the thirtieth day of September, 1876, at Midgic. The above mentioned deed I receive only to be examined, and if lawfully and properly executed, to be kept; if not lawfully and properly executed, to be returned to Edward Anderson. When the said deed is lawfully and properly executed to the satisfaction of my attorney, I, the said Charles Fawcett, will pay the amount of balance due on said deed—five hundred and seventy-two dollars—provided I am given a good warranty deed, and the mortgage, which is on record, is properly cancelled if required." The deed was not returned to A., and an action was brought by him to recover the said sum of $572, named in the above memorandum.

The action was tried twice, and on the last trial a verdict was given for the defendant, under the direction of the judge, and leave was reserved to the plaintiff to move for a verdict in his favor for nominal damages, the purchase money having in the meantime been paid to W. On plaintiff moving for such leave, a majority of the Supreme Court of New Brunswick set aside the verdict of the jury, and entered a verdict for the plaintiff. (19 N. B. R. 34.)

On appeal to the Supreme Court of Canada,

Held, reversing the judgment of the court below, (Strong, J., dissenting), that the said memorandum did not constitute a new contract between the plaintiff and defendant to pay the purchase money to the plaintiff, who was merely the agent of W., and therefore the verdict for the defendant should stand.

Per Strong, J., that the said writing did constitute a new agreement between the parties; but that if A. was merely an agent of W. in the transaction he could still sue, as his principal had not interfered.

Appeal allowed with costs. *Fawcett v. Anderson*, 22nd June, 1885.

Assessment and taxes — Inhabitant of the city of St. John—Taxation—Wife's separate property.

Plaintiff was a resident of the city of St. John up to June, 1877, when he went with his family to Nova Scotia. In 1878 he returned to the Province of New Brunswick with his wife and family, and after leaving them in the town of Portland, went to Boston, in search of employment. He remained in Boston until the spring of 1880, having been employed in business, and paid taxes there. Whilst plaintiff was absent, his wife's father assigned to her a lot of leasehold property in the city of St. John. In the fall of 1878 she and family moved into the city and resided on her property until the spring of 1880, when the plaintiff returned from Boston and lived with his wife. For the taxes for 1879, assessed against him in respect of his wife's property, and for an income tax against himself, both being included in one assessment, he was afterwards arrested and taken to jail, where he remained two days, when he paid the amount under protest, and was released. He brought an action for false imprisonment, and obtained a verdict for $150.

The full Court of New Brunswick set aside the verdict, and granted a new trial, a majority being of the opinion that the plaintiff was constructively an inhabitant of St. John, and as such was liable to be assessed, and that there ought to be a new trial, as it did not very distinctly appear that objections were taken at the trial, or upon what the motion for a non-suit was to depend.

On appeal, to the Supreme Court of Canada

Held, that the plaintiff was not liable to assessment, and that the verdict should stand.

Appeal allowed with costs. *Edwards v. The Mayor, etc., of St. John*, 1st May, 1883.

Canada Temperance Act, 1878—Justice of the Peace—Conviction—Canada Temperance Act, 1878; sec. 105—Absence—Wrongful arrest—Justification.

A. and B., Justices of the Peace for King's county, were sued for issuing a warrant of commitment under which B., (appellant) was imprisoned. The facts, as proved at the trial, were as follows:—A prosecution under the Canada Temperance Act, 1878, was commenced by two justices, A. and B., and a summons issued. On the return of the summons, on the application of the defendant, A. and B. were served with a subpœna, to give evidence for the defendant on the hearing; whe. upon two other justices (the respondents) at the request of A. and B., under the provisions of sec. 105 of the Act, heard the case and convicted the appellant. A. and B., though present in the court room as witnesses, took no part in the proceedings.

The Supreme Court of New Brunswick ordered a non-suit to be entered.

On appeal to the Supreme Court of Canada:

Held, affirming the judgment of the court below, Henry and Taschereau, JJ., dissenting, that, as the conviction was good on its face, until set aside it was a justification for respondents for anything done under it.

Held, also, that upon the facts disclosed, A. and B. were "absent," within the meaning of sec. 105 of the Canada Temperance Act, 1878.

Appeal dismissed with costs.

Byrne v. Arnold, 22nd June, 1883.

Chattel mortgage—Passing after acquired property—*Partus sequitur ventrem*—*Novus actus interveniens*—Trover against sheriff.

The plaintiffs were the grantees, and one Hackett, the grantor in a bill of sale, by way of mortgage, which conveyed among other property a certain mare. In the mortgage there was a proviso that until default Hackett might remain in possession of all the property mortgaged, but with full power to the plaintiffs, in default of payment, to take possession and dispose of the property as they should see fit. After default in payment of principal and interest the mare dropped a foal. This foal, together with a horse, also in possession of Hackett, were seized by defendant (sheriff) under an execution against Hackett.

 ADDENDA.

On appeal from the Supreme Court of New Brunswick. See 4 Pugs. & Bur. 218.

Held, that the foal, having been dropped while plaintiffs were owners and entitled to possession of the mare, was their property—*partus sequitur ventrem*.

Appeal dismissed with costs.

Temple v. Nicholson, 3rd March, 1881.

Contract—Condition precedent—Direction to jury—Implied promise, when part performance.

In April, 1872, the defendant Morrow, gave the plaintiffs, Waterous, *et al.*, an order by letter for certain mill machinery, which the plaintiffs were to put in complete operation to the defendants satisfaction in a building to be provided by the defendant. All the machinery, with the exception of a slab-saw, was supplied, and the mill was put in operation in the summer of 1872. The defendant found fault with the machinery, and after alterations and repairs made by the plaintiffs in 1873, the defendant put additional machinery into the mill and worked it until 1875, when it was destroyed by fire. The defendant had insured the whole machinery, including that supplied by the plaintiffs, for $7,700; the additional machinery put in by himself being valued at $2,500. The defendant received the benefit of the insurance to the full amount of the loss. The contract price was $4,250, together with freight and expenses, making in all $4,730. Some payments were made, but the defendant refusing to pay a balance of $1,900, the plaintiffs brought an action of assumpsit, adding the common counts.

At the close of the plaintiffs' case a non-suit was moved for on the ground that it was a condition precedent to the defendant's liability accruing that the work should be done to his satisfaction, and it was contended that the plaintiffs' own evidence showed that the defendant never was satisfied, but that he was complaining all along. This point being overruled, the defendant undertook to show that the machinery was not what was represented, but defective, and in many parts had to be repaired, and that he had already paid as much as it was worth. Much evidence was given on this issue, and the plaintiffs endeavored to show that any defect in the working of the mill was attributable to the shifting of the foundation, erected by the defendant himself, and to the want of skill of the men employed by him. The learned judge left it to the jury to say whether the machinery was reasonably fit and proper for the purpose for which it was intended, and if not, directed them that the defendant was only bound to pay as much as it was worth. The jury returned a verdict for the plaintiffs for $1,620, having deducted $200 for the defects and $80 for that part of the machinery not supplied.

A rule *nisi* to set aside the verdict and grant a new trial was made absolute by the Supreme Court of New Brunswick (2 Pugs. & Bur. 11), on the ground that the learned judge should have directed the jury that, the length of time that the defendant used the machinery, the complaints he made about it from time to time, and all the circumstances connected with it, should have been left to the jury, with a direction for them to consider whether from the defendant's dealings with it they could infer a new implied contract on his part to keep the machinery and pay what it was worth, though less than the contract price.

On appeal to the Supreme Court of Canada,

Held, that in suing upon this contract it was not necessary for the plaintiffs to have averred, as a condition precedent to their right to recover, that the work, besides having been skilfull , properly, sufficiently, and in a workmanlike manner executed, was completed to the satisfaction of the defendant.

In cases in which something has been done under a special c...ract, but not in strict accordance with the terms of the contract, although the party cannot recover the remuneration stipulated for in the contract because he has not done that which was to be the consideration for it, still, if the other party has derived any benefit from the work done, as it would be unjust to allow him to retain that without paying for it, the law implies a promise upon his part to pay such a remuneration as the benefit conferred upon him is reasonably worth. The jury in this case having decided upon the evidence that the defendant had derived a greater benefit from the work done than was compensated by the amount he had already paid, and the plaintiffs were entitled to retain the benefit of the verdict, and the rule granting a new trial should be discharged with costs.

Appeal allowed with costs. *Waterous v. Morrow*, 12th December, 1879.

Contract—Contract to cut lumber—Vesting of property—Writ of replevin—Sheriff's possession under—Trespass—Pleading—*Jus tertii*—Justification by sheriff under writ—Amendment, power of, by Supreme Court of Canada.

In November, 1874, one Arbo entered into a written agreement with one Muirhead to get logs off land under Muirhead's control, the logs to be Muirhead's property as cut. In December following one Marooney agreed with Arbo to cut and haul logs for him from land specified in the agreement between Arbo and Muirhead, which logs were to be Arbo's property at the landing, Arbo agreeing to furnish Marooney with supplies to get the logs. Marooney cut logs under this agreement and hauled them to the landing. In November, 1875, the logs not having been driven, and Arbo not having furnished sufficient supplies, he and Marooney rescinded their agreement, Marooney giving his note to Arbo for the supplies delivered. The logs remained on the landing, and in February, 1876, they were seized as the property of Arbo, who had become insolvent, under a writ of attachment issued under the Insolvent Act of 1875. In May, 1876, Marooney sold the logs to the plaintiff, who drove them to the boom of the S. W. Miramichi, where they were replevied by the assignee of Arbo's estate. The plaintiff put in a claim of property in them, and the sheriff returned the writ of replevin, with such claim, to the attorney who issued the writ. No writ *de prop. prob.* having been issued, the sheriff kept possession of the logs, and the plaintiff brought trespass against him for taking them.

The defendant pleaded: 1. Not guilty. 2. Goods, not the plaintiff's. 3. Goods the goods of the assignee of Arbo, and defendant did acts complained of by license of such assignee. 4. Goods, the goods of Muirhead, and defendant did acts complained of by license of Muirhead. 5. Goods, property of defendant.

A verdict was entered for plaintiff by consent for $1,554, the value of all the logs, subject to be reduced to $420.47, the value of the logs not cut by Marooney, if the court should be of opinion that plaintiff was not entitled to Marooney's logs.

The Supreme Court of New Brunswick reduced the verdict to the said sum of $420.47. See 4 Pugs. & Bur. 25.

On appeal to the Supreme Court of Canada,

Held, per Ritchie, C.J., that the judgment appealed from should be affirmed on the following ground: It having been proved on the trial, without objection and made part of the case, that the logs in question were seized by the defendant, as sheriff, under a writ of replevin issued out of the Supreme Court of New Brunswick, directing him to take the logs in question, the sheriff was justified in taking the logs thereunder, and that as against the plaintiff it was no wrongful taking or conversion; that this defence could be given in evidence under the pleadings in the cause, or if it could not be so given, this being a strictly technical objection, and this defence having been put forward on the trial without objection, and no such technical point reserved on the trial, if necessary the record should be amended.

Per Strong and Gwynne, JJ.—The parties at the trial having rested their rights upon the question of title, viz., were the logs the property of the plaintiff, or were they the property of Ellis, as assignee of Arbo, or of Muirhead; and the plaintiff claiming title through Marooney, it was necessary for him to show title in Marooney, which he had failed to do, and therefore he could not recover for the Marooney logs.

Per Fournier and Henry, JJ.—The logs when taken were the property of the plaintiff, and he was therefore entitled to judgment on all the issues raised.

Per Fournier, J.—The defendant might have justified under the writ, and the court might grant leave to add such a plea, but in that event the costs should be paid by defendant.

Per Henry, J.—No effort having been made in the court below to add such a plea, it was too late and contrary to precedent and justice now to admit it.

Per Gwynne, J.—When the plaintiff fails to show in evidence that he was in actual possession at the time of the taking, and is therefore driven to rest on the goodness of his title to the property, a defendant may, in rebuttal of the evidence of such title, set up a *have jus tertii* without showing he had any authority from the third person having such title. So a sheriff, sued for taking the goods of the plaintiff, may show, under this issue, that the goods belonged to a third party against whom he took them in execution. The several matters therefore alleged in the 3rd, 4th and 5th pleas were matters which could have been given in evidence under the issue joined upon the 2nd plea. As to the 5th plea, in view of the evidence, it was quite inappropriate to such evidence, for the writ of replevin placed in the hands of the defendant as sheriff to be executed, did not vest in the defendant any property in the goods, the taking of which was complained of, so as to enable him to justify the taking as his own property, as is done in the 5th plea.

Appeal dismissed with costs. *Scire v. Sheriff*, 10th June, 1881.

Corporations—St. John city—Power of Mayor, etc., to raise the level of the streets—Raising a street in part and erecting fence on part so raised in which access to the street is cut off—Non-suit—Charter of city—Municipal councils, powers of.

By the charter of the city of St. John the corporation was given power to alter, amend and repair streets, theretofore laid out, or thereafter to be laid out. The charter is confirmed by 26 Geo. III., cap. 46, and the right to alter the levels of streets is recognized by 9 Geo. IV., cap. 4. Church street was not one of the streets originally designated on the plan of the city. It was made a public street in 1811, on petition of the owners of the land through which it passes, who gave the land for the street. In 1871, the corporation raised Church street below Canterbury street, filling it in to within four or five feet of the plaintiff's house and shop. On the embankment so made in front of the plaintiff's house and shop the corporation erected a fence. By reason of this the plaintiff had no access from the street to his house and shop; but reached them from the narrow passage left next the house and shop running easterly towards Canterbury street and westerly toward Prince William street.

An action having been brought against the Mayor, etc., of the city for the damage sustained by the plaintiff by reason of so filling in the street and erecting the fence, the plaintiff was non-suited by Duff, J., on the ground that the Charter and Acts of Assembly gave the defendants full authority to raise the level of the street, and that in them was vested the sole discretion as to the time and manner of doing it, and that having exercised a *bona fide* discretion in the matter and raised it the damage sustained by the plaintiff was not the subject of an action; that as to the erection of the fence on the wall it was necessary for the protection of the public, and that it was the duty of the defendants to put it there for that purpose. This non-suit was set aside by the Supreme Court of New Brunswick, it being there held by Weldon, Fisher and Wetmore, JJ.; (Allen, C.J., and Duff, J., dissenting), that the corporation had no right to fill in the street in the manner in which they did it, and to erect the fence on the embankment in front of the plaintiff's house and shop, and that the manner in which the corporation had filled in the street and erected the fence, was of itself evidence that they had acted carelessly and without reasonable skill and care, and that the consideration of this should not have been withdrawn from the jury. See 2 Pug. & Bur. 636.

On appeal to the Supreme Court of Canada.

Held, that the non-suit should not have been set aside; Fournier and Henry, JJ., dissenting.

Per Gwynne, J., (Taschereau, J., concurring), that the defendants have, under the several Acts of Parliament which confirm and amend their charter, complete legislative power to raise or lower the level of the streets to any extent that the irregularities of the ground may seem to the corporation and its council, as representing the public, to require for the benefit and convenience of the public, cannot be doubted; the councils of these municipal corporations are themselves a deliberative law-making assembly, chosen by the people to do whatever, within their jurisdiction, may in their judgment be necessary for the public benefit, and the power conferred upon them must therefore have a liberal construction in view of the public rather than of private interests. The power of altering, amending, repairing and improving the streets, which is a power vested in the corporation for the benefit of the public, whose representatives the council of the corporation are, is restricted by no condition save only the implied condition that what shall be done in the name of the public, and ostensibly for their benefit and convenience, shall not be done in such a manner as in reality to constitute a public nuisance.

The plaintiff has never rested his right to maintain this action upon the ground that the act complained of is a public nuisance, from which he sustained peculiar injury, and as he could not succeed without establishing the act of which he complained to be such public nuisance, the non-suit was right and should be affirmed.

Appeal allowed with costs. *The Mayor, etc., of St. John v. Pattison*, 23rd February, 1880.

Damages—Action on the case—Injunction, declaring alleged order for, obtained maliciously—Demurrer.

Action for maliciously obtaining an *ex parte* injunction order from a judge, whereby the plaintiff was restrained from disposing of certain lumber, in consequence of which he had sustained damage as was alleged.

The declaration set out that plaintiff was possessed as of his own property of certain lumber; that defendants wrongfully, improperly, maliciously, and without any reasonable or probable cause, and without any notice to plaintiff, made an *ex parte* application to a judge of the Supreme Court of New Brunswick for an injunction in a suit commenced by them in said Supreme Court on the equity side, in which suit defendants were plaintiffs, and the now plaintiff with others were defendants, and procured from said judge an *ex parte* order of injunction whereby, etc., which order defendants caused to be served on plaintiff; that plaintiff afterwards appeared to the said suit and put in his answer, but defendants did not further prosecute their suit, which was dismissed with costs, and the order of injunction became of no further effect; that by reason of obtaining a service on plaintiff of said order he was hindered and prevented from manufacturing, etc., said lumber for a long space of time, whereby said lumber was greatly injured and part thereof lost, and the plaintiff lost large gains, etc. To this declaration plaintiff demurred.

The demurrer was sustained by the Supreme Court of New Brunswick. See 2 Pugs. & Bur. 469.

On appeal to the Supreme Court of Canada,

Held, affirming the judgment of the Court below, that the declaration disclosed no cause of action.

By the Statute of New Brunswick, 2 Rev. Stats., p. 77, such an order is granted on a sworn bill, or on the bill and an affidavit, and may be granted *ex parte*, subject to be dissolved on sufficient ground shown by affidavit on the part of the defendant. Here there was no allegation that the injunction was dissolved, or that any application was made for its dissolution, or that the order was obtained by any *suggestio falsi*, or *suppressio veri* on the part of the plaintiff, and for ought that appeared in the declaration, the judge exercised a sound discretion in granting the order.

Appeal dismissed with costs. *Collins v. Everitt*, 12th December, 1879.

Damages — Adjoining land owners — Where defendant has allowed cellars to remain after building destroyed—Damage from water collecting in them and running against wall of house built by plaintiff—Whether defendant liable—Action on the case—Declaration—Non-suit.

The plaintiffs owned a building lot in the city of St. John, on which they excavated a cellar and foundation, and built a large and valuable building. The soil of the bottom of the cellar and under the foundation was clay. The defendants owned the adjoining lot, on which, in 1848, the time their ancestor Stephenson purchased it, there was a house. There was a cellar under the house adjoining the plaintiffs' land. Stephenson, or his tenant, dug another cellar joining the first one, and put up another house on the same lot. These houses stood until 1871, when they were burned, leaving the cellars uncovered, thus making one large uncovered hole, bounded on the west by Charlotte street, and on the north by the plaintiffs' lot. These holes collected large quantities of water in them from the street and from the surface, and also by percolation from the land adjoining. When the plaintiffs' house was built, the cellars being co-terminous with the foundation of the plaintiffs' building, and the soil being clay, these holes retained the water, until it gradually softened the clay under plaintiffs' foundation wall, and also gradually destroyed the foundation wall itself, and escaped in that way into the plaintiffs' cellar, and thereby caused the side of the plaintiffs' building to settle and the building itself to topple over, and damaged it to a large extent.

The declaration contained two counts, the first count for wrongfully, carelessly, negligently and improperly removing the earth and soil off the defendants' lot, and negligently continuing it so removed, so that there remained holes and excavations, which the defendant so negligently managed and left uncovered that large quantities of water collected and remained in the holes, which they permitted to flow and escape against, under and through the plaintiff's foundation wall, and thereby did damage.

Second count, that the defendants improperly and negligently collected water, etc., and by their carelessness caused it to flow into plaintiffs' premises and did damage.

The only plea was the general issue of not guilty. A rule for a non-suit pursuant to leave reserved at the trial was made absolute by the Supreme Court of New Brunswick, on the ground that damage and injury must both concur to afford a party a right of action, and the evidence showed only an ordinary and legitimate use of the defendants' own land, which did not constitute an injury, and therefore they were not liable. See 2 Pug. & Bur. 523.

On appeal to the Supreme Court of Canada,

Held, that the declaration did not cover the appellants' case, and therefore the non-suit was correct.

Appeal dismissed with costs. *The Trustees of the St. John Young Men's Christian Association* v. *Hutchinson, et al.* 23rd February, 1880.

Easement—Light and air — Twenty years' uninterrupted use of—Prescription—Misdirection —Damages—Measure of.

Action on the case for obstructing plaintiff's lights. The plaintiff and defendant were owners of contiguous houses. The defendant's house was built some time prior to 1853 for one Burns, who in April of that year sold and conveyed it to one Seely, who afterwards deeded to one Hogan, from whom the plaintiff purchased under a registered deed. In the summer of 1853, whilst the defendant's house was in the occupation of one Mrs. Kanny, a tenant of Seely, the house owned by the plaintiff was built for one Adams, from whom, through several mesne conveyances, the plaintiff derived his title. In the fall of 1853, whilst the plaintiff's house was in course of erection, two windows were placed in the gable end of it to afford light and air to the bedrooms in the attic. These windows overlooked the house which Burns had erected. Mr. Adams began to live in the house about December, 1854. The windows remained where they were placed, and unobstructed until August, 1874, when the defendant by raising his house and putting a mansard roof upon it, caused the obstruction complained of, by closing up the lower half of the windows.

There was no evidence of an express grant of an easement, the plaintiff relying upon the fact of twenty years' uninterrupted enjoyment as entitling him to recover. For the defendant it was shown by Seely that he never gave Adams permission to put the windows there, and also that he did not notice them till after he had parted with his title (which was in 1857). Seely stated, however, that he saw Adams' house being built. The defendant swore that he had examined the county records, and that there was no grant of an easement in the lights in question on record. He also testified that he was ignorant of the windows when he bought, which was in the spring of 1874, and did not know of them till the obstruction was made. The evidence was not certain to when Mrs. Kanny's tenancy terminated. No question appears to have been raised at the trial as to the time her lease terminated, nor was this point left to the jury, the contention of the plaintiff's counsel being that the time began to run from the period when the windows were put in, and that tenancy had nothing to do with the question.

The learned Chief Justice of New Brunswick, before whom the case was tried, directed the jury that "if Mr. Seely, the owner of the land, did not occupy the land himself, but it was occupied by his tenants, then he would not be bound by the user, unless he knew of the windows being there; if he knew of the windows being there, and did not obstruct them within twenty years, he would be bound, and the tenancy had nothing to do with the question."

And as to the measure of damages the learned Chief Justice charged that: "The fair measure would be what it would cost the plaintiff to make such alterations in his house as would admit the same quantity of light and air as he had before the defendant raised his roof."

The jury found a verdict for the plaintiff for $400.

A rule *nisi* for a new trial was discharged.

On appeal to the Supreme Court of Canada,

Held, 1. That the duration of Mrs. Kanny's tenancy was a proper question for the jury, and it should have been left to them without the qualification that it made no difference if Seely had knowledge of the existence of the windows; for if the tenancy continued subsequently to August, 1854, there was manifestly no user for twenty years with the consent or acquiescence of the defendant and those through whom he claimed, for Seely, the then owner of the fee, would have no right to enter upon the possession of his tenant for the purpose of obstructing the light.

2. There was also a misdirection as to the measure of damages; the plaintiff should have been limited to a recovery in respect of the loss and inconvenience caused by the darkening of his windows up to the time when the action was brought, and for future damages he could bring successive actions from time to time as long as the nuisance continued.

The court below went at length into the question regarding the nature and effect of the presumption of a lost grant arising from twenty years' use of an easement, and the right of rebutting such presumption by evidence, and also dealt with the question as to the effect of a registered conveyance upon a title to an easement founded upon such a presumption. See the case as reported in 2 Pugs. & Bur. 303. As to the first of these questions see *Angus* v. *Dalton*, 6 App. Cases, 740.

Appeal allowed with costs, and rule *nisi* for a new trial made absolute. *Pugsley* v. *King*, 12th December, 1879.

Insolvency—Insolvent Act—Demand of assignment, when annulled, action for making—Reasonable and probable cause—Order of judge annulling demand not *primâ facie* evidence of.

In 1874, the firm of James Domville & Co. was composed of James Domville and James Scovil; and the firm of Estabrooks & Gleeson was then composed of John F. Estabrooks and the plaintiff. The latter firm carried on business then in the city of St. John as dealers in flour, meal, etc., and there had been dealings between the firms for about two years previously, but not, so far as appeared, to any very large extent.

In the fall of that year, three promissory notes, made by Estabrooks & Gleeson in favour of Domville & Co., which had been endorsed by the latter firm, and which had been discounted for them by the Bank of Montreal, were lying in that bank when they matured. The first was a note for $409.81, and it fell due on the 23rd November, 1874; the second was for $100.71, due 4-7 December, and the third was for $137.13, due 11-14 December.

On the 23rd November, when the first of these notes became due, the plaintiff called at the office of Messrs. Domville & Co., where he saw Mr. Scovil, and told him that he was unable to pay the note in full that day, but he offered Mr. Scovil 25 per cent. on account of it then, and asked to be allowed to renew for the difference. Mr. Scovil promised to speak to the defendant on the subject, and requested the plaintiff to call again and get his reply. The plaintiff accordingly called again shortly afterwards and found both Mr. Scovil and Mr. Domville in their office. The defendant then at once refused peremptorily to accept the offer which the plaintiff had made to Scovil, or to accept 50 per cent. and to renew for the balance for one month.

After three o'clock on the same day, the defendant called at the office of Estabrooks & Gleeson, and told the plaintiff that if the note was not taken up by one o'clock the following day an attachment would be issued against the firm of Estabrooks & Gleeson. The plaintiff urged him not to issue any attachment, assuring him that, not only Messrs. Domville & Co., but every one of the creditors of Estabrooks & Gleeson should be paid in full every dollar due them. The defendant, however, refused to listen to these assurances.

The note for $400.81 was not then retired, neither was the next one for $100, when it became due; but the third was paid in full at the maturity.

Sometime in the month of December, (the plaintiff thought about the 7th), Estabrooks & Gleeson received a letter from F. E. Barker, purporting to have been written by him as the solicitor, and on behalf of Domville & Co., intimating that Domiville & Co's., claim must be paid, or that Estabrooks & Gleeson must go into liquidation.

As the solicitor of Domville & Co., Mr. Barker, on the 16th December, 1874, issued an attachment at their suit against the property of Estabrooks & Gleeson, but which so far as appeared on the trial, was never executed. The Deputy-sheriff, in whose hands it had been placed for execution, testified that no property was pointed out to him, and that he found none to attach under it.

On the 12th January, 1875, a demand was served on Estabrooks & Gleeson at the instance of Domville & Co., requiring Estabrooks & Gleeson to make an assignment under the Insolvent Act of 1869.

Within five days after service of such demand, a petition, under the 15th section of the Act, signed by John F. Estabrooks and Patrick Gleeson individually, was presented to Judge Watters, the Judge of the County Court of St. John, praying that no further proceedings should be taken under it and due notice of the presentment of such petition having been given, and all parties being present either in person or by their counsel, before Judge Watters, he proceeded to enquire into the subject matter of it, and made the following order: "After hearing the parties and their evidence, as adduced before me, and it appearing to me that the said John F. Estabrooks and Patrick Gleeson have not ceased to meet their liabilities generally at the time of such demand, I do order that the prayer of the said petitioners be granted, and that no further proceedings be taken on such demand, with costs to be paid by the said James Domville and James Scovil to the said petitioners or to their attorney upon demand."

Estabrooks & Gleeson effected an arrangement with Domville & Co. for the amount of the indebtedness for which the demand had been made by giving them an endorsed note, payable, with interest, in twelve months, which note the makers subsequently paid in full.

The plaintiff brought this action on the ground "that the defendant falsely and maliciously, and without reasonable and probable cause, made, or procured to be made, a demand under the 14th section of the Act of 1869, signed by the defendant and by one James Scovil, partners, under the name, style and firm of James Domville & Co., requiring plaintiff and the said John F. Estabrooks to make an assignment of his estate and effects for the benefit of his creditors, and falsely and maliciously, and without reasonable or probable cause, caused the same to be served upon the said plaintiff and the said John F. Estabrooks, according to the provisions of the said Act; and the said plaintiff and the said John F. Estabrooks, in pursuance of the provisions of the same Act, applied by, and presented to Charles Watters, Esquire, the Judge of the County Court of the city and county of St John, their petition praying that no further proceedings under the said demand should be had against them under the said Act; and such proceedings were thereupon had under the said petition, that the said Judge being authorized to act, and having competent authority in that behalf, ordered that the prayer of the said plaintiff and of the said John F. Estabrooks should be granted, and thereafter and thereby such demand so made and served as aforesaid, became and was of no force, etc., and the proceedings thereon were determined; and by reason whereof the plaintiff was put to inconvenience and anxiety, and was prevented from transacting his business and carrying on his said trade with the said John F. Estabrooks, and was injured in his credit and incurred expense in procuring the said demand to be annulled, etc."

At the trial, Duff, J., directed the jury that the annulling of the demand by the order of Judge Watters was *prima facie* evidence of the absence of reasonable and probable cause, and threw upon the defendant the burthen of proving the affirmative.

This ruling was upheld by the Supreme Court of New Brunswick. 3 Pugs. & Bur. 77.

On appeal to the Supreme Court of Canada.

Held, reversing the judgment of the court below, that such order was not in itself even *prima facie* evidence of the absence of reasonable and probable cause; but further, the evidence sufficiently established the existence of reasonable and probable cause for making the demand of assignment.

Appeal allowed with costs. *Domville v. Gleeson*, 10th June, 1880.

Insurance, fire—Condition in policy—Not to assign without written consent of company—Breach of condition—Chattel mortgage.

Appeal, by consent, from the decree of Mr. Justice Palmer, Judge in Equity for the Province of New Brunswick, in favor of the respondent (plaintiff below).

The firm of Peters & Sutherland, of the city of St. John, N. B., effected an insurance for the sum of $2,000 with the Sovereign Fire Insurance Company on their stock of boots and shoes in the premises in which they did business. Not long after, the said Peters & Sutherland executed a chattel mortgage on their stock of boots and shoes, being the property covered by the said insurance in favor of Charles H. Peters, the respondent, who allowed them to remain in possession of and sell the said stock. While the said mortgage was outstanding, the said stock was destroyed by fire, and the company refused to pay the insurance thereon, on the ground that the chattel mortgage was a breach of the following condition in the policy: "If the property insured is assigned without the written consent of the company at the head office endorsed hereon, signed by the secretary or assistant secretary of the company, this policy shall thereby become void, and all liability of the company shall thereupon cease."

Held, affirming the judgment of the court below, that a chattel mortgage of the property insured was not an assignment within the meaning of such condition.

Appeal dismissed with costs. *Sovereign F. Ins. Co. of Can.* v. *Peters*, 8th March, 1886.

Insurance, marine—Condition of policy—Not to load more than registered tonnage with stone, etc., without agent's consent—Loading with phosphate rock—Evidence of consent by agent—Proof of contract—Prior insurance.

A voyage policy on the plaintiff's vessel *Pretty Jemima*, contained *inter alia*, the following clauses:—"Warranted not to load more than registered tons with stones, marble, lead, ores, or brick, without the consent of the agent of the Providence Washington Insurance Company of Providence, provided always, and it is hereby further agreed, that if the said assured shall have made any other assurance upon the premises aforesaid, prior in date to this policy, then the said Providence Washington Insurance Company of Providence shall be answerable for only so much as the amount of such prior insurance may be deficient towards fully covering the premises hereby assured."

In an action on the said policy, it appeared the vessel was loaded with phosphate rock, and the plaintiff gave evidence of a conversation with the company's agent in which the latter wanted to charge more premium than on a previous policy, because the vessel was going to carry phosphate. He also cautioned plaintiff about loading the vessel, how to lay the floor so as to distribute the weight over the ship. The plaintiff's evidence on this matter closes as follows: "Ranney (the agent) said I could load down to the mark, the load line, same as if loading coal." It also appeared that there was $1,100 prior insurance on one-eighth of the vessel, which plaintiff had bought, but of which he had never received the title.

Held, affirming the judgment of the Supreme Court of New Brunswick, (Gwynne, J., dissenting), that the agents consent had been obtained to the loading of the vessel beyond her registered tonnage, and there was consequently no breach of the above condition of the policy.

Held, also, that the defendants were liable up to the amount insured, only for so much of the assessed value as was not covered by the prior insurance of $1,100.

Per Gwynne, J., that the consent of the agent should have been alleged by the plaintiff in his pleading, and not having been so alleged could not be set up as an answer to the defendants' pleas; that the jury should have been requested to find whether or not phosphate rock was stone within the meaning of such condition, and that there should be a new trial to have such a finding by the jury.

The policy was signed by Ranney, as the company's agent throughout as such agent, and was so recognized by the president of the company.

Held, that this was sufficient in the first instance, if uncontradicted, to justify the jury in finding that Ranney was the agent of the company.

Robertson v. *Provincial Insurance Company*, 3 All. N. B., 379, followed.

Appeal dismissed with costs. *Providence Washington Insurance Company* v. *Chapman*, 12th January, 1885.

Insurance, marine—Policy to be countersigned by agent—Proof of agency.

A policy of insurance on the respondent's vessel contained the following reservation: "But this policy shall not be valid unless countersigned by Henry R. Ranney, the said company's duly authorized agent, at his office in St. John, N. B." The policy was not countersigned by Ranney, and in an action thereon the respondent gave evidence to shew that it was issued by Ranney and sent by him, as directed by the respondents to a person in Nova Scotia. A verdict was given for the plaintiff at the trial, and the company moved for a non-suit on the ground, *inter alia*, that the policy was invalid on account of not being so countersigned.

The non-suit was refused.

On appeal to the Supreme Court of Canada,

Held (Fournier and Henry, JJ., dissenting), that the appeal must be allowed and a non-suit entered.

The policy, as set out in the plaintiff's declaration, contained a stipulation that the vessel was not to load more than register tonnage with stone, ores, etc. The defendants pleaded to this count that she did load more than her register tons with stone or ores, namely, phosphate rock, contrary to such condition.

The plaintiff replied that phosphate rock was not stone or ore within the meaning of such condition; the defendant demurred to the replication, and, on argument on the demurrer, the replication was held good. 19 N. B. Rep. 3 P. & B., 24. *The Delaware Mutual Insurance Co.* v. *Chapman*, 16th February, 1885.

Jurisdiction—Appeal quashed for want of jurisdiction—Verdict against weight of evidence—Secs. 20 and 22 Sup. C. Act—Costs.

Appeal from a judgment of the Supreme Court of New Brunswick, making absolute a rule to set aside a verdict for the defendants, and for a new trial, on the several grounds of improper reception of evidence, misdirection, and because the verdict was against the weight of evidence.

Held, that the court below having proceeded as well on the ground that the verdict was against the preponderance of the evidence, as on the law, the appeal came within sec. 22 of the Supreme Court Act, and would not lie. But see now S. & Ex. Ct., Am. Act, 1880, sec. 4.

Appeal quashed for want of jurisdiction, but without costs, the appeal having been heard *ex parte*, the respondent not appearing. *Domville v. Cameron*, 9th February, 1880.

New trial—Evidence—Where improperly received and afterwards withdrawn by judge from jury—License to cut timber.

The plaintiff was the licensee of certain crown lands, under license from the crown, to cut timber and logs thereon. These licenses did not contain any description or boundaries, but were described as (1) "No. 192 east half block 176 Muzzerall Brook, containing three square miles," and (2) "South of Main S. W. Miramichi River, north-east quarter of block 42, and the southern 1¼ miles of block 41." The plaintiff endeavored by the evidence of one Braithwaite and one Freeze to identify the lands alleged to be included in these licenses, and in their evidence and that of one Flynn, proved that logs had been cut upon these blocks by two parties, respectively named Sutherland and Kirwan, and on the trial the plaintiff offered to prove the statements of these two parties and admissions made by them. The defendant's counsel objected to these statements as no evidence against the defendant, and on the objection being taken, the Chief Justice only admitted it on the plaintiff's counsel undertaking to connect the defendant with these parties, Sutherland and Kirwan. This he failed to do, but called one Coleman, an agent of the plaintiff's, to depose as to certain statements of the defendant. The plaintiff's counsel addressed the jury upon the whole evidence, commenting upon all the facts, but the learned Chief Justice, in charging the jury said that if the case rested on the evidence of Braithwaite, he was opinion that the plaintiff failed to make out his case, and also stated his opinion that the declarations of Sutherland and Kirwan were not evidence against the defendant, and that the plaintiff's case must depend upon the conversations between Coleman and the defendant respecting the logs. Upon this charge, the jury found a verdict for the plaintiff for $965.

A rule *nisi* was obtained for a new trial, and after argument, the rule was discharged by the first division of the Supreme Court of New Brunswick, the judge holding, under authority of *Wilson v. Fawsset* (1 P. & B. 496), that when evidence, which has been improperly received, has been withdrawn by the judge from the consideration of the jury, such improper admission of evidence is not a ground for a new trial.

On appeal to the Supreme Court of Canada,

Held, that the Supreme Court of New Brunswick was correct in refusing a new trial on the ground of the improper admission of evidence; the plaintiff having failed to connect the statements of Sutherland and Kirwan with the defendant, such evidence was properly and sufficiently withdrawn from the jury. But as regards Coleman's evidence, there was not sufficient to go to the jury, and the learned Chief Justice should have left nothing to the jury. On this ground the rule *nisi* for a new trial should be made absolute.

Appeal allowed with costs. *Snowball v. Stewart* 16th February, 1881.

New trial—Verdict against weight of evidence.

An action was brought to recover the price and value of goods sold by the plaintiff to the defendant's brother, and on the trial the plaintiff gave evidence of an agreement with the defendant whereby the latter, as the plaintiff alleged, undertook to give notes at four months to retire notes at three months given by his brother, the purchaser of the goods.

The plaintiff swore that this agreement was carried out for a time, but that the defendant finally refused to continue it any longer. The evidence showed that the defendant always gave his notes to his brother, who carried them to the plaintiff. The defendant, on the other hand, swore that he never made any such agreement, but only gave notes to his brother to help him in his business. The evidence of the plaintiff was entirely uncorroborated. A verdict was found for the plaintiff, and the Supreme Court of New Brunswick refused a new trial.

Held (Ritchie, C.J., and Taschereau, J., dissenting), that the weight of evidence was not sufficiently in favor of the plaintiff to justify the verdict, and there must be a new trial.

Appeal allowed with costs, and new trial granted. *Fraser* v. *Stephenson*, 8th March, 1886.

Railways and railway companies—Intercolonial Railway—Negligence of conductor—Accident to passengers—Right of action—Contributory negligence.

Plaintiff having a first-class ticket from Sussex to Penobsquis by the Intercolonial Railway, intended going to Penobsquis (her home) by the mixed freight and passenger train, which was due to leave Sussex at 1.47 p.m. The train on that day was an unusually long one, and when the passenger cars were brought up to the platform the engine was across the public highway. When the train came in it was brought up so that the forward part of the first-class car was opposite the platform. It was then about ten minutes after the advertised time of departure. Plaintiff was standing on the platform when the train came in, but did not then get aboard. The conductor of the train (the defendant) got off the train and went to a hotel for dinner. While he was absent the train was, without his knowledge, backed down so that only the second-class car remained opposite the platform. The jury found that the first-class car did not remain at the platform long enough to enable plaintiff to get on board. The defendant after finishing his dinner came over hastily, (being behind time, and therefore in somewhat of a hurry), called "All aboard," glanced down the platform, saw no person attempting to get on board, crossed the train between two box cars to signal the driver to start, (it being necessary to cross the train in order to be seen by the driver, owing to a curve in the track), and almost immediately the train started.

The 124th regulation for government of the Intercolonial Railway prescribes that conductors must not start the train while passengers are getting on board, and that they should stand at the front end of the first passenger car when giving the signal to the driver to start, which was not done in this instance. Plaintiff and a lady friend F., who were going on the same train, were standing on the platform, and when they heard the call, "All aboard," they went towards the car as quickly as they could. F. got on all right, but plaintiff who had a paper box in her hand, in attempting to get on board, caught the hand rail of the car, when she slipped, owing to the motion of the train, and was seriously injured. The jury found that the call, "All aboard," was a notice to passengers to get on board.

The Supreme Court of New Brunswick held that although the plaintiff's contract was with the crown, the defendant owed to her as a passenger a duty to exercise reasonable care, and that there was ample evidence of negligence for the jury.

The facts will be found fully reported in 19 N. B. R., 3 Pugs. & Bur. 340, and 21 N. B. R., 586.

On appeal to the Supreme Court of Canada,

Held, that the judgment of the court below should be affirmed, (Taschereau and Gwynne, JJ., dissenting).

Per Ritchie, C.J., there was no obligation on the part of the passengers to go on board the train until it was ready to start, or until invited to do so by the intimation from the conductor, "All aboard." It was the duty of the conductor to have had his first-class car up in front of the platform. Should circumstances have prevented this, it was his duty to be careful before starting the train to see that sufficient time and opportunity were afforded passengers to board the car in the inconvenient position in which it was placed, and the evidence shewed the defendant exercised no care in this respect.

Per Henry, J., there was no satisfactory proof of contributory negligence on the part of the plaintiff. The package she carried was a light one, and such as is often carried by passengers, with the knowledge and sanction of railway conductors and managers, and a tacit license is therefore given to passengers to carry such with them in the cars.

The plaintiff violated one of the regulations in attempting to get on the car while in motion. But the defendant could not shelter himself under those regulations, for when he gave the order, "All aboard," he knew, or ought to have known, that the first-class car was away from the platform, and he ought to have advanced the train, and stopped it so that the plaintiff could have entered such car. The conductor was estopped from complaining that the plaintiff did what by calling "All aboard" he invited her to do. After the notification, "All aboard," is given by a conductor, it is his duty to wait a reasonable time for passengers to get to their places.

Per Taschereau and Gwynne, JJ., dissenting, whether the omission to stop the first-class car at the platform, or the not waiting a reasonable time after calling "All aboard," were or were not breaches of the defendant's duty, such breaches could not be said to have caused the accident if the plaintiff had not voluntarily attempted to get on the train while in motion, which she was not justified in doing.

Appeal dismissed with costs. *Hall* v. *McFadden*, 1st May, 1888.

Sale of goods—Contract, parol evidence to establish when admissible—As to whether a mem. in writing contained the terms of agreement, a question for jury—Statute of frauds—Damages—Common counts.

The plaintiff sued defendants upon a contract alleged to have been made by them with the plaintiff to deliver to the plaintiff at St. John, N. B., 200 cords of good merchantable hemlock bark, suitable for tanning, at $4 per cord, the plaintiff paying freight from Shediac. He also declared upon the common money counts.

The plaintiff at the trial gave evidence to the effect that the contract was wholly verbal, and that the defendants had agreed that the bark should be all good bark, that it was to be delivered at St. John and measured on the cars there; that the defendants were to send some one to measure it, and that if they did not, plaintiff's son was to measure it; that the plaintiff was to pay freight from Shediac, where the defendants were to load it on the cars. And as to payment, plaintiff gave evidence that $304.81 then due by defendants to plaintiff, was to be applied upon the bark, and that the defendants were to take leather from the plaintiff in payment of the balance; that the bark was to be delivered in two or three months, as the plaintiff wanted it. In answer to plaintiff's order to forward bark, the defendants sent forward three car loads, which proved to be utterly worthless. The plaintiff also gave evidence that at the solicitation of the defendants he gave them his note for $500 at 4 months on the defendants promising that the bark would be all in before the note was due, and that notwithstanding the giving of the note, the defendants would take leather in payment of the bark as agreed, that when plaintiff asked defendant at Hamilton for a receipt for the note for $500, the latter wrote out the following paper:—

C. H. Peters, Esq.,

1876. To Hamilton & Smith.

April 20.	To 200 cords hemlock bark at Shediac, $4..	$800.00
"	....	4.84.
		$804.84.

Cr.

By note at 4 mos..............	$500.00
" goods per statement of acct.	304.84
	$804.84.

The above bark to be measured on the cars in St. John.

Settled as above,

Hamilton & Smith.

Upon this document being produced the defendants insisted that it contained the contract, and that the plaintiff's evidence of the contract must fall to the ground. Both parties were permitted to give oral testimony to establish what the contract was. The evidence was chiefly that of the plaintiff and defendant Hamilton, and was very contradictory. The jury believed the plaintiff and rendered a verdict for him for $945.80 damages.

The Supreme Court of New Brunswick made a rule for a new trial absolute, being of opinion that the contract had been reduced to writing and was contained in the memorandum of the 20th April, 1876; that the words "at Shediac" in the mem. showed that the bark was at Shediac at that time, and that the parties were contracting with reference to that particular bark. That being the case, it was unnecessary to make any stipulation about the delivery, because by the sale the property vested in the plaintiff without any delivery, and the evidence of the plaintiff as to delivery should not have been received, for it was either immaterial or the effect of it was to vary the terms of the written contract, which, being for the sale of goods above the value of £10 were required by the statute of frauds to be in writing.

On appeal to the Supreme Court of Canada,

Held, that whether the mem. of the 20th April, 1876, was or was not drawn up by the consent of both parties with intent to be that should settle and contain their contract in whole or in part, was a question for the jury, and the onus of proving that the document was drawn up for that purpose lay upon the defendants. That the nature of the case required that both parties should be permitted to give oral testimony to establish what the contract was, and as the jury had wholly disbelieved the defendant's evidence, the plaintiff was entitled to recover both on the common counts and on the special counts, and the verdict of the jury should not have been set aside.

Appeal allowed with costs. *Peters v. Hamilton*, 10th June, 1880.

Sale of goods—Contract of sale—Goods not specified—Intention to pass property—Appropriation.

T., a brickmaker, sold, by sample, 50,000 bricks out of a kiln containing

100,000, to the plaintiff, who paid the contract price, and hauled away about 16,000. The balance remained in the kiln in T.'s yards, and were never in any way separated from the rest of the kiln, or appropriated to the plaintiff. The defendant (the sheriff) subsequently sold them under an execution at the suit of W. against T. Plaintiff brought trover against the defendant, claiming property in 34,000 of the bricks.

The Supreme Court of New Brunswick held (Wetmore, J., dissenting), that the contract was executed, and the property in the bricks passed to the plaintiff at the time of sale. 4 Pug. & Bur. 234.

On appeal to the Supreme Court of Canada,

Held, reversing the judgment of the court below, that the sale was one by sample; the bricks sold were not specifically ascertained, and there was no evidence from which it could be inferred that it was the intention of the parties the property in the bricks should pass before delivery.

Appeal allowed with costs. *Temple* v. *Close*, 16th February, 1881.

Sale of goods—Agreement for sale of deals—Contract not complete—New trial.

Action for an alleged agreement contained in the following letters:—

MONCTON, September 13th, 1880.

Messrs. T. L. De Wolf, Halifax:—

DEAR SIRS,—I will send and deliver to you on the cars at Point du Chene, all the merchantable deals and deal ends I can manufacture at my mill at Meadow Brook, this season and next, during the shipping season, an estimated quantity from two to three millions. Deal ends not to exceed what may be required for broken stowage, and to be from three to eight feet long.

Price—Nine dollars per thousand superficial feet for deals, and two-thirds price of deals for ends, and fourths, if any.

SPECIFICATION.

34 per cent.,		7x3 and 8x3.
35	"	9x3.
10	"	10x3.
14	"	11x3.
8	"	12x3 and upwards.

Average length, fourteen feet or more.

About ten per cent. pine, balance spruce.

The pine I will stick and pile well, and keep on my wharf until you require them sent forward.

About two millions to be ready for shipment by the first of July next, and a large portion ready as soon as navigation opens.

Terms—Cash on delivery.

This offer to hold good until the first of October next.

Yours truly,

(Signed) ABNER JONES,
Halifax.

HALIFAX, 29th September, 1880.

Abner Jones, Esq., Moncton:—

DEAR SIR,—We wired you this morning that we accepted your offer for next season's cutting of deals, which we now beg to confirm. If you have any deals sawn this fall we might be able to take them here, we paying the difference of railway freight between Point du Chene and Halifax. Please let us know what quantity you think you will cut this fall, what railway freight per car is to Halifax, and also to Point du Chene.

Please let us know if you would ship what you cut this fall to Halifax if we required them.

We accept your offer, as made in your letter of the 13th inst., in all particulars.

We think this will serve instead of writing out a contract, but if you require it, will fill one up and send you.

Yours truly,

T. L. De Wolf & Co.

The action was tried before Mr. Justice King, at the Westmorland Circuit, in December, A.D. 1881, and resulted in a verdict for plaintiff for $3,500. The jury were directed to find for the plaintiff, and that the only question related to the damages to be awarded plaintiff.

The defendants' counsel moved for a non-suit at the close of the plaintiff's case.

The defendants applied to the Court *en banc* to set aside the verdict, and that a new trial be ordered on the grounds set out. This was granted. The learned judge at the trial held that the letters of the 13th September, 1880, and 29th September, 1880, constituted a complete and binding agreement, and that the subsequent correspondence between the parties did not show that such agreement was rescinded.

The Court (Allen, C.J., Weldon, J., Wetmore, J., Palmer, J., and Fraser, J. —King, J., delivering a separate judgment), in granting a new trial, dealt only with these points, and held that the two letters above quoted constituted a complete binding contract between the parties, but that both agreed to abandon it —or, at all events, that certain letters were evidence of such abandonment—and that in this respect the direction to the jury was incorrect.

King, J., while also of the opinion that the two letters constituted a complete and binding contract, was inclined to think that there was a question for the jury whether the conduct of the plaintiff, after receiving the defendant's letter of the 17th December, and that in reply to his of the 16th December, was not such as to show that plaintiff acquiesced in the defendant's notice of refusal to abide by the bargain.

On appeal to the Supreme Court of Canada,

Held, that the two letters of the 13th and 20th September, 1880, did not constitute a complete contract between the parties. The rule having been taken for a new trial only, the court refused to direct a non-suit or verdict for defendant, but affirmed the rule for a new trial. (Counsel for respondent not called on.)

Appeal dismissed with costs. *Jones v. DeWolf*, 27th February, 1884.

Trespass—Telegraph Company—Erection of line—Right to cut trees—Company bound to show necessity—34 Vic. cap. 52, incorporating Dominion Telegraph Co.

The Act, 34 Vic. cap. 52, incorporating the Dominion Telegraph Co., declares in the 4th section that the company may enter upon lands or places, and survey, set-off and take such parts thereof as may be necessary for such line, etc., and in case of disagreement between the company and owners of lands so taken, or in respect of any damage done to the same, it may be settled by arbitration in the mode therein described. By section 20 the company are authorized and empowered to enter upon the lands of any person or persons, and survey and take levels, and to set out and ascertain such parts thereof as they shall think necessary and proper for making the said intended telegraph, and all such other works, matters and conveniences as they shall think proper and necessary for the making, effecting, preserving, etc., the said telegraph, and to build and set upon such lands, such station houses and observatories, watch-houses and other works, etc., as and where the said company shall think requisite and convenient, etc. Provided always, that the said company shall not cut down or mutilate any tree planted or left standing for shade or ornament, or any fruit tree, unless it be necessary so to do, for the erection, use or safety of any of its lines.

In an action against the company to recover damages for cutting down ornamental trees, the defendants pleaded that the trees were standing by the side of a public highway, and the defendants were erecting their line of telegraph along the highway; and because the trees were in the way and obstructed the passage of the line of telegraph, and because they deemed it necessary and advisable to do so, they committed the acts complained of, by virtue of the statute, and not otherwise.

The Supreme Court of New Brunswick.

Held, 1st. That the arbitration clause in the 4th section did not apply to a case like this, where the complaint was that the defendants had wrongfully destroyed plaintiff's trees; 2nd. That the proviso in the 20th section imposed on the defendants, if the ornamental trees should obstruct their line on the side of the highway where they located it, the burthen of showing that it was necessary for them to take it on that side, and that the defendant's pleas were bad for want of an averment that it was necessary to cut the trees, not merely that they deemed it necessary. See 3 Pug. & Bur. 353.

On appeal to the Supreme Court of Canada,

Held, that the judgment of the court below should be affirmed.

Appeal dismissed with costs.

The Dominion Teleg[illegible]h Co. v. Gilchrist, 15th February, 1881.

Table of Cases.

A

	Vol. of Reports and Page.	Index Page.
Abell, ex parte	19, 22; 18, 600	41, 115, 171
Abbinnett v. The Northwestern Mutual Insurance Co.	21, 216; 24, 137	50, 212
Ackman v. Town of Moncton	24, 101	20
Adams, et al., v. National Insurance Co.	20, 569	126
Albert Railway Co., ex parte	19, 48	141
Mining Co. v. Sparr	22, 316	52
Allen v. McDonald, et al	20, 533	93
Alward v. Mayor, etc., of St. John	23, 317	107
Alexander v. Mayor, etc., St John / v. Cowie	19, 599	190
v. Cowie and Torrie	20, 476	194
Almon v. Lewin	20, 284	234
Anderson v. Fawcett / v. Mowatt	24, 313; 19, 34; 20, 82	9, 49, 60
Appleby v. Black	24, 528	205
v. Devine	22, 198	223
v. Second	20, 403	93
Armstrong v. McGourty	22, 29	224
v. The Mayor, etc., St. John	20, 349	191
v. Botsford	24, 284	97
v. Grand Trunk Ry. Co.	18, 445	40
Avon Stone Co. v. Dunham	18, 460	5

B

Bank of New Bk. v. Brown	19, 106	2
v. Flaherty	19, 407	121
ex parte Deveber	21, 401	121
Bank of Nova Scotia v. Steeves	20, 338	121
v. Cushing	21, 498	29
Barbour v. Roberts	24, 211	11, 47
Barry v. Logan	18, 465	121
v. Hogan	18, 465	167
Beckwith, in re	21, 101	26
Bell v. Carlyle	22, 453	7
v. Moffat	19, 261; 20, 721	168, 182
v. Wetmore	19, 531	114
Belyea v. Merritt	23, 225	158
Bennet v. Murdock	20, 317	57
Best v. Bernstein	20, 106	16

	VOL. OF REPORTS AND PAGE.	INDEX PAGE.
Birmingham, ex parte	18, 364	101, 148
Bishop of Chatham v. Western Ass. Co.	22, 242	120
Black v. Cogswell	19, 44	229
Black v. Doherty	22, 215	199
v. Municipality of St. John	23, 249	153
Boice, ex parte	24, 159	177
Bolser v. Crossman	25, 556	244
Bolstead, ex parte	21, 227	14
Boss v. Millar	22, 494	175
Boston Belting Co. v. Gabel	20, 347	47
Botsford v. Trites	19, 135	23
Bourgeois v. Gilbert	19, 353	120
Bowes v. National Insurance Co.	20, 438	125
Boyce, ex parte	24, 159, 345	177, 215
Boyer v. Town of Woodstock	24, 521	181
Boyne, ex parte	22, 228	36
Brewer v. Brewer	22, 450	117
Briggs v. McBride	19, 202	189, 221
Brown v. Maltby	20, 92	43
v. Vaughan	22, 258	204
ex parte	25, 508	242
Brownell v. Raworth	21, 11	8
Buckley v. Russell	24, 205	149
Burke v. Clarke	18, 602	6
Burns v. Botsford	19, 5	66
v. Cassels	25, 18	45
Burpee v. Smith and Mann	20, 468	163
Burton v. Dougherty	19, 51	113
Byrne, ex parte	22, 427	112
v. Arnold	24, 161	39

C

Cahill v. Cahill	18, 438	6
Calhoun v. Rourke, et al	19, 591	84
v. Un. M. Ins. Co.	19, 18	122, 167
Canada Life Ins. Co. v. Calkins	24, 276	169
Carleton Ry. Co. v. Grand Southern Ry. Co.	21, 339	186
Carman v. Dunn	23, 385	76
Carter v. Landry	19, 516	49
Casey v. Hannington	19, 262	93
Chapman v. Doherty	25, 271	65
v. Providence Washington Insurance Co.	19, 496; 20, 91; 23, 105	59, 60, 122, 130
v. Delaware M. Safety Ins. Co	19, 496; 23, 121	59, 130
v. Mutual Safety Ins. Co.	19, 28	122
Cheeseman and wife v. Hatheway	23, 415	229
Chestnut v. Doyle	24, 505	65
Clark v. Griffiths	24, 567	164
v. Kimball	23, 412	52
v. Town of Portland	19, 180	213
ex parte	21, 128, 623	67, 77

	VOL. OF REPORTS AND PAGE.	INDEX PAGE.
Clemenston, ex parte	20, 413	121
Clarke v. Calkin	20, 98	121
Close v. Temple	20, 241	183
Coates v. Gosling	20, 323	31
v. Town of Moncton	25, 605	213
Coleman, ex parte	23, 574	38
Collins, ex parte	23, 38	37
v. Everett	18, 469	5
Colwell v. Robinson	21, 489 ; 23, 69	15, 130
Commeau v. Burns	22, 573	82
Connagher v. Parlee	24, 585	55
Connell v. Yerxa	19, 537	145
v. McLeod	22, 310	62
Connelly v. Shives, et al. exts	18, 606	5, 148
Coram, in re	25, 404	117
Cormier v. Ottawa Agl. Ins. Co.	20, 526	125
v. McKee	21, 1	61
Cook, ex parte	22, 557	195
Coughlan, ex parte	24, 308	149
Coughlin, ex parte	22, 632	37
Coulthard v. Caverhill	25, 84	8
Copp v. Read	19, 455, 641	14, 217
Courser v. Kirkbride	23, 404	94
Cox v. McMann	19, 121	198
Cruikshank v. McAvity	20, 352	3
Currie v. Stairs	25, 4	209
Cyr v. Ouilette	20, 264	160

D

	VOL. OF REPORTS AND PAGE.	INDEX PAGE.
De Forest v. Holland	23, 411	62
Delaney v. McDonald	23, 139	104
Delong v. Burrill Johnston Iron Co.	25, 140	155
Derry v. Derry	20, 90 ; 19, 621	6[illegible], 76
Develier, in re, ex parte	21, 307, 401	32
Dexter, in re	20, 267	11
Dibble, ex parte	25, 119	See Errata
Dickie v. The Western Ass. Co.	21, 544	126
Diffin v. Dow	22, 107	93
Doe dem. Appleby v. Second	22, 377	171
Barnes v. Belyea	19, 541	86
Barnett v. Roe	19, 102	85
Bennett v. Murdock	20, 317	57
Black v. Cogswell	19, 44	220
Brideau v. Budreau	22, 550	145
Chambers v. Douglas	23, 484	115
Crothers v. Roe	19, 138	173
Doherty v. Brown	19, 605, 608	87, 91
Durion v. Roe	23, 307	86
Estabrooks v. Towse	22, 10 ; 24, 387	158, 173
Elliott v. Flangan	25, 154	21
Ferguson v. Roe	19, 337	85
Gallant v. Roe	22, 423	87

	VOL. OF REPORTS AND PAGE.	INDEX PAGE.
Doe dem. Jones and wife v. Nevers	18, 627	78
Hazen v. Laskey	23, 181	145
v. Rector St. James' Church	18, 479	83, 156, 179
Heathcote v. Hughes	19, 368	142
Jarvis v. Trites	19, 471	88
Mason v. Chittles	20, 113	199
Mayor of St. John v. Roe	21, 357; 25, 149	87, 88
Rankin v. Andrews	22, 125	120
v. Charlton	21, 119	117
Simons v. Gilbert	22, 575	233
Wood v. DeForest	23, 209	159
Doherty, ex parte	25, 38	67
Domville v. O'Brien	18, 656	4
Doolan v. LeForest	21, 553	219
Dorsey v. Connell	22, 564	115
Douthrite v. Stevens	21, 545	194
Dowling v. McNeilly	19, 42	93
Driscoll, et al. v. Mellville Ma. Ins. Co.	23, 160	131
Drury's Will, in re	22, 318	238
Dunn v. Allen	25, 1	28
Dwyer, et ux. v. Town of Portland, in re	20, 123	213

E

Estabrooks v. Sears	20, 510; 25, 543	111, 137
ex parte	19, 284	18
v. McGowan	22, 455	66
Eastern Townships Bank v. Hannington	18, 631	26, 180
Earle v. Botsford	23, 407	83, 134
Edwards v. Burgoyne	21, 228	148
v. Mayor, etc., St. John	22, 257	118
Elliott v. Parks	23, 611	53
Ellis v. Powers	20, 40	195
Everitt, et al. v. Lynds	20, 384	24

F

Fahey, ex parte	21, 302	42
Fairley and Wilson, in re	25, 568	212
Farrel, ex parte	25, 167	38
Fawcett, ex parte	24, 228	111
Ferguson v. Domville	19, 576	22
v. Johnston	19, 279	92
ex parte	19, 117	153
in re	21, 71	14, 245
v. Savoy	23, 87	66
v. Troop	25, 440	144

	VOL. OF REPORTS AND PAGE.	INDEX PAGE.
Fleming v. N. British and Mercantile Ins. Co.	20, 153	158
Flewelling, et al. v. Lawrence	21, 529	57
Flood v. Morrissey	20, 5	60
ex parte	23, 86	26
Forbes v. Temple	22, 511	212
Ford v. Reid	23, 220, 580	3, 176
v. Browser and wife	24, 510	147, 227
Fox, in re	20, 391	45
Fox and wife v. Mayor, etc., St. John	23, 244	115
Foxwell v. Smith	18, 439	156
Frank, et al. v. McGrath	25, 499	120
Fraser v. Ullock	25, 55	65
in re	24, 245	200, 214
Friar v. McGowan	19, 25	228
v. Wilmot, et al. exrs	23, 546; 19, 521	110, 520
Furling v. Russel	24, 478	54

G

Gagnon v. Chapman	21, 251; 18, 449	62, 156
Gallant v. Calder	23, 73	107
Gerow v. Prov. U. Ins. Co.	25, 279	63
v. Holt	25, 412	182
Gitchell v. Burchill	22, 631	74
Gibson v. Gill	19, 565	192
v. N. B. & Mercantile Ins. Co.	19, 652	157
Gilbert v. Raymond	19, 315	28
Gilchrist v. Dom. Tel. Co.	20, 211	223
Gillis v. Morrison	22, 207	94, 142
Gleason v. Domville	19, 17	120
Glidden, ex parte	24, 250	29
Golding, ex parte	19, 47	213
Good v. Good	22, 439	208
v. Merithew	24, 160	63
Goodeus, ex parte	25, 151	216
Green v. St. John & M. Ry. Co.	22, 252	187
v. Harris	24, 496	55
Grey v. Chapman	24, 542	177
Grieves, ex parte	19, 4	146
Griffiths v. Town of Portland	24, 579	171
Gruggain v. Langis	21, 549	91
Groves, ex parte	22, 629; 23, 38; 19, 4	24, 37, 146
Guy, et al. v. Rankin, et al.	24, 49	143
v. Brady	24, 563	148

H

Hackett, ex parte	21, 513	36
Halifax Banking Co. v. Smith	25, 610	242
Hall v. McFadden	19, 340; 21, 586	189, 190

	VOL. OF REPORTS AND PAGE.	INDEX PAGE.
Hamilton, et al. v. Dumphy	21, 214	13
v. Simpson	19, 497	191
v. Calder	23, 373	223
Hannington, in re	20, 413	121
Hanson v. Venning	22, 639	225
Harvey, in re	24, 623	67, 77
Harnett v. Wry	25, 258	67
Harris v. Clayton	21, 237	208
v. Green	25, 451	201
v. Fowle	22, 398, 572	107, 175
Harrison v. Alton	20, 371	111
Hayes, ex parte	23, 313	37
Hasen v. Hasen	20, 70	232
Hasen v. Town of Portland	24, 332	173
Henry v. Bostwick	24, 414	53
Hickey, ex parte	23, 467	42
in re	24, 245	200, 214
Hickson v. Loban	24, 354	137
Hilyard v. Wood	19, 309	23
Holstead, in re	20, 512	6
Hoar v. Lewis	22, 286	56
Hotham v. Philips	23, 136	52
Howard and Crangle, ex parte	25, 191	39
Hutchinson v. Shireff	20, 25	193
v. Trustees, etc	19, 65	220
Hyneman, ex parte	23, 480	176

I

Ingraham v. Parks	19, 101	220
Intercolonial Express v. McKenzie	24, 616	63

J

Jack v. Lyons	19, 336	60
Jackson v. McLellan	18, 694; 19, 432	14, 46
Jonas v. Gilbert	20, 61	33
v. Marshall	20, 64	33
Jones v. McMillan	19, 378	111
v. Municipality of Albert	21, 200; 20, 78	77, 152
v. Dewolfe, et al	23, 356	52
v. Tuck	23, 447	135
v. Maritime Bank	20, 544	33
v. Landry	22, 417	28
v. Milliken	22, 315	25
v. Morgan	24, 338	5
ex parte	19, 104	59
Jordan v. Great Western Ins. Co	24, 421	133

K

	VOL. OF REPORTS AND PAGE.	INDEX PAGE.
Kaue, ex parte	21, 370	42
Kerry, in re		
Keiller v. Charters, et al	23, 493	137
Keenan v. Trustees of Leinster St. Baptist Church	22, 11; 21, 211	62, 154
Kerr Executrix, etc. v Squires	22, 448	1, 144
v. Stevens, et al	22, 124	168
ex parte v. Thorne	18, 625	24
King, et al. v. Murray	22, 582	239
Kingston v. Wallace	23, 573	243
Kinnear v. Black	21, 272	14
Knox, et al. v. Gregory	21, 196	25

L

La Banque Nationale v. Beckett	25, 145	28
Ville Marie v. Lordly	21, 273	81
Landry v. Town of Moncton	24, 103	20
Lantoleon v. Anchor Marine Ins. Co.	22, 14	127
Law v. Landry	19 590	23
v. Harding	19, 590; 20, 120	23, 60
Lawless, ex parte	18, 520	18
Leighton v. Deering	21, 410	195
Lemon, ex parte	20, 563	113
Leonard, et al. v. Griffin	21, 188	121
Lewin, ex parte	19, 425; 23, 591	18, 20
Lipsett, ex parte	25, 66	42
Loane, ex parte	22, 629	24
Lockhart, exr. v. Ray, et al	20, 129	232
Lynds v. Turner	22, 286	36
Lunt, et al. v. Lloyd	21, 2	154
Lyon v. Barnes	22, 55	175

M

Maher, ex parte	22, 633	37
Magee v. Mayor, etc., St. John	23, 275	85
Magner v. Hutchinson	21, 221, 537	212, 238
v. Sullivan	21, 537	212
Manchester, ex parte	25, 532	78
Manser, ex parte	23, 314	37
Maritime Bank v. Carvill	24, 250	29
v. McKean	22, 526	175
v. Guardian Ass. Co.	19, 297	122
Warehousing Co. v. Nicholson	24, 170	151
Marks v. Newcomb	22, 419	105
Marshall v. Armstrong, et al	22, 162	95, 102

	VOL. OF REPORTS AND PAGE.	INDEX PAGE.
Mayor, etc., St. John v. Patchell	22, 173	170
v. Lockart	23, 430	95
v. Masters	19, 585	170, 213
McBean, ex parte	24, 362	216
McCall v. Gillespie	24, 98	109
McCann v. Kearney	20, 84	207
McCully, ex parte	20, 87	18
v. Noonan	24, 142	177
McCatherine v. Lewis	25, 429	65
v. Lunt		
McCarthy v. Prov. W. Ins. Co.	21, 165	61
in re		
McCleave, ex parte	21, 315	35
McCormick v. McBride	23, 12	94
McDonald v. Mayor, etc., St. John	21, 370; 25, 318; 20, 114	157, 188, 199
ex parte	20, 542; 21, 57	31, 214
v. Potts	22, 146	146
McFee v. Mowatt	19, 252	162
McGilvray v. Grant	19, 217	104
McGibbon v. Burpee, et al	25, 81	97
McHugh v. Murray	24, 12	53
McIndoe, ex parte	23, 38	37
McIntosh v. Hamilton	19, 1; 18, 654	23, 128, 156
McKean v. Commercial Union Ins. Co.	21, 583	126
McKnight, ex parte	23, 272	241
McLaughlin v. McLeod	19, 539	121
McLeod v. James	18, 439	135
v. Pye	21, 212	26
McLellan v. Barnes	19, 590; 21, 228; 19, 374	59, 61, 174
v. Davidson	20, 388	29
v. Rankine	22, 116	66
McManus v. Blakeney	25, 216	92
v. Walsh	22, 332	87
McMillan v. Walker	21, 31	50, 153, 174
McMullin, in re	24, 382	181
McNair v. Stewart	24, 471	97
McPherson v. McKeenan	19, 3	141
McRory v. McAlpine	23, 357	27
McSorley v. Mayor, etc. St. John	19, 645; 20, 429	17, 19
McQuarrie ex parte	24, 287	6
Medoamkiak Boom Co. v. Dalton	23, 28	149
Michaw v. Finnigan	24, 327	169
Mecker, et al. v. Peters	23, 95	175
Mercer ex parte	25, 317	29
Merritt v. Wright	21, 135	61, 237
Miller v. Basset, et al	24, 439	189
Milbur v. Jones	19, 586	174
Moffat v. Lunt	18, 673	22
Moore v. May	19, 564	25
ex parte	23, 221	1
Moran v. Taylor	24, 39; 23, 222	47, 132, 176
Morrice v. Foster	25, 1	64
Morrison v. Bank of Montreal	24, 109	69
Morrow v. Waterous, et al	21, 412; 18, 580	54, 76, 231
v. Waterous Engine Co	18, 580	76
Muirhead v. Lober	24, 360	137
Mullin v. Frost	20, 122	12
Municipality of Kent v. McArthur	22, 111	212
Murray v. Burgoyne	20, 149	183
v. Moffat	19, 481	211

N

	VOL. OF REPORTS AND PAGE.	INDEX PAGE.
National Park Bank v. Ellis	18, 517	4
Nevins, et al. v. Schoefield, et al.	18, 435	167
New Brunswick Ry. Co. v. Armstrong	23, 193; 21, 124	187, 226
Nicholson, et al. v. Temple	20, 248; 21, 192	31, 61
Nevers, ex parte	19, 5	41

O

O'Brien v. Churchill	21, 509	177
Orr, ex parte	20, 67	84
O'Regan v. Quebec & Gulf Ports Steamship Co.	19, 524	7
O'Sullivan v. O'Sullivan	19, 396	16
Otty, et al. v. Crookshank, et al.	21, 102	237
Oulton and Allan, in re	25, 19	27
Oulton v. Allan	25, 369	61
Owen, ex parte	20, 187	83

P

Palmer and Calhoun, in re	24, 211	27
v. Harding	19, 281	26, 162
Paran v. Barnett	19, 497	221
Parlee, ex parte	25, 51	114
v. Snider	23, 221, 271	164, 176
Parks v. Ingraham	19, 195	221
Pattison v. Mayor, etc., St. John	18, 636	4
Peabody v. N. W. Boom Co.	19, 195	174
Perkins, ex parte	24, 66	162
People's National Bank v. Stewart	18, 268	30
Peters v. Waterbury	21, 151	183
v. Hamilton	19, 284	197
Phair v. Venning	22, 362	108
Phoeny v. Aiken	22, 635	94
Philip v. McLaughlin	21, 532	216
Philips, ex parte	21, 119	215
Pitfield v. Kimball	25, 193	3, 44, 163
Pomares v. Minas Ins. Co.	18, 654	159
Porter v. McMahon	25, 211	71, 209
Pourier, ex parte	23, 541	28
Powell v. Wark	19, 57; 20, 15	157, 201
v. Hannington	22, 520	135
Price, ex parte	23, 87	42
Prince of Wales Coal Co. v. Osman	22, 115	163
Purchase v. Seelye	19, 519	171

Q

	VOL. OF REPORTS AND PAGE.	INDEX PAGE.
Quiddy River Boom Co. v. Davidson	23, 380	243

R

Rand, ex parte	24, 374	39
Randolph v. Taylor, et al	20, 264	160
Ranney v. Sheraton	25, 521	78
Raymond v. Dom. Tel. Co	24, 387	63
Record v. Record, et al	21, 277	102
Regina v. Blair, in re McCarthy	24 245 ; 24, 71	200, 214
in re Hickey	24, 72	214
in re Keary	24, 74	214
v. Blair and Stapleton	24, 245	200
v. Burtt	22, 51	86
v. Budge	23, 531	93
v. Close	19, 502	2, 116
v. Corey	21, 543	70
v. Dayton, et al	21, 195	174
v. Dibble, ex parte Shaw	23, 30	87
v. Dewitt, ex parte Shaw	23, 30	37
v. Dewitt	24, 17	68
v. Ellis	22, 440	5
v. Ferguson	20, 259	4, 71
v. Fredericton	19, 139	38
v. Gilbert	18, 629	33
v. Grimmer	25, 424, 480	140, 181
v. Hannington and Walsh	23, 340	71
v. Horseman	20, 529	71, 133
v. Long, et al	21, 208	116
v. Marsh	25, 370	6, 216
v. Mayor of Fredericton	19, 139	279
v. McCafferty	25, 396	98
v. Morrison	18, 682	68
v. Mulholland	20, 478	112, 116, 192
v. Municipality of Charlotte	22, 636	146
v. O'Neil	19, 49	17
v. Risteen	22, 51	86
v. Rose	22, 309	37
v. Rose Milne	20, 394	41
v. Simpson	20, 472	41
v. Perley, in re White	25, 43	215
v. Shannon	23, 1	71
v. Sullivan, in re Dwyer	24, 149	215
v. Theal	21, 449	69
v. Tower	20, 168, 478	68, 71, 97, 112
v. Waddell	25, 93	108
v. White and Perry	25, 484	182
v. Wilson, et al	21, 178	19
Richard v. Simpson	20, 118	182

	VOL. OF REPORTS AND PAGE.	INDEX PAGE.
Richardson v. Vaughan	21, 75	165
Robertson v. Jones, et al	20, 267	58
Robinson v. Clarke	20, 156	69
v. Ellis	19, 6	121
v. Ferguson	24, 332	226
v. N. B. Ry. Co	23, 323	186
v. Shireff	25, 68	202
v. Topley, et al	20, 361	106
v. Colwell	23, 69	159
Rogers v. Wallace	24, 459	83
Rose v. Schoefield	25, 127	121
Ross, ex parte	21, 257	69
v. Citizen's Ins. Co	19, 126	122
Ross and Wife v. Town of Upper Mills	22, 108	162
Russell, ex parte	20, 536; 25, 187	34, 39
v. Buckley	25, 264	63, 143
v. Bishop	24, 298, 322	158
v. Legere	24, 298, 322	158
Ryan, ex parte	24, 528	177

S

Saint John and Maine Ry. Co. v. Montgomery	21, 441; 22, 252	186, 187
Sayre v. Le Blanc	23, 147	56
v. Harris	18, 677; 22, 142	24, 63, 119
Schoefield et al. v. Corwill et al	21, 558	41
N. Bk. Patent Tannery Co.	22, 509	129
v. Nevins	17, 329	23
Scott v. Palmer	21, 304	203
v. McKenzie	18, 470	111
Shannahan, ex parte	19, 499	210
Shaughnessy, in re	21, 182	112
Shaw, ex parte	23, 30	37
Shehyn v. Milliken, et al.	22, 58	151
Sheraton v. Sheraton	25, 534, 544	79, 80
v. Whelpley, et al.	20, 75	13, 32
Shireff v. Campbell	24, 554	98
v. Vye	24, 572	31, 143
v. McKeen	24, 184	31
v. Muirhead	25, 1, 5	98, 202
Seelye, in re	19, 549	121
Seery v. Temple	19, 302	147
Simpson, ex parte	22, 132	42
Sinclair v. Holland	24, 529	143
v. Sinclair et al	20, 564	61
Small v. Belyea	24, 16	40
Smith, et al. v. Morrissey	20 1	59
v. and Wife, Sherriff, etc.	18, 143	226
v. Chapman	25, 206	6, 158
v. Cormier	25, 487	151
Snowball v. Muirhead	22, 561	15
v. Stewart	19, 567	157
Somers v. Wilbur	20, 502	12, 43
Southwest Boom Co. v. Fauley	25, 41	67

	VOL. OF REPORTS AND PAGE.	INDEX PAGE.
Spurr v. Venning	22, 639	225
Stadacona Ins. Co. v. Rainsford	21, 309	95
Star Kidney Pad Co. v. McCarthy	23, 83	17, 168
Stather, ex parte	25, 374	113
Steadman v. Venning	22, 639	225
v. Robertson	18, 580	108
Steeper v. Harding, et al	24, 143	3
Steeves et al. v. Foxwell	23, 476	23
v. Sovereign Fire Insur. Co.	20, 394	123
v. ex parte	22, 558	195
Stephenson v. Fraser	24, 482	38, 139
v. Hoar	24, 614	6
v. Clinch	24, 182	10
v. Haywood	22, 104	158
ex parte	23, 38	37
Stewart v. Snowball	19, 597	157
Strather, ex parte	25, 374	113, 231
Street v. Swinton	22, 185	29
Stockton v. Beatty	19, 104	226
Swim v. Sheriff	20, 25	193

T

Tait, assignee, v. Dowling	20, 265	60, 121
v. Strenach	19, 93	58
Taylor, et al. v. Burnett	20, 165	200
Taylor v. Dom. Tel. Co.	24, 327	63
Tennant v. Belyea	24, 238	146
Tierney, in re	25, 286	147, 239
Thomas v. Geldart	20, 95	191
Thomson v. Simonson	25, 122	65
Torrens, et al. v. Currie	22, 342	83
Tower v. Outhouse, et al	21, 302; 20, 113; 23, 354; 22, 570	12, 103, 176, 195
Trueman v. Wood	19, 522	182
v. Bain	25, 238	227
Trustees St. John Young Men's Association v. Hutchinson	18, 523	4
Tufts, et. al. v. Chapman	23, 187	29
Tucker, ex parte	23, 311	19
Turner v. McMann, et al	22, 231	206
v. Burtt	24, 547	27
ex parte	22, 634	42

U

Union Mutual Life Ins. Co. v. Gilbert	25, 221	89

V

	VOL. OF REPORTS AND PAGE.	INDEX PAGE.
Vassie v. Vassie	22, 76	84
Vaughan v. Roberts	23, 313	23
Vernon and wife v. Oliver	23, 392	89
Vernon v. Thompson	20, 116	194
Vose v. Duff	19, 50	168

W

Wallace Huestis Grey Stone Co v. Foxwell	20, 64	91
Waterbury v. Dewe	19, 225	207
Waterhouse Engine Works Co. v. Campbell	22, 503	134
Watt v. Scrith W. Boon Co.	19, 646	14
Watters v. Milligan	22, 628	8
Ward v. Oathouse et al.	21, 209	104
v. Reed	22, 279, 433	66, 140
Weldon v. O'Sullivan	19, 402, 441	16, 217
West v. Trustees School District	22, 56	119
Wetmore, in re	19, 632	25
White, ex parte	20, 509, 532	31, 41
v. Riley	24, 476	63
Wheeler and Wilson Manuf. Co. v. Charters	21, 480	51
Wilbur v. Jones	21, 4; 19, 536	13, 63, 91
Willett v. Lockhart	19, 637	164
Wilson, ex parte	25, 209	109
Williamson, ex parte	24, 64	140, 162
Woods v. McKay and wife	21, 109; 20, 262	93, 207
v. McCann	25, 258	11, 67
Woodward, ex parte	21, 221	135
Woodman v. Town Council of Moncton	19, 348	174
Worral v. Brideau	22, 562	195

Y

Youngclaus v. Wallace	21, 365	27

www.ingramcontent.com/pod-product-compliance
Lightning Source LLC
Chambersburg PA
CBHW021219270326
41929CB00010B/1194